CAPTURING WEALTH
FROM TUNA

CAPTURING WEALTH
FROM TUNA
CASE STUDIES FROM THE PACIFIC

Kate Barclay

with Ian Cartright

ANU
THE AUSTRALIAN NATIONAL UNIVERSITY

E PRESS

Asia Pacific Press
The Australian National University

ANU

E PRESS

Copublished by ANU E Press and Asia Pacific Press
The Australian National University
Canberra ACT 0200 Australia
Email: anuepress@anu.edu.au
This title is available online at http://epress.anu.edu.au/capturing_tuna_citation.html

Asia Pacific Press
Crawford School of Economics and Government
The Australian National University
Canberra ACT 0200
Ph: 61-2-6125 0178 Fax: 61-2-6125 0767
Email: books@asiapacificpress.com
Website: http://www.asiapacificpress.com

National Library of Australia Cataloguing-in-Publication entry

Author:	Barclay, Kate.
Title:	Capturing wealth from tuna : case studies from the Pacific / authors, Kate Barclay ; Ian Cartwright.
Publisher:	Canberra : Asia Pacific Press, 2007.
ISBN:	9780731538164 (pbk.)
	9781921313639 (online)
Notes:	Includes index.
Subjects:	Tuna fisheries--Islands of the Pacific.
	Tuna fisheries--Law and legislation--Islands of the Pacific.
	Tuna fisheries--Economic aspects.
Other Authors:	Cartwright, Ian.
Dewey Number:	338.3727783

Cover design: Teresa Prowse, ANU E Press

Contents

Tables

Appendix tables

Figures

Maps

Symbols used in tables

..	not available
n.a.	not applicable
-	zero
.	insignificant

Acronyms and abbreviations

access agreement	Distant water fishing vessels are members of fisheries associations that negotiate access to the waters of coastal states for fishing. Often these follow Head Agreements between the governments of the negotiating countries.
ACP	Africa Caribbean Pacific country, a category under the Cotonou Agreement.
ADB	Asian Development Bank
agent	Locally based businesses that provide contractual and other services for distant water fleets. Usually includes obtaining fishing licences; can include handling trans-shipping, buying the catch and procurement. Can be legally responsible for fleet while it is in the country.
AusAID	Australian Agency for International Development
automatic location communicator	A device approved by the FFA, which transmits data about the location and fishing activities of the vessel on which it is placed (as part of the VMS).
bunkering	Supplying fuel from one vessel to another.
Competent Authority	Designation for a government department accredited to monitor food safety and quality in line with EU requirements, such that the products of that country may be exported to the European Union.
Cotonou Agreement	Successor to the Lomé Agreement. It gives certain ACP countries tariff-free access to EU markets.
CPUE	Catch per unit of effort. A productivity measure for fisheries. When CPUE declines, this often means fish stocks have declined.
CSPOD-II	Canada–South Pacific Ocean Development Program, funded by the Canadian International Development Agency (CIDA).
DWFN	Distant water fishing nation. The term distant water fishing *nation* is not a good one because a nation is a subjective construct usually based on feelings of ethnic belonging and historical ties to particular territories. States are the administrative political and economic units associated with nations. So, strictly speaking, the term should be distant water fishing *states*. This study, however, uses the term DWFN because it will be more familiar to readers than DWFS.
EEZ	Exclusive Economic Zone (200 nautical miles out from the coastline)
EPIRB	Electronic Position Indicating Radio Beacon (safety equipment for vessels in case they need to be rescued)

EU	European Union
FAD	Fish aggregating device, also called *payao* (Filipino)
FFA	Forum Fisheries Agency
FFC	Forum Fisheries Committee (governing body of the FFA)
FIAS	Foreign Investment Advisory Service
FOB	Free on board
FOC	Flag of Convenience. When a country allows a fishing vessel owned by a company in another country to be registered in the first country for reasons of mutual convenience. It becomes a problem if the flag state is unwilling or unable to undertake flag-state responsibilities, such as righting any wrongs done by the vessel under International Maritime Law.
FSM Arrangement	Reciprocal access agreement for PNA Group countries, with priority accorded to local and locally based fleets, signed in the Federated States of Micronesia.
GDP	Gross domestic product
GEF	Global Environment Facility, a funding scheme under the UN Development Program.
GRT	Gross registered tonnage, a measure of volume, being the total cubic content of the permanently enclosed spaces of a vessel, with some allowances or deductions for exempt spaces such as living quarters (1 gross registered tonne = 100 cubic feet = 2.83 cubic metres)
gt	gross tonnes
HACCP	Hazard Analysis Critical Control Point, a system for assuring safety and hygiene in food production.
Head Agreement	Agreements between governments of distant water states and coastal states for fisheries access. Access agreements often come under Head Agreements.
katsuobushi	Smoke-dried and cured skipjack used extensively as a stock base and flavouring in Japanese cuisine.
Lomé Agreement	Trade agreement between the European Union and certain former European colonies in Africa, the Caribbean and the Pacific (ACP) for tariff-free access to EU markets. Superseded by the Cotonou Agreement.
longline	The predominant style of fishing for large sashimi tuna. A longline is set out behind the vessel with short lines hanging off it dangling hooks under the surface of the water. Large tuna (and sometimes other species) snap at and become caught on the hooks to be pulled aboard when the longline is reeled in.
MCS	Monitoring, control and surveillance of fishing activities for fisheries management.

MHLC	Multilateral High Level Conference. The series of meetings preceding the Preparatory Conferences (Prep Cons) that developed the Western and Central Pacific Fisheries Convention and Commission.
MIDA	Marshall Islands Development Authority
MIMRA	Marshall Islands Marine Resources Authority
monofilament line	A technological development that allowed greater efficiency and accuracy in longline fishing.
MSY	Maximum sustainable yield
Multilateral Treaty	At the time of writing, still the only distant water fishing access agreement negotiated multilaterally with the Pacific island countries (FFA members) by the United States in 1988 (renewed for another 10 years in 2003).
NGO	Non-governmental organisation
OFCF	Overseas Fisheries Cooperation Foundation, a Japanese quasi-government organisation that conducts fisheries development assistance.
Palau Arrangement	An arrangement within the PNA group to limit the total number of purse-seine vessels allowed to fish in the EEZs of their countries to 205. There is a set number for domestic and locally based foreign vessels. This system is likely to be superseded by the VDS.
PDF	Project Development Fund. A proportion of the funds from the US Multilateral Treaty that are set aside by the FFA for member countries to apply for special projects. Often the projects are related to fisheries.
pelagic	Belonging to the open ocean, rather than in shallow waters near the coast.
PITIC	Pacific Islands Trade and Investment Commission
pole-and-line	One of the main types of industrial tuna fishing, widely practised, especially by the Japanese fleet, to fish for skipjack until the 1980s, when the more efficient purse-seining method gained ascendancy. At the time of writing, the Solomon Islands had one of the few remaining pole-and-line fleets, along with Japan. Long flexible rods with fixed lines and barbless L-shaped hooks are dipped into schools of tuna feeding on the surface; the tuna bite at the hook, are swung up and over the shoulders of the fishers where they slip off the hook and land on the deck.
PNA	Parties to the Nauru Agreement. The group of countries in whose EEZs the majority of purse-seine fishing is done. They formed a group soon after the establishment of the FFA to expedite purse-

seine-related issues: Federated States of Micronesia, Kiribati, Marshall Islands, Nauru, Palau, Papua New Guinea, Solomon Islands and Tuvalu.

PNG	Papua New Guinea
Prep Con	The Preparatory Conferences that developed the Western and Central Pacific Fisheries Convention preceding the establishment of the WCPFC.
purse-seine	The predominant style of fishing for skipjack since the 1980s. Dense schools of fish near the surface are encircled by the net, which is then pulled closed at the bottom, creating a bowl or purse shape in which the fish are trapped before being hauled on board.
RFMO	Regional Fisheries Management Organisation
SPC	Secretariat of the Pacific Community
STCW	Standards for the training and certification of watchkeepers
TAC	Total allowable catch
trans-shipment	Moving a load of fish from one vessel to another, usually from a fishing vessel to a carrier vessel that will take it to the market destination.
tuna coffin	Chilled sashimi tuna are packed in individual large cardboard boxes called tuna 'coffins' for airfreight.
ultra-low temperature (ULT)	Ultra-low temperature technology freezes tuna to about –60ºC, which means the flesh does not oxidise and turn brown, which means it can still be sold as *sashimi* (tuna frozen at higher temperatures cannot easily be sold as fresh fish).
UNCLOS	United Nations Convention on the Law of the Sea
VDS	Vessel days scheme. The proposed measure for limiting effort in the region to replace the Palau Arrangement 205-vessel cap. PNA countries will be allocated a number of vessel days that they can then allocate as they see fit. They can choose to auction them to the highest bidders or allocate them preferentially to domestic companies. The Palau Arrangement allocated vessels to fishing states; the VDS allocates effort units to coastal states.
VMS	Vessel monitoring system, used by Pacific island states to monitor the position and activities of fishing vessels to manage their fisheries, maintained by the FFA.
WCPFC	Western and Central Pacific Fisheries Commission. The fisheries management organisation for the Pacific region, operating under the Western and Central Pacific Fisheries Convention.
WCPO	Western and Central Pacific Ocean

Acknowledgments

The research for this book was undertaken while Kate Barclay was an AusAID Postdoctoral Fellow at the Asia Pacific School of Economics and Government (now called The Crawford School), The Australian National University. Additional funds for the research were provided by the Pacific Branch of the Australian Government Agency for International Development (AusAID) and the International Fisheries section of the Australian Government Department of Agriculture, Fisheries and Forestry (DAFF). The revision of the report into a manuscript was undertaken while Dr Barclay was working at the Institute for International Studies, at the University of Technology Sydney.

The research and the book were immeasurably improved through the mentorship of Ian Cartwright, with his decades of experience of fisheries management and policy advice in the Pacific and Australia. Mr Cartwright had extensive input into the Introduction and Chapter 1. The other chapters were written by Dr Barclay. The population and land and sea area data are from Secretariat of the Pacific Community (2004a) and Chapman (2004b).

Many thanks to research assistant Justin Liang for his excellent contributions.

A great number of people assisted in the production of this book, by giving interviews as well as providing documents, contacts and feedback on early drafts. The authors gratefully acknowledge these contributions from people in industry, government departments, international organisations, non-governmental organisations and consulting companies. Interviewees and other contributors are listed by name and organisation below. Any mistakes are the authors' own. The opinions expressed are those of the authors, except where attributed to interviewees. The opinions expressed do not represent the views of The Australian National University or the Australian government.

Thanks to the following people for their support of this project through interviews, passing on reports, sending information by email or passing on useful contacts.

Ailan Seafoods (PNG): Reinhard Mangels
Ailan Awareness (PNG): John Aini
Asian Development Bank: Thomas Gloerfelt-Tarp
Australian Council for International Agricultural Research: Barney Smith, Ken Menz
Australian Government: Glenn Hurry, Sue Erbacher, Mary Sertich, James Lee, Jacinta Innes, Deahne Turnbull, Hannah Birdsey
Australian National University: Maree Tait, Satish Chand, Chakriya Bowman, Mike Bourke, Hannah Parris
Lesley Barclay
Bismark Barramundi (PNG): Ian Middleton
Blue Pacific (Cook Islands): Jack Cooper, Chris (Operations Manager)
Central Pacific Producers (Kiribati): Barerei Onorio, Ariera Tekaata
Judy Chiota
Les Clark

Cook Islands Government: Carl Hunter, Ian Bertram, Peter Graham, Myra Moeka'a, Vaitoti Tupa, Pam Maru, Garth Broadhead, Mark Short

European Union Rural Coastal Fisheries Development Program (PNG): Seán P. Marriott

Fiji Fish Marketing Group Limited: Grahame Southwick, Russell Dunham

Fiji Government: Apolosi Turaganivalu

Fish Bites Incorporated (Cook Islands): Navy Epati

Fisheries Training Centre (Kiribati): Teorae Kabure

Forum Fisheries Agency: Nakada Masao, Transform Aqorau, Steve Dunn, Len Rodwell, Chris Reid, Ben Hall

Frabelle (PNG): Nestor Defensor, Augusto C. Natividad

Gillett, Preston and Associates: Bob Gillett, Garry Preston, David Burgess, Hugh Walton, Peter Watt

Anthony V. Hughes

Takuzo Ishizaki

John Kennedy

Jeff Kinch

Keith Kingston

Kiribati Fisherman's Services Company Limited: T. Nauan Bauro

Kiribati Government: David Yeeting, Raikaon Tumoa, Maruia Kamatie, Beero Tioti, Temwaang, Teea Tira, Terieta (Personal Secretary to the President)

Barry Lalley

Land Holdings Limited: Trevor York

Latitude 8: Maurice Brownjohn

Antony Lewis

David and Tina Mamupio

MAPS Tuna (PNG): Tet Merin, Lyanna Sete

Marshall Islands Government: Glen Joseph

Matira South Fishing Limited (Cook Islands): Frances Garnier

National Fisheries Development (Solomon Islands): Adrian Wickham

Neptune Fishery (PNG): Adrian Chow

Overseas Fishery Cooperation Foundation (Japan): Echigo Manabu

Pacific Fishing Company Limited (Pafco) (Fiji): Jean Claude Guenegan, Inoke Navuetaki, Joy Prakash Gupta, Ashok Raj

Papua New Guinea Government: Samol C. Kanawi, Noan Pakop, Julius Onkau, Norman Barnabas, Yaosa Kaikar, Clarence M. Hoot, John Adani, Terry Sibanganei (Madang Province), Roboam Paka, Julius Onkau, Emmanuel Tamba (New Ireland Province), Peter Wagi, Aquina Kango, Ludwig Kumoru, Sylvester Pokajam

Porter Group (Cook Islands): Glenn Armstrong

RD Tuna (PNG): Pete C. Celso, Danilo D. Zamudio

Sanko Bussan (PNG) Limited: Blaise Paru

Phillip Siaguru

Solander (Fiji): Charles Hufflett, David Lucas

Solomon Islands Development Trust: John Roughan

Solomon Islands Government: Tione Bugotu, Rudolph Dorah, Derek Aihari, Sylvester Diake, Peter Ramohia, Edwin Oreihaka, Pauline Beseto

Soltai Fishing and Processing Limited (Solomon Islands): Milton Sibisopere, Asery Kukui, Mr Nakamura, Afredo D. Sevillejo, Godfrey Manebosa, John Pina

Secretariat of the Pacific Community: Aliti Vunisea, John Hampton, Patrick Ledohey, Lindsay Chapman, Colin Millar, Youngmi Choi, Tim Lawson

South Pacific Regional Environment Program: F. Vitolio Lui

South Seas Tuna (PNG): Ian Boatwood

Robert Stone

Nancy Sullivan

Tarawa Fishermen's Cooperative Society Limited (Kiribati): Maerere Baiteke, Bateriki Baree

The Nature Conservancy (Solomon Islands): William T. Atu

Simon Tiller

Tosa Bussan (Fiji): Nakano Toru

University of the South Pacific: Sandra Tarte, Vina Ram-Bidesi

University of Papua New Guinea: Wilson C. Go, Kirpal Singh, Augustine Mungkaje, Lance Hill, Ross Hines

Gert van Santen

Worldfish Centre: Johann Bell, Chris Ramofafia

World Wide Fund for Nature (WWF): Stephen Kido Dalipanda, Liz Wilson, Luanne Losi

1

The Pacific tuna fishery

The Western and Central Pacific Ocean (WCPO) is home to the largest tuna fishery in the world, representing a vital economic resource for Pacific island countries.[1] This book is intended for readers interested in the development[2] and management[3] of the region's tuna resources. It adds to debates on how best to achieve aspirations for development of the tuna industry without compromising ecological sustainability.

Research for this book consists of interviews with stakeholders conducted during 2005 in six Pacific island countries: Papua New Guinea, Solomon Islands, Marshall Islands, Kiribati, Cook Islands and Fiji (Map 1.1).[4] It also draws on the plethora of previous reports written by fisheries management and development experts on similar topics and discussions with a range of specialists, including those at the Pacific Islands Forum Fisheries Agency (FFA).

To better understand Pacific island countries' aspirations for economic and human development based on their tuna resources, we sought the views of Pacific islander interviewees on a range of issues, including: the current use of tuna resources in the region; the benefits being realised; and whether existing tuna industries look like achieving Pacific islanders' development aspirations. In addition, we obtained interviewees' preferred strategies for future tuna management and development.

The most prominent desire expressed was to capture more of the wealth generated by regional tuna industries in their domestic economies, sustainably and according to principles of social equity. The main ways to capture more wealth propounded by Pacific island governments are by encouraging domestic tuna industry development and maximising returns from distant water fleets. The two approaches are not necessarily mutually exclusive. The ability of Pacific island countries to safeguard their tuna resources relies on their capacity to successfully assert their position within the Western and Central Pacific Fisheries Commission (WCPFC),[5] whose membership includes many of the world's largest and wealthiest states.

The first section of this book is a synthesis of the research conducted in each country about how Pacific island countries can better realise their aspirations for this unique global resource. One of the disturbing findings of the study is that there is a lack of clearly thought out and articulated vision for the future in fisheries management and development in most of the countries researched. Interviewees' hopes for the future were rarely coordinated with each other or the general economic direction of the country, and there was little strategic planning for how to achieve those hopes, or a sense of how what was being done now would contribute. Lack of a clear vision for the future and strategies for how to achieve that vision can lead to short-term, unrealistic, reactive policies and are likely to be a major constraint on the management of and development from tuna resources.

Nevertheless, four of the countries visited have made considerable progress towards increasing the benefits from their tuna resources. Papua New Guinea, Cook Islands and Fiji have moved away from simple access agreements and have various forms of licensing that favour domestic involvement and onshore investment. Marshall Islands, while still having extensive access agreements, has also attracted substantial trans-shipment activity, with flow-on economic benefits. Kiribati, with challenging geographical and socioeconomic environments, has yet to move beyond standard access agreement arrangements. Solomon Islands' fishing industry was one of a number of economic casualties of the social and political upheaval of 2000–03, and is struggling with governance, business confidence and capacity issues to regain previous levels of benefits from tuna.

Nearly all interviews and documents examined for the study showed that Pacific islanders' major aspiration was to capture more wealth from regional tuna fisheries in a sustainable manner. The 2005 meeting of the WCPFC Scientific Committee highlighted overfishing on two of the four main target species of tuna (yellowfin and bigeye), particularly in the most productive areas of the region, and recommended reducing fishing mortality. Decisions taken by the WCPFC in 2005, however, seem to allow for an increase on 2001–03 levels, against the recommendations of the Scientific Committee.

It is clear that the WCPFC must take further effective action to address overfishing. The issue for Pacific island countries is the form that action will take. Recent research has suggested that the sorts of management measures that could appear on the WCPFC table have the potential to result in very different impacts across Pacific island countries and distant water fishing nations (DWFNs),[6] in Exclusive Economic Zones (EEZs) and on the high seas. Means to address these impacts must be incorporated in management measures if agreement is to be reached in a timely manner. While the effects of expanding or reducing fishing pressure are complex, one clear lesson from other fisheries is that failure to manage the fishery will be disastrous for the prospects of capturing wealth from tuna in the long term.

Map 1.1   Western and Central Pacific Ocean

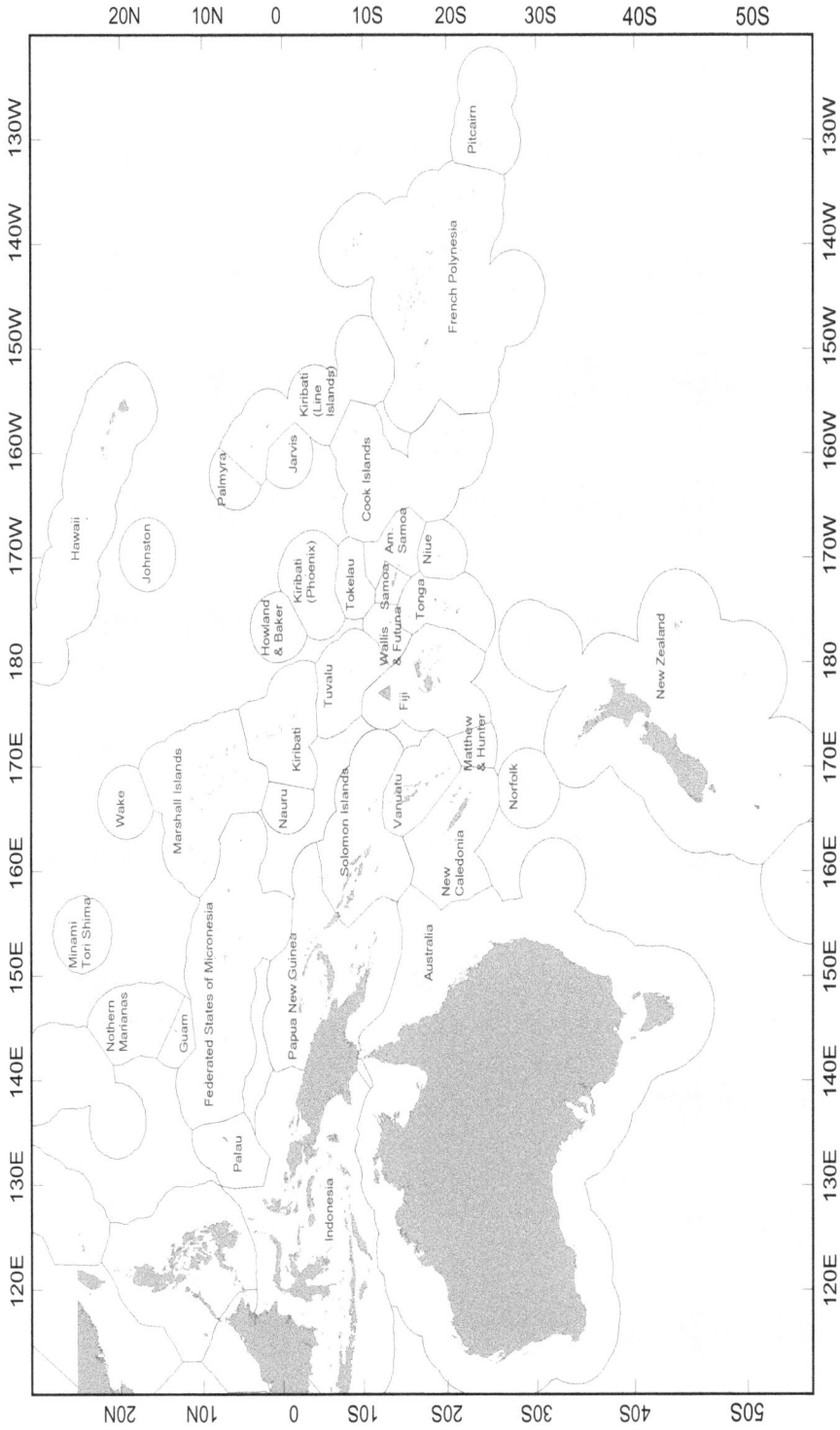

Source: Colin Millar, Secretariat of the Pacific Community, Noumea, New Caledonia.

Western and Central Pacific Ocean tuna fisheries

The resource

The Western and Central Pacific oceanic tuna fishery[7] is based on four key species: skipjack, yellowfin, bigeye and albacore tuna. The resource is of global significance; in 2004, it produced 51 per cent of the world's tuna catch (SPC 2004b). The Western and Central Pacific Ocean tropical tuna species are more productive than the more temperate tuna, including the heavily overfished Pacific bluefin and southern bluefin. The most productive area for tuna lies in the equatorial zone (10°N–10°S), where about 80 per cent of all tuna from the WCPO are caught. Skipjack and small yellowfin and bigeye tuna school (frequently together) on the ocean surface and are commonly found in the tropical and subtropical waters of the WCPO. Larger yellowfin and bigeye are generally found in deeper water, where they are more widespread, although some larger yellowfin (two to three years) are also caught in free-swimming schools. In contrast with skipjack and yellowfin tuna, albacore concentrate in temperate areas where food is abundant.

The oceanic environment

Climate fluctuations have direct impacts on the productivity of the WCPO and the associated tuna fisheries. The most dominant effect is the development of El Niño (and La Niña) or ENSO events,[8] which have direct effects on the distribution of tuna, associated fisheries and industry activity, and on levels of revenue that Pacific island countries can expect to derive on an annual basis from their fisheries. For example, purse-seine effort and catches are generally displaced eastwards during El Niño conditions and westwards during La Niña, indicating a spatial shift in the distribution of surface-swimming (predominantly skipjack) tuna (Figures 1.1 and 1.2), which respond to changes in the availability of food in the surface layers of the ocean. The implications for management are also clear in terms of the overarching need for arrangements that manage the impacts of fishing throughout the range of the stock, including in EEZs[9] and on the high seas.

The highly mobile distant water fleets, subject to negotiating access agreements in EEZs, are able to follow the fish and take advantage of areas of high-catch rates as ENSO conditions dominate. Domestically based fleets using smaller vessels, such as the Pacific island country longline fleets, are less able to do this, so are frequently faced with environmentally driven 'boom and bust' cycles. Processing plants and service and supply industries are also inevitably impacted by these changes.

The Secretariat of the Pacific Community Oceanic Fisheries Program has developed a model for predicting the distribution of skipjack across the region, which could be useful in developing policies in countries such as Marshall Islands, where the availability of the skipjack resource fluctuates (Langley 2004). If, as some scientists fear, global climate change means a more or less permanent El Niño effect, this could have a dramatic effect on the economic potential of the tuna resources for countries such as Marshall Islands, which lose skipjack stocks under these conditions.[10]

Figure 1.1   **Distribution of US purse-seine catches in a typical El Niño year, 1994**

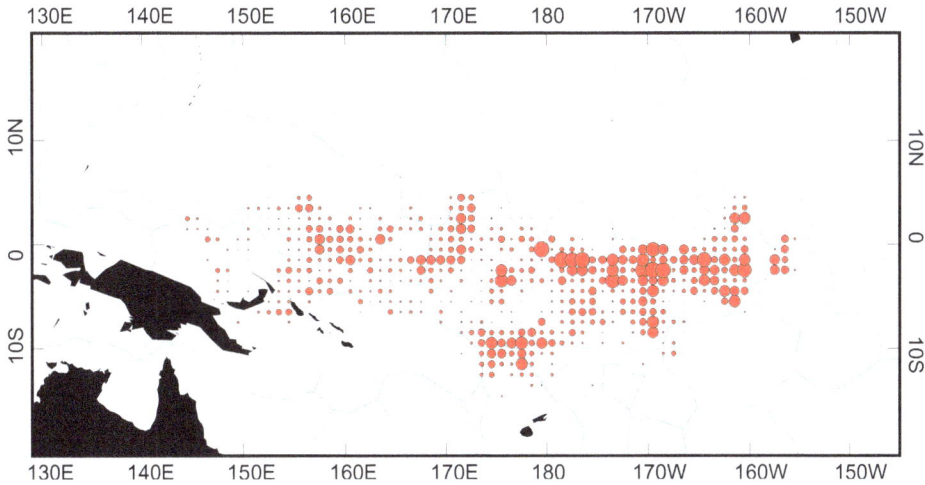

Source: Secretariat of the Pacific Community as presented in Asian Development Bank (ADB), 2003. *On or Beyond the Horizon: a discussion paper on options for improving economic outcomes from the Western and Central Pacific Tuna Fishery*, ADB TA 6128-REG 226, Technical Assistance for Alternative Negotiating Arrangements to Increase Fisheries Revenues in the Pacific, Asian Development Bank, Manila.

Figure 1.2   **Distribution of US purse-seine catches in a typical La Niña year, 1995**

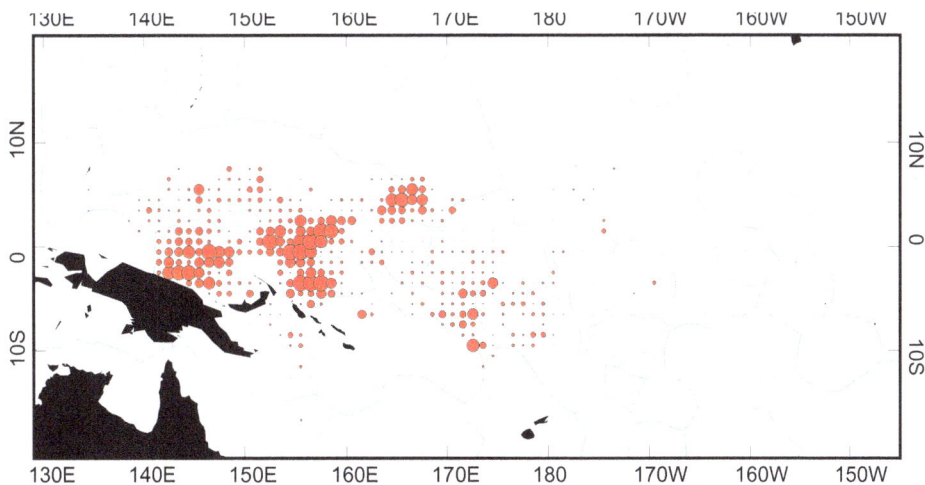

Source: Secretariat of the Pacific Community as presented in Asian Development Bank (ADB), 2003. *On or Beyond the Horizon: a discussion paper on options for improving economic outcomes from the Western and Central Pacific Tuna Fishery*, ADB TA 6128-REG 226, Technical Assistance for Alternative Negotiating Arrangements to Increase Fisheries Revenues in the Pacific, Asian Development Bank, Manila.

The fisheries

There are three major components to the WCPO tuna fishery, each associated with a particular fish behaviour. In order of importance these are purse-seine, longline and pole-and-line. Table 1.1 provides a summary of these components.

Purse-seine. The provisional 2004 purse-seine catch of about 1.2 million metric tonnes was the highest on record and the catch has been around this high level for the past three years (Williams and Reid 2005). Purse-seine vessels target primarily skipjack, with associated catches of small yellowfin and bigeye. The operation is highly mechanised and technology and capital intensive, with modern vessels costing in excess of US$25 million. Despite these barriers to entry, some Pacific island countries still seek national involvement in the ownership and operation of these vessels, because of the significance of purse-seining to the overall WCPO tuna fishery. While the DWFNs of Korea, Taiwan, Japan and the United States still account for about 75 per cent of the purse-seine catch, vessels based in Pacific island countries fishing under the FSM Arrangement[11] and Philippines vessels catch the balance (Williams and Reid 2005). This reflects an increasing involvement of these vessels in Pacific island country economies, particularly in the case of Papua New Guinea, where the bulk of the FSM Arrangement fleet is based, and where there is a correlation between shore-based investment and access.

The fishery is high volume with relatively low value (per tonne). In recent decades, most fleets have suffered from a profitability squeeze with increasing fuel and other costs, and oversupply has depressed prices. While prices have trended upwards in recent years, and the catches per unit of fishing effort (CPUE—a measure of efficiency) have increased substantially for some fleets, the fact that the fuel price has increased by about 300 per cent since 2002 (Krampe 2006) has tended to offset these gains. The substantial increase in the Taiwanese fleet during this period can be considered an indication of relatively profitable operations and confidence in the future. It would be useful to understand more about the price structure of this fleet, including any possible hidden subsidies that might apply. The high-cost US fleet has been hit particularly hard and has reduced in numbers from about 50 vessels when the US multilateral access treaty was first signed in the 1980s to less than 20 vessels in 2005. Overall, in real terms, the value of tuna fisheries has shrunk by half since the early 1980s (ADB 2003).

Longline. The longline fishery continues to account for about 10–12 per cent of the total WCPO catch (about 220,000 metric tonnes in 2004), but is about the same in value as the larger purse-seine catch, reflecting its uses for premium sashimi and other higher (than canning) value products (Williams and Reid 2005). The method targets fewer, larger, deeper-swimming tuna using hooks set over a minimum of tens of kilometres of ocean. Longline vessels in the WCPO are of two main types: large distant water freezer vessels and smaller (less than 100 gross registered tonnage [GRT]) offshore vessels specialising in chilled fish. This latter class is based locally and has formed the backbone of Pacific island country efforts to expand domestic fishing operations, particularly in more southern countries.

Table 1.1   Main industrial gear types used in Western and Central Pacific Ocean tuna fisheries

Gear type	Catch	Typical vessel that uses gear	Notes
Purse-seine	Mainly skipjack and small yellowfin, with an incidental catch of small bigeye. Most catch is for canning		About 60 per cent of the tuna catch in the WCPO region is by purse-seine gear: about 1.2 million tonnes in 2003. Most of the purse-seine catch is taken within five degrees of the equator. These are high-technology and expensive vessels, so few are based domestically in the Pacific. Most are run by DWFNs.
Longline	Mainly large-size yellowfin, bigeye and albacore. The prime yellowfin and bigeye are often exported chilled to overseas markets. Most of the albacore is for canning.		About 11 per cent of the tuna catch in the WCPO region is by longline gear: about 213,000 tonnes .in 2003. There are two major types of longliners: 1) relatively large vessels with mechanical freezing equipment (often based outside the Pacific islands), and 2) smaller vessels that use mostly ice to preserve fish and are typically based at a port in the Pacific islands. Small and medium-scale longline vessels have been favoured in domestic industry development schemes since the 1990s.
Pole-and-line	Mainly skipjack and small yellowfin. Most catch is for canning, katsuobushi or the Japanese fresh skipjack market		About 15 per cent of the tuna catch in the WCPO region is by pole-and-line gear: about 295,000 tonnes in 2003. In the 1980s, several Pacific island countries had fleets of these vessels, but most no longer operate due to competition with the more productive purse-seine gear. The Japanese distant water, larger scale pole-and-line fleet, however, remains active in the region.

Source: Gillett, R., 2005. 'Tuna for tomorrow? Some of the science behind an important fishery in the Pacific islands', in RETA 6128: alternative negotiating arrangements to increase fisheries revenues in the Pacific, Asian Development Bank, Manila.

Domestic longline opportunities were opened up by the introduction of medium-scale longliners of less than 60GRT using monofilament gear in the mid to late 1980s. Until then the major fleets from Taiwan, Japan and China had been using 200–500GRT vessels. The first domestic medium-scale longline fleet emerged entirely from the private sector in Fiji in the late 1980s. A fleet emerged in Papua New Guinea in 1995. Successes in these countries meant other Pacific island countries became interested, and regional fisheries development advisors pushed the idea. All six of the countries covered here have had some form of domestic longline development. After a promising start, most Pacific island country-based longline fisheries were stagnating by 2005. Table 1.2 provides a summary of the progress of the expansion of tuna longline fishing in Pacific island country waters, highlighting in most cases a rush to enter the fishery, a period of relatively stable catches and profitability, followed by severe declines due to falling catch rates, rising costs of inputs including fuel and air freight, and other logistical difficulties.

Pole-and-line. Catches by pole-and-line vessels in the WCPO have been about 270–300,000mt in recent years. Most (more than 90 per cent) is taken by the Indonesian and Japanese fleets, with very little being caught in Pacific island country EEZs, with the exception of Solomon Islands. Since pole-and-line fisheries target the same species as purse-seiners (skipjack), the overall efficiency of purse-seining has resulted in a marked decline in the number of pole-and-line vessels in the WCPO. The medium-scale shore-based pole-and-line fisheries that have been based in Pacific island countries (as opposed to the larger Japanese distant water vessels) have much higher costs per tonnage of fish than the purse-seine method. Fisheries formerly operating in Palau, Papua New Guinea and Kiribati are no longer active, only one vessel is now operating (seasonally) in Fiji and fishing activities are only now starting to improve after problems in the Solomon Islands fishery in recent years (Williams and Reid 2005).

For the pole-and-line method to be economically viable, therefore, it needs markets that will pay a premium price for its product. Solomon Islands' pole-and-line fishery had such a market in the United Kingdom until 2000, which was one of the reasons why the company kept its head above water for so long (as well as because of the Cotonou Agreement's 24 per cent tariff advantage over competitor countries in Southeast Asia). The loss of this market is one of the reasons why the Solomon Islands fishery has had financial trouble since 2000.[12]

Downstream processing

Fiji and Solomon Islands have had the longest running canneries among the countries covered by this study, both starting in the early 1970s with Japanese investment.[13] The next large-scale cannery was opened by the Philippines-based company RD in Papua New Guinea in 1997. The RD initiative was part of a PNG domestication policy to entice distant water fishing companies to establish shore bases by tying fisheries access to the building of processing facilities and offloading a proportion of their catch each year. After the success of RD, several other large-scale plants have been initiated. Marshall Islands also had a loining plant for about five years in the early 2000s.

Table 1.2 Domestic longline development by country, 1995–2005

Country	Fishery type	Fishery status 1995	Fishery status 2002	Fishery status 2005
Cook Islands	Small to medium scale targeting sashimi tuna in the south, larger scale catching albacore for canneries in the north	A couple of distant water fleet vessels operating in the south; no domestic players	Domestic southern and northern fisheries experienced a boom (to 19 vessels from 3 in 2001)	CPUE decline and lack of profitability led to stagnation in southern fishery; many who entered fishery in 2002 left in 2004–05. Northern fishery continuing strong
Fiji	Small to medium scale targeting tuna for sashimi markets	Private-sector companies Fiji Fish and Solander started in the 1980s, picked up momentum, joined by Chinese companies (total 90 vessels)	Boom of late 1990s continued (peaked at more than 100 vessels)	CPUE decline and lack of profitability led to stagnation. Domestic private-sector veterans hanging on, new entrants dropping out (60 vessels active)
Kiribati	Small scale targeting sashimi tuna	One government-owned pole-and-line vessel converted to longline	Specially designed, locally constructed small-scale vessels being developed under an aid project	Two locally built vessels being trialled by government, not yet exporting
Marshall Islands	Medium scale targeting sashimi tuna	Government and aid-sponsored medium-scale vessels (5). Ting Hong distant water vessels based locally (peaked at more than 100)	Government and aid-sponsored vessels failed. Ting Hong replaced by MIFV Chinese vessels (49) based locally	No domestically owned vessels, MIFV vessels (38) based locally
Papua New Guinea	Medium scale targeting tuna for sashimi markets, and shark	Beginning of private-sector driven domestic medium-scale fleet	Booming, with 40 vessels at several centres around the country	Freight costs and logistical difficulties, and CPUE decline, led to stagnation; all centres but Port Moresby closed down; all but one company wound back operation
Solomon Islands	Medium scale targeting tuna for sashimi markets	One foreign-owned, locally based operation in Honiara (Solgreen)	Solgreen continuing (about 10 vessels)	Solgreen closed. New company Global in Tulagi (31 vessels)

Other kinds of commercial tuna processing conducted in the Pacific include: packing and preparing chilled and/or frozen tuna into loins or steaks for fresh-fish markets; smoke-drying skipjack for *katsuobushi* (a commonly used stock flavouring and condiment in Japanese cuisine);[14] and in recent years small-scale factories have started up in several countries producing various kinds of gourmet processed fish—cold smoked tuna ham and tuna jerky.

While large-scale fish processing in the form of canneries and loining plants has generated employment and spin-off benefits in Fiji, Solomon Islands and more recently in Papua New Guinea, uncompetitively high-cost production environments mean almost all of these developments have relied on government revenue in one way or another. They are also vulnerable to erosion of trade preferences under the Cotonou Agreement. Processing of fresh chilled and frozen fish connected to longline fisheries in Papua New Guinea and Fiji—as purely private-sector ventures—has been more economically sound, but is currently suffering from falling CPUE in the fishery and the high costs of freight. Small-scale gourmet processing plants are a new initiative that might prove to be well suited to Pacific island country conditions.

Effects of trade barriers on domestic processing industries

The European Union and the United States have tariffs on imports of canned tuna, to protect their domestic canning industries. For this reason, Fiji's Pafco exports loins rather than cans to the United States. As former European colonies in Africa, the Caribbean and the Pacific (ACP), Papua New Guinea, Solomon Islands and Fiji are exempt from the 24 per cent tariff under the Cotonou Agreement. The EU tariff thus gives processed tuna from these countries a trade advantage in lucrative EU markets over more competitive industries in Southeast Asia, although with quotas this has begun to change. Under the EU Economic Partnership with Pacific island countries, it is possible that the complex Rules of Origin for fisheries products will be simplified and relaxed to also allow fish processed in Pacific island countries but caught by vessels owned in other countries to be included in the definition of 'ACP' (Rodwell, pers. comm.).[15] For the first few years of operations, the RD cannery in Papua New Guinea relied mostly on US markets, but in 2005 the managing director said that without the trade advantage in the European Union the cannery would 'close tomorrow' because the high costs of processing in Papua New Guinea meant that it could not compete against Southeast Asian producers (Celso, pers. comm.). Pacific island country developments in tuna processing are therefore vulnerable to erosion of EU trade preferences.

Food safety requirements

Food safety regulations for the European Union and the United States are very strict. Nevertheless, Solomon Taiyo managed to meet interim EU standards in the past, while RD and Pafco currently export to the European Union and the United States. The EU Partnership Agreement includes assistance to Pacific island countries for achieving the technical capacity to test and monitor food safety, and the United Nations Food and Agriculture Organisation (FAO) gives assistance with implementing hazard analysis critical control point (HACCP) systems. These food safety requirements can be seen as an incentive to develop human resources and facilities capacities, with positive spin-offs for other industries where food safety is important, such as tourism and hospitality, as well as for the health systems of Pacific island countries.

Management of tuna fisheries in the WCPO

In common with many other fisheries worldwide, fisheries management in the WCPO has on the whole been reactive. According to one industry representative, national fisheries managers either have not had the vision to step in and make the hard decisions early enough to avoid 'a big bust after the boom', causing the fishery to settle at a level far below optimal sustainable rates, or have had the vision but not the power to enforce their decisions on unwilling fishing companies (Southwick, pers. comm.). Messages of gradually increasing concern have been delivered by the SPC in the past decade regarding bigeye, and latterly yellowfin. Stocks were, however, generally considered to be healthy enough not to signal the need for strong management action until more recent times.

Ecological sustainability is the basic prerequisite for being able to capture wealth from tuna industries. For governments to be able to deliver on sustainability outcomes, they need to have appropriate and consistent policies at three political scales

- sustainable management at the domestic level
- effective cooperation and coordination and some management at the regional level (FFA and subregional groups such as the Parties to the Nauru Agreement[16] [PNA])
- sustainable management at the international/multilateral level (WCPFC).

The latest stock assessment from the WCPFC First Regular Scientific Committee Meeting held in August 2005 shows that resource sustainability is now a serious issue. The WCPO used to have a buffer of relatively healthy stocks giving it time in which to work out the best regional management measures, but as the stocks have been fished down, these measures have to be decided on and implemented as a matter of urgency for some species (WCPFC 2005). The increasingly worrying scientific advice coming from the SPC contrasts with the lack of concrete action to manage the burgeoning increases in tuna-fishing activity (Greenpeace c.2005).

An interesting point about the WCPO tuna fishery is that the biological and economic components of sustainability are in different relationships with each other in different sectors. Most notably, economic unsustainability for the longline fisheries in the south kicks in long before significant impacts on the stocks as a whole occur. Yet the equatorial purse-seine skipjack fishery could remain economically viable even after the overall yellowfin and bigeye stocks are driven well below sustainable target levels. FFA-wide views and aspirations on tuna management and development vary as a result of this.

It is clear that allocation and effective management measures must be achieved sufficiently quickly to halt and reverse the impacts of fishing on bigeye and yellowfin stocks. If not, the WCPO tuna fishery seems likely to trend towards becoming a high-volume, skipjack-oriented purse-seine fishery, dominated by the low-cost Chinese and Taiwanese fleets, with minimal input from Pacific islanders.

Table 1.3   A history of constraints identified for development from tuna resources

ADB report (ADB 1997)	FFA report (Gillett 2003)	This book (2007)
Direct involvement of government in tuna businesses deterring the private sector; protected economies; government-oriented business interests	Widespread belief among fisheries officials that the role of government is to enable private-sector development, although officials without knowledge of the history of failure of state-owned enterprises still favour them	Most interviewees with a fisheries background believe state ownership of vessels or other means of direct involvement in tuna fisheries is a bad idea, but some influential officials still call for state ownership of tuna enterprises.
High-risk, capital-intensive nature of tuna fishing industry; difficult access to markets; high-cost production environments.		Declining profitability of tuna fishing since 1970s; lack of trading/marketing skills a problem; high-cost production environment.
Inadequate and inadequately managed sea and airfreight infrastructure.	Airfreight availability problems; inefficient harbour management.	Diseconomies of scale for air and sea freight in most locations.
Lack of commercial credit	Credit availability problems	Credit availability only a problem for those with no/bad commercial track record
Economies unstable; industry and investment policies unsound; unfriendly environment for foreign investors	Policies unstable; taxation difficult; administration expensive and prone to blockage; poor government–industry dialogue; low attractiveness to investors	General economic environment and policy development polices leading to over-promotion framework not conducive to industrial development; of fishing as an investment opportunity, lack of consultation with industry, in turn creating boom/bust cycle in between government departments, with other stakeholders; tuna fishing
Human resources not competitive on cost/productivity; inadequate pools of skills in some areas (technical, business)	Low levels of entrepreneurial development and industrial fisheries skills	Lack of business experience a problem for indigenous fisheries development; lack of human resource capacities in private and public sectors
Policies unclear and inconsistent	Instability of policies affecting tuna industries	Overarching need for strong, sound domestic policies to promote sustainable development and underpin regional and multilateral negotiating positions

Environmental laws not enforced

Inadequate supplies of fresh water for processing in all but a few Pacific island locations; difficult to access land for commercial purposes

Heavy reliance on preferential trade access likely to be eroded in future

Environmental and social/political aspects of fisheries management inadequately addressed, detracting from development benefits and damaging the business environment

Lack of fresh water and land for commercial development

Heavy reliance on preferential trade access likely to be eroded in future

Sources: Asian Development Bank (ADB), 1997. *The Pacific's Tuna: the challenge of investing in growth, Pacific Studies Series*, Asian Development Bank, Office of Pacific Operations, Manila. Gillett, R., 2003. *Domestic tuna industry development in the Pacific islands. The current situation and considerations for future development assistance*, FFA Report 03/01, Pacific Islands Forum Fisheries Agency, Honiara, Solomon Islands.

The FFA's Economics and Marketing Manager, Len Rodwell, considers that one major key to addressing the bigeye (and to a lesser extent the yellowfin) issues is to regulate the catches of purse-seiners. In addition, improving observer and port-sampling programs would more accurately differentiate between bigeye and yellowfin catches and assist with the regulation and accuracy of stock assessments. While there are some limits on purse seine fishing effort imposed through the PNA-based Palau Arrangement and its replacement, the much-anticipated Vessel Days Scheme (VDS), these are insufficient to halt the current trend towards overfishing and stock decline.

Given that the majority of the purse seine fishery in the WCPO (about 65 per cent) is carried out in the waters of FFA countries, and access to their waters by DWFNs is essential for economic operation, the FFA must effectively exert control over the purse seine fishery. The longline fishery is more difficult to control, given that the reverse situation prevails, with most fish taken on the high seas.

Good governance and clear and well-informed national policies on tuna management, strengthened through regional cooperation at the PNA/FFA level, given effect throughout the range of stocks by agreeing suitable measures in the WCPFC, offer the best way forward for the region.

Past recommendations for development from tuna

Tables 1.3 and 1.4 compare constraints and recommendations for developing Pacific tuna resources made close to a decade ago with more recent studies, including this one. The tables show that Pacific island countries have made good ground in some areas. In particular, most governments have come to see the private sector as a more appropriate driver of tuna development than state-owned enterprises. Service and supply industries have been promoted successfully in some Pacific island countries as an alternative to domestic fishing industries, and generally there has been a shift from simply desiring tuna development towards realising tangible results.

It is not easy to determine the precise degree to which tuna industry developments have occurred as a result of previous recommendations and reports, although in some cases (for example, Marshall Islands, Cook Islands), advice and technical assistance from regional organisations and aid donors have had clear results in terms of domestic industry expansion.

Cook Islands

Cook Islands has learnt much from its brief foray into tuna fisheries development, going through a boom–bust cycle in about 10 years. Even at current levels, however, the benefits to the domestic economy far outweigh the meagre access fees (US$5,000 per longline vessel, per annum) that were formerly the only income from offshore tuna resources. Much of this development arose from advice from the FFA and the SPC, and an administration willing to accept that advice. The government was also highly committed to domesticating its fishery. If Cook Islands' tuna industry recovers from the slump it was experiencing in 2005 and develops into an economically sustainable industry, it could be a valuable part of Cook Islands' overall economy, relieving some of the heavy dependence on tourism.

Table 1.4   A history of recommendations made for development from tuna resources

ADB report (ADB 1997)	FFA report (Gillett 2003)	This book (2007)
Maximise distant water access fees (rentals)		Distant water access fees are an important source of revenue for some countries, and can be increased but consider alternative approaches:improving governance of negotiations, regional cooperation and by managing fisheries such that profitability is maintained/restored
Concentrate domestic development on service and supply		Service and supply is another way to gain returns from DWFNs, as is supplying crew
Reorient role of government to enable private-sector investment (from state ownership); stimulate domestic private sector to invest; encourage foreign investors to base locally	Create investment-friendly economic climate; tuna management plans help with policy and administration environment; fisheries associations help with industry–government dialogue; revise taxation, especially for fuel; disseminate reports	Improve fisheries management, policymaking and administration for the business environment, and exchange of information in order to capture more wealth from tuna fisheries
	Seek leaders for local, medium to large-scale tuna businesses from business backgrounds, not small-scale fisheries	Develop business training and experience to achieve greater indigenous leadership in tuna industries
	Fish aggregating devices (FADs) are one of the few initiatives in small-scale tuna fisheries that have been successful, but few countries in the region have effective FAD programs	Small-scale fisheries development can be assisted with FAD programs (but likely to require continuing subsidies), greater understanding and protection of coastal marine environments, trust funds from industrial tuna fisheries and improved consultation
	Increase the FFA's role in domestic industry	In addition to the planned provision of development advice for individual countries, the FFA couldcoordinate/promote regional development initiatives
	Scrutinise development schemes (cost–benefit analysis) before committing government money	Ensure projects chosen are most likely to be economically sustainable; match individual country circumstances and those least likely to be a drain on revenue,noting that despite evidence that tuna fishing enterprises often do not generate wealth, countries still wish to develop them

Sources: Asian Development Bank (ADB), 1997. The Pacific's Tuna: the challenge of investing in growth, Pacific Studies Series, Asian Development Bank, Office of Pacific Operations, Manila. Gillett, R., 2003. Domestic tuna industry development in the Pacific islands. The current situation and considerations for future development assistance, FFA Report 03/01, Pacific Islands Forum Fisheries Agency, Honiara, Solomon Islands.

Fiji

The development of Fiji's domestic longlining industry can be considered a success story that emerged purely from the private sector. For a period, Fiji's longline fishery and related fresh-fish processing businesses were clearly financially viable, but they were hit hard in recent years with falling CPUE and rising fuel prices. While domestication has been a success in one sense, in common with other fisheries considered during the study, some of these gains were lost due to the lack of effective management and inadequate licensing. Fiji's large processing company, Pafco, has required large inputs of government revenue, but it has provided jobs and human resource training opportunities for people outside Suva.

The use of fisheries as a tool to address self-determination issues and implement affirmative action polices has been problematic, and has contributed to the downturn of the domestic longline industry. Bringing more indigenous Fijians into ownership and leadership roles in tuna industries is a long-term policy of the government.

Kiribati

Numerous plans and reports have been provided and a management plan completed, which has not been implemented. Most recommendations have pointed to a poor macroeconomic environment, fragile land environment and small economy as almost insurmountable barriers to competitive shore-based tuna development. The government, however, believes that there are good prospects for large-scale processing (a loining plant), apparently backed up by a positive feasibility study. There is also a strongly expressed but ill-defined desire to 'become more involved' in tuna fisheries. A number of failed government-driven small-scale tuna operations have not deterred clear preference by government for continuing involvement in tuna operations. The small-scale domestic fishery selling direct to the public has, however, flourished.

Marshall Islands

Marshall Islands has experienced a number of setbacks and generally overcome them, moving from operational involvement by government in fishing operations to successfully encouraging and supporting private-sector investment. This success was also donor led, through a major ADB institutional strengthening project. Marshall Islands' resource potential, freight and transport connections, and the pragmatic, relatively business-friendly approach of the government means Marshall Islands is in a good position to maintain and increase the wealth it generates from tuna industries. The shortage of local managers, a small labour pool and relatively high wages are constraints to development. These factors are caused at least partly by the ability of Marshallese to go to work in the United States. The social impacts of hosting a busy international port in the lagoon detract from the economic benefits gained from tuna industries, so this is another area in need of policy attention. The fluctuations in the fortunes of the tuna sector are somewhat tied to El Niño cycle-driven resource availability and strategies to smooth (or adapt to) this variation need to be factored into development strategies.

Papua New Guinea

In terms of the full range of raw materials and infrastructure required for successful domestic industry development, Papua New Guinea is in the best position of any of the Pacific island countries included in this study. In addition, Papua New Guinea's tuna resources are so rich it can make a great deal from distant water fleets. After a major donor-led restructure of national fisheries bodies into the National Fisheries Authority (NFA), substantial gains were made and investment attracted. While some impressive progress has been made, one main factor constraining Papua New Guinea from achieving its development aspirations is the capacity of the government to improve the business environment. Of particular concern to industry and investors has been the uncertainty surrounding governance, especially the politicisation of decision-making at the NFA. The other main factor is implementing sound management of the tuna fishery for its long-term sustainability. The large processing venture RD has been more commercially viable than previous attempts by Pacific island countries to trade access fees for onshore development, proving the domestication model is possible despite a challenging competitive environment.

Solomon Islands

Solomon Islands has a long history of domestic fisheries development. There has been some success with a pole-and-line fleet and a cannery as major contributors to the economy, especially through employment. Lack of capacity in the public fisheries sector and poor governance have been longstanding issues. Immediately before the social and political breakdown of 2000–03, however, the Solomon Islands tuna industry was relatively healthy and its fisheries management was among the best in the region. While the breakdown in law and order and governance in 2000, rampant corruption, escalating costs and loss of confidence destroyed much of the industry, there is proof-of-concept for a viable Solomon Islands domestic tuna industry. The tuna plan, which was reviewed after peace was restored, has yet to be implemented, and the largest domestic company, Soltai, faces an uncertain future.

Despite the progress outlined above, a number of the constraints identified nearly a decade ago in the major ADB study remained in 2005.

Clearly, there is no lack of ideas about how Pacific island countries can achieve more from their tuna resources. Many seem feasible but have yet to be tried by Pacific island governments. In some cases, there has tended to be a cycle of identifying a problem, commissioning a report, failing to act on the report, re-identifying the same problem, commissioning a report, and so on. Indeed, there is a no guarantee that this book will not suffer the same fate.

Given the political, economic, social and cultural background prevailing in Pacific island countries, however, it is perhaps not surprising that progress is slow. Many of the issues that remain to be addressed are deep-seated structural issues that will take time to overcome. While on occasion the problem is a lack of commitment on the part of officials to try recommendations, in other cases the commitment is there but insurmountable obstacles prevent movement. It is one thing for consultants and others to make pronouncements, frequently assuming an open and transparent market economy, and quite another to make them happen. Much remains to be done, but it is heartening to look at the progress that has been achieved despite governance problems, capacity constraints, stifling bureaucracy and political pressures.

Regional cooperation by Pacific island countries on tuna

There are increasing calls for greater regional cooperation among Pacific island countries from the highest level, as embodied in documents such as the *Pacific Plan* (Eminent Persons' Group 2004; Pacific Islands Forum 2005). Calls for greater regional cooperation in the Pacific have been made for some decades; new factors in such calls include the mounting evidence of the failure of many Pacific island countries to assert 'effective sovereignty' due to lack of government capacity. One study estimates that poor governance has cost US$75 billion in forgone income in Papua New Guinea, Fiji, Solomon Islands and Nauru since independence (Grynberg et al. 2005). Increasing interventionist Australian government policy towards its Pacific islands neighbours since 11 September 2001 is another new factor (Fry 2005).

Regional cooperation in oceanic fisheries has been seen as a 'shining example' of governments working together in the Pacific (Tarte 2004). Due to the migratory nature of the resource, for tuna fisheries management in the WCPO to be effective, it must be managed regionally, multilaterally and nationally. Regional bodies such as the FFA (established in 1979) and the Oceanic Fisheries Program at the SPC (established in 1980) have coordinated and assisted Pacific island countries in various regional initiatives relating to research, management and development of their tuna resources.

One the other hand, there are several significant areas in which Pacific island countries have not achieved cooperation in fisheries. Most notably, they have not shared economic information about tuna industries or aid, or negotiated access/licensing arrangements collaboratively, despite the US multilateral treaty providing evidence that regional negotiation could yield substantial benefits.[17]

With the establishment of the WCPFC, Pacific island countries also have to work with distant water fishing countries, some of whom oppose Pacific island countries on key issues. Japan was a difficult opponent for Pacific island countries in the negotiations leading up to the establishment of the WCPFC.[18] Japan promises to continue to be a strong opponent of Pacific island countries being allocated the tuna resources in their EEZs, arguing that fishing states have at least equal rights to the resources and that highly migratory resources do not 'belong' to the zone in which they are caught. The fact that Japan has fishing relations with some Pacific island countries (mostly PNA states) has tended to create divisions in regional cooperation to achieve recognition for issues such as allocation by fishing zones. In particular, Japan's past practice of engaging with, or paying travel expenses for, only Pacific island countries with which it has fishing agreements has been divisive. Other distant water fishing states/entities in the WCPFC include the United States, Korea, China, Taiwan and the European Union. These states and entities are highly industrialised, with considerable wealth and other resources at their disposal to underpin negotiating strategies. Pacific island countries will need every tool at their disposal to further their interests, the most powerful of which is an ability to win votes through regional cooperation, combined with strategic alliances with like-minded states.

Summary of recommendations

Based on case studies of tuna industries and distant water fleet activities, we specify 10 strategies for working towards the goal of capturing more wealth domestically in a sustainable and socially equitable manner. Specific policies necessarily vary from country to country because each has very different economic, cultural and geographic environments, including different endowments of tuna resources. Some general strategies, however, can be more or less usefully applied across the region.

The most fundamental strategy is effective fisheries management. We suggest that in light of Pacific islanders' aspirations in this context, fisheries management should be understood and applied more broadly than just in terms of conserving the resource. At the same time, fisheries management measures should optimise productivity and hence profitability of fisheries. At a regional level, management measures must be designed to take account of economic factors and the complex interactions between gear and species across EEZs and the high seas. Furthermore, fisheries management is most effective when it takes into consideration the social, cultural and political contexts in which it operates.

Recommendation 1
Place greater emphasis on predicting economic outcomes—particularly across fisheries, gear types and WCPFC members—when designing and determining management measures, including levels of fishing effort by domestic and foreign fleets.

Recommendation 2
Follow up the 2002 FFA Rights-Based Workshop, possibly through a series of in-country seminars, to increase awareness among domestic policymakers and fisheries managers of such approaches.

Recommendation 3
Base tuna management and development on the principles of ecologically sustainable development—balancing economic, environmental and social goals and outcomes.

Another basic strategy for capturing more wealth from tuna is for Pacific island countries to make the most of DWFN companies, especially since access fees from these fleets are the easiest way to capture wealth. The case studies demonstrate than in addition to access fees and fisheries aid, some Pacific island countries have drawn benefits from DWFNs through spin-off supply and service businesses based on fleets trans-shipping in port. Many reports have already been written about how Pacific island countries could increase their level of access fees, so our recommendation for access fees is to follow up on ideas raised in those reports and make a more concerted effort to reform the basis for granting access and the associated fee negotiations.

Recommendation 4
Hold an access-fee summit (hosted by the FFA) including Pacific island fisheries officials, other stakeholders and experts to discuss various ways of licensing DWFN vessels, including improving the existing access fee-based arrangements and alternatives,

such as appropriate rights-based licensing and chartering arrangements. The summit should revisit the many reports on increasing access fees that have been produced over the years and consider seriously which ideas will work in practice.

While other stakeholders, including the community and industry, can use the democratic process to influence public policy, Pacific island governments hold the key to creating an environment to enable private-sector development. Pacific island governments will determine the nature and success of fisheries management measures to protect the resource and investors' rights in the resource, and it is governments that negotiate and agree on distant water access and other licensing agreements.

Based on the case study material, we suggest a range of areas where governments can improve the economic environment, including: more consultative and informed decision making; policy stability; non-discriminatory taxation regimes; effective, efficient government services; developing investment hubs; departmental structures and planning; transparency and accountability; and industrial policy, including human resources development.

Recommendation 5
Pacific island government officials, with industry representatives, review the delivery of government services with industry representatives, to highlight ways of streamlining bureaucratic processes to increase industry efficiency and profitability.

Recommendation 6
Review successes and failures in tuna management and development planning processes to date and base future efforts on lessons learned. Develop tuna management plans such that they are 'owned' by nationals and have agreed, achievable goals and timelines. Plans should have legislative force. Progress needs to be assessed on a regular basis, and goals and strategies revised to ensure alignment with national and regional policies, as well as tuna fisheries and market dynamics.

Recommendation 7
Appoint a professional regional representative (possibly part-time) to represent the interests of Pacific island country tuna industries, working closely with the FFA. The representative should be adequately funded to travel and liaise to improve consultation and inclusion. In particular, the representative should attend regional meetings and set up information networks with industry players.

Recommendation 8
Bring industry, environmental and social/community NGOs into consultative decision-making processes as envisaged in tuna management plans.

Recommendation 9
Sponsor agencies to make consultants' reports publicly available as a general rule. The FFA or the SPC should develop and manage a publicly accessible bibliographic database of publications with relevance to tuna in the region.

Recommendation 10

Build capacity in Pacific island country fisheries departments in the following fields: fisheries management (including working knowledge of stock assessments); economics; business management; and public policy.

The remainder of the strategies are about the possibilities for private-sector regional cooperation in generating wealth, the roles of bodies such as the FFA and the SPC in facilitating industrial fisheries development, and exploring possibilities for generating wealth from small-scale coastal tuna fisheries and recreational fishing.

Notes

[1] For the purposes of this book, Pacific island countries are synonymous with the members of the Pacific Islands Forum Fisheries Agency (FFA).

[2] 'Development' in this book refers to specific fisheries industry development and to general economic development.

[3] 'Management' in this book is used for fisheries resource management and business management, within fisheries bureaucracies and in the private sector.

[4] The tables in the Appendices show some of the statistical similarities and differences between these countries, in terms of their general economy as well as their tuna fisheries.

[5] Fisheries targeting highly migratory species such as tuna cannot be managed effectively by individual countries, so the world's tuna fisheries are managed multilaterally through Regional Fisheries Management Organisations (RFMOs). The WCPFC is to administer the *Convention for the Conservation and Management of Highly Migratory Fish Stocks in the Western and Central Pacific Ocean* and met for the first time in December 2004. The convention establishing the Commission and laying down the basis for its work entered into force in June 2004. Before the convention was adopted, the negotiations were in the form of a Multilateral High Level Conference (MHLC).

[6] The term distant water fishing *nation* is not a good one because a nation is a subjective construct usually based on feelings of ethnic belonging and historical ties to particular territories. States are the administrative, political and economic units associated with nations. So, strictly speaking, the term should be distant water fishing *states*. This report, however, uses the term DWFN because it will be more familiar to readers than DWFS.

[7] Scientific information used here might not be as up to date as a specialist fisheries management for this region might be able to find. This book, however, aims to go across disciplines, and in that vein the information used is the best the authors were able to find at the time of writing.

[8] The ENSO (El Niño/Southern Oscillation) is an oscillation between a warm (El Niño) and cold (La Niña) state that evolves under the influence of the dynamic interaction between the atmosphere and ocean, with an irregular frequency of two to seven years.

[9] Exclusive Economic Zones (EEZs) are the areas of ocean 200 nautical miles out from coastlines, over which states have sovereign rights.

[10] SPC reports on this include Lehodey et al. 2003 and SPC 2005.

[11] Reciprocal access agreement for Nauru Agreement countries, with priority accorded to local and locally based fleets, signed in the Federated States of Micronesia (FSM).

[12] For further information about the importance of the environmentally aware UK market to the Solomon Islands tuna fishery, see Barclay 2005.

[13] For more information on Solomon Islands' cannery, see Barclay 2000, 2001, 2004, 2005.

[14] During the production phase, loins are often called *arabushi* (literally 'rough loin'), with the final cured product called *katsuobushi* ('skipjack loin').

[15] For further information on the Cotonou Agreement, its predecessor, the Lomé Convention, and the Rules of Origin, see Grynberg 1998 and 2003.

[16] The Parties to the Nauru Agreement (PNA) are a subgroup of the FFA countries whose EEZs encompass most of the equatorial belt of rich skipjack fishing grounds in the region.

[17] Opinions of the 'success' of the US (tuna) treaty vary widely. Some member countries (for example, Kiribati) feel it is inequitable because some countries benefit without having the US fleet fish in their waters, while others feel that such an agreement and fee level would not have been possible without FFA-wide cooperation, and that the regional spirit of the treaty is, of itself, a valuable benefit. These views aside, the treaty was struck under a unique set of circumstances (Anderson 2002; Ram-Bidesi 2004; Tarte 2002, 2003a, 2003b), which cannot be applied simply to other multilateral agreements.

[18] For a history of these negotiations, including the prominent role played by Japan, see Anderson 2002; Ram-Bidesi 2004; Tarte 2002, 2003a, 2003b.

2

Capturing more wealth from tuna

Almost without exception, Pacific islanders interviewed and documents analysed for this project indicated a strong motivation towards capturing more of the wealth generated by regional tuna resources in the domestic economies of Pacific island countries. Interviews and documents used in this project assumed that the two main ways in which Pacific island countries could do this were: i) domestic industry development, and ii) maximising returns from distant water fleets.

Domestic industry development

In this study, we use examples of domestic tuna industries in Pacific island countries to highlight strategies that are likely to lead to the kinds of domestic industry development that will capture more wealth within Pacific island countries' own economies. There are two important principles to bear in mind when considering these strategies.

One is that domestication should be economically sustainable and contribute to government revenue rather than detract from it, which means it should be wholly private-sector driven and independent of financial inputs from government. This means that tuna development is, in effect, the same as business development. For domestic tuna development to work, the economic and policy environment has to enable private-sector development.

In the early 2000s, Forum Fisheries Agency (FFA) member countries decided that reducing their reliance on distant water access fees and growing domestic tuna industries was the way to improve economic benefits from their tuna resources (Gillett 2003). Most Pacific islander interviewees and recent reports from Pacific island governments indicate that this view remains current. That is, the best way to capture more wealth from tuna resources is through 'domesticating' tuna industries. The region's prime ministers have said they see 'domestic [tuna] industry development…as an important means of increasing returns to Pacific Island Countries' (Pacific Islands Forum Secretariat 2004a). Domesticating the benefits from tuna resources is most often understood as Pacific island nationals as resource owners displacing DWFNs, establishing locally based tuna fishing operations and doing the actual fishing. It is also, albeit less often, imagined as developing locally based tuna-processing industries.

In the past, many Pacific island country domestic tuna industries—vessels and processing plants—were wholly or partly government owned. These all failed within a few years or limped along with heavy government and aid donor subsidies, meaning their contribution to the host country's economic development was questionable, although when they employed large numbers of people they at least spread income and human resource development opportunities among Pacific island populations. Due to the overwhelming evidence that government ownership of tuna industries is not the best strategy for domestic development, Pacific island countries tend now to seek more private-sector driven development. Because Pacific island countries have high-cost, difficult business environments, however, governments have had to induce shore-based investment through policies such as tying fishing access to onshore developments and offering generous taxation incentives. Furthermore, many of these companies rely on preferential trade access to the European Union under the Cotonou Agreement. The lack of independent private sector investment (all investment is induced, based on incentives and/or reliant on trade preferences) would seem to indicate that Pacific island countries do not have competitive advantage in tuna industries. Improving the business environment so that inducements and incentives are not necessary is crucial for domestic development.

The second principle for success is that national domestication plans must take account of geographic, economic and biological realities. For instance

- the geographic and economic environment for loining or canning tuna at a financially viable price
- the availability of suitable resources for particular fishing methods, for example, bait and schooling fish for pole-and-line fisheries
- an ability to adapt to/weather downturns due to variations in fish abundance driven by ENSO effects
- the ratio of albacore to sashimi-quality species to support an economically viable longline fishery
- the real cost of policies to 'share' domestic development opportunities between provinces/regions in a given country for political purposes rather than business logic
- economic circumstances: a lack of infrastructure, land, water, labour and other endowments mean that for some Pacific island countries, domestic tuna industries are unlikely to capture as much wealth as licensing DWFN vessels.[1]

Maximising returns from distant water fishers

Based on interviews and government documents explored for this project, Pacific island countries' strategies for maximising returns from DWFNs seem to revolve mostly around negotiating with DWFNs to pay as much as they can for access, and negotiating with

DWFN governments to top up industry payments with aid packages. Another strategy that has been employed in recent years is to attract DWFN vessels to trans-ship, take on supplies and undertake repairs in Pacific island ports. Some Pacific island countries have also gained value from DWFNs by having them employ nationals as crew.

Given the particular geographic and economic potential of some Pacific island countries, returns from DWFNs are, for the foreseeable future at least, likely to remain their most important source of wealth from regional tuna fisheries. Other Pacific island countries' tuna resources are not rich enough to attract large fleets of DWFNs so the returns to them will be small. Approaches to maximising returns from DWFNs thus cannot be uniform for all Pacific island countries. Two other important principles affecting how much wealth Pacific island countries can capture from DWFNs are: i) to populate the fishery with the most efficient vessels (and thus those with the potential to be most profitable), and ii) to maintain the value of catching opportunities.

Unless effective management measures (in biological and economic terms) are implemented, overfishing in the Western and Central Pacific Ocean will inevitably lead to falling CPUE and revenue streams, from domestic and DWFN vessels. Good fisheries management to optimise the economic and ecological sustainability of tuna fisheries is therefore an important determining factor. If effective fisheries management improves the profitability in tuna fisheries, it will in turn increase the capacity and willingness of DWFNs to pay more for fishing opportunities.

Pacific island country policies: the key to achieving Pacific island countries' aspirations

A single principle underlies all strategies designed to capture more of the wealth from tuna resources: Pacific island governments are the main bodies capable of making the changes necessary to capture more wealth from tuna through domestication and returns from DWFNs.

Only Pacific island governments can make regional tuna fisheries economically and ecologically sustainable, by implementing sound fisheries policies in their own jurisdictions and strengthening these through regional cooperative initiatives. This is not to say that Pacific island countries are the only stakeholders or the most powerful ones in general terms, but that the political and economic nature of the situation means coastal states collectively (which for this fishery includes Indonesia and the Philippines as well as Pacific island countries) have the most crucial role to play in improving returns from tuna resources.

While domestic development must be driven by the private sector, the private sector cannot improve Pacific island countries' business environments; it can only be part of governance improvements implemented through Pacific island governments. For example, industry representatives have arguably been the prime movers behind improvements to the business environment in Papua New Guinea and Fiji, but it is the government itself that must implement those improvements. Likewise, aid donors cannot fix Pacific

Figure 2.1   Western and Central Pacific Ocean fisheries management

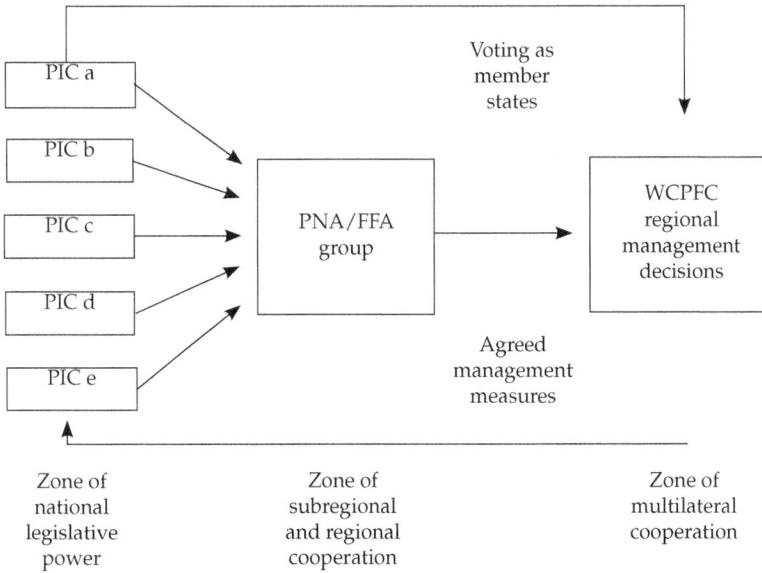

Figure 2.2   Two-way adversarial model of distant water access

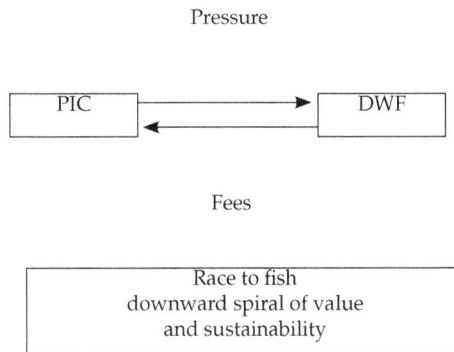

Notes: PIC: Pacific island country; DWF: distant water fishing.

island economies or create an enabling environment for the private sector; Pacific island governments must do that, with or without donor assistance.

Regional bodies such as the FFA and the Secretariat of the Pacific Community (SPC) can provide advice but it is up to Pacific island countries whether they use the advice. The Western and Central Pacific Fisheries Commission (WCPFC) is the forum in which regional management initiatives will be decided, but Pacific island governments must drive this process. Regional bodies can exert influence on individual countries and, through cooperation, can initiate regional measures, but Pacific island governments are the only legislative and executive authorities within their own Exclusive Economic Zones (EEZs) (Figure 2.3).

There are externalities beyond the control of Pacific island countries that will affect management and development policies, such as international fuel prices, fisheries in Indonesian and Philippines EEZs, DWFN interests and binding decisions from the WCPFC. Nevertheless, Pacific island governments have more power than any other bodies over the factors that affect their countries' capacity to capture more wealth from regional tuna resources.

Bearing in mind the central importance of Pacific island governments in this process, there are many things that can be done to enable Pacific islanders to capture more of the wealth generated by the region's tuna fisheries. Going beyond the dichotomy of domestic industry versus maximising distant water access fees, the remainder of this section outlines 10 strategies for capturing more wealth from tuna.

Effective fisheries management

Sustainability is often included within the aspirations of Pacific island countries to capture more wealth from regional tuna resources, as exemplified in the FFA vision: 'We will enjoy the highest levels of social and economic benefits for our people through the sustainable development of our fisheries resources' (FFA 2005). The word 'sustainable' is also prominent in tuna management plans and other government statements regarding tuna industries. Despite frequent use of the word, however, Pacific island governments thus far seem to have displayed limited commitment to the ideal. Some have introduced exclusion zones to try to reduce the impact on coastal fisheries, but overall they have taken limited steps to protect the marine environment from the negative effects of tuna industries. Moves to protect the environment associated with shore-based facilities have often been driven by stakeholders other than governments, such as importing markets (Solomon Islands) and local chiefs (Fiji).

As with fisheries worldwide, Pacific island countries are faced with conflicts between a duty to protect stocks and the environment and their aspirations to capture more wealth from tuna; to gain access to, be allocated and use a fair share of the tuna resource. On the one hand, it is obvious that without enough fish to catch there can be no wealth generated from fisheries, but on the other hand individuals at the state and enterprise level naturally hope that any necessary cuts to catch or effort will fall on someone other than themselves.

Figure 2.3   **Mutual incentives model of distant water access**

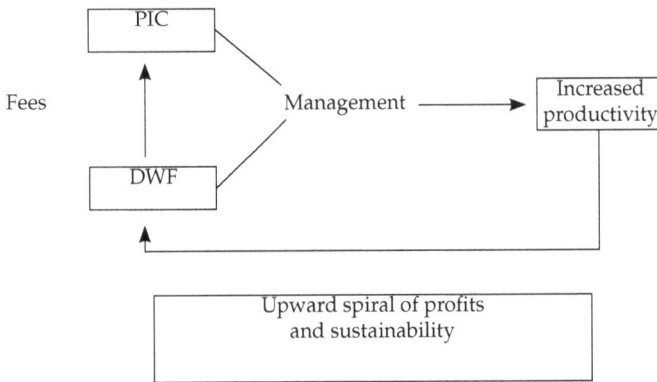

Notes: PIC: Pacific island country; DWF: distant water fishing.

In such situations, governments feel political pressure to argue to this effect at regional forums and at the WCPFC, or to argue that the proposed cuts are not necessary at all.

Managing for economic as well as biological sustainability

The need to manage for biological sustainability (maintaining stocks at levels capable of producing the maximum sustainable yield—'Bmsy' in the Western and Central Pacific Fisheries Convention) is well established. There is also a need to strive for optimal economic outcomes,[2] including for Pacific island countries, which is an area where individual states can play a significant role.

The rush to license vessels, as if the relationship between fishing effort and catch (revenue) was a straight line, and the resulting 'busts', was remarked on in a number of countries visited, particularly in reference to longline fisheries.[3] Some interviewees in PNA countries noted the need to ensure that management regimes involved economic as well as ecological considerations. One suggestion was that the PNA group members could gain substantial increases in access fees if they were to: i) extend the FSM Arrangement and fully pool their WCPFC allocation; ii) put in place credible measures to maintain CPUE; and iii) use rights-based management approaches to sell long-term rights (for example, 10 years) and give DWFNs maximum confidence in their investment. Certainty of the future economic viability of tuna stocks and access to them are also important for domestic investment in fisheries industries.

Early bioeconomic modelling work by the FFA and the SPC suggested that reductions in purse-seine effort could yield substantial overall increases in economic benefit, principally by reducing catches, increasing CPUE and price (by restricting supply) and reducing the costs of fishing. Some of these findings led to assertions that the key to Pacific island countries increasing economic benefit from the purse-seine fishery was to restrict effort (see, for example, ADB 2003), and thereby increasing the prospects of raising access fees. More recent bioeconomic modelling work (Reid et al. 2006) has questioned this perspective, noting that as skipjack catches have increased, CPUE has been maintained, or in some cases increased. Revenue streams from access fees have increased, by 10 per cent between 1999 and 2003 (Lewis 2004a). Using an updated bioeconomic model, the economic benefits (rent) of reducing effort in the purse-seine fishery, while present, are forecast to be substantially less, although the effect on reduced supply in terms of increased prices could increase that benefit. In any event, the more recent work has thrown into doubt some of the original assertions about the value of the PNA group striving to reduce effort in the purse-seine fishery, and indeed, who would benefit from such constraint. It has also highlighted the need to continue to work on refining the bioeconomic model and, equally importantly, extending the results to Pacific island countries to support consideration of management options.

Notwithstanding this debate, the major constraint for the purse-seine and longline fisheries lies with yellowfin and bigeye. The challenge will be to balance the requirements of the Western and Central Pacific Fisheries Convention with respect to these species with the largely economic-driven aspirations of Pacific island countries.

Recommendation 1

Place greater emphasis on predicting economic outcomes—particularly across fisheries, gear types and WCPFC members—when designing and determining management measures, including levels of fishing effort by domestic and foreign fleets.

Fisheries management planning

It is important that Pacific island governments have a clear idea of where they wish to see their tuna fisheries heading in the future. All too often tuna fisheries management objectives are vague. Another common problem is a conflict between the objective to maximise economic returns and policies aimed at distributing benefits from tuna developments for social reasons.

In the late 1990s and early 2000s, the FFA and the SPC, with Canadian government funding through the Canada–South Pacific Ocean Development (CSPOD) Program II assisted Pacific island countries to develop management plans for their tuna industries. Most Pacific island countries now have tuna management plans, which provide at least some guidance, even if few have formal statutory status. The FFA *2005–07 Business Plan* notes that the agency will assist with the review of existing plans and work towards 'ecosystem based management'.[4] After spending a large amount of resources on this process, it might be timely to review what has been learned from management and tuna industry planning processes, and most importantly share the knowledge resulting from that review with Pacific island countries.

Monitoring, control and surveillance (MCS)

Australia, which has a large budget to spend on monitoring its maritime borders, has in recent years been unable to prevent multiple incursions in a relatively small area of its northern EEZ by Indonesian fishers.[5] Compared with Australia, Pacific island countries' EEZs cover areas several orders of magnitude larger relative to the amount of government funds available for surveillance and enforcement, so they are unable to conduct MCS effectively on their own. Regional pooling of surveillance and enforcement is a necessary part of effective fisheries management for Pacific island countries.

Regionally, the FFA has been successful in generating regional MCS initiatives, but there is considerable scope to build on these efforts, including

- expanding the existing US Treaty regional observer program to allow observers on vessels as they transit different EEZs and, by negotiation at the WCPFC, on the high seas
- expanding activities under the Niue Treaty in respect of joint operations and shared facilities.

As the WCPFC builds its MCS framework, Pacific island countries should strive to gain the greatest level of adoption possible of current in-zone fisheries compliance measures. The aim should be to transfer (and strengthen) the existing in-zone compliance environment onto adjacent high seas, leading to more cost effective and efficient MCS outcomes.

Rights-based management

The value of rights-based management in fisheries is well known as a means of addressing economic and biological sustainability (Cartwright and Willock 1999). The concept of rights-based fishing in a tuna fishery is not well developed, but was considered in some detail at a regional workshop in Nadi, Fiji (FFA 2002). This workshop noted that consideration should be given to strengthening property rights at three levels.

- National—using enhanced licensing conditions, for example, by extending terms to five years or more, making them transferable and using more flexible units of rights (such as hook numbers) for catch allocations; and by using the increasingly valuable rights to be allocated under the WCPFC to reduce DWFN effort and leverage domestic involvement/industry development.
- Regional—using the power of FFA members to determine total allowable catch or level of effort for areas under national jurisdiction, with allocations of high seas fishing opportunities among all participating countries, and FFA members cooperating for reciprocal access for longline vessels, mirroring the FSM Arrangement. The rights afforded under the Vessel Days Scheme (VDS) among the PNA group will be pivotal in at least two ways: i) to deal with ENSO-driven variations, and ii) through options to reduce days and make the right more valuable.
- Multilateral—using the power of the FFA group, and the PNA subgroup, to influence negotiations for participatory rights for allocation of catch/effort at the WCPFC.

Gillett (2003) sees that rights-based management could be useful for development but that two things are needed before aid donors can try to support it: i) a greater awareness among domestic fisheries managers of the benefits of rights-based regimes; and ii) improved infrastructure necessary for rights-based regimes, including policy stability and protection of use rights. Corruption is another issue that needs to be addressed by Pacific island countries before rights-based management could produce maximum benefits for national economies.

Another role for rights-based approaches is as a potential means for solving the gear interaction issue. As 'real' management measures (that is, those that effectively constrain) are introduced (or in the case of the VDS begin to take effect), there will be opportunities to introduce methods that enable trade-offs between gear types and target species. For instance, bigeye and yellowfin could be traded for skipjack in equatorial waters, and albacore in tropical and temperate waters.

Recommendation 2

Follow up the 2002 FFA Rights-Based Workshop, possibly through a series of in-country seminars, to increase awareness among domestic policymakers and fisheries managers of such approaches.

Managing social, political and environmental issues

Fisheries managers tend to see politics as something that ideally should be kept out of fisheries management. Some politically motivated fisheries management decisions have certainly been disastrous. On the other hand, decisions for ecologically sound fisheries management, and economically sound development strategies, are political decisions as much as anything else.

The Marshall Islands government's decision to go for service and supply industries rather than attempting to domesticate fisheries was a political decision, based on astute technical advice, which had good economic outcomes. Since fisheries management is more about managing people's impact on fish rather than about managing fish *per se*, fisheries management will always involve dealing with political issues.

Social issues are not usually given high priority, and are often listed simply as 'negative impacts' with the inference that they should be avoided if we could only work out how, and if the resources were available. Social issues are, however, not simply unintended by-products of fisheries development. Social and environmental problems arising from tuna developments must be addressed, not just for the general good of society, but because the ill will generated by socially divisive developments rebounds negatively on those developments. In other words, it is easier for a company to be successful if it has good public relations than if it has bad public relations. Public relations are a company responsibility, but the way fisheries developments fit with their social context is a matter of government policy.

As with the desire for sustainable tuna fisheries in the offshore area, the desire to minimise negative social and environmental impacts in coastal and port areas was one of the aspirations mentioned by virtually all interviewees and documents studied for this project. Despite the widespread nature of this aspiration, however, very little has been done by governments to alleviate social and environmental problems associated with tuna industries. None have developed and implemented concrete strategies to minimise these impacts.

The impacts on coastal areas of commercial tuna developments generally fall into two categories: impacts on coastal fisheries and impacts on the surrounding environment as a result of pollution.

Impacts on coastal fisheries. One of the factors contributing to widespread social ill will against industrial tuna developments is the pervasive belief that commercial tuna industries are depleting the resources villagers catch for food and income. Near-shore fisheries are of paramount importance for the food security, health and income of coastal Pacific island populations.[6] Some studies suggest that the economic value of the informal catch in Pacific island countries would far exceed the value of the commercial catch if it were calculated systematically (King, pers. comm.) (although comparisons involving multiplier effects can be problematic).[7] Most coastal fisheries concentrate on reef fish, because it is easier to catch reef fish from small vessels than it is to venture out to the open sea to catch tuna. The available evidence, however, indicates that fishing pressure on reef fisheries should be alleviated in many Pacific island areas (Bell, pers. comm.; King, pers. comm.). In this case, refocusing near-shore fisheries on relatively healthy tuna stocks, facilitated by the use of near-shore fish aggregating devices (FADs), would seem a sound policy, although research indicates that FADs are not always used by villagers in ways that reduce pressure in other coastal fisheries (Gillett 1999). Several Pacific island countries, including Papua New Guinea, are following Samoa's lead and establishing community-based resource management regimes for coastal areas. Solomon Islands is doing this in conjunction with Marine Protected Areas under the sponsorship of several non-governmental organisations (NGOs).

Small-scale coastal fisheries targeting tuna based on the Samoan model were seen in the 1990s as a major opportunity for domestic fishers. The experience of Samoa, however, where hopelessly overcapitalised small-scale fisheries led to a collapse in near-shore tuna resources (Watt, pers. comm.), demonstrates the need for sound resource management. Furthermore, part of Samoa's success was based on a unique economic opportunity for trade with nearby American Samoa, a situation not replicable in other Pacific island countries. Examples where Pacific island governments have acted to manage fishing pressure on coastal resources include Morobe Province in Papua New Guinea, which has decided to limit the number of pump boats that may operate out of Lae and increase effort incrementally to avoid local depletions.

Since shark can be targeted by longline and handline gear that also target tuna, shark fisheries are connected to tuna fisheries. The escalating price of shark's fin presents a growing risk for shark populations. The reported export value of shark's fin from Milne Bay, in Papua New Guinea, rose to more than K1 million annually in the mid 2000s (the real value could be higher). As traditional stocks in Southeast Asia are depleted, buyers are likely to turn increasingly to Pacific island shark fisheries.

It is also important to know whether offshore commercial tuna fisheries have an impact on coastal tuna fisheries. It is common to hear from small-scale and recreational fishers in Pacific island countries that is it now much harder to catch tuna than it was 10 to 15 years ago, and commercial tuna fisheries are usually seen as the main cause of the apparent decline in resources (Bauro, pers. comm.; Dunn, pers. comm.; Kingston, pers. comm.; Ramohia, pers. comm.; Tamba, pers. comm.).[8] While increasing levels of exploitation can reduce CPUE, particularly if focused within a particular area, industrial fishing does not always equate with overfishing. Where scientific research into interactions between small-scale and industrial fisheries has been conducted, the connections between catch rates in the fisheries can be quite complex (Hampton et al. 1996). Despite the high mobility of tuna populations, and depending on the circumstances, it seems likely that the availability of particular tuna stocks to near-shore fisheries can be impacted significantly by large-scale industrial fishing activity.

Impacts of pollution. It is commonly believed that large-scale tuna-processing plants in Papua New Guinea and Solomon Islands pollute the surrounding environment, including damaging reef-fish stocks (Barclay 2001; Sullivan et al. 2003). Some research has been conducted into the pollution effects of the large-scale canneries Solomon Taiyo and RD (Benet Monico 2003; Mani 1994; Wallis 1999), but there have not yet been continuing environmental monitoring or enforcement schemes implemented by Pacific island governments to minimise negative environmental impacts.

The effect of commercial fisheries, including processing industries, on near-shore areas, however, is not only a resource management issue, it is about social and political management of fisheries. Scientific data about the effects of tuna industries and policies to mitigate any negative effects are only part of the solution. It is also necessary to effectively disseminate the results of such research to all stakeholders, including villagers, to enable better informed debate about the merits or otherwise of tuna industries. Village-level stakeholders should also be part of consultative advisory and decision-making committees to enable their input, and to act as a conduit for information between fisheries officials and villagers affected by tuna developments.

Social policies. The optimal public policy mix should manage the development of tuna industries such that it facilitates a widespread sense of social progress rather than social dislocation and polarisation of groups for and against the development. Furthermore, while it is extremely unlikely that a tuna-related coup will eventuate, the social ill will generated by many tuna developments in the region, which results in petty sabotage, adds to already difficult business environments, and, if not addressed, it could escalate. It is part of the social and political instability that discourages investment in several Pacific island countries.

One of the notable features of the tuna-processing factories in Fiji, Solomon Islands and Papua New Guinea is that while people appreciate the employment opportunities, the factories have had bad public reputations. They have been seen widely as offering unpleasant, unsafe work for substandard wages, as causing social breakdown and as polluting the surrounding environment (Emberson-Bain 1994; Hughes and Thaanum

1995; Sasabe 1993; Sullivan et al. 2003). Based on our research, these companies have been more responsible corporate citizens than their reputations suggest. It is worth bearing in mind, however, that although developing tuna processing is clearly a national government aspiration, there are large sectors of Pacific island populations who have different opinions about the desirability of such development. Failure to address the negative social reputations of tuna-processing companies has meant social groups continue to attack them. RD has been tied up in legal battles with landowner groups and an NGO that RD perceives as having slandered the company (Friends of Kananam c.2003), and RD has been the target of petty extortion rackets (*Post-Courier* 2005).

Social issues around ports and factories. Apart from Cook Islands, all of the Pacific island countries covered by this study have significant numbers of DWFN fleets visiting local ports and/or large-scale onshore processing factories. International ports and tuna factories are magnets for a range of social problems, including prostitution, substance abuse and violence. Some 35,000 men from the southern Philippines work overseas on fishing vessels and call into ports including those in Solomon Islands, Papua New Guinea, Indonesia, Malaysia and Taiwan. According to a health official from General Santos City in Mindanao, many of these fishermen engage in 'extremely risky behaviour' when they finish a trip, including sex with multiple partners (often involving binge drinking and sex workers), injection of recreational drugs and insertion of penile implants. Some people in this part of the Philippines have tested positive to HIV. While no cases of HIV/AIDS had been reported among the fishermen at the time the article was published, it noted that there appeared to be a high rate of tuberculosis among the fishermen, which is recognised as an indicator of AIDS (*Solomon Star* 2004). Papua New Guinea's rates of HIV/AIDS are now very high. Fishing crews visiting Papua New Guinea could contract the disease and spread it around the Pacific very quickly.

To ensure that development benefits from tuna industries are not cancelled out by social disruption, a range of social welfare and health services are needed around international ports and industrial processing centres. Local women and incoming men could benefit from advice about sexually transmitted infections (STIs). Women who are subject to violence related to substance abuse or the stress of fishing crew lifestyles need particular kinds of welfare services, as do those ostracised for being perceived as prostitutes. The lifestyles of fishing crews are very difficult, and many have mental health problems. The 2005 Forum Leaders' Communiqué pointed out the importance of regional strategies for dealing with HIV/AIDS, and the role of the Pacific Health Fund to help fund initiatives to combat health challenges (Pacific Islands Forum Secretariat 2005).

In addition to help when problems arise, a greater range of 'normal' activities (not involving sex or substance abuse) should be provided for visiting fishing crews. While vessels are in port, crews can have little to do, and crew who do not want to engage in sex or substance abuse have nowhere to escape these activities occurring onboard. The kinds of activities crews often appreciate include visiting restaurants, shopping and recreational fishing. Many simply miss social contact outside the crew, with whom they are incarcerated for the duration of the fishing trip. Houses for crew to stay at while ashore, such as the 'Seafarer's Angel' houses around the world, would help normalise visiting crew behaviour.

Gender issues. Gender is a social issue for tuna industries, especially around relationships with fishing crews and disparities in pay and seniority in shore-based tuna businesses. Inequitable gender relations is one of the problems that foments social ill will against tuna developments, although previous research indicates that gender inequity is less likely to cause social disruption in the way that perceived ethnic tension has (Barclay 2004). One reason for this is that people do not consider inequity between men and women to be as serious an issue as inequity across ethnic groups. Nevertheless, addressing gender inequities was one of the aspirations for tuna development mentioned in government documents, so Pacific island countries clearly feel that gender inequities need to be addressed in best-practice fisheries management.[9] (Alternatively, Pacific island governments could simply be reproducing the mantras of gender analysis stipulated in most aid projects.)

Distribution of benefits. Almost all documents outlining strategies for tuna development listed equitable distribution of benefits among the citizenry as a key aspiration. Indeed, one of the main reasons domestication is so popular is because benefits from access fees have largely not been felt by Pacific island populations. With domestic developments, at least some of the wealth from tuna is distributed among the people via salaries and wages.

Pacific islander interviewees were particularly concerned that benefits from tuna developments should be felt in rural or outer-island areas. In strictly legal terms, villagers have no claim in customary tenure to offshore resources (Turaganivalu, pers. comm.). The social reality of customary marine tenure in Pacific island countries is, however, that villagers sometimes assert rights over resources they did not use in custom (Kinch et al. 2005). Furthermore, anecdotes suggest that industrial fishers often come much closer to shore than they should. The belief that commercial tuna fisheries are taking villagers' resources without giving any return to villagers is one of the factors contributing to social ill will towards commercial tuna industries in Pacific island countries.

Interviewees often hoped that rural fishers could somehow become involved in commercial tuna fisheries, but there were intractable problems with this, mostly because the perishable nature of the product made it difficult to transport to markets at a reasonable cost. Other ways for coastal villagers to benefit from commercial tuna industries include channelling proportions of commercial fisheries licence fees into trust funds for rural coastal development projects. Most of the tuna management and development plans in the region included such ideas, but Marshall Islands was the only one of the countries covered by this study that had instituted such a fund by 2005.

The most significant strategy employed to distribute benefits has been shifting industrial tuna developments away from established industrial or urban centres. In Papua New Guinea, this has led to large-scale processing ventures in Madang, Wewak and Lae, with longline developments spread even more widely. In Solomon Islands, there are fisheries bases at Tulagi and Noro, with many people hoping for an additional base in Malaita

(Bina Harbour). In Fiji, the Pafco cannery/loining plant is located at Levuka on Ovalau, rather than in Suva (substantially increasing operating costs).

The problem with spreading tuna developments geographically is that it exacerbates the diseconomies of scale that already damage the economic viability of Pacific island country developments. Having many locations for industrial development means each suffers from infrastructure and human resources deficiencies that make them uncompetitive internationally. RD has been trying to attract more businesses to Madang for some years but the Papua New Guinea government seems to want 'a tuna factory in every port', echoing the 'meat cannery in every town' scenario of the late 1980s that saw the establishment, and subsequent collapse, of several competitors to James Barnes Pty Ltd's monopoly (Bowman 2005). Political and social aspirations to spread developments around the country thus constrain the economic viability of domestic industries, thereby confounding the overarching economic aspiration to capture more wealth from tuna resources via domestication. Policy decisions about the geographic locations of tuna developments are a juggling act between the economies of scale and synergies provided by consolidating industries, with social and political imperatives to bring developments to particular locations.

Recommendation 3

Base tuna management and development on the principles of ecologically sustainable development, balancing economic, environmental and social goals and outcomes.

Increased access fees

Access fees for DWFNs constitute an important source of revenue for four of the Pacific island countries covered by this study (Marshall Islands, Kiribati, Papua New Guinea and Solomon Islands), all of which are members of the PNA group. Revenue shortages mean many PNA countries are unable to provide adequate health and education services for their populations, and income from access fees provide vital discretionary budget support. Many commentators—for example, at the Pacific Islands Forum—have remarked on how little of the gross value of the tuna fishery (usually 5–6 per cent, with 7–8 per cent achieved in some years by some countries) is returned to states through access fees. This complaint is somewhat misleading, because access fees must be taken out of profits. It is arguable that with the current economic status of tuna fisheries, especially with fuel cost increases, 5–8 per cent of gross value is possibly as high as DWFNs can be expected to pay (Tumoa, pers. comm.; van Santen and Muller 2000). Nevertheless, there are three main ways in which Pacific island countries can increase the revenue raised through access licence fees (in addition to making the licence more valuable through improved management).[10]

Reconsider the basis of access agreements

While it is assumed here that DWFN-driven fishing will be a continuing feature of tuna fisheries in many Pacific island countries, there should be careful consideration of alternative models. One is DFWN fishing that acts as a 'kick start' for appropriate domestic industries. Clark (2002) considers a range of options for replacing access agreements, using approaches introduced successfully in Namibia, based on fishing rights. It is a basic economic principle that by restricting rights their value increases. To introduce rights-based management of fisheries means establishing rights and empowering the individuals and locally registered companies holding the rights, who are in turn obligated to pay fees and are expected to meet certain standards in terms of investment, job creation and so forth. Clark suggests that through this approach the role of distant water access agreements is reduced or eliminated because vessels from outside the region are allowed to operate only under charter to or in joint ventures with domestic rights holders.

Papua New Guinea has been successful in pursuing a strong domestication policy by providing preferential access to fishing opportunities to those companies prepared to make onshore investment, particularly in the area of processing. Having one of the most productive EEZs in the region has strengthened Papua New Guinea's capacity to implement these policies.

An approach similar to the one Clark recommends has been applied in longline fisheries in three of the countries studied (Papua New Guinea, Fiji and Cook Islands), with definite increases in domestic industry activity. Various factors, including ineffective fisheries management, governance problems and policy instability, have tended to erode some of the potential gains. Nevertheless, the results show the potential benefits arising from careful review of distant water access agreements and the pursuit of alternatives.

Other approaches include reconsidering the current form of bilateral access arrangements, many of which are based on agreements between distant water fisheries associations and Pacific island governments. Such agreements tend to result in a large number of vessels being licensed, some of which are relatively inefficient. It makes good economic sense to look for the most profitable vessels (and thus those most able to pay the maximum fees) through more direct licensing arrangements, possibly directly with individual companies. If current plans for the VDS are successful, these more efficient vessels will then take up the limited (and therefore more valuable) fishing opportunities (licences).

Improved administration and governance

Pacific island countries' fisheries administrators prefer to keep information about the real price of licence fees secret, and regional bodies such as the FFA and consultants working in the region often support them. It has been argued that in order to be able to make a useful assessment of the economics of tuna fisheries in the region, economists must know how much the access fees are, as well as the level of tied aid and other features of the agreements, which many consider form part of the access equation (Gloerfelt-Tarp, pers. comm.).[11] Fishing operators also need clear information about fees to make long-term strategic decisions about their investments. In addition, a more transparent exchange of access agreement information, including fee levels, would help deal with the longstanding divide-and-conquer tactics employed by DWFNs, who thrive on intense bilateral negotiations.

Another improvement that could be made is to increase the level of expertise available to coastal-state negotiation teams. Usually DWFNs host negotiations and offer to pay only for a limited number of fisheries officials (often two) to come to negotiate. One interviewee suggested that FFA advisors should join coastal-state negotiation teams, as was the case in the early days of establishing fisheries agreements in the region. A number of interviewees also said that it would be of value to have negotiations conducted in the coastal state, so that experts from all relevant government departments could participate, strengthening negotiation teams.

Some form of 'gift' to coastal-state negotiators was widely assumed by interviewees to be part of distant water access negotiations with at least several of the DWFNs. It was felt that such gifts were probably a negative influence on the outcome for Pacific island countries, because they carried an expectation that the recipients would not push so hard for higher fees. An added advantage of having negotiations conducted in coastal states would be to diminish the opportunity for the passing of 'brown envelopes' to influence negotiations. Dealing with governance problems in access fee negotiations has an immediate positive effect on the amounts of revenue generated. Papua New Guinea's fisheries bureaucracy reforms led to revenue from access fees jumping from an estimated US$5.8 million in 1999 (Gillett and Lightfoot 2002) to more than US$9 million in 2002 (Lewis 2005), and US$13.6 million in 2003 (Preston, pers. comm.).

Governance issues in access fees are not just about corruption and setting up systems that are transparent and accountable; they are about capacity. Small government departments without experts in fisheries finance find it difficult to know the best basis for calculating fees and how to independently check market figures to make sure DWFNs are paying the appropriate amounts (McCoy and Gillett 2005; van Santen and Muller 2000; FFA 2001). The FFA has provided assistance in the form of bilateral briefs to individual countries to inform bilateral negotiations, but could do considerably more if FFA personnel were included, at least on an occasional basis, as advisors on national delegations.

Alternative negotiating models

Over the years there have been many studies of alternative access arrangements that could enable Pacific island countries to increase fees. The most obvious one is that countries should negotiate collectively with DWFNs rather than bilaterally. Lewis (2004a) suggests at the very least sharing information among neighbours or like-minded countries to enabling a semi-coordinated approach to access negotiations. He notes that coordinated or semi-coordinated approaches have not been tried in the atmosphere of secrecy and mistrust that pervades access negotiations in the region.

Pacific island countries have never tried most of the ideas raised in previous studies[12] on how access fees can be increased. Some of the reasons for this include

- most studies were done by consultants who submitted reports to the FFA Secretariat, who are already aware of the issues; they were not discussed in consultative forums/ workshops, at a national or regional level

- a perception that cooperation would mean surrendering sovereignty and decreasing the ability to negotiate 'tailor-made' agreements suited to each country
- unwillingness to redistribute benefits to recompense for cooperation from less endowed Pacific island countries in the FFA group
- a perception that Pacific island countries might lose out from bilateral aid deals if they join a multilateral push to negotiate fees (a threat Japan has made)
- unwillingness to forgo personal 'perks' of bilateral arrangements
- inertia of small government departments trying to get by on limited resources with limited capacity and simply being unable to try new things or to organise joint negotiations.

Recommendation 4

Hold an access fee summit (hosted by the FFA) including Pacific island country fisheries officials, other stakeholders and experts to discuss various ways of licensing DWFN vessels, including improving the existing access fee-based arrangements and alternatives, such as appropriate rights-based licensing/chartering arrangements. The summit should revisit the many reports on increasing access fees that have been produced over the years and consider seriously which ideas could work in practice.

Creating a business environment to capture wealth

Probably the biggest impediment to domestic tuna industry development in Pacific island countries is that the business environment is largely not conducive. Production environments are high cost and macroeconomic policies encourage investor mentalities of short-term gain rather than long-term commitment. While the much maligned Ting Hong company was infamous for this kind of mentality in the 1990s, it should be noted that Pacific island governments have attracted this style of operation by making it difficult for foreign and even locally based companies with long-term visions to be successful. Improving macroeconomic policies and fixing some of the policies obstructing business development will improve levels of foreign and local investment in business in general, including in tuna industries. Following is a list of areas in which Pacific island governments can facilitate investment, including for tuna industries, drawn from ideas put forward by interviewees and the literature (especially Gillett 2003).

The role of government

Our research found that few fisheries officials believed state ownership of enterprise was a good idea. State ownership has continued in places such as Kiribati, where it is not clear how the government might best withdraw from commercial operations it set up years ago, and how public-sector involvement can be avoided when there is a negligible private sector (Onorio, pers. comm.). Most fisheries officials interviewed felt that the private sector was the appropriate engine of development, so the government's role was to set up a policy environment that would encourage private-sector investment. Translating this aim into reality has some way to go in most Pacific island countries and should be a key objective for those states wishing to attract and hold appropriate investment in tuna fisheries.

Coordinated approach

With tuna being one of the major economic resources for many Pacific island countries, it is important that the whole of government has a working knowledge of tuna fisheries development policies, not just fisheries departments. Sometimes senior government officials in other parts of government, who are not aware of the history of failure of virtually all government-owned fisheries enterprises in the Pacific, keep the call for state ownership alive. If such calls become influential in policymaking, vast amounts of revenue could again be wasted.

Another reason why it is important for other government departments to be aware of developments in fisheries is that they can unintentionally obstruct tuna industries. For example, Papua New Guinea's national carrier, Air Niugini, did not effectively have the capacity, competitive prices or the route connections to be suitable for chilled fresh tuna exports, so PNG longline fishing companies tried to organise charter flights from an airfreight company. Air Niugini, however, wanted to retain its monopoly status, so it lobbied effectively to prevent departmental approvals for regular use of the airfreight company and prevented any tuna shipments from using the cold-store facilities at Port Moresby airport (*The National* 2005b). After several years, the company Heavylift secured permission to run regular tuna freight flights from Port Moresby, without access to the cold store, but by that time all of the longline fisheries outside Port Moresby had closed down, largely due to the high price and logistical difficulties of Air Niugini's services (Tai 2004). Everything from taxation on inputs and immigration rules for staff to port infrastructure and roads affects tuna businesses, so interdepartmental coordination is vital.

Policy stability

Policy uncertainty is a major constraint to industry development in Pacific island countries (Bowman 2005). Without certainty, businesses cannot estimate their future costs and options. The nature of politics in many Pacific island countries is not conducive to policy stability. Frequent changes of ministers and government means the policies of the previous government are discarded. Our research uncovered many instances of policy instability, and industry interviewees cited it as a problem.

Taxation and other government fees

Fisheries managers understand that excessive taxes can threaten development, but taxation officials might see tuna developments as a source of revenue to be 'milked' (Gillett 2003). Locally based foreign fleets left Papua New Guinea in the 1980s because of increasing duties on fish exports. Economists recommend a stable, fair, effective tax regime as beneficial, while 'rubbery' tax regimes in which companies feel they can pressure government to avoid certain taxes as an incentive to invest are not helpful to business development (Hand 1999). Previous reports have found that investors in general tend to prefer stable, reliable policies and trading environments over financial concessions (Gillett 2003; ADB 1997).

Our research found that Pacific island countries still tend towards punitive taxation regimes with *ad hoc* tax relief offered to some investors. In Papua New Guinea, one report estimates that the level of incentive given to RD in its first five years of operation means lost revenue cancelled out the development gains in those years when the large processing factory employed 3,000 people in Madang (Gillett, Preston and Associates 2000). Kiribati has had charges of up to 60 per cent on some tuna industry inputs. The Solomon Islands government contributed to NFD leaving the pole-and-line fishery by charging 35 per cent duties on a new vessel. On the other hand, the Marshall Islands government's decision to cut taxes on fuel for tuna vessels was one of the factors that enabled its service and supply industry to take off, in line with Gillett's (2003) finding that low fuel taxes were directly related to domestic industry development.

Effective, efficient government services

One of the main ways governments can create an enabling environment for business is through providing timely, accessible, effective, consistent and reasonably priced services. The World Bank's Foreign Investment Advisory Service (FIAS) Sydney office could assist with implementing such changes in Pacific island countries. Some of the main government services raised by interviewees as important for tuna industries include

- fisheries licensing
  - In Papua New Guinea, lengthy delays in fishing licences for domestic operators add to investor uncertainty.
- foreign investment and working visa approvals
  - In Cook Islands, the Development Investment Board facilitates investment applications through other government departments. The board can facilitate three-year working visas in a two-week turnaround.
  - 'Silo' departmental approaches in Solomon Islands, Papua New Guinea and Kiribati mean investment authorities can do little to facilitate applications; business and work visa application processes are said by investors to be cumbersome and add considerably to costs.
- meeting food safety requirements for export destinations
  - Meeting the requirements for the US Food and Drug Administration and the European Union's 'list-one' status on monitoring and regulating food safety standards to enable fishery producers to export easily to these lucrative markets. Currently only Papua New Guinea has EU list-one status.
  - Marshall Islands has used FAO assistance with hazard analysis critical control point (HACCP) systems to improve market access for its fresh-tuna exports.
- administration of land tenure
  - Access to land for business development was a constraint in all of the Pacific island countries covered in this study—for reasons of limited space in Kiribati, Marshall Islands and Cook Islands, but also because customary land tenure systems make it difficult to acquire secure, reasonably priced access to land in many countries.

Recommendation 5

Pacific island government officials, with industry representatives, review the delivery of government services, to highlight bottlenecks and ways of streamlining bureaucratic processes to increase industry efficiency and thus profitability.

Infrastructure

Domestic and service and supply industries for DWFNs have been constrained in many Pacific island countries by a lack of infrastructure, and by inadequate maintenance and management of infrastructure (Gillett 2003). To some extent, the private sector will provide its own infrastructure where necessary. On the other hand, the RD and Soltai[13] processing companies have had to install infrastructure (such as a fresh water supply) that in competitor countries would be provided for them, which has added to already high production costs, detracting from their economic viability and therefore their capacity to generate wealth for Pacific island countries. Seaport and airport infrastructure were most commonly cited as being in need of improvement.

Freight

An FFA study into airfreight from 2002 identified regional domestic longline industries as being at risk because of their reliance on passenger routes for provision of low-capacity, high-cost airfreight (Tamate 2002). Conditions have deteriorated since then, with fuel price increases and new passenger planes having lower freight capacities. Of the countries covered by this study, only Cook Islands and Fiji had large enough tourist industries to have the connections for reasonably priced airfreight on passenger planes to the appropriate destinations (Japan, Europe and the United States). The remaining countries used a combination of dedicated freight and passenger flights. Among many other recommendations, the FFA report recommended regional coordination of airfreight to address these problems. This report was one of those that failed to be disseminated to people who might be able to use it: apparently only one industry person saw the report during the period when it was 'fresh' and its recommendations might have been useful (Gillett, pers. comm.). It seems likely, however, that if regionally organised commercial freight routes for tuna industries were commercially viable the private sector would already have moved into this area.

High-cost infrequent sea freight was also cited as a major impediment by industry interviewees. Sea freight added greatly to canning/loining production costs in Papua New Guinea, Solomon Islands and Fiji. Marshall Islands' loining plant had a sea freight advantage, with a high volume of vessels bringing fresh food and drink for US military personnel based there.

There is a limited amount Pacific island governments can do to effectively facilitate freight, especially if they have small populations and are geographically remote from major trade routes. Getting goods in and out at competitive prices effectively limits domestic tuna development in many Pacific island countries. The only way freight costs can become economical in these circumstances is if freight is consolidated and its volume increases, for example, through large-scale domestically based production.

The private sector can work out for itself whether a particular location has adequate transport links, and whether air and seaport infrastructure is adequate and efficiently run. There is a great deal of scope for government improvement of infrastructure facilities and management, but investments in expensive infrastructure should be made only after extensive industry consultation.

Finance

Interviewees for Gillett's 2003 study raised government facilitation of credit for fisheries as a necessary intervention for development of tuna fisheries. In our study, credit seemed to be a constraint only when a commercial track record was lacking. Interviewees from profitable companies, such as Land Holdings in Cook Islands and NFD in Solomon Islands, said they had no problem with access to commercial finance. Companies such as Soltai, with a poor profitability record, did have problems accessing finance. Access to finance is thus directly related to profitability.

Gillett (2003) pointed out that failed domestic development attempts in the past have had negative effects on the availability of credit for fisheries industries. Most Pacific island countries have made finance available for domestic fisheries development via development banks or aid projects to businesses that would not be financed under commercial lending criteria. Most of these have failed, with negative financial consequences for the borrowers. Giving Pacific island fishers access to credit when they are not credit worthy and are unlikely to make a commercial success is generally worse than not helping them. The resulting financial ruin and damage to their confidence as well as that of the lending institutions impacts severely on future development.

Fisheries entrepreneur Robert Stone's experiences in Fiji illustrate how credit for commercial fisheries development can work successfully. After managing the Fiji government-owned fishing venture Ika Corp for some years in the 1970s, Robert Stone wanted to enter the industry himself. He approached the banks for a loan to buy a tuna pole-and-line vessel, but was refused on the basis that he had no track record as a commercial fisherman. He then bought a small boat with his own money and fished commercially for snapper for three years. He returned to the Development Bank with the records from his snapper-fishing venture and was given 100 per cent credit for his first pole-and-line boat. He successfully operated this vessel, and others he bought, for more than a decade before declining skipjack prices encouraged him to leave the fishery.

Investment hubs

Fisheries, fishery service and supply industries and fish-processing industries can all enjoy economies of scale and synergies from consolidating in industrial investment 'hubs'. China's 'export processing zones' have become the centre of the economic boom on the east coast. Other countries have also successfully generated business development through clusters of firms with operational synergies, which share a pool of infrastructure and resources (including human) that improve as more companies join the hub. Business studies have long recognised clusters as drivers of innovation, facilitating business development by increasing the productivity of the companies in the cluster, and by stimulating new businesses (Bowman 2005).

Economic viability has been a major constraint on Pacific island countries generating more wealth from their tuna resources, especially because of high-cost business environments. Policies encouraging the development of hubs with core competencies and supporting infrastructure can assist with tuna industry development. RD in Papua New Guinea has attempted to attract other investors to a marine industrial park north of Madang, but Pacific island governments have not employed the idea of hubs in development policy. Indeed, for social and political reasons outlined earlier, Pacific island governments have done the opposite and damaged the economic viability of domestic industries in order to spread the benefits of development, often for political reasons.

A hub approach to development policy would help alleviate diseconomies of scale for freight and make it more likely that governments could afford to provide and maintain adequate infrastructure.

Creating public policy systems to capture wealth

Fisheries policy reform and departmental restructuring in some Pacific island countries has led to improved business environments and therefore greater private sector development. On the whole, however, fisheries departments have not tried most of the ideas suggested in the many reports on fisheries development produced by the FFA, SPC and ADB. Pacific island countries unable or unwilling to adopt governance reforms in recent years have had stagnant private sector development. Some of the key changes that can enable Pacific island countries to capture more wealth from tuna are

- reorienting public policy towards enabling private sector development
- greater openness with useful information about tuna
- improving governance.

Below are some suggested improvements to fisheries governance systems and related processes that could improve returns to Pacific island countries.

Fisheries authorities

The experiences of Papua New Guinea in restructuring from a government department oriented to fisheries extension services to a relatively independent statutory authority oriented to provision of services to industry and collecting fees on behalf of government (ADB 1998) offer many lessons for the region. Most Pacific island fisheries bureaucrats are paid extremely low salaries, which is not a good incentive. Under the National Fisheries Authority (NFA) reform, staff were paid more and were expected to work at a higher level than they had in the old department. The NFA was well funded and equipped to do its work, which had a positive influence on outcomes, such as greatly increased revenues gained through access fees. Improved policies and administration also contributed to a boom in domestic development. The value of Papua New Guinea's tuna exports went from about K3.5 million in 1996 to more than K220 million in 2002 (Gomez 2005). The

NFA's main problem proved to be that which devils statutory authorities the world over: it was difficult to ensure good financial governance. A number of Pacific island countries in this study were considering a move to the fisheries authority model because it had much to offer—in terms of staff incentives to excel, arms-length operation from the minister, the ability to make decisions and accountability—but these countries hesitated because the authority model requires a high level of governance and trust. A powerful but dysfunctional board structure open to bias and corruption presiding over many millions of dollars of public funds could be worse than existing bureaucratic structures.

Tuna management and development plans

Gillett (2003) found that countries that adopted tuna management plans had positive outcomes in policymaking for and administration of tuna industries in terms of transparency, stability of policies affecting the sector and government–industry consultation. Based on our observations, it would appear that the tuna management plans were not the causal factor behind improved policies and administration; rather, the improvements came from the will and capacity to improve governance, and the plans were a valuable guide. For example, Fiji and Papua New Guinea made extensive reforms to their governance of tuna industries in the past decade, and actively used their tuna management plans as part of that. Marshall Islands and Cook Islands did not have such plans, but they also made governance improvements, some of which were along the lines suggested in reports commissioned as preparation for tuna management plans, such as Chapman (2001, 2004b), and Aldous (2005). Solomon Islands and Kiribati had comprehensive tuna management plans, but did not follow them.

Some form of publicly available plan or charter of fisheries policy is important for transparency and for the private sector to be able to rely on policy directions. For the plans to be reliable, however, they should have legislative force. One of the problems with the plans drafted in the past five to seven years is that they were not well 'owned' by Pacific islanders, being drafted by short-term consultants. In addition, there has been limited follow-up in terms of evaluating progress with the plans and regularly revising them to take account of the highly dynamic nature of the tuna fishery.

A great deal of effort and resources have been put into tuna management plans regionally in the past decade. It could be a good time to review this process.

Recommendation 6

Review successes and failures in tuna management and development planning processes to date and base future efforts on lessons learned. Develop tuna management plans such that they are 'owned' by nationals and have agreed, achievable goals and timelines. Plans should have legislative force. Progress needs to be assessed on a regular basis, and goals and strategies revised to ensure alignment with national and regional policies, as well as tuna fisheries and market dynamics.

Consultative and transparent decision making

Consultative decision making can lead to more effective policies in various ways.

- Industry can help make better-informed management and development policies and administration.
- Environmental NGOs can help with resource management and public relations.
- Social and political stakeholders can help make more socially and politically apt policies and administration, and help with public relations.
- Other government departments can promote consistent policies and help address relevant issues outside fisheries' jurisdiction (such as taxation).
- Other Pacific island countries can improve and harmonise management and development initiatives.

Pacific island governments, however, tend not to see the potential value of external input to decision-making processes. Tuna management and development plans included institutionalising and regularising intergovernment departmental and other stakeholder input into decision making through consultative committees, but none of these ideas have been implemented in a significant way, although some governments among those covered by this study have *ad hoc* cross-sectoral consultation. On the whole, Pacific island countries have been 'slow to embrace the concepts of transparency and consultative processes' (Cartwright 2004).

Non-governmental organisations (NGOs). NGOs can act as a conscience to help moderate government policies and keep governments in contact with their constituents, but NGOs have not thus far played much of a role regarding tuna management or development in the region. Pacific island governments are not used to including NGOs and do not really see them as being legitimate voices in decision-making processes. Pacific island governments fear that a range of problems will arise if NGOs are allowed into government processes (Cartwright 2004). Some Pacific island countries take an adversarial approach to industry NGOs (INGOs) (Gillett 2003), and many are suspicious that environmental NGOs (ENGOs) are anti-government and/or anti-development. One of the problems with accepting NGOs into decision-making processes seems to be the perception that NGOs are 'Western', so developing a 'Pacific Way' for NGOs could help them to be seen as legitimate stakeholders by Pacific island governments.

Fishing associations. Strong fishing associations seem to be correlated positively with industry development, while poor industry–government dialogue correlates with difficult business environments (Gillett 2003). The relationship between industry and government should ideally be one in which industry can freely provide constructive criticism without fear of reprisal, and governments are able to respond constructively and make changes where appropriate. Pacific island countries' presentations of issues in the Multilateral High Level Conference and PrepCon processes leading up to the WCPFC showed the lack of INGO input, being government focused rather than tailored to meet the needs of domestic industry development (Cartwright 2004). INGOs are important because they are at the 'coal face' of fisheries management, so understanding of their situation is crucial for effective management, especially in terms of setting fees and compliance (Cartwright 2004).

Notwithstanding a general reluctance to include other stakeholders in decision-making processes, Gillett (2003) found that INGOs were seen by Pacific island governments as a positive thing. And Pacific island countries have included INGOs in some decision-making and negotiating processes, certainly more often than ENGOs (Cartwright 2004).

Interviewees noted that the regional fishing industry association (Pacific Islands Fisheries Industry Association [PIFIA]) established in September 2004 had, despite a promising start, not worked as planned because company owners were mostly too busy to participate effectively. This reflects findings from another study that found industry representatives did not have the time to attend lengthy regional fisheries management meetings (Cartwright 2004). The Tuna Boat Owners Association of Australia worked around this problem by employing a professional representative familiar with government processes and able to effectively disseminate information and lobby government on behalf of the industry. This could be a useful model for PIFIA to consider.

Recommendation 7

Appoint a professional regional representative (possibly part-time) to represent the interests of Pacific island country tuna industries, working closely with the FFA. The representative should be adequately funded to travel and liaise to improve consultation and inclusion. In particular, the representative should attend regional meetings and set up information networks with industry players.

Constraints relating to environmental issues are becoming increasingly important for tuna industries. These issues might be relatively minor compared with tuna stocks and by-catch management, but they impact on Pacific island countries' ability to sell their products in the sensitive markets of the United States and Europe. A recent study found that 79 per cent of European consumers, supermarket buyers, chefs and restaurateurs said that the environmental impact of seafood was an important factor in their purchasing decisions (WWF 2005). International campaigns to ban longlining because of stock depletion in some tuna species and incidental deaths of birds, turtles and sharks damage the public image of tuna as a product, as does damage caused by pollution from vessels and ship groundings. If brought into the decision-making process, some ENGOs can work with governments and industry to make improvements in these areas.

Recommendation 8

Bring industry, environmental and social/community NGOs into consultative decision-making processes as envisaged in tuna management plans.

Availability of information

One of the contributing reasons for the lack of action by Pacific island governments in exploring the feasibility of more of the ideas in reports already commissioned on developing tuna is that they are often not easily available. The SPC and ADB have made many of their reports available on their web sites, although the SPC web site is not very easy to use. The FFA, however, keeps country-specific reports confidential, leaving it up to Pacific island governments to disseminate them as they see fit. The SPC treats its very useful national tuna status reports the same way. Pacific island governments rarely make reports freely available within relevant departments, let alone to industry or other stakeholders. As a result, the usefulness of the many expensive reports produced is curtailed, the main beneficiaries being researchers and consultants such as ourselves, who have the contacts to be able to access them. The second step therefore is to make the reports more widely (in most cases publicly) available so that other stakeholders, especially industry, can make use of the ideas in them.

Recommendation 9

Sponsor agencies to make consultants' reports publicly available as a general rule. The FFA or the SPC to develop and manage a publicly accessible bibliographic database of publications with relevance to tuna in the region.

Accountability in tuna governance

Papua New Guinea's reforms in fisheries governance since the late 1990s demonstrate useful lessons for other Pacific island countries. On the one hand, the improvements to government capacity and policy were reflected in booming domestic industries and increased revenue from licence fees. On the other hand, improvements in the fisheries sector could not be quarantined from the governance problems remaining in the PNG government system as a whole (Pitts 2002; Lewis 2005). Current thinking on corruption prevention indicates that it is best approached as a whole of government (or even whole of society) issue (Larmour and Wolanin 2001). In this sense, fisheries policymakers can improve transparency and accountability within fisheries, while collaborating in wider efforts to improve these factors in government as a whole.

In recent years, the Fijian and Solomon Islands governments have taken steps to make fisheries officials accountable for apparent corruption with licence fees. In addition, the Solomon Islands Fisheries Department, as part of a government-wide initiative, has started improving its administrative systems to be more accountable, through tying the budget to documented planning, budget estimates and annual reporting of achievements and expenditure.

While high levels of corruption have not necessarily impeded economic growth in countries around the world (China is one example), industry interviewees for this study were unanimous in describing corruption as a constraint on their business.

Industrial development policies

It is a widely held belief that because most Pacific island countries have a high-cost production environment, and they do not have a competitive advantage for developing domestic tuna fishing or processing industries. Some economists therefore advocate that Pacific island countries would gain more wealth from maximising access fees from fleets from countries that do have competitive advantage in tuna fisheries, while concentrating on improving economic institutions and business conditions so that private sector development can occur independently (Petersen 2002a, 2002b). On the other hand, many of the fisheries development projects of the past were government owned, and were very inefficient. And, as we have discussed in a previous section, individual Pacific island countries have very different potentials for achieving domestic tuna industry development.

Nevertheless, domestic tuna industry development, even if somewhat economically skewed, at least brings some benefits in terms of employment and human resources development (Rodwell, pers. comm.; Barclay 2000, 2005). In any case, most Pacific island countries strongly desire to develop domestic tuna industries and use taxation incentives and tied fishing licences to encourage such development.

The many failed domestic development attempts from the past contain lessons about what does not work. These have damaged Pacific islanders' faith in business as a way to achieve development and negatively influenced the confidence of banks and other lending institutions in fisheries, as well as wasted a lot of government revenue. One of the important recommendations from Gillett's (2003) report was that any new developments should be technically and economically evaluated before any investment was made. The following sections detail strategies for industry development based on what has worked in the six Pacific island countries covered by this study.

Developing domestic fishing industries

Natural resources specialist with the ADB Thomas Gloerfelt-Tarp is puzzled by Pacific island countries' determination to domesticate industrial tuna fishing as a way to bring more of the profits in-country, considering that tuna fishing has not been very profitable for more than a decade (Gloerfelt-Tarp, pers. comm.). Many of the Pacific islander fisheries officials interviewed for this project were aware that it was difficult to make a profit in tuna fisheries, but they still aspired to have locally owned and managed tuna-fishing companies. Kiribati's Permanent Secretary for Fisheries, David Yeeting, explained that this aspiration was 'an emotional thing'. The sea and fish are so important in Kiribati culture, I-Kiribati want to be involved in tuna fishing despite the difficulties (Yeeting, pers. comm.). This being the case, it is vital that Pacific island countries learn from previous fisheries development successes and failures to help identify those projects that are most likely to cover their costs and least likely to cost Pacific island governments scarce revenue.

Many reports have outlined potential fisheries development policies for purse-seine, longline and pole-and-line fisheries (ADB 1997; Chapman 2004b; Gillett 2003).[14] We do not therefore present an exhaustive list of all possibilities for domestic fisheries development; rather, we present a list of principles underpinning successful domestic fishing companies in the countries under study. Most of these relate to longlining, as this is the option pursued most commonly for domestic development.

Decreasing the fuel bill helps viability

Rising fuel prices are part of the reason why fishing is less profitable these days. Governments can provide some relief by making sure their taxation regimes and infrastructure for fuel delivery do not unnecessarily add to prices. Some companies with fleets of 10 or more vessels have been working out ways to reduce their fuel consumption by using carrier vessels to take fuel to their fishing fleets in the fishing grounds, and bring back the catch, rather than having each fishing vessel steam to and from port to offload catch and fill up with fuel.

Fisheries should be targeted precisely to local resource endowments

The case of Cook Islands' southern longline fishery demonstrates clearly the importance of matching fishing style to local resource endowments. Taiwanese company Gilontas used vessels and crews accustomed to fishing for albacore for the cannery market, but Cook Islands albacore stocks were not productive enough for this kind of relatively high-volume, low-value per unit style of longline fishing. Gilontas withdrew from Cook Islands within a couple of years of entering the fishery. Land Holdings Limited focused on maximising the quality and therefore the value of each fish through careful handling on board and getting the fish to market quickly. Cook Islands' southern waters contain fish that can fetch high prices on the sashimi market, including bluefin. This approach to fishing has built the reputation of Cook Islands' tuna in the Japanese chilled-sashimi market. Land Holdings Limited has achieved prices of up to NZ$60,000 per fish and is financially successful, despite the seasonal nature and relatively low productivity of the southern Cook Islands fishery.

Chilled fish export businesses need suitable airfreight arrangements

No matter how good catches are, if the fish cannot be brought to market in good condition for an economical cost, they cannot form the basis of a successful business. Logistically suitable, viably priced airfreight continues to be one of the major problems faced by the longline business managers interviewed for this project. Successful companies used one of two kinds of airfreight arrangements.

1. The first kind is where large international tourist industries mean there are frequent passenger flights on planes with suitable freight capacity (and there are local markets in the hospitality industry for B and C-grade tunas). In this study, that was Fiji and Cook Islands; however, even in countries with large tourist industries, businesses focused on exports of chilled tuna were facing difficulties. With recent CPUE declines in Fiji's fishery, the business has been marginal. One of the major carriers in Cook Islands recently changed to using the new generation of passenger jets that maximise passenger space at the cost of freight space, meaning Cook Islands logistics are less favourable than they were.

2. In countries without large international tourist industries, a few companies arranged workable airfreight by using dedicated freight planes to get fish to a hub, where it was transferred to large passenger jets going to chilled-fish market destinations.

Ultra-low temperature frozen tuna can be sea-freighted to lucrative markets

The difficulties and expense involved with airfreight means it is good if fishing companies can use sea freight. Because tuna oxidises when frozen under normal conditions, frozen tuna cannot be sold in the most lucrative fresh-fish markets, which is why most Pacific island countries have relied on airfreight to export chilled tuna. Tuna frozen to ultra-low temperatures (ULT, –60° Celsius), however, does not oxidise, but maintains its red hue, so it can still be sold as sashimi and tuna steaks. ULT is usually considered too high-technology to be done as part of a domestic industry, but a small second hand ULT machine was being used by one company in Suva, demonstrating that ULT technology may feasibly be part of domestic operations.

Suitable markets for B and C-grade tuna strongly influences longline fisheries' viability

The highest price can be achieved on the sashimi market, but only a small proportion of each catch is A-grade bigeye or yellowfin. The rest of the catch must also be sold at reasonable prices, for which there are a range of markets. Expanding sashimi markets outside Japan and tuna steak/fillet markets accept fish of lower grades and smaller sizes than the Japanese sashimi market. In Fiji and Cook Islands, the tourist industry provides a relatively high-priced domestic market. PNG operators also sell a small amount of fresh tuna locally, or to Australia. Southern fisheries that include a high proportion of albacore in the longline catch can sell that to canneries, although the price is low.

Tuna-fishing businesses need large cash reserves

Fluctuations in the availability of the resource due to oceanographic effects and the volatility of tuna markets mean that inevitably tuna companies have bad years when they make losses. Some fisheries, such as Cook Islands' longline fisheries and Fiji's skipjack fishery, are highly seasonal. Companies need to be sufficiently profitable and/or diversified to generate cash reserves or loan equity to survive the bad years/ off seasons. The revenues from fishing or, in the short-term, from other sources, need to be adequate and sufficiently well managed to allow for the maintenance and replacement of fleet and equipment.

Can pole-and-line fisheries be revived through premium markets?

The pole-and-line method is higher cost than the purse-seine method, so for it to be viable pole-and-line-caught skipjack need to be sold at a higher price than purse-seine-caught fish. It seems possible that with some (private sector) effort in marketing and trade connections for the wealthy markets of Japan, Europe and the United States, premium markets for pole-and-line products might support a revival in Pacific island country-based pole-and-line fishing (Rodwell, pers. comm.). A marketing campaign could differentiate pole-and-line product in the minds of quality and ecology-conscious consumers, particularly if purse-seine fisheries are adequately controlled. Marine Stewardship Council (MSC) accreditation could be sought as part of marketing the pole-and-line method as environmentally friendly. The Japanese distant water pole-and-line fleet survives, albeit in a highly subsidised form, so it seems worth investigating opportunities in the Japanese market for pole-and-line-caught skipjack. The *tataki* market could be explored further, as could fresh (ULT frozen) skipjack markets in Japan.[15] Pole-and-line product from the Pacific has never been differentiated from purse-seine product in the Japanese *katsuobushi*[16] market (Nakamura, pers. comm.), but it may be possible to do so and improve prices. There could also be the potential for premium prices for pole-and-line-caught skipjack in the gourmet smoked smallgoods being made in Fiji, Cook Islands and Kiribati (Rodwell, pers. comm.; Stone, pers. comm.). Lower-quality fish could also be smoked for local markets. In many Pacific island countries, fresh skipjack is not a preferred eating fish but smoked and/or dried it could be more popular. A study of these possibilities could be provided by regional and/or donor organisations and supported by governments, but decisions to explore the possibilities should be made by the private sector on commercial considerations.

Supply side measures to increase profitability of fisheries

Pacific island countries have considered the idea that falling prices could be due to an oversupply of fish, and that if the FFA group of countries could restrict catches in their area it could push the prices for fish up. An economic study of this option found that the necessary conditions—such as total demand for tuna being insensitive to price changes, and the support of all member governments to impose catch restrictions—were met only partially in the case of the FFA fishery, but that small price increases in the short term should be possible (Owen 2001). The World Tuna Purse-seine Organisation (WTPO) has had some success pushing prices up by restricting the fishing activities of its members, and therefore supply. Models that consider economic as well as ecological sustainability could inform supply side measures, however, the difficulties of developing such measures in a global, highly competitive market should not be underestimated.

Developing domestic processing industries

All of the Pacific island countries covered here had aspirations to develop domestic processing industries, because 'value-adding' processing was seen as a good way to capture more of the wealth from international tuna industries, and also for spreading the wealth among the population through employment, procurement and spin-off businesses. Papua New Guinea's aspirations in this regard are the most ambitious: it hopes to replace Thailand as the world centre for tuna processing.

Chilled and frozen fresh tuna can be processed to a certain extent before export, but the most labour-intensive tuna processing is associated with canning, in particular the loining process. Because of the high-cost production environment in Pacific island countries compared with competitor countries in Southeast Asia, canneries/loining plants in Solomon Islands, Papua New Guinea and Fiji have all relied on preferential trade access to European markets and hefty tax remissions or other kinds of subsidies to be economically viable. Marshall Islands had a loining plant connected to the Starkist cannery in Pago Pago for a few years, but it eventually failed for lack of appropriate management. Kiribati is interested in establishing a loining plant but is likely to face substantial challenges, including those associated with fresh water supply and diseconomies of scale with freight.

Another kind of processing that has potential for domestic development is small-scale gourmet plants. Because small-scale processing plants are cheaper and easier to build and operate than large-scale canneries, they constitute a form of development that could feasibly be owned and run by Pacific islanders. This kind of processing proportionately adds a great deal of value. In the words of one interviewee, 'You can take a fish worth $2 a kilo and turn it into a fish worth $15 a kilo.' Stonefish in Fiji established a small plant with HACCP systems and sold smoked fish, tuna bacon and tuna jerky, mostly as exports to the United States. Based on that, a similar plant was built in Cook Islands, with its produce sold domestically. A small plant focusing on tuna jerky for export to Asia via Fiji was built in Kiribati. A plant that could be used for smoking and related kinds of processing was built under an aid project in Kavieng, Papua New Guinea, but so far has been used only for fresh-fish filleting and packing.

Tying distant water fisheries access to domestic industry development

In recent years, Papua New Guinea has been the main proponent of tying fisheries access to investment in shore-based developments, and has had some success. Where access is preferential, however, or fees are waived, there is not always an adequate assessment of whether the value of the investment to the Pacific island country is greater than the fees forgone. Allowing exclusive access to particular waters for domestic fleets is another strategy employed with some success.

The 2002 FFA Workshop on Property Rights in Nadi, Fiji, discussed an alternative approach to access fees. Broadly speaking, this was based on taking strong national participatory rights to access, as strengthened by the WCPFC allocation process, and allocating them to domestic companies as a means of increasing indigenous involvement and domestic industry development. Under such an approach, DWFNs could still fish in Pacific island EEZs, but only under charter or through joint ventures with a domestic participatory right-holder. The right-holders are then required to make investments and create jobs rather than simply pocket the earnings from the sale or lease of the licence (Clark 2002).[17] The country profiles in this study note that this strategy has not domesticated benefits from fisheries as much as hoped, and one regional commentator saw benefits from these arrangements going to more individuals than governments or national economies (Gillett, pers. comm.).

Domesticating trading and marketing

Almost no interviewees cited trading and marketing as their aspirations for capturing more wealth from tuna; they talked primarily about fishing and processing. Since the 1980s, however, there has been much more money in tuna trading than in fishing (Reid 2005; Schurman 1998). 'Foreign investment in the tuna fishing sector of new and upcoming fishing nations has in the past been mainly from trading houses that stand to benefit from marketing and not necessarily from fishing operations' (McCoy and Gillett 2005). Luen Thai Fishing Venture, which operates in Micronesia, is not primarily a fishing company. It contracts a fleet to which it sells supplies and from which it markets the catch. It is believed Ting Hong operated this way too (McCoy and Gillett 2005). Taiyo Gyogyo, the Japanese partner in Solomon Taiyo, was also motivated by a trading aim: it wanted a high-quality reliable supply of canned fish for its UK buyers (Hughes and Thaanum 1995). Lack of international trading networks seems to have been an important factor in Soltai's financial downturn since 2003 (Barclay 2005). The sophisticated accounting systems and active international trade networks used by veteran Fijian longline companies Solander and Fiji Fish have undoubtedly played a role in their success.

Fisheries managers used to believe that as markets matured, fishers would start to take over the role of middlemen, marketing their products more directly (Dunn, pers. comm.), but this has not happened and the middlemen have taken profit away from the fishing end of the business (McCoy and Gillett 2005). Increasing competition in the fishery seems to have resulted in a large enough supply that in times of high landings, traders have been able to push the prices down (ADB 2003).

Some kinds of fish marketing and trading do not require much capital outlay—an office with reliable telecommunications is enough—but this business does require contacts, business acumen and knowledge of markets. The difficulty for Pacific island countries lies in acquiring the skills and experience needed for marketing and trading. A first step might be supplying gear and food for vessels. At the other end of the spectrum is marketing high-price seafood products in the wealthy markets of Europe, Japan and the United States, and supplying in sufficient bulk with sufficient quality and reliability. Nothing in most Pacific islanders' background prepares them for a career in international trading and marketing. On the other hand, Pacific island economies are no more suited to industrial fishing or processing than they are to international trading, and Pacific islanders see it as reasonable to become involved in those sectors. It will be a challenge to successfully facilitate the development of seafood trading and marketing businesses, but it should be possible, especially with plenty of consultation with industry and other relevant stakeholders, and some capacity building. Governments can assist by coordinating marketing and trading initiatives through agencies such as the Pacific Islands Trade and Investment Commission (PITIC 2002), which Cook Islands has used to establish markets for its marine resource exports, and the World Bank's Foreign Investment Advisory Service (FIAS 2005).

If Pacific island countries can develop seafood marketing and trading expertise, this could revolutionise the ways in which countries with substantial tuna resources, but with a geographic environment not conducive to domestic industrial development, think about generating wealth from tuna. For example, instead of selling the rights to fish to DWFNs, they (through the domestic private sector) could organise lucrative markets for their fish and then contract DWFNs to catch the fish for them at an agreed price, and make profits on selling the fish to the buyers.

Service and supply industries for DWFNs

Of the countries covered in this study, only Cook Islands did not have some kind of service and supply industry for trans-shipping DWFNs. Governments in Solomon Islands, Kiribati, Fiji and Marshall Islands have actively encouraged the development of such industries. Marshall Islands in particular chose this option over domestic fishing as the way to generate local business development with a great deal of success, generating revenue in trans-shipping fees and spin-off businesses in minor repairs and procurement.

Constraints on domestic service and supply industry development are similar to those for business as a whole in Pacific island countries. Fiji's longline trans-shipping businesses are constrained by a lack of wharf infrastructure, and somewhat by the range of skilled tradespeople. Kiribati cannot attract longliners because of a lack of air connections to export sashimi-grade fish. Kiribati does attract purse-seiners, but has limited and expensive supplies of fresh food and water for them.

The most intractable problem for service and supply industries is fluctuations in the availability of the resource. The numbers of purse-seine and pole-and-line vessels operating in Marshall Islands' EEZ dropped dramatically in 2002–03 when oceanographic effects moved the fish further west. Solomon Islands' purse-seine fishery declined just as Marshall Islands improved, in mid 2003, and stayed bad until mid 2005. Kiribati suffered a downturn in 2003 and 2004, with almost no vessels trans-shipping in Tarawa, then picked up again in 2005. Like fishing companies, service industries have to be able either to follow the fish or to earn enough in the good years to see them through the bad years.

Another point to note about service and supply industries is that while they bring economic activity within the domestic economy of Pacific island countries, a large proportion of this activity is simply funnelling imports and so is not of much developmental value. McCoy and Gillett (2005) found that more than half of the total expenditure of Chinese longliners operating in the Pacific was spent on fuel, and about 30 per cent on bait. None of the countries covered here had a fuel refinery or commercial bait fishery so this expenditure did not add value domestically. The negative impacts of prostitution and substance abuse around busy international ports where there are insufficient health and welfare services to mitigate these impacts should also be considered.

Developing human capital

Human capital is often considered an industrial policy issue for encouraging development in particular sectors. We have drawn it out as a strategy for capturing wealth for tuna on its own because we believe it is vital for Pacific island countries, and because we are envisaging the development of human capital not only in terms of producing employees for the private sector, but in terms of building public-sector capacity.

Public-sector capacity

Fisheries revenue has not historically been reinvested in fisheries governance, but has been directed to central government revenue, although this is changing in some countries with moves towards self-funding statutory authorities. Governments have not prioritised training or education in areas relating to fisheries management by specific allocation of scholarships (Tarte 2004). Fisheries management and development are hampered by government departments with insufficient numbers of staff and without the appropriate levels of education. One of the reasons why Pacific island governments have not taken on ideas for improvements for fisheries development and management from the many reports on the topic is that they have not had the time or the background to be able to make the recommended changes. Areas where Pacific islander interviewees said public-sector capacity needed improvement included fisheries science, fisheries management, economics and fisheries law.

The PNG examples mentioned earlier have shown how improved fisheries bureaucracy capacity improved the amount of revenue generated by access fees, and improved policies contributed to the generation of a great deal of domestic industry development. On the other hand, there are many examples where lack of capacity means losses for Pacific island countries in terms of fisheries management and development. Pacific islander interviewees noted that some Pacific island delegates to international meetings showed through their questions that they had not grasped the information in the briefs for the meetings. Delegates who do not understand the issues or the discussion properly are unable to contribute, and they are also unable to act as effective conduits for their governments. Pacific island politicians are sometimes not briefed sufficiently about regional and domestic fisheries issues to be able to make consistent workable policies.

One of the other ways in which government capacity has a direct influence on the ability of Pacific island countries to capture wealth from tuna is the capacity of their distant water access negotiation teams. Many of the strategies identified by interviewees and in reports for ways to secure greater revenues from DWFNs require building the capacity of Pacific island government negotiators. Instituting systems whereby negotiators have an incentive to perform well in these negotiations would also help (Gillett, pers. comm.).

In addition to skill and experience levels, there is the issue of adequate resourcing of fisheries departments. For some states, such as Kiribati, the need for adequate numbers of qualified fisheries staff cannot be overemphasised. Sound advice from fisheries departments is essential to making the right decisions and creating the right policies to guide sustainable fisheries management and development. Poor governance is driven by under-resourced and pressured government officials, a lack of direction and planning, low accountability and low productivity.

Fisheries managers' understanding of tuna industries

Interviewees for this project and reports on similar topics raised a range of areas where Pacific island countries' ability to capture wealth from tuna was being constrained by a lack of understanding of tuna businesses. Several interviewees noted a naivety on the part of Pacific island officials who felt they were capable of making advantageous deals with the representatives of large international fishing companies. The same circumstances apply to fisheries access negotiators, who need a great deal of understanding about the economics of tuna industries, which few Pacific island government staff currently have. McCoy and Gillett (2005) interviewed Chinese longline business managers who found local officials they dealt with 'very inexperienced' and sometimes lacking competence; this was then seen as a business opportunity.

One NGO worker from Solomon Islands felt that this naivety was due partly to the dual economy existing in most Pacific island countries, meaning many Pacific islanders lack experience in capitalism, and he also thought it was due to the prevalence of cargo cult-style beliefs that there was a simple road to wealth somewhere out there.

While financial and economic literacy are important skills for fisheries managers, it is probably unrealistic to expect that each Pacific island country will develop the expertise necessary for all leadership and decision making. As well as institutional strengthening, including further education in these areas for fisheries managers, utilising skills from other government departments and from organisations such as the FFA can add to Pacific island countries' capacities in economics and business management. It is essential that the skills and experience shortage within the public sector with respect to human capacity is addressed.

Much of the technical assistance provided to fisheries departments in the region is of a 'fly-in, fly-out' nature—from consultants and staff of regional fisheries organisations. While regional fisheries agency staff are able to make multiple visits and thereby build corporate history, there is a lack of systematic mentoring and leadership capacity building in fisheries. Such mentoring could be provided by well-qualified technical advisers (especially fisheries economists and managers) appointed for two to three-year posts with fisheries departments.[19] These should not be line positions because of the risk that the mentor instead of the local official ends up 'owning' institutional development; the mentor's role should be to facilitate improvements by local officials, not make improvements themselves.

Recommendation 10

Build capacity in Pacific island fisheries departments in the following fields: fisheries management (including working knowledge of stock assessments); economics; business management; and public policy. Where capacity gaps exist, consider recruiting suitably qualified and motivated staff from other government departments and externally.

Private-sector capacity

A great deal has already been written on strategies to improve Pacific island countries' pool of qualified and experienced fishing crews, technical managers for processing facilities and tradespeople for service industries,[20] so such strategies are not canvassed here.

One point worth noting here, however, is the synergies and cost savings that can result from greater regional coordination of training. The 2005 Forum Leaders' Communiqué noted the importance of expanding regional technical and vocational education training and having technical qualifications 'portable' (Pacific Islands Forum Secretariat 2005). Papua New Guinea's National Fisheries College has successfully run some short courses on fisheries small business development in other Pacific island countries. Kiribati's Fisheries Training Centre has a long record of training crew and placing them in work on DWFN vessels, and looks soon to expand into officer training. Some other Pacific island countries might want to extend this opportunity for their citizens through cooperation with Kiribati.

Business skills and experience

The main issue in private sector human resources addressed here relates to one of the principles raised at the outset of this discussion on capturing more wealth from tuna: tuna development equals business development. One of the greatest constraints on greater Pacific islander involvement in management and ownership of tuna businesses is a lack of skills and experience in business. One of the tendencies in Pacific island country strategies for tuna business development noted in this study, as well as Gillett's 2003 study on domestic industry development, is the expectation that small-scale fishers can upscale to medium and larger scale fishing enterprises, because they are skilled at fishing. Gillett noted that there have been 'very few cases' of small-scale operators successfully upgrading to become medium or large-scale operators. He explained this by pointing out that fishing was different to managing fishing and medium and larger-scale fisheries businesses, and small-scale fishers were unlikely to have management skills.

Many Pacific island small-scale fishers live in a social context in which they have had little or no exposure to business principles, where business as an economic activity might not be highly valued, and where other social obligations might be prioritised more highly than the covering of one's operating costs and generating a profit—meaning, for example, strong pressures to 'dip into the till' to pay for family obligations. Business failure rates are still high in cultures where people are exposed to business principles from childhood, and where business is highly valued as a social and economic activity, so it is understandable that there is limited business acumen to support commercial tuna development projects in Pacific island countries.

We therefore agree with Gillett's (2003) suggestion that businesspeople who have had success in other sectors are more appropriate targets for commercial tuna development than small-scale fishers. There are two problems, however, with attracting lateral movement of established businesspeople as a strategy for achieving Pacific island countries' aspirations regarding domestication. One is the small pool of Pacific islanders with any business skills and experience, since in most Pacific island countries other ethnic groups have tended to dominate the business world. The other problem is the lack of profitability in tuna fisheries, which means they are unattractive as businesses, especially for businesspeople with no technical expertise in fishing. The many fishery development failures in the past contribute to wariness about investment in fishing. Processing or trading projects could have greater success in attracting lateral movements of established businesspeople.

All recent projects for tuna development covered by this study included feasible-looking business plans as a criterion for participation, and all of the tuna management plans included business training as a strategy to improve success rates, especially for small-scale tuna businesses. In light of the assertions above, however, business plans and short training courses could only be a first step in inculcating the major cultural shift that could be necessary for large numbers of Pacific islanders to become successful businesspeople. The important lesson from Robert Stone's experience, cited earlier, seems to be that he started off his fisheries business independently at a financially manageable level (one small boat fishing for snapper), and gained experience operating as a commercial fisherman for some years before taking out a large loan. Perhaps tuna business development strategies should be aimed at encouraging Pacific islanders to gain training and experience in managing low-risk businesses for some years before facilitating their access to large loans in the high-risk tuna-fishing sector.

One strategy for achieving this could be to design projects for Pacific islanders to gain extended exposure to the management of tuna businesses—through internships, for example—and encourage Pacific islanders to undertake tertiary studies in business and enterprise to lay the groundwork for management and ownership of tuna businesses. Rights-based management could also be a strategy for encouraging Pacific islander fisheries entrepreneurship. Finally, projects that facilitate business learning rather than distribute largesse are more likely to be successful in achieving indigenous participation in tuna businesses. The entry requirements for tuna business projects should be left to normal business processes.

Who is best for the job?

The desire for domestication of tuna industries could be seen as part of a broad historical process emerging from decolonisation, whereby Pacific islanders were to take over from expatriates in all areas of government and business. It is related to the term 'localisation', which has usually referred to the replacement of expatriate employees with locals, and which has also been a long-term concern for Pacific islanders in regional tuna industries.

The small populations and economies of Pacific island countries, however, have meant that there has been a limited pool of trained and experienced managers, for the public and private sectors. For this reason, the most senior positions in tuna businesses have been held mostly by people who are not ethnic Pacific islanders. This is a fact of life even for much larger, wealthier countries—sometimes the best people for particular jobs, particularly very specialised jobs, come from overseas. Some public-sector reforms have also involved expatriate consultants. As agents of change, non-national consultants can be very effective in the short term, not least because they have no vested interests in the status quo compared with permanent employees. Non-nationals are not as susceptible to pressure from relatives, or other political/cultural issues that can negatively affect governance. But there are often problems with maintaining changes engendered by non-national contractors because nationals do not gain a sense of 'ownership' over the reforms. Furthermore, the great pay disparities between non-national consultants and their national colleagues can generate resentment against the reforms.

This situation is a conundrum, whereby non-national input at senior levels is sometimes the most pragmatic option, but it is politically unacceptable, especially if non-nationals are seen to dominate senior positions and localisation does not appear to increase over time. It would be best to achieve some kind of middle ground between the problem of expert expatriates sidelining their local colleagues and therefore failing to engender long-term skills improvement, and the problem of completely local but insufficiently experienced management. There is no easy solution to this dilemma in the Pacific, where there is a chronic shortage of qualified and trained local managers, and where prevailing levels of remuneration do not offer a good incentive for training and retaining high-calibre local staff. Some contributions towards addressing the issue are suggested below.

- Non-national leadership input in fisheries management and businesses could be more developmental and less detrimental by assessing the success and achievement of their national colleagues, not how much the non-national achieves.
- For the medium to long-term, Pacific island countries and aid donors can continue to build the pool of trained and experienced private and public sector managers through human capital development.
- Encourage suitably skilled and motivated Pacific island nationals from public and private sectors to enter the fishing industry to inject new blood, rather than retraining existing staff or starting from scratch.

Cooperating regionally to capture wealth

The cyclical migratory nature of tuna resources means that businesses frequently need to have the flexibility to follow the fish. DWFNs have long had vessels capable of achieving this, shifting between oceans to seek profitable catch rates and species. Businesses that operate in only one Pacific island country have to suffer inevitable bad years, and since economic pressures on domestic operators have increased in recent years, businesses can rapidly become unviable. Organising locally based industries into national units also has impacts on domestic industry development. For example, employment opportunities are disrupted if locally based companies have to scale back in years of heavy losses due to poor catches and/or economic circumstances. For Pacific island governments, access fees plummet in the years that DWFNs do not fish in particular EEZs, but if fisheries access were pooled across a suitable group of EEZs (such as the PNA group), access fees to individual countries could be more even across the years. The existing FSM Arrangement, the new PNA Vessel Days Scheme (VDS) and arrangements to 'trade' fishing entitlements between members will go a considerable way in this regard, through developing fishing rights that are not tied to a geographic area but can be used throughout the region. This means for years when the fishing is not good in one country's EEZ, they can still raise revenue through selling rights to fish elsewhere in the region, thus smoothing out revenue fluctuations.

Even with these mechanisms in place, national borders make it difficult for businesses to operate regionally. For example, Fiji Fish has vessels that operate in Solomon Islands and Vanuatu as well as Fiji. Licensing the fishing vessels to operate in more than one EEZ was quite easy, but Fiji Fish found it extremely difficult to gain the necessary permissions from the Solomon Islands and PNG governments to use carrier vessels to take fuel out to its fleet and bring the catch back to Suva. It is apparent that there would be considerable benefit from developing arrangements for reciprocal access between Pacific island countries.

Increased labour mobility within the region, including fishing crews and skilled tradespeople, could also be beneficial for capturing more wealth from tuna. Lack of labour mobility is one of the factors inhibiting general regional economic development (Pacific Islands Forum Secretariat 2005; Chand 2005b; Peebles 2005). Labour mobility could also alleviate some of the human capital constraints mentioned earlier. Easier flows of labour and conceiving of the resource regionally or subregionally could enable Pacific island countries to gain benefits from the industrial hub principle mentioned earlier. For instance, Pacific island countries could conceive of a tuna-processing hub in Madang as something they could participate in and benefit from. If Papua New Guinea were to make it possible for other Pacific island countries to gain employment and investment benefits from a hub in Madang, this could improve the economic viability of processing in the region, and therefore make capturing wealth from tuna more possible.

National borders build in economic constraints for businesses exploiting this migratory resource. Attempts to protect perceived national interests by throwing up barriers to regional operation through difficult immigration procedures, difficult business-licensing procedures and protection of domestic businesses are preventing Pacific islanders from capturing more wealth from tuna. The current conventional view in which each country wants its own processing plant in its national economy and sees developments in other Pacific island countries as competition perpetuates the diseconomies of scale that make Pacific island countries' production environments high cost in comparison with Asian countries. Below are some ideas for potential regional economic opportunities.

Regional approaches to marketing and trading

Europe would be an excellent market for fresh (chilled and frozen) tuna from the Pacific because it is large, consumers pay high prices for fish and there is great demand because Europe has severely restricted supplies of fish. EU buyers, however, require large, regular supplies. Pacific island country fishing companies as they currently exist, fragmented across national borders, cannot achieve the scale and reliability of supply needed for the EU market. Any one EEZ might not be able to produce the same amount all the time because of seasonal and yearly fluctuations, but a marketing business sourcing fish from fishing companies across the region could guarantee large reliable supplies (Gloerfelt-Tarp, pers. comm.). Such an initiative should be private-sector driven, but to be attractive and feasible Pacific island governments would need to assure potential investors that they would facilitate the necessary approvals and licences to enable it to happen.

Mobile processing, service industries and crews

Although floating factories are used in other parts of the world, in the Pacific they tend to be imagined as representing the worst kind of foreign investment that makes no commitment to local development. Floating fish-processing factories could, however, be managed such that they benefit Pacific island economies. Such a factory could employ Pacific islanders.

Small ultra-low temperature freezing machines fit in shipping containers, so small mobile plants for processing fresh chilled and frozen tuna could work the waters with longline fisheries in Cook Islands, the Line Islands in Kiribati and Fiji. Floating factories could also help with the uncertainty involved in large capital infrastructure in places such as Kiribati and Marshall Islands, where fixed land-based infrastructure may be rendered inoperable by rising sea levels in the future.

The roles of the FFA and the SPC in facilitating development

The SPC has long offered technical developmental advice for small-scale and near-shore fisheries in the region. Until recently, the FFA has concentrated mostly on providing fisheries management advice, with minimal development advice. From now on, however, the FFA's activities will include far more industrial developmental advice (FFA 2005). The agency is to provide better information on the economic benefits to Pacific island countries from tuna fisheries, especially DWFNs, including access fees and how many people are employed by tuna businesses (van Santen 2005). Part of the FFA's increased role in development will occur under the European Union-funded EDF9 project, 'Development of Tuna Fisheries in Pacific ACP Countries' (DevFish). The DevFish project is designed to work through stakeholder consultation in each country, and aid donors, to dovetail with non-fisheries areas such as general governance, investment and environmental issues. It is to be hoped that this will facilitate an integrated process of developmental change, which should be more effective than previous 'one-point interventions' have been.

To be able to facilitate industry effectively, the FFA will need to adapt the services it offers, to include constructive criticism of Pacific island country policies and direct contact with the private sector and to improve its ability to disseminate information. For example, the agency's studies on airfreight would have been useful for industry, but industry did not have easy access to them. Another example is that the agency's *Tuna Products Catalogue* has not been widely available for investors interested in processing. There is little value in donors funding reports that gather dust on fisheries departments' shelves, when the agreed agent of development, the private sector, is asking for more information on which to base investment decisions. The FFA and the SPC will need to be more honest than they have been in the past about the economic potential of development options. This is a difficult ask when political and other interests are clearly wedded to a particular development option, however, it is essential that regional organisations 'tell it as it is', even when that is 'bad news'.

Based on the analysis and comments from interviewees, we suggest the following ideas for action, a number of which form part of the FFA's operational plan

- more effectively utilise the Overseas Fisheries Cooperation Foundation expert on Japanese markets hosted by the FFA
- coordinate commercial consultation about freight availability and costs
- coordinate studies to explore market possibilities for Pacific island country tuna products, especially value-added products
- assist Pacific island countries to develop capacity in seafood marketing and trading
- coordinate activities between businesses in the region
- coordinate and assist with regional economic initiatives, including trading, mobile industries and regional training and recruitment
- host industry liaison officers (perhaps one each for purse-seine, longlining and processing)
- expand and update the economic database on key longline and purse-seine fleets (DWFN and domestic) so as to build a time series of prices and operational costs
- continue with bioeconomic modelling to underpin the successful development and adoption of management measures at the WCPFC
- coordinate with FIAS to improve Pacific island countries' foreign investment environments.

Small-scale and indigenous fisheries development policies

Our research indicates that Pacific island governments are keen to see that benefits from tuna industries are felt at the village level. Most rural fisheries development projects based on reef fish have failed to be economically self-sustaining and Pacific island governments have not had the resources to sustain them. Recent versions of small-scale fisheries development projects based on the assumption that economic viability is important, such as the EU Rural Coastal Fisheries Development Program in Papua New Guinea and the Outer Islands Fisheries Project under Central Pacific Producers in Kiribati, have had greater success thus far in facilitating coastal fishers to supply domestic urban markets. Tuna makes up only a small part of these catches, as they are often difficult to catch from small vessels close to shore, and sometimes are not the preferred species for domestic consumption.

Models of small-scale, indigenously owned tuna fisheries

The Samoan *alia* longline fishery has been hailed as a successful model of an indigenously owned small-scale tuna-fishery development. Many Pacific island governments sent teams to Samoa to investigate, although none then established an *alia* fishery at home (Gillett 2003). As Samoa was not included in this study, a detailed evaluation of the model is not presented here, but it is worth noting that despite some successes, the *alia* model also had many problems. Dozens of fishers were lost at sea in the small vessels in the first couple of years, the fishery did not have HACCP systems in place so there was a danger of a health scare in export markets, and effort exceeded the maximum economic sustainable yield of the fishery, leading to a CPUE collapse (Watt, pers. comm.; Chapman 2004b). The *alias* then mostly left the fishery, leaving it dominated by larger-scale longliners that could more easily fish offshore and which were mostly owned and managed by non-nationals. This is considered to be one of the first material demonstrations showing that while a regional stock (albacore) is in good condition, it is possible for ill-conceived domestic approaches to have a severe localised impact arising from over-expanding the locally based fleets. Cook Islands and Fiji have experienced similar results, albeit from the impact of larger, locally based longline vessels, as well as from stock damage being done further north in the equatorial zone.

In some parts of the Philippines, small-scale, locally owned and built wooden vessels called 'pump boats' using handlines have had success in commercial tuna fisheries. Filipino resident expatriates in Papua New Guinea have been involved in a move to have this model adopted in Papua New Guinea, as a way for indigenous small-scale fishers to enter commercial tuna fisheries. Pump-boat trials were conducted in the late 1990s and early 2000s, without much success, although in 2005 some government and industry interviewees still had hope for this model. The pump-boat/handline model is being included in the next revision of the PNG National Tuna Management Plan (Government of Papua New Guinea 2004).

Recreational fishing

Recreational fishing based on international tourism is often raised as a development option, since there is a huge economic return per fish caught by recreational fishers, if international tourists utilise locally owned and run businesses. Recreational fishing can be suitable for village-level ecotourism. Since this development option relies on international tourism, however, it is constrained by the same factors that limit tourism potential in Papua New Guinea, Solomon Islands, Kiribati and Marshall Islands. Even in Fiji and Cook Islands, which have large tourism industries, recreational fishing has not been a significant business. None of the six countries covered in this study had a recreational fishery attracting international tourists fishing for pelagic species such as tuna. Marshall Islands and most of the other countries covered have active local recreational fisheries targeting tuna and like species, but these have no significant economic development effects.[21]

Notes

[1] Where large-scale domestic development (loining or canning plants, major port/infrastructure facilities, etc.) is not feasible, there are other domestic development options that should be pursued. For some Pacific island countries, however, these options are unlikely to generate greater benefits to the economy than revenues from various forms of licensing DWFN operations.

[2] According to Article 5(b) of the Western and Central Pacific Fisheries Convention, Bmsy as a target can be modified 'by relevant environmental and economic factors, including the special requirements of developing States in the Convention Area, particularly small island developing States, and taking into account fishing patterns, the interdependence of stocks and any generally recommended international minimum standards, whether subregional, regional or global'.

[3] The degree to which these busts are a result of localised depletions depressing CPUE, or of environment-driven changes (oceanographic factors, for instance) is a matter of some conjecture.

[4] See also the section 'Tuna management and development plans'.

[5] Some of these fishers come from the island of Roti in Indonesia, whose people have for centuries been fishing in areas now considered to be part of Australia's EEZ. Since the 1970s the Australian government has tried to prevent them entering their customary fishing grounds (Balint 2005).

[6] For an overview of near-shore fisheries development in Pacific island countries, see Chapman 2004b.

[7] Thus far little work has been done on the economics of small-scale fisheries, although the Asian Development Bank-supported Coastal Fisheries Management and Development Project and the EU Rural Coastal Fisheries Development Program in Papua New Guinea collected socioeconomic data in 2004 and 2005.

[8] Provincial fisheries officers in Solomon Islands, however, feel that increased populations in coastal areas, pollution, overfishing and unsustainable fishing practices (such as dynamite fishing) are also having a negative impact on the health of coastal fisheries resources (Government of Solomon Islands 2005c).

[9] For details of gender issues in tuna industries in Solomon Islands, Fiji, Kiribati and Marshall Islands, see Pacific Islands Forum Secretariat 2004b.

[10] Using fisheries access as an inducement for onshore development can also be seen as a way of generating benefits from DWFNs. See section 'Tying distant water fisheries access to domestic industry development'.

[11] Although Pacific island countries have kept information about the precise amounts of aid connected to fisheries access secret, the extent to which aid from sources such as Japan and the European Union is tied directly to fisheries access might not be as great as is often assumed. For example, Japan and the European Union have large aid programs in Tonga, which gives them no particular fisheries advantage.

[12] Lewis (2004a) provides an excellent summary of the current status of access agreements, including possible strategies for improving the outcomes of access fee negotiations.

[13] While the Japanese partner company was involved, this company was called Solomon Taiyo Ltd. When the company was reconstituted after the withdrawal of the Japanese partner in 2000, it was called Soltai Fishing and Processing Ltd.

[14] See also the many reports available on the SPC and FFA web sites.

[15] *Tataki* is a skipjack loin that has been seared on the outside but is still raw in the middle. It is served in a similar way to sashimi.

[16] *Katsuobushi* is a popular stock flavouring in Japan, and is also used as a condiment. Cooked skipjack loins are smoke dried at a high temperature for several days then treated with a special mould. This is then crushed to a powder or shaved finely. Solomon Islands' Soltai has the largest skipjack-smoking factory outside Japan.

[17] See also the discussion and recommendation under 'Rights-based management'.

[18] The idea of commodity chains in relation to tuna is discussed by Schurman 1998.

[19] This suggestion is not advocating a return to colonial fisheries officers. These days, many regional fisheries technical advisers are Pacific islanders.

[20] Chapman 2002, 2003, 2004a; Gillett 2003; McCoy and Gillett 2005.

[21] Lindsay Chapman covered recreational fisheries in his extensive regional study of near-shore fisheries (Chapman 2004b).

3

Cook Islands

Population: 14,000
Land area: 237 km²
Sea area: 1,830,000 km²

After frequent contact by Spanish, British and French explorers from 1595, Cook Islands was named by Russian cartographers in the early 1800s in honour of the British Captain James Cook. Cook Islands was formally annexed by New Zealand in 1900 and gained independence in 1965. The country is self-governing in association with New Zealand and Cook Islanders have rights to New Zealand citizenship. About 50–70,000 Cook Islanders live in New Zealand and about 10,000 in Australia.

Potential of Cook Islands tuna fisheries

The Secretariat of the Pacific Community (SPC) estimated a total allowable catch (TAC) for the Cook Islands Exclusive Economic Zone (EEZ) of 44,000mt for the surface fishery (purse-seine and pole-and-line) and 6,000mt for the longline fishery (Chapman 2001). A surface fishery has not been developed[1] but there is a small longline fishery; the maximum annual catch (3,004mt in 2004) has remained below the TAC. This started out mostly as a distant water access fishery, but since 2000 distant water access has been banned as part of a domestic tuna industry development policy.

The southern fishery is seasonal (particularly yellowfin), apparently affected by water currents, sea surface temperatures and algal levels in the waters (Mitchell 2001). In the southern fishery, the best months are August and November, with low catch months from January to March (MMR 2004). It is commercially viable to fish only from May to November (York, pers. comm.). The northern fishery runs from March or April to November, with peak months in July, August and November (Garnier, pers. comm.).

History of development

Cook Islands' commercial tuna fisheries started in the 1990s as two distinct longline fisheries. A small fishery of two to three vessels started in 1994 in the southern group of islands based at Rarotonga, targeting chilled sashimi-grade fish airfreighted to Japanese

Map 3.1   Cook Islands

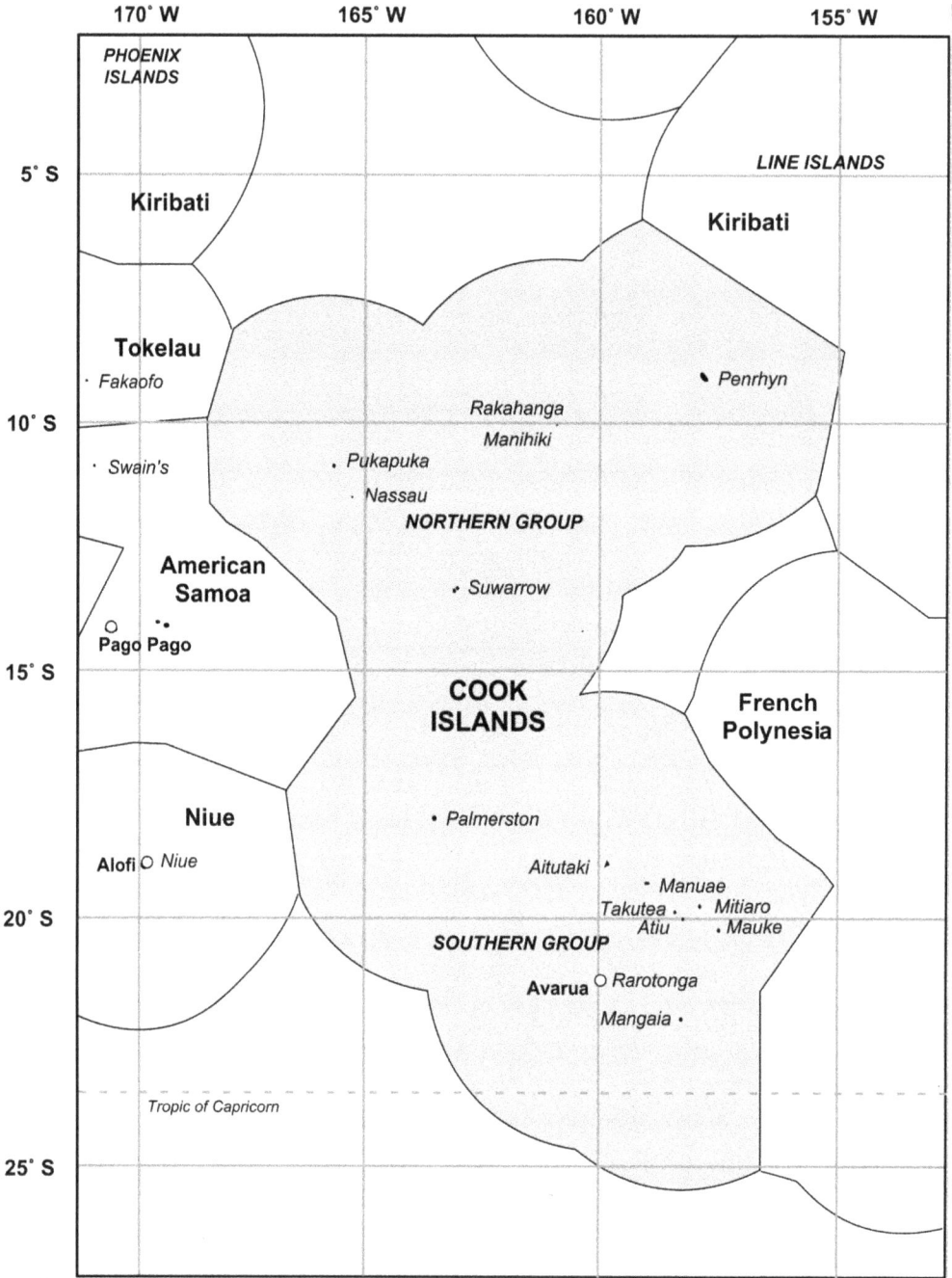

170° W   165° W   160° W   155° W

PHOENIX ISLANDS

LINE ISLANDS

5° S

Kiribati

Kiribati

Tokelau

· Fakaofo

· Penrhyn

Rakahanga

Manihiki

10° S

· Pukapuka

· Swain's

· Nassau

NORTHERN GROUP

American Samoa

· Suwarrow

○

Pago Pago

15° S

COOK ISLANDS

French Polynesia

Niue

· Palmerston

Alofi ○ Niue

Aitutaki

· Manuae

Takutea · · Mitiaro

Atiu · Mauke

20° S

SOUTHERN GROUP

Avarua ○ Rarotonga

Mangaia ·

Tropic of Capricorn

25° S

Source: Youngmi Choi, Secretariat of the Pacific Community, Noumea, New Caledonia.

and US markets (via Auckland). Some was also sold to New Zealand and to local restaurants and hotels. These companies targeted bigeye and yellowfin, but also caught albacore, swordfish, marlin, mahi mahi, wahoo and similar species. These companies were joint ventures with foreign-owned vessels based locally. The vessels ranged from 16 to 32m in length, 30–180 gross registered tonnage (GRT). In 1996, the first fully locally owned and operated longline vessel was registered.

Another longline fishery started in Cook Islands in 1998 in the northern part of the EEZ, targeting albacore to be frozen on the fishing vessels, which then took the fish back to base in Pago Pago, American Samoa. This fleet was made up of three to four vessels with large enough frozen storage capacity to stay out fishing for two to three months at a time. These companies were entirely foreign owned and operated. The northern albacore is less seasonal than the southern fishery targeting yellowfin and bigeye (Mitchell 2001). In the north, the best fishing months are May and September–October, with low months in March and July–August (MMR 2004).

The catch per unit of effort (CPUE) has been greater in the northern fishery than in the south. The average CPUE in 1998 for the northern albacore fishery was 55kg per 100 hooks, which was favourable compared with the regional average, but this dropped to less than 30kg per 100 hooks in 1999, possibly due to a La Niña event (Mitchell 2001). From 1995 to 2000, 1,230mt of fish (mostly albacore) from the Cook Islands EEZ was landed at Pago Pago (MMR c.2003). The northern fishery has always been larger than the southern fishery by volume, in 2004 accounting for 77.1 per cent of the catch (MMR 2004).

Albacore has always made up the largest part of the total catch. Even in the southern fishery, which does not target it, albacore made up the largest single species in the catch (Mitchell 2001; MMR c.2003, 2004). For the three years from 2002 to 2004, albacore made up 43 per cent of the southern catch (Bertram, pers. comm.). Other species in the southern catch composition for 2003 included bigeye (11 per cent), yellowfin (8 per cent), swordfish (25 per cent),[2] blue marlin (13 per cent), mahi mahi (4 per cent), striped marlin (3 per cent) and others (8 per cent) (MMR 2005a).

The largest market destination for Cook Islands tuna in the 1990s was the United States, which bought albacore for canning, some sashimi tuna and swordfish for the fresh-fish market (Table 3.1). The next largest market was the local one, which absorbed 15 per cent of the catch, comprised mostly of lower grade tunas and other species that were not worth exporting (Mitchell 2001).

By 2000, it became clear that the Western and Central Pacific Fisheries Commission (WCPFC) would probably involve some form of allocation of fishing rights to member countries. It was considered to be in Cook Islands' interests to develop an active tuna fishery and to be recording the fish caught in its waters and under its flag to strengthen its case to receive a reasonable portion of the regional allocation (Mitchell 2001). In addition, the Cook Islands government wanted to foster the growth of the local commercial fishing sector (Epati, pers. comm.). So in 2001, a technical advisor from the SPC came to Cook Islands to write a strategy for developing tuna fisheries (Chapman 2001).

Table 3.1   **Cook Islands: market destinations by percentage and product, 2005**[a]

Destination	Frozen	Chilled
United States (California, Hawai'i)	0	75 (for sashimi and tuna steaks)
United States (Pago Pago)	90 (for canning)	0
Japan	0	24 (for sashimi)
Taiwan	10 (for processing)	0
New Zealand	0	1
Domestic market	0	15 (for direct retail, for fish shops, hotels and restaurants, for processing at Blue Pacific)

[a] January–June, 2005

Source: Ministry of Marine Resources (MMR), 2005b. *The commercial tuna longline industry*, Information Paper for Cabinet, Cook Islands Ministry of Marine Resources, Avarua, Cook Islands.

The strategy identified several key areas that needed work to enable Cook Islands to make more from its tuna resources. These included (Chapman 2001)

- infrastructure, especially harbour and port developments
- options for post-harvest activities to increase the proportion of domestic value-added tuna products
- continuing fish aggregating device (FAD) program for small-scale fisheries
- long-term data collection system with regular analysis and distribution of reports for the benefit of the industry
- review of government taxes and duties to encourage domestic development, including looking at the possibility of tax holidays
- information dissemination and liaison to help encourage investment
- training for small-scale operators in fishing techniques and business management
- exploration of options for various boat designs and various modes of ownership (such as cooperatives) to develop the most viable domestic small and medium-scale fisheries
- institutional strengthening for the Ministry of Marine Resources
- work with lending institutions to ensure that adequate capital is available under viable terms and conditions for local ownership of businesses.

According to the Secretary for the Ministry of Marine Resources at the time, Navy Epati, the government preferred to foster a local industry rather than have distant water access fleets take the fish, so foreign licences were effectively banned. Foreign-owned vessels could be used in Cook Islands only if they were chartered as a 'demise' or 'bare boat'[3] charter to a locally based company at least partly owned by a Cook islander, and registered in Cook Islands. The local company was legally liable for obligations regarding catch reporting and so on. There was initially an effort to tie licences to employment of local crew, but since there is a labour shortage in Cook Islands and Cook Islanders, as New Zealand citizens, may go to work in New Zealand for better wages if they want to do manual work, crew had to be sourced overseas, especially for the boats that worked out of port for more than a day at a time. Koreans, Taiwanese, Tongans, Indonesians, Filipinos, Samoans and Fijians have all worked in the Cook Islands fleet (Bertram, pers. comm.; Graham, pers. comm.).

The northern fishery has not yet substantially changed through this domestication policy. Local people are agents for the foreign-owned vessels, do some administrative work for their companies in Rarotonga and receive a portion of the profits, but the vessels continue to come and go from their preferred port of Pago Pago in American Samoa, source all their supplies there and are operated and crewed exclusively by foreigners. The government considered making the northern fishery vessels land their catch in Rarotonga, but they ultimately decided that adding the extra length to the vessels' steaming time (3.5 days) would be an unnecessary setback to profitability (Epati, pers. comm.). In addition, Pago Pago is a fully established port with all the necessary goods and services available, much cheaper than in Rarotonga (Garnier, pers. comm.).

The southern fishery based on Rarotonga, however, underwent significant changes as a result of the domestication policy. It took about a year to get the basic policies and procedures in place. The old legislation covered access for distant water vessels, not the establishment of a domestic industry, so had to be revised in 2001 (Epati, pers. comm.). Before 2001, there had never been any more than two locally owned vessels working from Cook Islands ports. In late 2001 and early 2002, some of the new locally based companies began operations. In 2002, catches from the southern fishery were worth NZ$2.6 million, and the northern fishery was worth NZ$3.1 million (MMR c.2003). Tuna topped the export sector, surpassing pearls, and there were considerable expectations for the fishery. Investors rushed to enter the tuna fishery and, by 2003, fish made up 56.6 per cent of exports (pearls made up 19.5 per cent), and the fishing industry was cited as one of the four sectors contributing to real GDP growth from 2002 to 2003 (Tables 3.2, 3.3 and 3.4). This signalled substantial diversification in the economy since 2002, when pearls were the only significant export and tourism was the main income earner (Government of Cook Islands 2005). Because the policies and procedures were not thoroughly established, things were somewhat chaotic. Boats were lined up in the harbour and foreign fishing companies flocked to Avarua to find local business partners. The Department of Immigration was not ready to process all the working visa applications, and other government agencies such as health and the police were overwhelmed by the sudden social changes that took place around the harbour. In 2002, a vessel was caught fishing illegally for the first time, so procedures for prosecuting illegal fishers had to be worked out. The pace of the growth in the domestic industry 'took everyone by surprise' (Epati, pers. comm.).

The domestic industry went from three vessels in 2001 to 19 in 2002 (catch: 1,143mt) and 44 in 2003 (catch: 2,335mt) (MMR 2004). It had been believed widely that there were not enough fish in Cook Islands' EEZ for a viable tuna fishery, but now it looked like it did have sufficiently valuable tuna resources on which to build an industry (Epati, pers. comm.).

CPUE, however, started to drop off. The Ministry of Marine Resources asked the minister to cap the licences in 2003 because there were too many boats. Companies

Table 3.2   **Cook Islands: indicators of domestic development, 2001**

Locally based vessels active	Cannery/ loining facilities	Sashimi packing facilities	Cook Islands nationals jobs on vessels	Cook Islands nationals jobs on shore	Frozen tuna exports (metric tonnes)	Fresh tuna exports (metric tonnes)	Cooked loin exports (metric tonnes)
10 longline	0	3	50	15	0	5	0

Source: Gillett, R., 2003. *Domestic tuna industry development in the Pacific islands. The current situation and considerations for future development assistance*, FFA Report 03/01, Pacific Islands Forum Fisheries Agency, Honiara, Solomon Islands.

Table 3.3   **Cook Islands: value of fresh chilled tuna exports, 1994–2004**

Year	Value (NZ$)	Year	Value (NZ$)
1994	382,000	2000	-
1995	1,067,000	2001	-
1996	250,000	2002	2,334,000
1997	-	2003	8,258,000
1998	-	2004	135,000
1999	2,000		

Source: Government of Cook Islands, 2005. *Cook Islands Annual Statistical Bulletin 2004*, Avarua, Cook Islands.

started collapsing. Foreign companies could see that the returns were low and pulled out, especially in the southern sashimi and fresh-tuna oriented fishery (Bertram, pers. comm.). While licence numbers dropped to 38 in 2004 and catch increased to a record 3,000mt (a 30 per cent increase on 2003), CPUE was lower (MMR 2004). By 2005, the CPUE was still declining, while at the same time fuel prices had escalated significantly, causing economic difficulties (Bertram, pers. comm.). Thirty-two vessels were licensed to fish in the Cook Islands EEZ in 2005, but in September only about seven of these were active in the southern fishery, and 11 in the north. Some of the foreign-operated vessels licensed for the northern albacore fishery were fishing elsewhere or were offloading in Pago Pago. Some vessels from the southern sashimi-oriented fishery were awaiting repair, or were tied up for economic reasons (Maru, pers. comm.).

The optimism that blossomed in 2002 had subsided by 2005. The 25 vessels from New Zealand that came in 2003 had all left. Five vessels owned by the Taiwanese company Gilontas that came from Panama in 2004 left in August 2005. One of the three processing facilities that had been operating in 2003 was shut down, and another was scaling back due to insufficient turnover. Morale in the sector was low (Epati, pers. comm.). Marine ministry officials became increasingly pessimistic about prospects for further development in the southern fishery, citing the inability of companies to catch sufficient quantities of fish relative to the operating costs from Cook Islands—particularly fuel and freight prices (MMR 2005a).

With the first burst of activity in the fishery, Cook Islanders rushed to invest with no long-term strategy and lost money. By the mid 2000s, the Cook Islands tuna industry was still in the testing phase so failures were to be expected (Short, pers. comm.). Despite the

Table 3.4   Cook Islands: indicators of domestic development, 2004

	Locally based vessels facilities	Sashimi packing/ fresh-tuna loining	CI: non-CI jobs on vessels	CI: non-CI jobs on shore	Whole frozen tuna exports (for canneries)	Whole chilled tuna exports (sashimi)	Deli-style processed tuna products
Land Holdings Ltd	2 LL south	-	1:8	1:1			-
Blue Pacific	-	1	-	8–12:1			240kg per week
Cook Islands Fish Exporters	-	1	-	20–40:5		500mt	-
FBI and Te Maroro	2 LL south, 4 LL north	1 (fish shop)	1:5 (southern)	5:0			-
Pamatatau	1 LL south	-					-
Cook Islands Marine Export	2 LL north	-					-
Fish CI Ltd	2 LL north	-					-
Aitutaki Fishing	4 LL north	-					-
Matira South	3 LL north	-	0:30				-
CI Tuna Fisheries Ltd	3 LL south	-					-
Taio Shipping Services	1 LL south	1 (container)					-
Cook Islands Fish Ltd	1 LL south	-					-
Cook Islands Seafood	1 LL north						-
Cook Islands Fishing	1 LL north						-
Total	30	4	CI: >2, CI: up to 58	non-CI:>35, non-CI: 7	2,500mt		12mt per year

Notes: LL: longline. CI: Cook islander. NCI: non-Cook islander, The Ministry of Marine Resources was not collecting a breakdown of the types of exports, just the total catch, which was about 3,000mt. Approximately 85 per cent of this was exported, with the remaining 15 per cent consumed locally.
Sources: Interviews with: Epati, Navy, 2005. Co-owner Fish Bites Incorporated fishing company. Former Secretary, Ministry of Marine Resources. Interview, 20 September. Avarua, Cook Islands. Maru, Pam, 2005. Ministry of Marine Resources employee working in the areas of monitoring, control, surveillance and licensing. Interviews, 19–23 September. Avarua, Cook Islands. York, Trevor, 2005. Master Fisherman and co-owner Land Holdings Ltd tuna-fishing business. Interview, 20 September. Avarua, Cook Islands. Garnier, pers. comm.

somewhat 'boom–bust' nature of the early southern Cook Islands tuna fishery, however, some industry interviewees still had faith in its potential. Navy Epati, former fisheries bureaucrat turned owner of fishing company Fish Bites Incorporated, characterised the events of the past four years as a learning phase. People invested in the fishery because of early successes without knowing anything about fishing, and as a result they lost money. But they also gained considerable knowledge, and Epati believed that by building on their experiences the fishery should be able to grow again with a more stable trajectory. 'We learned more about fishing in the last four years than we did in the previous 40 years' (Epati, pers. comm.). Trevor York from Land Holdings, a company that continues to do well and is looking to expand, also feels that the Cook Islands tuna fishery is potentially profitable for operators who 'know what they are doing'.

Longline fishery

One of the more successful of the local companies in the southern fishery was Land Holdings Limited. The company was 70 per cent owned by Cook Island resident Bill Dougherty, an established local businessman in the construction industry. The remaining 30 per cent was owned by a New Zealand citizen with a working visa, skipper Trevor York. York had been fishing most of his career around New Zealand before coming to the Cook Islands to work for another company in 1998. He had been in charge of a vessel before, so had some idea of how to balance the costs of running a vessel and make it profitable. The company started fishing in 2001 with one vessel. As of September 2005, Land Holdings operated two longline vessels.

One of the problems for local fishers is that replacement parts for vessels can take weeks to arrive. Land Holdings imports also had sufficient cash reserves to import its own bait in bulk, and keeps a stock of spare parts on hand so it does not have to wait (York, pers. comm.). It thus avoided the problem facing many of the other operators in September 2005 when the company that had been supplying bait ceased importing it.

As of September 2005, Land Holdings employed seven deckhands, two skippers and an office administrator. The company had two vessels but was in the process of buying a third, for which it would need a third skipper, and was considering expanding the fleet even further (York, pers. comm.). When the company began, it tried to recruit Cook Islands deckhands, but few local people were interested in the work. When Land Holdings bought its second boat it went to Fiji to find crew. As of September 2005, it employed six Fijians and one Samoan as deckhands, one Cook islander and one New Zealander as captains, with one Cook islander working in the office (York, pers. comm.). Land Holdings keeps its vessels out as much as it can during the season, bringing them in only to offload for at most one day before going back out to fish again.

According to Trevor York, it is possible to be successful in the Cook Islands fishery as long as operators are willing to work hard and focus on quality product. Land Holdings' vessels gut and ice up the catch on board then bring it back to the factory, where it is wrapped, boxed and airfreighted out (York, pers. comm.). Land Holdings does well in its markets because its quality is good. It receives maximum value for each fish.

One of the more difficult parts of the business is working out the balance between costs and prices to see if it is worthwhile exporting, which involves fairly complicated financial calculations. Land Holdings' agents in the United States and Japan can give ballpark figures on what the prices are like, but since the fish is sold at auction there is no guaranteeing the exact price. Then there is the cost of freight to consider. Also, for local sales the price includes the head, whereas for exports to the US the head is taken off first, meaning the price per fish may end up being lower in the USA even if the price offered per kilogram is actually higher in the USA.

Fish Bites Incorporated was formed in March 2005 from two other fishing companies: Te Maroro (established in 2003) and Fresh off the Boat (established in 2004). Fish Bites operated two vessels in the southern fishery, with two Fijians, three Samoans and one Cook islander working on the vessels, and five Cook Islanders working on shore. Its vessels could catch 800kg a day (they do not stay out overnight). Its southern fishery was in a difficult financial situation at the time of interview.

Fish Bites was also the local partner for three longliners operating in the northern albacore fishery out of Pago Pago. It received a percentage of the value of the catch and was the legal owner of the company with all the attendant responsibilities, but in practice did not operate the vessels. The vessels were Korean owned, with Tongan crews.

The cost of fuel and freight and the supply of bait fish were all causing problems for Fish Bite's southern fishery at the time of interview in September 2005. Airfreight to Japan cost NZ$4.50 per kilogram. Fish Bites was effectively selling fish for export at $4/kg, which left no margin, so it started selling locally direct to the public for $16/kg (Epati, pers. comm.). Locals and tourists bought from Fish Bites because the fish was well presented and slightly cheaper than at other fish retail outlets in town (Graham, pers. comm.). Fish Bites was selling as much as it could catch through the shop as well as to eight local restaurants. The company also had plans for expansion into reef fin-fish aquaculture in partnership with the Australian company McRoberts (Epati, pers. comm.).

Fish Bites was one of the small operators that did not have the capital to import its own bait (one container load cost NZ$40–50,000) (Epati, pers. comm.). Epati was hoping that if an industry association could be established it could administer a plan put forward to the marine ministry for funds to buy the first container load of bait as a 'revolving fund'. The association would then administer bait sales to the smaller operators to cover the costs of buying future loads. The ministry approved this plan in principle and was thinking of contributing to the revolving fund if a viable industry association could be established (Bertram, pers. comm.).

The large New Zealand company Sealord came to the Cooks in 2003. It was in partnership with Cook Islands Fishery Exporters, which was going to do the packing and freighting. Sealord is one of the biggest fishing companies in Australia and New Zealand, involved mostly in trawling. It also has international marketing connections and produces processed seafood, such as fish fingers. After just one year (the worst year in the southern fishery to date), Sealord decided that fishing in Cook Islands would not give a good return on its investment and it withdrew.

During 2004, five vessels owned by Taiwanese company Gilontas came to work in the southern fishery. These vessels were unable to make a profit and left in August 2005. The vessels and the crews proved to be unsuitable for the southern fishery (Armstrong, pers. comm.). The vessels were too large and had brine freezers, which meant they used too much fuel. The crews, mostly ethnic Chinese, with some Indonesians and Filipinos, were unwilling or unable to change their fishing practices from a style focusing on volume suited to cannery product, to a style that would maximise the quality and value of each fish. For example, apparently they treated bluefin tuna, which exported fresh can fetch tens of thousand dollars per fish, the same as cannery albacore, freezing it and taking it back to port days after it had been caught. This meant the company missed out on potential profits.

Matira South Fishing Limited started in early 2004 with four vessels, two owned outright by the company and two chartered Tahitian vessels. The aim was to fish in the south, but because the low season dragged on two months longer than usual in 2005 due to high water temperatures, the company needed to make some money fast, so it sent the vessels to the north to earn some cash in the albacore fishery. These vessels are larger than the size that seems to be suitable for the fishery targeting the sashimi market in the south. One of the vessels was equipped for fishing for the sashimi market with ice, so the company tried that for a while, but because of the size of the vessel this was not cost effective.

Matira South felt it would be possible to improve profits in the northern fishery by reorienting from the low-value cannery market for albacore by loining and freezing fish on board for fresh-fish markets. In the high season, the catch in the west of the fishing grounds can be up to 60–70 per cent albacore, but further east the catch composition is more mixed. Because albacore gets the best price from the canneries (US$2,300 per short tonne for albacore, compared with $1,100 for yellowfin, and down to $600 for skipjack and wahoo), the vessels try to bring back mostly albacore, which means discarding some of the other species. This in turn means vessels have to stay out longer before filling the hold. By loining and freezing all species on board, Matira South hoped to get more value for the catch, to utilise all species and thus to improve productivity. Another measure necessary to improve productivity is to ensure the vessels can fish year round, which means fishing the high seas during the off season in Cook Islands.

The prices for frozen loins offered by an agent in Tahiti were US$3.80–4.50/kg (depending on the species), and a buyer in Australia had offered A$10/kg. So the prices for frozen loins are much better than cannery prices, and because frozen loins can be transported by sea the freight prices are much cheaper than for sashimi exports by air. Freight prices in reefer containers for the loins were quoted at NZ$0.20/kg.

The two vessels from Tahiti freeze the loins to −25°C, which means the fish remains at the same quality for 18 months. In order to be able to sell to the lucrative EU market, it will be necessary to establish Hazard Analysis Critical Control Point (HACCP) systems on board the vessels and establish a Competent Authority in Cook Islands. Matira South established market connections for loins in Australia in 2005. Some samples were sent to buyers there and the necessary preparations made with Australia's Quarantine Investigation Service. The company could have been selling loins to Australia already except that all four vessels were, at the time of interview, unseaworthy with mechanical problems.

Distant water access fleet

In the early years of the Cook Islands tuna fishery, most of the vessels in the southern fishery and all of those in the northern fishery were foreign, paying access fees. In 2000, when the government decided to develop the domestic fishery, it banned foreign vessels.

Bait fishery

There has never been a local bait fishery supplying tuna fisheries in Cook Islands. There is a possibility for milkfish aquaculture for bait fish in the northern group, where there are some ponds made by US forces during World War II, when they built airstrips (Bertram, pers. comm.). Navy Epati's partnership for aquaculture in the outer islands is considering farming milkfish in ponds to cut this cost for its longline ventures. Apparently milkfish aquaculture was tried in Cook Islands in the past but the breeder fish were too attractive as a food fish for locals so it did not last long (Epati, pers. comm.).

Fish aggregating devices (FADs)

In the 1990s, the Ministry of Marine Resources deployed several FADs (using the recurrent budget, US multilateral treaty Project Development Fund [PDF], United Nations Food and Agriculture Organisation [FAO] and NZAid money) for local small-scale fishers, who had learned to use them and become reliant on them (Chapman 2001). Fishers contributed a NZ$50 annual fee to the FAD program. Chapman recommended long-term funding be made available, especially for maintenance, in the ministry's recurrent budget or fees from the US multilateral treaty (Chapman 2001:10). In 2005, FADs continued to be important for small-scale fishers using handline, trolling and harpoon methods, and the ministry had instituted a program to maintain the FADs (Bertram, pers. comm.).

Small-scale coastal

Artisanal and small-scale commercial fisheries including trolling and midwater fishing techniques around FADs were targeted by a development strategy in 2001 (Chapman 2001). Small-scale coastal fishers around Rarotonga were able to sell tuna in local markets, although some of them withdrew from the fishery during the boom period when larger-scale operators were offloading non-export fish in the local market for NZ$5 a kilogram, and the small-scale fishers had to charge $10/kg to be viable (Hunter, pers. comm.). By 2005, however, the price of local tuna had gone up to $15–20 a kilogram, so it was possible that small-scale coastal fishers would re-enter the market.

In 2001, there was talk of the government developing jetty facilities and freezing and ice-making facilities for the outer islands (Chapman 2001); however, the viability record of such government-sponsored rural developments in the Pacific is not good. By 2005, the Ministry of Marine Resources had not established a program for tuna fisheries development in the outer islands because of the same kinds of problems that inhibit rural commercial tuna fisheries around the region, including difficulties and expenses for transporting the fish by sea or air, difficulties in maintaining fish quality and difficulties in establishing and maintaining ice supplies (Bertram, pers. comm.; Chapman 2004b).

Game fishing

Cook Islands has had some sports and game fishing associated with the tourism industry. As of September 2005, there were eight sports-fishing vessels in Rarotonga and four in Aitutaki (Bertram, pers. comm.).

Port and trans-shipment base

Cook Islands has not offered trans-shipping or port services to foreign fishing vessels and is not planning to do so in the foreseeable future.

Onshore processing

Cook Islands has never had a cannery or cooked-loin processing facility and it seems unlikely one will be developed. There was, however, a small local sashimi-processing industry. Chapman's tuna industry development strategy cited expensive electricity as a possible inhibiting factor for onshore sashimi-processing factories and businesses such as ice supply. He also cited shortage of land as a possible deterrent, since one fishing company was trying to build a plant at the time but was unable to access suitable land (Chapman 2001). As soon as the fishery took off in 2002, however, investors rushed to establish plants. With hindsight, investors were too optimistic about the volume that would require processing so there were more plants in Rarotonga than were viable at current fishing levels.

In 2001, Chapman identified one small fish-processing facility that supplied small amounts of ice and bait and purchased small amounts of fish. That operator was interested in expanding but given the fish shortage fishers were paid more to sell direct to hotels and restaurants than to him as a middleman, so he could not access a larger supply (Chapman 2001).

In 2003, there were three industrial-scale fish-processing plants operating in Rarotonga, but by the end of the year one (Matia) had closed (Bertram, pers. comm.; Garnier, pers. comm.; Graham, pers. comm.). Two remained operating in 2005 but there was not really enough fish coming through to keep both of them in business. In addition to the industrial-scale plants, there were a couple of fish shops operating locally, buying local catch and filleting it ready for retail, or packing high quality fish for air freight export (Bertram, pers. comm.; Graham, pers. comm.).

Cook Islands Fish Exporters was formed in 2002 by Cook Islands businessman Brett Porter as a joint venture between his Avarua-based company, Meat Co., and a New Zealand-based fishing company Hawkes Bay Seafoods, in partnership with Sealord. Cook Islands Fish Exports built a high-quality plant and exported chilled yellowfin and bigeye by airfreight via Auckland as sashimi to Japan, with B-grade and other species such as broadbill and mahi mahi to the United States, depending on relative prices in each market. Frozen albacore was sent via sea freight to Pago Pago (Bertram, pers. comm.; Graham, pers. comm.; Armstrong, pers. comm.). The Cook Islands Fish Exports plant packed the export product for Land Holdings, and was also supplied by the five Gilontas vessels during 2004–05.

The Porter Group had recruited 25 longline vessels from New Zealand to come to fish in the southern fishery in 2003 to supply Cook Islands Fish Exports' plant. By November 2003, the first of these went broke and returned to New Zealand. By September 2005, only two vessels owned by a consortium of Cook Islands businesspeople were still active in the Cook Islands (Garnier, pers. comm.), and one of those vessels was offered for sale in September 2005 (Bertram, pers. comm.).

At the peak of production, the Cook Islands Fish Exports plant employed about 40 people, mostly locals, with five non-nationals. As of September 2005, the plant had scaled down activities due to a lack of fish and was employing about 20–25 people. At the end of the season, the plant was going to close entirely until the fishing season started again (Armstrong, pers. comm.).

Blue Pacific Foods was a company that processed a small amount of chilled fish for airfreight export and also sold chilled and frozen fish retail for local customers, but its main business was a small facility value adding by making smallgoods from tuna and other species caught by the longliners. Its products were vacuum packed in clear plastic and included cold and hot smoked fish, tuna ham, frozen packages of fish soup and tuna sausages. Blue Pacific was also considering niche-market, high-value canned tuna and tuna sold in olive oil in glass jars (Blue Pacific Operations Manager, pers. comm.).

Blue Pacific utilised the species and grades of fish that could not be exported as sashimi. 'Smoking turns fish that can be bought at NZ$2 a kilo into fish that can sell for $15 a kilo. All it takes is a bit of wood, salt and time' (Blue Pacific Operations Manager, pers. comm.). The highest value product, cold-smoked marlin, retailed at NZ$5 per 150g ($333 a kilogram). Hot-smoked marlin and tuna ham were cheaper at less than $20 a kilogram. The local market buys everything Blue Pacific can produce—240kg a week—so it has none left over to export.

One of the features of this venture which enabled it to survive was that one of the investors was the owner of a well known local bar and restaurant (Trader Jacks). The plant facilities were used to prepare food for the restaurant, so it was not reliant only on fish for its business (Bertram, pers. comm.; Graham, pers. comm.).

Determinants of success

Some of the main lessons that seem to have been learned about Cook Islands' southern fishery in recent years are that it is not a high-volume fishery, fish that are taken are high quality and require good handling practices and the fishery is seasonal (Armstrong, pers. comm.; Broadhead, pers. comm.; Short, pers. comm.; York, pers. comm.).

Food quality and safety

Successful companies focused on maintaining quality through fish-handling practices from the moment the fish was caught, thus maximising the value of each fish. For example, when they caught large bluefin, they send them to market as soon as possible (back to the packing plant within 24 hours of being caught, and onto the auction floor in Japan within 60 hours) to maximise the value of the fish, achieving up to NZ$60,000 for a single fish (Armstrong, pers. comm.).

Failures occurred with companies that went for volume without paying enough attention to maintaining the quality of the fish—the style of fishing used when targeting albacore for the cannery market.

Addressing food-quality issues in the domestic market was also a factor in the success of the southern fishery. Quality has improved in the local market a great deal since 2000. In 2001, Chapman identified that few operators of small vessels were using ice to preserve fish at sea (Chapman 2004b). There was lack of market awareness of quality and food-safety issues, so the Ministry of Marine Resources engaged SPC technical advisor Michael Blanc to do some training on fish handling. Fishers as well as some local buyers did the course, and soon most were using ice and cool boxes to store their fish promptly after being caught.

Until 2005, Cook Islands had no laws about food safety, so market pressures were the only thing making local producers careful about quality and hygiene. As of September 2005, however, a new food act was before Parliament, requiring seafood exporters (not producers for the local market) to comply with EU regulations on food safety and hygiene, using HACCP methods on fishing vessels and in processing facilities. Fishing vessels interested in exporting to the European Union under the Cotonou Agreement were working with the government to establish these systems (Broadhead, pers. comm.; Garnier, pers. comm.; Short, pers. comm.). In addition, the government was considering incorporating *Codex Alimentarius* standards for fish and fishery products into the legislation (Graham, pers. comm.). Achieving European Union-approved status was a long-term plan, since it required the development of testing facilities as well as institutional arrangements and scientific expertise (Broadhead, pers. comm.).

Local market

Partly as a result of quality improvements, a domestic market emerged that paid good prices for fish of high quality that could be used to feed international tourists. This high-end domestic market helps make the southern tuna fishery viable by providing good prices for fish that is non-export grade, or when freight and price conditions make it unviable to export fish. Smaller indigenously owned and run operations relied exclusively on the local market. Local people looked out for the small vessels coming back to harbour and rushed to buy straight from the boat (Bertram, pers. comm.). Rarotonga can consume more than 5mt of fish a week and most weeks only half of that is supplied (York, pers. comm.).

Tourism contributed to the health of Rarotonga's local fish market. In a country with a population of 14,000, 78,328 tourists visited in 2003, and this number has risen slightly each year (Government of Cook Islands 2005). Restaurants and hotels catering to tourists made up about half of the local market for fish (Armstrong, pers. comm.). In addition, the boost tourism has given to the local economy in the past 15 years has increased Cook Islanders' incomes such that local people also pay good prices for fish.

Synergies with tourism

The Cook Islands shows that tuna fishing can have important synergies with the tourism sector in the areas of the local market and airfreight. Air New Zealand's decision to use planes with more space for passengers and less for freight, however, has not been beneficial for the tuna industry, so it is not ideal to rely on tourism for freight. And some tourism operators apparently feel that tuna fisheries detract from tourism. Sport-fishing charter operators have complained that commercial fisheries deplete the resource so that tourists can't catch any fish, despite the fact that longliners are prohibited from letting their lines drift within 12 nautical miles of the coast (6nm for vessels less than 14m in length), and the Ministry of Marine Resources enforces this rule (Bertram, pers. comm.; Graham, pers. comm.). Resort owners have been also been known to complain that the fishing industry detracts from the image of a 'pristine' island environment, which attracts tourists (Armstrong, pers. comm.).

Costs of operation

Having small fuel-efficient vessels of 12–14 metres in length was one of the features of successful companies in the southern fishery (Armstrong, pers. comm.). The major cost components (as a proportion of total costs) for vessels operating in the southern fishery in 2002 were: airfreight (25–40 per cent); fuel and oil (10 per cent); and bait (8 per cent). Fishing companies paid wholesale bulk rates for fuel of about NZ$1.25 per litre and fuel costs were considered to be a problem for the fishery (MMR c.2003). In 2003, the government responded to claims that the high cost of fuel was damaging the industry and removed the tax on fuel for fisheries. This dropped the cost to $0.87 per litre. International fuel cost rises then brought the price back up to $1.20 in 2005 (Bertram, pers. comm.). In contrast, the 2004 price for fuel in Pago Pago was just NZ$0.50 per litre (US$1.34 per gallon) (Garnier, pers. comm.). Other costs included wages, ice, food, replacing gear, marketing, loan repayments and insurance (MMR c.2003). Overall operating costs from Rarotonga were estimated to be twice as expensive as from Pago Pago.

Managing costs to accommodate the seasonality of the fishery was another determinant for success. Successful companies worked crews and vessels extremely hard during the fishing season and were structured such that they could afford to close operations during the off-season (Armstrong, pers. comm.). Companies that needed to operate year round to cover their costs pulled out.

Harbour and insurance concerns

Insurance was considered to be a problem by fishers. Only the hull of a boat was covered, not the expensive engine parts, and vessels could not be insured against risks such as cyclones (Epati, pers. comm.). The harbour was not a safe anchorage in all weather. After a damaging cyclone in 1987, insurers refused to cover waterfront investments against sea-surge damage during cyclones. Fishing vessel owners told Chapman they were reluctant to invest in larger vessels until they had safer anchorage (Chapman 2001). In 2005, the lack of protection offered by the harbour against cyclones was still a problem. During the five cyclones that hit Rarotonga in January 2005, some vessel owners took their vessels out to deeper water and rode out the storms (clearly a dangerous strategy) because their vessels would have been destroyed in the harbour (Bertram, pers. comm.). Other vessel owners hauled their vessels out of the water and took them to high ground, which apparently voided their insurance (Epati, pers. comm.).

Cook Islanders have been discussing building a stronger sea wall against cyclone damage for many years. Protection using COPED or Tetrapod technologies would cost millions of dollars, however, and spoil the aesthetics of the coastline, which draws tourists (Bertram, pers. comm.). There is protection in the area around the airport, however, and since the harbour area is also away from the major tourist resorts, similar protection for the harbour might not significantly damage tourists' enjoyment of Rarotonga's lagoon scenery. Chapman also recommended a range of other improvements to the harbour, including dredging it to a minimum depth of 3m at low tide, building a good launching ramp for trailer vessels, and using dredged material to reclaim some land to use for services such as slipways, engineering and supplies (Chapman 2001). In 2003, when the numbers of fishing vessels increased greatly, and when international port security measures meant the container section had to be separated from the rest of the port, a new section of the wharf was built for small fishing vessels and yachts. In 2005, further extensions and improvements to this area were planned (Graham, pers. comm.).

Availability of credit

Interviewees mentioned credit as a problem for the fisheries sector in general. When the domestic industry first started, the commercial banks in Cook Islands were not interested in extending loans to fishing companies; they felt fishing was a less safe investment than tourism. After some pressure from politicians, the Development Bank finally agreed to start lending to fishing companies. The first Development Bank loan went bad within months and a second vessel considered too big for the southern fishery was bought by inexperienced operators and sat virtually unused at the wharf for a couple of years (Epati, pers. comm.). However, the financial sector gradually worked out how to service the new industry. Land Holdings, a local construction company with a thriving longline business, said it had no problem with credit from the commercial banks because it was financially healthy (York, pers. comm.).

Freight

For the northern fishery, freight was not an issue, since the vessels stored their own catch onboard frozen, delivering it to the cannery in Pago Pago when returning to base for supplies. Albacore and other frozen fish exported by sea from the southern fishery were stored in freezers in Rarotonga until there was enough to fill a container. Large container vessels could not fit in the Rarotonga harbour, but small container vessels visited every 7–10 days (Bertram, pers. comm.; Graham, pers. comm.).

Chilled fish for the sashimi market was airfreighted out of Rarotonga via Auckland. Industry people cited airfreight issues as a 'real headache'. Air New Zealand had increased its freight prices in line with recent fuel price increases. It also changed scheduling and plane types in 2005. Previously, there had been 10 or more outbound flights a week in Boeing 767s, which have plenty of freight capacity. There was a quick turnaround in Auckland to markets in the United States and Japan. In 2005, the airline started using Airbus A320s on many of the runs to Cook Islands, an aircraft that displaces freight in favour of increased passenger space. In addition, schedule changes meant a 16–18 hour wait in Auckland before the fish could get onto planes to market (Armstrong, pers. comm.).

Because chilled sashimi tuna depreciates about 10 per cent per day once it is taken from the boat, airfreight schedules as well as prices were thus two of the many factors to consider in the decision to export or not.

Value adding

One of the interesting things about the Cook Islands tuna industry is that there is a small-scale value-adding processing facility producing gourmet smallgoods from tuna. This model seems to be well suited to the Pacific islands, especially where there is a hospitality market to hand, being small-scale and involving much less capital investment than a cannery. According to the managers, the facility was not difficult to set up or run.

Another direction in value adding being explored in 2005 was longliners with onboard loining and freezing capacity. The whole of the catch can then be utilised, rather than what currently occurs, where the northern fishery wants only albacore of a certain size and discards most other fish, and the southern fishery targets sashimi fish but also catches a lot of albacore. High-quality albacore frozen quickly to a very cold temperature can be sold for good prices as tuna steaks in the United States and the European Union. The EU supermarket trade could be opened to Cook Islands exporters as a result of bilateral negotiations continuing in 2005 under the Cotonou Agreement (Broadhead, pers. comm.). Even with much higher freight costs, this would be more profitable than selling to canneries. Utilising the whole catch means ships can be more productive.

Miscellaneous

Finding crews was cited as a problem. Cook Islanders were willing to work only on the small vessels that did day trips, not on the slightly larger vessels that stayed out for several days at a time. Crews were thus sourced from Fiji, the Philippines or China. Managers and owners interviewed said that among local and foreign crew there were few with either the potential or the incentive to work their way up to become first mates, skippers and eventually boat-owners. Many vessels operated irregularly due to mechanical problems and difficulties in accessing spare parts (MMR 2004; Bertram, pers. comm.; Graham, pers. comm.). In September 2005, vessels were also slowed by a bait shortage in Rarotonga.

Governing tuna industries

The Ministry of Marine Resources is the government department responsible for most aspects of fisheries management. Its duties include: data collection; monitoring, control and surveillance; observer programs; infrastructure development; extension services and training programs; disseminating information; and liaising with industry and other stakeholders, including investment agencies and government departments (Chapman 2001).

Until September 2005, the ministry's main focus in tuna-fishery management was establishing new legislation. The *Marine Resources Act* went through Parliament in July 2005 and in September was ready to be gazetted pending a review of the licensing regulations. The ministry's next priority was to finish its tuna management plan. Work had started on the management plan with Forum Fisheries Agency (FFA) consultant Les Clark. The ministry had not yet set a total allowable catch (TAC) for Cook Islands' tuna fisheries, but the Minister for Fisheries capped the number of licences for longline vessels at 60. As part of Cook Islands' commitment to the WCPFC, the ministry planned to have the tuna management plan finished and vested with regulatory powers by Cabinet by the end of 2006 (Graham, pers. comm.).

Governance problems, specifically corruption and other mismanagement by government officials, have been less of a problem in the Cook Islands than other Pacific island countries (Hunter, pers. comm.; Moeka'a, pers. comm.; Short, pers. comm.).[4] Possibly, the greater incomes of Cook Islanders relative to incomes for other Pacific islanders, as well as the lower ratio of dependents to wage earners, means there is less of an incentive to succumb to bribery or corruption (Short, pers. comm.). The Ministry of Marine Resources produces annual reports to acquit its budget (Graham, pers. comm.), and was being audited as part of normal governance processes during the period of fieldwork in September 2005. There were no significant abnormalities discovered.

Improvements to tuna-fishery management suggested by the Chapman report included: improving surveillance and enforcement; moving access boundaries for larger longline vessels further away from shore; having reliable data provided to the ministry; the ministry keeping the disaggregated data confidential to protect the commercial interests of fishers; developing an observer program and an automatic location communicator system; and undertaking port sampling (Chapman 2001).

To address some of these issues, funding was requested from the New Zealand government for an institutional strengthening project. As of September 2005, that project was almost ready to recruit technical assistance, and the ministry had worked on these issues in the meantime by setting and enforcing rules regarding longline boundaries.

Marine ministry staff felt that fishing companies were at first reluctant to give them information about the location of their fishing, but came to trust the agency over time. The ministry is confident of the quality of information on the logsheets presented by boats in the southern fishery but less sure of the accuracy of northern fishery vessels, and the statistics from the small-scale (non-longline) FAD fishery were described as poor (Bertram, pers. comm.). The ministry developed an observer program but hit a problem with a labour shortage: no one wanted to take the job and go to sea. It was thinking of trying to source observers from Fiji or another country in the region.

By 2005, there were two automatic vessel locator systems in place, the FFA VMS and a national system. A port sampling service was introduced to the fishery based around Rarotonga, with the following coverage rates: 2002, 60 per cent; 2003, 70 per cent; 2004, 30 per cent (when there was a huge jump in the number of vessels in the fishery); 2005, 50 per cent. In 2003, ministry staff trained to teach longline fishing techniques and also undertook studies in international fisheries law and general management.

Biological data about the fishery are important for obvious reasons, but for industry development and socioeconomic management of the industry more economic data would be useful. For example, in 2005 there were no comprehensive data available on amounts or values of tuna exported and sold locally. The government statistician published the value of chilled tuna exports, but frozen albacore exports (which make up the bulk of the fishery) were included in 'other' exports rather than being separated as an individual item, and there were no figures for local fish sales.

As part of its flag-state responsibilities, the Cook Islands government enforces minimum requirements regarding safety and equipment, policies regarding waste disposal, public liability insurance and insurance for medical treatment and repatriation of crews (Broadhead, pers. comm.).

Chapman recommended the establishment of a Cook Islands Tuna Fishery Development Committee, with representatives from all relevant sectors including the financial sector (2001). As of 2005, no such committee had been established. An industry association would also help in this regard.

Government consultation across agencies seems to work better in Cook Islands than in some other Pacific island countries. The marine ministry works with the National Environment Services Department and other related departments on plans to minimise the damage caused by pollution from vessels. The marine ministry and Environment Services also collaborated with their media and education programs aimed at schools, communities and the private sector.

The government saw its role as providing an 'enabling environment' for private-sector activity, rather than in owning or managing fisheries businesses (Chapman 2001), and the general impression of government philosophy from interviews in 2005 was that companies should succeed or fail according to their commercial viability, and not be bailed out by government.

During the boom phase, the government was firmly behind tuna fisheries as a major development opportunity, as evidenced by their willingness to forgo the revenue of foreign access fees to encourage the development of a locally based industry. With widespread disappointment in the industry in 2005, some felt there was a risk that government interest might wane (Epati, pers. comm.).

The Development Investment Board aims to provide a transparent system for business development applications based on the core criteria of benefits for the Cook Islands economy. In order to facilitate business applications, it works with other ministries. For example, it consults with the Ministry of Marine Resources about marine-related applications; immigration procedures for employees are facilitated by the Development Investment Board. If the board recommends a three-year working visa, the turnaround on the visa application can be as short as two weeks (Short, pers. comm.).

The Cook Islands government supported industries by facilitating marketing relations internationally. For the tuna industry, the Development Investment Board has utilised networks available through the Pacific Islands Forum Secretariat's Pacific Islands Trade and Information Commission offices (PITIC 2002). The board used these offices to set up trade shows and introductions to potential importers in Japan and China for Cook Islands tuna-industry representatives.

From the short study conducted in September 2005, it appears that the Cook Islands government has provided an enabling environment for private-sector development, especially the domestic private sector. The Foreign Investment Board and other departments facilitate investment for a reasonable cost and application procedure with a reasonable turnaround period. The general state of the economy and economic policies do not seem to be impeding development from tuna resources, as they have in other Pacific island countries. Credit is available for investors with the commercial record and assets necessary to give banks confidence in lending. The main impediment to tuna industry development thus far has simply been the commercial viability of the fishery, which is something the private sector needs to work through itself.

Conclusion

Cook Islands has learnt much from its brief foray into tuna fisheries development, going through a boom–bust cycle in about 10 years. If the Cook Islands tuna industry recovers from the slump in 2005 and, through effective management and sound business decisions, develops into an economically sustainable industry, it could be a valuable part of Cook Islands' overall economy, relieving some of the heavy dependence on tourism. At the same time, if social and ecological issues attached to tuna fisheries are managed well, the tuna industry shares important synergies with tourism. Tuna fisheries provide high-quality fresh product, which is increasingly important in international gastro-tourism, while tourists' passenger flights (subject to aircraft type) provide freight routes to sustain the portion of the fishery aimed at chilled sashimi exports. Fishing and processing companies provide human resources development potential for Cook Islanders in technical and management roles, as well as in international trading and marketing.

Development aspirations and tuna

One of the early expressions of the Cook Islands government's aspirations for the tuna industry was quoted by Lindsay Chapman in his strategy for tuna fisheries development: 'To have a sustainable and profitable industry harvesting at or near the total allowable catch fully owned by Cook Islanders, employing the maximum number of Cook Islanders, with maximum retained value in the country' (Chapman 2001). The tuna development strategy itself included a set of aspirations for 2001

- create an enabling environment to encourage private-sector development in fishing, processing and support sectors
- establish sustainable, environmentally friendly and responsible domestic development and harvesting for local consumption and export-oriented income
- maximise benefits and economic returns to Cook Islanders as a whole as well as local communities
- create employment opportunities for Cook Islanders, especially in the outer islands
- institute accurate data collection, including by-catch and interactions with protected species
- have domestic tuna management and development consistent with international and regional obligations.

After the boom-and-bust phase between 2002 and 2004, however, aspirations changed somewhat. As far as economic development goes, tourism is still much more prominent than tuna in the national psyche (Broadhead, pers. comm.). Aspirations for development from tuna resources expressed by interviewees in 2005 ranged from seeing tuna as having very little or no role in the wider economic development of Cook Islands, to seeing it having an important role as one part of a diversified economy, but with a more limited vision about what type of industry was possible than was envisaged at the outset of the domestic industry in the early 2000s.

Domestic development

In 2005, retaining maximum value in the country for Cook Islanders remained an aspiration in Cook Islands, as elsewhere in the Pacific. The domestication policy and development of the southern fishery went some way to achieving this aspiration, as did the value-adding processing conducted on shore. It is hard to see how to capture more of the value from the northern fishery while it remains tied to the cheaper operating costs and the cannery market in Pago Pago without damaging the commercial viability of that fishery. The large and fairly high-value local market meant that virtually the whole value of the 15 per cent of the catch that was sold locally was retained in the country. Further work on retaining more of the value of the catch in Cook Islands should probably be deferred until the industry stabilises and it becomes clear what kinds of tuna industries can be sustained.

Full ownership of fishing ventures by Cook Islanders remains an important aspiration, but the losses suffered by those who invested in tuna fishing in the early 2000s means there is greater wariness about committing to investment in tuna-fishing companies. The policy of forcing local ownership through tying it to fishing licences had gone only so far in generating meaningful local ownership of fishing ventures. For some of the northern fishery vessels, local ownership was little more than a 'rubber stamp', the only domestic benefits being a stream of income for the local vessel owners and some limited catch history linked to the Cook Islands flag. Some local owners are active participants in the running of their fishing companies, but because the northern fishery is conducted a long distance from Rarotonga it is easy to remain inactive as a vessel owner. It is possible that through the domestication policy, over time the level of meaningful local ownership of fishing companies might grow.

Full investment through equity by Cook Islanders is in any case difficult because of the large capital reserves necessary for even a small vessel. To run a fleet of six 10–12m vessels requires an outlay of NZ\$2.5 million for the first year and few Cook Islanders have access to this kind of capital (Armstrong, pers. comm.). Foreign investors thus tended to give their local partners the equity necessary to get licences, but structured the company such that the local owners were unable to have real control over the company.

The tuna development strategy mentioned business management training for small-scale operators using specific fisheries business training modules to be developed by the Ministry of Marine Resources working with an institution specialising in business training. The strategy report also recommended that the ministry work with lending institutions to make capital available for locals under workable conditions (Chapman 2001). These plans appear not to have progressed much since the downturn in the industry discouraged further investment.

Many Cook Islanders, especially in Rarotonga, have in recent years invested increasing time in cash work, so as to be able to afford imported goods. Many people hold two jobs (Armstrong, pers. comm.; Hunter, pers. comm.). In the past decade, many people have started small businesses. With the boost to the economy provided by tourism, many of these businesses have gone well, meaning Cook Islanders have developed confidence in their business skills and in business as a source of income. There is also a growing culture of entrepreneurialism (Armstrong, pers. comm.; Short, pers. comm.). As of 2005, however, few Cook Islanders were treating work in foreign-owned and managed tuna businesses as an opportunity to learn about the business in order to get into management and ownership themselves (Armstrong, pers. comm.; Cooper, pers. comm.).

Domestic development was aspired to within the boundaries of 'consistency with international and regional obligations'. Cook Islands has to date been a team player with regard to regional fisheries management obligations, such as the vessel monitoring system (VMS) and scientific data collection.

Another of the aspirations Cook Islanders had for tuna fisheries was to develop small-scale fisheries to help with rural and outer-island development. Unfortunately, tuna fisheries and processing are not feasible in the more remote parts of the Cooks, largely due to the costs and difficulties in storing and freighting a perishable product. Tuna fishing and processing businesses work best in industrial areas with economies of scale for freight and infrastructure. Bait-fish aquaculture, however, could be conducted in the outer islands. Tuna industries could also contribute to development in rural and outer-island areas through a small portion of access fees or fees from the US multilateral treaty being made available for a development fund that could be accessed for small-scale developments to improve standards of living.

Employment for Cook Islanders

The early aspirations for the employment of Cook Islanders fell by the wayside, particularly on fishing vessels. Cook Islands has a labour shortage: there simply is not the unemployment problem that exists in other Pacific island countries such as Papua New Guinea, Solomon Islands and Fiji. Work on fishing vessels is physically hard and the life can be very uncomfortable. Some of the vessels in the northern fishery stay out fishing for months at a time and the pay is not high for ordinary crew. Cook Islanders have taken up employment opportunities on some of the small vessels operating from Rarotonga that do not stay out at sea, and in processing facilities.

An ecologically sustainable fishery

The type of fishery Cook Islands seemed to be heading towards in 2005—with a focus on quality over quantity and small-scale value adding—was an ideal type for economic development from tuna resources while not significantly damaging fish stocks. Related to aspirations for having the fishery conducted in an ecologically sustainable manner were stated objectives about accurate data collection.

Stocks of tuna, however, are only one of the ecological sustainability issues raised by tuna fishing and processing; pollution in coastal and harbour areas is another. Several Cook islander interviewees expressed hopes that pollution from fishing and processing activities would be carefully monitored and infringements punished (Short, pers. comm.; Tupa, pers. comm.). The director of the National Environment Service felt that regional cooperation, in the form of sharing information and equipment and jointly working out policies and guidelines for fishing and processing activities, should be employed to prevent and manage pollution problems related to tuna fishing (Tupa, pers. comm.).

Minimising negative social impacts

Another aspiration not mentioned specifically in the tuna development strategy but raised by several interviewees was the desire to minimise negative social impacts from the fishery. When the fishery first boomed in 2002, Avarua had to cope with an influx of several dozen fishers from Asian countries, New Zealand and other Pacific island countries (Garnier, pers. comm.; Hunter, pers. comm.). There were apparently a few brawls in bars and concerns were raised about whether Rarotongans welcomed these immigrant workers. 'It is difficult for Pacific islanders to think of letting another culture in' (Short, pers. comm.).

According to Cook islander fishing vessel owner Frances Garnier, if Cook Islands is to host a tuna-fishing industry in the long term there is a need for specific social and health infrastructure to cope with fishing crews and to minimise negative social impacts for Avarua as well as for the crews themselves. The kinds of health infrastructure crews need include reasonably priced and accessible services for injured or sick fishermen, as well as specific services for substance abuse and for awareness, prevention and treatment of sexually transmitted infections (STIs). Pago Pago also has a mental health clinic, which is useful because life on board can be mentally stressful (Garnier, pers. comm.). Ideally, these health services need to have interpreter services attached, because of the multicultural nature of fishing crews. Women and girls who become involved with the sex industry around ports also need specialist sexual health services, as well as supportive welfare services to cope with violence against them, substance abuse and other negative social effects.

A good trans-shipping port should also provide normal recreational outlets for crews. While crews are in port in Pacific island countries, they often have nothing to do and can become bored (Garnier, pers. comm.). Church and other community groups concerned about fishing crews' less salubrious activities could do something constructive by hosting alcohol-free recreational activities such as fishing trips or picnics. Marine governance bodies could provide information and training sessions for crew spending time ashore, to update them on developments in fisheries management relating to their work, show them informational videos and develop awareness about best environmental practices for their activities (Garnier, pers. comm.). English conversation classes could also be offered.

Recommendations

Notwithstanding the need to learn from past experiences, the main recommendation for general development issues would be for the Cook Islands to continue doing what it has been doing, especially in the following areas.

- Continue with food safety and hygiene regulation improvements under the *Food Act* and bilateral negotiations with the European Union for trade access to increase the commercial options for tuna exporters.
- Continue encouraging Cook Islanders to take up more technical and managerial roles in fishing businesses. Some strategies towards this end could be to
  - increase understanding of the economic and operational realities of running a fisheries business based on a highly variable resource, from a relatively high-cost location
  - continue supporting Cook Islanders to acquire education, training and experience in technical areas and business management
  - encourage Cook Islanders to view working in a foreign-managed and owned business as an opportunity to learn the business so as to be able become a manager or business owner themselves
  - continue encouraging expatriate Cook Islanders with professional and technical skills and business experience to return to work or invest in Cook Islands.
- Balance economic benefits against environmental and social costs from tuna industries through government continuing to work on environmental regulation, monitoring and enforcement, and, if the numbers of fishing crews coming and going from Avarua looks like expanding, there will be a need to further develop social and health infrastructure.
- Undertake a cost–benefit analysis for installing storm and surge protection around the port along similar lines to the protection around the coastline near the airport.

The Ministry of Marine Resources could use more staff to enable it to cover the numerous diverse tasks required for regional and domestic fisheries management.

If fisheries policy is to shape the industry, which the domestication policy does, it is important for government officials to be well informed about commercial issues affecting the industry, so as to be able to effectively encourage development in the desired direction rather than distorting the industry meaninglessly, or worse, impeding it. In other words, in order to make the domestication policy effective, it will be important for marine ministry staff to learn from the boom-and-bust experience of the early 2000s. At the time of writing, the main lesson learned seemed to be rational development linked to economic sustainability. In this context, the ministry was discouraging investment in tuna businesses. Two other lessons that could be useful for policies affecting the industry, however, are that

- the southern fishery seems to suit a focus on quality rather than quantity, conducted from small to medium-sized, fuel-efficient vessels doing short trips
- the fishing end of the business is high risk and potentially not very profitable, so domestication via vessel ownership and operation might not be the best strategy.

In order to capture more of the value from tuna resources in Cook Islands, other options should be considered, such as domestication policies targeting onshore processing, or even tuna trading and marketing.

In order to improve the level of business savvy among Cook Islanders investing in tuna industries, the Ministry of Marine Resources could work with agencies such as the Development Investment Board, the Cook Islands Business Enterprise Centre and/or the University of the South Pacific Centre in Avarua to develop strategies to encourage Cook Islanders to treat foreign investment as a learning opportunity. The ministry could also continue with the suggestion raised in the tuna development strategy (Chapman 2001) to develop fisheries-specific business training courses.

The ministry's services relating to tuna industries could be further improved in the areas of consultation and information dissemination. The ministry produces an annual summary of tuna fisheries, which comprises mostly information from scientific and licensing data collection processes. The summary could also include other information on the projects and achievements of the ministry in each year, and be made available to the public via the ministry's web site or in printed form.

The marine ministry and industry players could consult with non-PNA group governments and industry organisations with shared interests in longline fisheries about setting up a subregional group within the FFA. This group could parallel the PNA group (equatorial counties where most purse-seine fishing occurs). The group could facilitate cooperative action among the public and private sectors to target regional initiatives such as those suggested by Cook Islands interviewees.

Notes

[1] There has never been a pole-and-line or a purse-seine fishery in Cook Islands, although Cook Islands is signatory to the US multilateral treaty for access for the US purse-seine fleet.

[2] By 2004, swordfish was being targeted. In previous years this species had constituted a lower proportion of the catch.

[3] The most basic kind of charter: simply renting a boat for a period, with no obligation about crewing or catch sales.

[4] Cook Islands is not completely free of these problems: a couple of cabinet ministers, including the leader of the Cook Islands Party, Sir Geoffrey Henry, were dismissed over governance issues in 2005 (ABC 2005a).

4

Fiji

Population: 847,000
Land area: 18,247 km²
Sea area: 1,260,000 km²

Fiji is made up of about 800 islands and islets, of which about 110 are inhabited. Fiji was a British colony between 1874 (with the island of Rotuma added in 1881) and 1970. Suva was the centre for British colonialism in the Pacific region, a status that set Fiji up to be the 'gateway to the Pacific' after decolonisation. It remains a hub for the Pacific. Several important regional initiatives, such as the Pacific Islands Forum Secretariat and the University of the South Pacific, are based in Suva. The British allowed colonial plantation owners to import large numbers of indentured labourers from India and entrenched the political position of indigenous Fijians as landowners, a situation that has led to an uneasy ethnic basis to contemporary Fijian politics and economics. This tension has been part of the mix of factors behind the coups in Fiji's recent history. Fiji has a booming tourist industry as well as struggling sugar and garment-production industries.[1]

Potential of tuna fisheries

Fiji, lying 17 degrees south of the equator, is on the periphery of the richest tuna grounds, which lie between 10° north and 10° south of the equator, so it does not have the same potential for development from tuna fisheries as some of the Pacific island countries further north. Fiji's total allowable catch (TAC) for the three main longline tuna species—bigeye, yellowfin and albacore—has been set at 15,000mt, as an interim measure according to the precautionary principle based on catch data from the 1990s, which was felt to be unreliable (Government of Fiji 2002). Consultative meetings for the Tuna Management and Development Plan set the number of licences at 90 (Turaganivalu, pers. comm.), which later was increased to more than 100. Based on many years' experience in the fishery, however, managers from Fiji Fish and Solander (Pacific) feel that the maximum economically sustainable annual catch for Fiji's Exclusive Economic Zone (EEZ) was less than the 15,000mt set in the Tuna Management and Development Plan, and that 60 licences should be the upper limit.

Map 4.1   Fiji

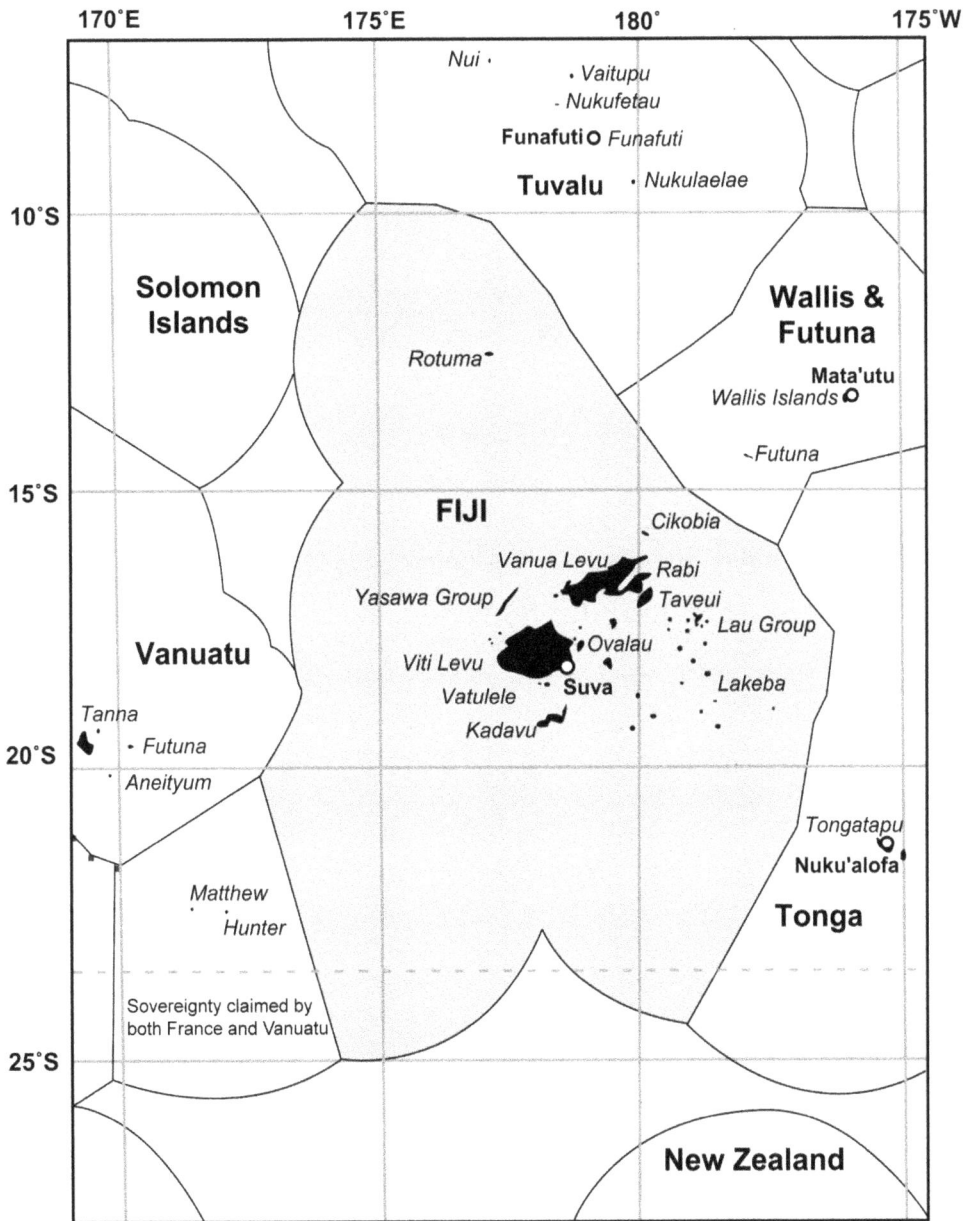

Source: Youngmi Choi, Secretariat of the Pacific Community, Noumea, New Caledonia.

History of development

Pole-and-line

A surface skipjack fishery started in Fiji in the 1970s with surveys of fish and bait fish from 1970 to 1973 under a United Nations Development Program (Pafco 2000). There was no private-sector interest in developing a pole-and-line fishery so the government established Ika Corporation under the Land and Development Authority (Stone, pers. comm.). In the early 1970s, the Fisheries Department built a pole-and-line vessel that was a cross between American and Australian-style pole-and-line vessels. The Fisheries Department also bought a second-hand Japanese pole-and-line vessel. These two vessels were used by Ika from 1975. Later in the 1970s, Ika acquired several more vessels from Japan, using aid money from New Zealand and other funds (Stone, pers. comm.). Fiji's pole-and-line catches increased from 700mt in 1976 to a peak of 6,000mt in 1989 (Government of Fiji 2002).

The Pacific Fishing Company (Pafco) cannery at Levuka on Ovalau had been the main market for the domestic pole-and-line fleet, but Pafco prices for skipjack fell to a level that was unprofitable (Hufflett, pers. comm.). By that stage, Pafco was loining albacore for Bumble Bee and did not rely on supply from the domestic skipjack fishery. The Fisheries Department did not intervene to have the government-owned Pafco support the domestic skipjack fishery, so the fishery declined (Stone, pers. comm.).

In 1983 Robert Stone, who had been managing Ika, set up a private company pole-and-line fishing for skipjack, eventually running two vessels. He explored new markets, including for the product *tataki*—seared then ultra-low temperature frozen packaged skipjack loins sold in Japan. By the early 2000s, Stone had sold his vessels and left the fishery due to falling margins.

Solander (Pacific) was registered as a Fijian company in 1988 and began as a pole-and-line fishing company targeting skipjack for the Pafco cannery. Since the cannery prices for skipjack were low, Solander moved out of the skipjack fishery and changed to longlining targeting sashimi markets in mid 1992.

In 2002, Tosa Bussan (Fiji) purchased a second-hand 59-gross registered tonnage (GRT) pole-and-line vessel from Miyazaki in Japan and started fishing in the Fijian EEZ. The vessel was crewed entirely by Fijians. Tosa Bussan intended originally to establish a small fleet to produce *tataki* for the Japanese market (see below) but discovered that the Fijian skipjack fishery was less productive than hoped because it was uneconomical to fish during the off-season for skipjack. Its skipjack vessel could catch only 500mt annually, whereas in Solomon Islands a pole-and-line vessel of similar capacity could catch 1,500mt annually. Tosa Bussan decided it would be unprofitable to expand its pole-and-line venture further. As of September 2005, this single pole-and-line vessel was still supplying the Tosa Bussan processing plant and it was intended that this arrangement would continue (Nakano, pers. comm.), but the main focus of the company had shifted to skinless yellowfin loins supplied by longline vessels.

Longline

When monofilament technology and smaller longliners (less than 60GRT) were introduced to the Pacific in the mid to late 1980s, Fiji was one of the first countries to develop a domestic industry using these vessels. The Fijian dollar was devalued by 35 per cent in 1987, which encouraged export industries. Air Pacific started direct passenger flights from Nadi to Japan in 1988 as part of a move to deepen the Fiji–Japan bilateral economic relationship, and this gave the longline industry airfreight connections to Japan. After the advent of these flights, there was a great deal of Japanese private-sector investment in tourism enterprises in Fiji (Turaganivalu, pers. comm.). Growth in the tourist sector increased demand for air links and increased prices in the domestic market for tuna.

Fiji Fish was the first to fish by the longline method in Fiji in 1988 with the FV *Sunbird*. The fishery targeted the sashimi market and also supplied albacore for the cannery market. Vessel numbers increased between 1992 and 1995, peaking at about 90 vessels, then declined, then increased again from 1999. Since 1997, Fijian longliners have also fished in the waters of other coastal states and international waters. In 2000, Fiji's longline catch was more than 11,000mt, with an estimated market value of F$150 million (Government of Fiji 2002).

Investment in the longline fishery boomed again in the early 2000s with many new vessels entering—peaking at more than 100 vessels—until falling catch per unit of effort (CPUE) rates caused many vessels to withdraw from the fishery from 2004. About only 50 vessels had been licensed by September 2005, and possibly another 10 would apply by the end of the year. The CPUE drop and increasing fuel costs meant many vessels were tied up in the harbour. Several owners had gone bankrupt. The companies that managed to survive the low catch years hoped that with fewer vessels the catches would start to increase. The drop in supply had already boosted prices, but for a sustained industry recovery the CPUE would also need to increase (Southwick, pers. comm.). Despite the decline in active vessel numbers in 2005, Fiji still had the largest longline fleet of any of the Pacific island countries (Langley 2005).

The longline fishery in Fiji's EEZ was not impacting significantly on the stocks of the target species. In conjunction with the heavy fishing mortality occurring along the migration paths in equatorial waters, however, Fiji's fishing effort had brought down the numbers of fish enough to damage the economic viability of the fishery in recent years (Langley 2005). The high-value (bigeye and yellowfin) proportion of the catch therefore decreased as fuel and other input costs rose, squeezing margins for the longline fishery since 2001. This trend pushed Fiji-based operators to travel outside Fiji's EEZ to find fish (Southwick, pers. comm.). Since 2002, 20 per cent of the Fijian fleet's catch was from the Vanuatu EEZ, 20 per cent from international waters, some from Solomon Islands' EEZ and a small amount from Tuvalu's EEZ (Langley 2005).

Interviewees from longline companies Solander and Fiji Fish said they believed Pacific stocks of yellowfin and bigeye were even more damaged by overfishing in 2005 than scientists from the Secretariat of the Pacific Community (SPC) were estimating at the time (Hufflett, pers. comm.; Southwick, pers. comm.). In 2002, Fiji Fish's fleet caught 20 yellowfin a day, but in 2005 they were lucky to catch two or three (Southwick, pers. comm.). Fiji Fish said it started 'sounding alarms' about the stocks in 1995 but was told by the SPC fisheries scientists that it was being too pessimistic (Southwick, pers. comm.). Solander managers also first picked up the CPUE decline in their company catch statistics in the late 1990s (Hufflett, pers. comm.). Based on a CPUE decline for albacore noticed since 2003, Grahame Southwick said he feared the same thing that happened with yellowfin and bigeye was happening with albacore: when it became economically unsound to target other species, fishers began targeting albacore (Southwick, pers. comm.).[2]

Albacore has made up the largest part of the catch from the Fijian EEZ. Albacore was sold mostly frozen for the US cannery market, with growing chilled sales for export to places such as the United Kingdom (Government of Fiji 2002; Dunham, pers. comm.). This species had a recruitment problem in the 1970s and 1980s but appeared to have recovered by the 1990s. There was a sudden drop in albacore CPUE in 2003, then a slight recovery in 2004. Some of the recent drop could have been due to increased fishing, but it also appeared to be caused by oceanographic effects. Albacore as a species is relatively resilient to longline fishing because it matures and spawns at a younger age (smaller size) than the relatively large, older fish caught by longliners (Langley 2005).

Yellowfin and bigeye catches were destined for the chilled and frozen sashimi markets. In 2002, Fiji's chilled tuna exports were worth about F$160 million annually (Government of Fiji 2002; Hufflett, pers. comm.). These species had declined as a proportion of the Fijian catch since the early 2000s, concurrent with a region-wide recruitment problem noticed by SPC stock assessments.

In the 1990s, Fiji Fish and Solander were joined by Chinese longline companies.[3] Since Fiji had relatively low wage costs, there were opportunities for locals to be employed on Chinese vessels. Some longline equipment was manufactured in Fiji. There were private and government slipways in Suva used by the Chinese fleet. Chinese vessels liked Fiji because of its infrastructure, services, cannery and airfreight. Most of the Chinese vessels' catch was albacore for the cannery market, with some bigeye, yellowfin and occasionally billfish sent to the chilled-fish markets overseas (McCoy and Gillett 2005).

By 1997, there were seven Chinese longliners based in Fiji. Since 2000, increases in the Chinese fleet in the Pacific have mostly been in Fiji (McCoy and Gillett 2005). Fiji was thought to be the most likely of the Pacific island countries to benefit from increases in China's ultra-low temperature (ULT) freezing technology longline fleet (McCoy and Gillett 2005), although falling CPUE meant a fall in the number of Chinese-owned Fijian-licensed vessels in 2005. As of 2005, an 'undetermined' number, possibly 20–30, of large-scale (more than 100 gross tonnes) Chinese vessels were based in Fiji without being licensed to fish there. They seem to have arrived in 2003. It was thought they fished in Vanuatu and on the high seas, and it was not clear whether they trans-shipped entirely in Fiji or trans-shipped a portion of their catch on the high seas (McCoy and Gillett 2005).

The China National Fishery Corporation (CNFC), a state-owned enterprise reputed to be the largest fishing company in the world with more than 65,000 employees, had a resident office in Lami. Connections between Chinese businesses and the vessels they represented, either through charter or ownership, were not entirely clear in Fiji. Fijian-based agents for Chinese longliners were less in control of the fleets than in Micronesia, where all supply and marketing was done by the agent. In Fiji, only three or four of 10 agent companies were involved in packaging for export. Chinese vessel operators sold their fish at a set price to these agents (McCoy and Gillett 2005).

Managers from the 'veteran' companies of Fiji's domestic longline fishery, Solander and Fiji Fish, felt that the increased numbers of mainland Chinese vessels operating from Fiji had damaged the fishery and they predicted they would cause more damage in future unless they were regulated more tightly (Lucas, pers. comm.; Hufflett, pers. comm.; Southwick, pers. comm.). Solander company statistics noted trouble with bigeye and yellowfin catches as early as 1997, but the drop was more pronounced after 2002. The sharp decline in CPUE, which caused large losses in 2003 and 2004, coincided with the influx of many more longliners (mostly Chinese) to Fijian waters than had fished there previously, and they believed the drop in CPUE was due to the increased effort in Fiji's EEZ.

Solander and Fiji Fish managers felt strongly that the Chinese vessels must be subsidised in some way, because it seemed impossible that they could be profitable. They also felt that the Chinese fleet was going to drive many other fleets out of business in the Pacific because the prices at which the Chinese fleet sold their catch on world markets brought the price down too low for non-subsidised fleets to compete (Southwick, pers. comm.; Hufflett, pers. comm.). Solander managers suspected that the Chinese vessels flagged elsewhere, such as Vanuatu, operated under less strict rules and therefore had unfairly lower operating costs.[4]

By 2005, the Fijian longline tuna fishing industry was composed of three main interest groups. The first was the veterans of the domestic industry, represented by Fiji Fish and Solander. The second was the sector of the industry substantially owned and managed by mainland Chinese companies. The third sector was the group of indigenous vessel owners who entered through the post-2000 affirmative action policies of the government to subsidise and encourage indigenous Fijian ownership of tuna industries (Turaganivalu, pers. comm.).

Solander Pacific began longline fishing in Fiji in 1992, after pole-and-line fishing in Fiji since 1988. Solander is a private family company based in Nelson, New Zealand. Until 1994, it was wholly New Zealand owned. In 1994, the Fijian government required Solander to sell down 30 per cent of its shareholding to Fijian citizens. As a consequence, Ratu Cokanauto Tu'uakitau—a senior member of the Great Council of Chiefs—became the chairman and local shareholder of Solander Pacific.

Solander Pacific generated gross sales of between F$12 and $20 million annually, turning a profit every year except 2003 and 2004, when substantial loses were incurred as the CPUE dropped drastically. As of September 2005, it seemed that catches had recovered somewhat, although concurrent increases in fuel and other costs meant margins were lower than they had been with similar catch rates in the past. To September 2005, the company calculated it had invested more than F$12 million in the country, including $8.9 million on the fleet and $2 million on onshore infrastructure for processing (Hufflett, pers. comm.).

Solander Pacific's fleet in 2005 consisted of 11 vessels, all of which were 20–30 years old. Most were second-hand Japanese vessels, and would soon need replacing. New vessels cost about NZ$2.5 million each. The company employed about 250 people and 100 casual workers. The total number of expatriates were: one New Zealander local director; one New Zealand superintendent engineer, who worked on the shore base; and two New Zealand staff on the fleet (all men). The number-two manager was an Indo-Fijian woman who managed the company's finances and marketing.

Fiji Fish, based in Lami, near Suva, is a group of 14 companies owned by Grahame Southwick. Fiji Fish's main business is longline tuna fishing for the sashimi market and associated businesses such as packing and marketing. The companies were split to maximise tax advantages, since fishing and processing were tax-free activities, but marketing, cold storage, fishing gear supply and other related businesses were not tax free. The group of companies had a combined annual turnover of F$120 million in the past, but with the bad conditions in the Fijian longline industry since 2002 the annual turnover was more like $90 million.

Of the 40 vessels Fiji Fish operated in 2005, it owned 15 outright, and 30 per cent of each vessel in the rest of the fleet was owned in joint ventures with Taiwanese vessel owners. Their vessels were all 20–25m, which Fiji Fish believed was the right size for the Fijian fishery. For the 15 fully locally owned boats, the whole crew were Fijian except the captains, who were Korean. For the 25 jointly owned vessels, half of the crew were Fijian (as per licensing regulations) while the other half were a mixture of Indonesians, Filipinos and mainland Chinese.

Fiji Fish sends sashimi to the Japanese market and fresh-chilled albacore to the United Kingdom. Airfreight from Fiji to London via Sydney cost about F$6–7 a kilogram in 2005 (Dunham, pers. comm.). Half of the Fiji Fish fleet did not fish in the Fijian EEZ in 2005, but on the high seas, and in Solomon Islands and Vanuatu, which were more productive for yellowfin and bigeye. Sashimi could not be offloaded in Solomon Islands or Vanuatu, however, partly because of a lack of processing facilities, but mostly because of a lack of airfreight routes out of these countries. The vessels spend 10 days each trip steaming to and from Suva, and two days in port, so many days each month are wasted fishing time and fuel. In addition, fishing so far away from the offloading base meant fish stayed on the vessels for up to 35 days, which meant the first 15 days or more worth of catch (40–50 per cent) was no longer of high enough quality to sell on the sashimi market. About 15 per cent of the fish that could no longer be sold chilled was sold frozen to canneries at a fraction of the price, and the rest was 'thrown out as pet food in the local market'.

Fiji Fish had analysed the economics of getting around this problem. One option considered was to loin and freeze the catch at sea for the first couple of weeks, but according to its calculations lower prices achieved for this product meant it was not economical. The fresh chilled market is the only one that 'pays a good enough price to justify going out and catching the fish' (Dunham, pers. comm.).

The solution Fiji Fish settled on was to invest in three large transport vessels that were to go out to the fishing grounds to collect the catch and bring it back to Fiji, while the fishing vessels stayed fishing. Fiji Fish estimated that even after the extra costs of buying and running the transport vessels were taken out, the increased productivity of the fishing vessels should amount to F$3–400,000 more in income per vessel a year.

Purse-seine fishery

From 1980 to 1985, a New Zealand company conducted purse-seining in Fiji with two vessels as a feasibility trial. The US fleet has also fished occasionally in Fijian waters on free-swimming schools or logs. Skipjack were usually not concentrated enough to make purse-seining in Fijian waters as attractive as in other, warmer waters, except during the prolonged El Niño event of 1993–94 (Government of Fiji 2002).

Distant water access fleet

The domestication policy basically meant a ban on distant water fleets operating in Fijian waters. Japanese purse-seine fleets operating in international waters and other areas near the edge of Fiji's EEZ boundary sometimes drifted over the boundary and fished in Fiji's EEZ. This was recorded through the vessel monitoring system so the Japanese fleet retrospectively paid access fees for these transgressions (Government of Fiji 2005).

Bait fishery

Fiji's longline fishery has relied on frozen imported bait. There was a local bait fishery in the past, attached to the pole-and-line fishery. According to Robert Stone, since the decline of the pole-and-line fishery, there were few people left with knowledge about local bait grounds and how to fish them effectively. Bait-fish access and costs could be affected by the 2004 Customary Fisheries Bill.

Fish aggregating devices (FADs)

FADs were first deployed in Fiji in 1981. The Fisheries Department and Ika fishing company maintained FADs during the 1980s and 1990s (Government of Fiji 2002). Without a substantial surface skipjack fishery, it has not been necessary to maintain a FAD program for the industrial fishery. FAD projects have been continuing for the small-scale and artisanal fishery (see below).

Small-scale coastal

Small-scale coastal fishing for tuna has been as difficult to sustain in Fiji as it has been elsewhere in the Pacific. Under the Commodity Development Framework funding, the Fisheries Division in 1999 promoted small-scale fishing around FADs by subsidising 36 locals in the Suva area to buy 7.2-metre fibreglass skiffs with 40-horsepower outboard motors and fishing gear. Local fishers used trolling, vertical longlining and mid-water handline methods. Larger yellowfin and bigeye were sold to local processors for export; the rest of the catch was sold direct to the public or buyers who sold locally. Proceeds from the catches were to be used to pay off loans for the vessels and gear. As of 2002, only six to 12 of the 36 fishers in the program were still fishing around the FADs; the rest were fishing inshore or had sold their vessels and gear (Government of Fiji 2002).

Game fishing

There were game-fishing clubs in Suva and Pacific Harbour that held regular tournaments. Several of the main tourist areas had vessels available for international tourists to charter (Government of Fiji 2002).

Processing

Pafco. The Pafco cannery was established by the Japanese company C. Itoh at the Pafco trans-shipping base at Levuka in the early 1970s. The first market in 1974 was canned albacore to Bumble Bee Seafoods of the United States. In 1978, the Lomé Convention opened up markets in the United Kingdom under the John West brand; in 1984, Pafco also started selling to Sainsbury's and other generic brand owners. In 1987, C. Itoh withdrew from the cannery and Pafco was left insolvent (Pafco 2000). The company was saved by a contract with Bumble Bee to loin albacore for its canneries. Pacfco lost interest in the skipjack market in the United Kingdom, so Solomon Taiyo became the main supplier from the Pacific (Stone, pers. comm.). In 1992, the Pafco cannery underwent a major overhaul funded by the Australian government (worth A$17 million) (Pafco 2000). A six-month long industrial dispute and Cyclone Kina meant that 1993–96 were bad years, so in 1997 the government injected F$10 million into the company. Then, in 1999, the first five-year agreement between Pacfo and Bumble Bee was finalised. The Fijian government injected about F$14 million in 2000–02 to upgrade the Pacfo facilities (Government of Fiji 2002) to enable the development of Hazard Analysis Critical Control Point (HACCP) systems and compliance with EU food safety regulations (as well as regulations for Australia, Canada, the United States and the international *Codex Alimentarius*) (Pafco 2000). A second five-year agreement was signed in 2004. Management thought it likely that, unless something happened to the resource, Pafco's five-year agreement with Bumble Bee would be renewed for a third time in 2009.

Pacfo was 98 per cent owned by the Fijian government, with the remaining 2 per cent owned by Ovalau landowners (Pafco 2000). As part of the arrangement with Bumble Bee, Pacfo was controlled by a non-executive board of directors headed by a non-executive chair—all of whom were government appointees—while the day-to-day operations were directed by Bumble Bee managers working with Pacfo managers (Pafco 2000). Bumble Bee and Taiwanese company FCF Fishery had an arrangement whereby FCF supplied all the fish to the Pacfo cannery. In addition, longline companies operating out of Suva supplied the Levuka base with albacore and other fish not suitable for chilled exports (Dunham, pers. comm.).

Since the first five-year agreement was signed between Pacfo and Bumble Bee in 1999, the Pacfo plant has operated under, and sold all exports through, Bumble Bee. Productivity rates and quality rose under Bumble Bee management. The plant processed about 30,000mt of round fish annually (27,000mt albacore and 3,000mt skipjack, bigeye and yellowfin), with a yield rate of about 55 per cent (for albacore; less for skipjack), making mostly cooked loins exported frozen to canneries in California. It was not worth exporting canned fish to the United States because of the duty on canned tuna in that country. Pacfo canned 38,000 cases of tuna (48 cans to a case) for Clover Leaf of Canada (which had no duties on imports of canned fish). Flake tuna left over from loining was canned by Pacfo for the local market—200,000 cases of 48 cans annually. The general manager did not think there was much point in the Pacific trying to export to the European Union because the market was too far away and too competitive, with producers from the Seychelles, Africa and Ecuador already producing canned fish with cheaper operating costs (Guenegan, pers. comm.).

In 2005, Pacfo employed about 800 locals, with five or so expatriates in senior management positions. The company had an employees' union that managed industrial negotiations in 2003 to secure a pay increase of 60 per cent over two years. This brought the average hourly rates of pay for unskilled labour to F$2.75, and for skilled labour to $3.50 per hour, which in addition to high freight costs made Levuka one of the more expensive places for tuna processing in the region (Guenegan, pers. comm.).

Pacfo's strengths included preferential EU market access (under the Cotonou Agreement), its strategic location near the rich fishing grounds of the Pacific Ocean, a good water supply and a skilled, trained workforce. Pacfo's weaknesses were the high costs of freight and other internal and external operating costs, no economy of scale and lack of capital (Pafco 2000).

The Fijian government was committed to maintaining Pafco at Levuka for social reasons, to make the communities on Ovalau Island economically viable. It was this commitment that influenced the Australian government's decision to fund the 1992 upgrade of the Pafco facilities. Up to 70 per cent of the available workforce in Ovalau worked for Pafco. Bumble Bee was committed also to being based at Levuka for social reasons, but managers pointed out that this increased their operating costs because of the additional leg for freight and a restricted labour supply. (Guenegan, pers. comm.; Gupta, pers. comm.).

The social aspects of Pafco's operations have always been important. According to the public relations officer, when Pafco was first established at Levuka people were able to build corrugated-iron houses. But there were also negative social impacts: Levuka became known as the 'boozing capital' of Fiji because a lot of money was spent on alcohol (Navuetaki, pers. comm.). Throughout the years, Pafco has caused social change on Ovalau, some of which has been viewed negatively (Emberson-Bain 1994). Social and political factors also impact on the viability of the company. As well as the extra costs incurred for being based at Levuka, social and political issues in the form of the 2000 coup damaged the company. Bumble Bee almost pulled out of the first five-year agreement with Pafco during 2000, when the base was occupied by militants, who took all the stored fish (Navuetaki, pers. comm.). In order to try to ameliorate some of its social issues, Pafco employed a public relations officer, whose job included liaison with local communities.

Fresh chilled/frozen tuna. With the development of domestic longline fisheries, several packing plants were established. The first was Fiji Fish's packing and freezing plant in 1989. In 2002, there were seven fresh-tuna processing and packing plants: one in Pacific Harbour, two in Lautoka, three for sashimi in Suva and one for *tataki* in Suva. Three more sashimi plants were planned by companies in 2002, as well as a cannery and two more post-harvest plants—all in the Suva area (Government of Fiji 2002). There were four sashimi-processing plants in the Suva area in 2005: Golden Ocean, Fiji Fish, Celtrock and Transpacific. A company called Hang Tong planned to open a fifth plant (Turaganivalu, pers. comm.).

Because there were so many packing plants, Solander did not have its own plant but contracted a facility next to its base to pack chilled fish for airfreight. Solander had its own small ULT freezing machine to process frozen sashimi for sea freight to Japan.

In 2000, Tokyo-based Tosa Bussan Inc. started a feasibility study around Pacific Harbour for pole-and-line fishing for a processing facility to produce *tataki*, a popular Japanese dish made of skipjack loins seared on the outside but raw on the inside.

The main mode of *tataki* production for Japan in recent decades has been large distant water pole-and-line vessels that travel around the globe for months at a time, processing the catch on board and storing it at ultra-low temperatures before returning to Japan to offload. This method was becoming too expensive in terms of fuel. Furthermore, Japanese regulations on the distant water fleet made them uncompetitive compared with other distant water fishing countries, and there has been declining interest among young Japanese people to go into distant water fishing.

Tosa Bussan could see that many Japanese companies were establishing processing factories in China, because labour there was cheaper than in Japan, but China was far away from the fishing grounds of the Pacific. Using China as a base for processing would thus be expensive in terms of freight. The richest skipjack fishing grounds were around Kavieng, Solomon Islands and northeast up to the Marshall Islands and Kiribati, but the business environment in all of those places was deemed unsuitable for establishing an onshore processing base. Tosa Bussan knew Fiji's fishing grounds were less rich than the countries to the north, but it was close to those fishing grounds. Fiji had regular, reasonably priced freight connections, adequate wharf infrastructure, good roads and telecommunications. In addition, it had a suitable labour force with wage rates comparable with those in China. Tosa Bussan thus selected Fiji as the location to try *tataki* production.

In 2001, Tosa Bussan (Fiji) built a processing factory in Walu Bay, Suva. Boxes of ultra-low frozen loins were exported by sea to Japan twice a month during the peak skipjack season. In 2002, Tosa Bussan's second-hand Japanese pole-and-line vessel came into operation supplying the factory but turned out not to be profitable.

Tosa Bussan (Fiji) incurred large losses during the first two years of operation and had no choice but to diversify. Its buyers in Japan helped out by paying for fish in advance.

To add to its *tataki* product, Tosa Bussan moved into ULT frozen skinless loins for the Japanese sashimi market. The company bought frozen bigeye and yellowfin from vessels that had been fishing outside the Fijian EEZ but which offloaded in Suva. In a month, Tosa Bussan (Fiji) exported five to six containers, or 100mt, of skinless loins. Since diversifying, the company had been profitable and, in 2006, it was planning to construct a new factory in Suva.

As of September 2005, Tosa Bussan employed 70 staff at the processing plant. Twenty-five Fijians were employed on the pole-and-line vessel. Two Japanese technicians came out to train the Fijian factory staff for the first year or two, but apart from them and the director, Nakano Toru, the entire workforce were Fijian citizens.

Small-scale gourmet products. There was one more kind of processing in Fiji: a small-scale gourmet processing plant at Pacific Harbour, producing a range of products, including cold smoked marlin, tuna jerky and tuna ham. According to the founder, Robert Stone, there were two keys to the success of this venture. One was finding a good distributor for export markets. The other was setting up systems in the small factory such that the quality and hygiene were up to importing-country requirements. (Stone, pers. comm.).

Trans-shipping, service and supply

According to Solander owner, Charles Hufflett, when he first visited Suva in the 1950s, it had a thriving service industry for ships. The Pafco base at Levuka started as a trans-shipping base for the Japanese distant water longline fleet in 1963, as a joint venture between the colonial Fijian government (which owned 10 per cent) and Banno Oceania, a company connected to the Japanese Ministry of International Trade and Industry (which owned 90 per cent) (Pafco 2000). The Japanese fleet had been operating from Kavieng in Papua New Guinea but was looking for a base closer to the centre of the Pacific Ocean. Fijians were against anything connected to Japan because of memories of World War II, but Levuka on the island of Ovalau at that time was suffering economic hardship because of the collapse of the copra market in the late 1950s, and the consequent shift of trading activities to Suva (Pafco 2000). The chiefs of the area convinced people that the continuity of their society depended on something like a fishing base, so they agreed. The copra-exporting facilities were transformed to a fishing base with large cold-storage sheds (Navuetaki c.2002). In 1973, the trans-shipment base was converted to a cannery and Levuka was no longer used as a trans-shipping base.

Since 2000, the Fijian government has aimed to develop the infrastructure and logistics networks needed to further encourage tuna vessels in the region to come to Fiji to offload their catch for processing, and for vessel repairs and maintenance (Turaganivalu, pers. comm.). Fiji's central location in the Pacific and its relatively good infrastructure and transport connections meant it was a natural choice for trans-shipping. The air connections were some of the best in the region for sashimi freight. The air links also made Fiji a good point from which to fly crew in and out. Fiji's roads and telecommunications are also better than many countries in the region. Suva has become a hub for the longline tuna fisheries of the region. As of the early 2000s, foreign vessels trans-shipped their catch under a permit issued by the Ministry of Fisheries and Forests. Most of the catch went into freezer vessels for export, with some by-catch sold for local markets, some catch going to Pafco and some bought by the Foreign Fish Traders Association in Suva. Some Fijian stevedores (six–eight per trans-shipment) were used for trans-shipping, along with the crews of the vessels offloading. Some local tradesmen were also employed servicing vessels in Suva (Government of Fiji 2002). Fiji's sea and air connections meant it could provide a quick turnaround for crew and provisions, as well as a port from which to send fish to international markets. By 2005, more and more agents for distant water longline fleets were basing themselves in Suva (Turaganivalu, pers. comm.).

Under national development objectives since 2000, the government wanted to improve the wharf facilities used by the longline industries, as part of a F$230 million plan to improve the port facilities around Suva. This plan included a fishing jetty at Lami, for which the Japanese government had committed up to F$10 million in aid money (Turaganivalu, pers. comm.). In addition, there was a plan to build a large slipway at Lautoka.

Citizens' groups in Lami, however, opposed the plans for the new jetty, arguing that they already had enough industrial infrastructure in their area and wanted future developments to be social amenities, such as sports and recreational facilities (Turaganivalu, pers. comm.). The Lautoka local government also decided that it was better to focus on tourism as a development opportunity rather than industrial fisheries infrastructure, and so rejected the plan for the slipway. The national Cabinet agreed that these concerns were reasonable and put aside the plans for Lami and Lautoka (Turaganivalu, pers. comm.). In terms of community consultation, this outcome was successful, but it frustrated the fishing industry and contributed to industry doubts about government support for their sector (Guenegan, pers. comm.; Hufflett, pers. comm.).

Domestication and indigenisation

One of the notable features of Fiji's fisheries development policy in the past decade has been the effort to domesticate and indigenise tuna fisheries. Distant water fleets have not been licensed to fish in Fiji's EEZ. Vessels owned by overseas companies have to be registered and flagged in Fiji, and fishing companies operating in Fiji have to be at least 30 per cent owned by Fijian citizens (Turaganivalu, pers. comm.).[5] As well as the expectation that locally based fishing companies will bring more benefits to the Fijian economy than distant water fleets, other motivations behind the policy to have vessels flagged in Fiji have included: i) the greater control government can exert over locally flagged vessels, and ii) the need to establish a solid catch history in Fiji's zone, the adjacent high seas and from landing for onshore processing of all vessels in ports, to strengthen Fiji's case for a reasonable allocation of the Western and Central Pacific Fisheries Commission (WCPFC) TAC (Turaganivalu, pers. comm.).

The domestication policy alone, however, resulted in a fishery largely owned and managed by non-indigenous nationals, resident expatriates or foreigners who established local companies. Especially since the 2000 coup, having indigenous Fijians own and manage companies has been a high political priority reflected in fisheries policies. For example, the Social Justice Bill passed by Parliament in December 2001 specified that indigenous Fijians be given preferential access to new fisheries licences (Government of Fiji 2002). The Fiji Customary Fisheries Bill 2004 gave administrative effect to the *de facto* recognition of Fijian and Rotuman resource ownerships rights in coastal areas in line with indigenous ownership under customary tenure of 83 per cent of Fijian land (Aqorau 2005).

The Customary Fisheries Bill emerged as part of a more general government blueprint for the protection of indigenous rights presented to the Great Council of Chiefs after the 2000 coup (Looking Glass Design c.2001).

The Tuna Management and Development Plan cited 'uneven distribution of wealth and [an] economic gap between the two major races…as the major cause of political turmoil and unrest in the country'. The plan therefore sought to 'enable Fijians and Rotumans to fully exercise their rights of self-determination within the unitary State of the Republic of the Fiji Islands' by 'bridging the economic gap' between indigenous Fijians and resident expatriates and Indo-Fijians through offering development opportunities in tuna industries to indigenous Fijians on a preferential basis (Government of Fiji 2002).

Indigenous Fijians were given preferential licensing conditions, and 20 longline licences were reserved for indigenous Fijians. 'Any application by an Indigenous Fijian or a company that is minimum 51% owned by an Indigenous Fijian is automatically eligible for an Offshore Licence for longlining tuna' (Government of Fiji 2002).[6]

The Seed Capital Assistance Revolving Fund (SCARF) Program in the Ministry of Fisheries and Forests was another affirmative action mechanism. Indigenous Fijians wishing to own tuna businesses were assisted by an investment program whereby the ministry put up one-third of the equity for the business while the Fiji Development Bank provided the other two-thirds of the loan, of up to about F$200,000.

The Development Bank required indigenous vessel owners to commit some of their own equity by using assets such as property as security against the loans (Turaganivalu, pers. comm.). Indigenous vessel owners whose businesses failed risked having their assets seized and sold to repay the loans (Turaganivalu, pers. comm.). The decline in CPUE in Fiji occurred just as indigenous Fijians became vessel owners under the SCARF program. The indigenous owners argued that even with subsidies in conditions with high fuel costs, low fish prices and low CPUE, it was too hard for them to meet the conditions of their loans and keep their businesses running (Turaganivalu, pers. comm.). Indigenous vessel owners were understandably discouraged by these setbacks, and their confidence in the feasibility of owning and managing a fishing business has been shaken considerably in recent years.

In 2005, the Fisheries Department was criticised because it was believed that the affirmative action policy was not having a noticeable improvement on the level of indigenous participation but was in fact enabling foreign investors to circumvent the rules.

Determinants of success

Synergies with tourism

In terms of chilled airfreight sashimi exports, Fiji's comparative advantage over other countries in the region lies in its tourism industry, which provides regular direct flights to markets in Asia and North America. In addition, the tourist population has generated a local market for sashimi tuna, just as it has in Cook Islands.

Human resources

Another advantage Fiji's tuna industries have is being close to the educational services of the University of the South Pacific (USP). For example, USP's Marine Studies Program runs a Seafood Safety (HACCP) Training Course, which is useful for the various post-harvest operations based in Suva and Levuka (Hufflett, pers. comm.). Fiji's pool of trained and experienced fishing crews from the now defunct Ika Corporation represents another advantage Fiji has over other countries in the region.

The manager of Tosa Bussan felt that Fijian employees were 'excellent' (Nakano, pers. comm.), and all interviewees agreed that Fijian fishers were as skilled as any, but interviewees also talked of difficulties with Fijian employees. Fishing company owners mentioned hiring Fijian crew who did one or two trips then quit or turned up to work drunk and had to be fired (Turaganivalu, pers. comm.). Fiji Fish owner, Grahame Southwick, said his Asian crews worked 'three times as hard' as his Pacific islander crews, reflecting their relative dependence on wage labour (Fijians are landowners). Fijian deck crew were paid about US$300 a month. Chinese crews were paid US$200–300 a month. Most Fiji-based Chinese longline operators believed that Pacific islanders would not work as consistently hard as Chinese crew, and that there might be language and cultural difficulties in a mixed crew (McCoy and Gillett 2005).

The fact that longline companies based in the Pacific can employ Asian crews is one of the factors contributing to their competitiveness. Fishing companies based in wealthy countries with regulations forcing them to employ expensive home-country crew (Australia, Japan, the United States) are being forced out of longline tuna fishing by their wages bills (Southwick, pers. comm.).

Trade access to the European Union

As an African Caribbean Pacific (ACP) country, Fiji's fishery products are exempt from tariffs in the European Union. Several interviewees said that Fiji had 'list-one' status with the European Union, meaning it was cleared to export to any European country. A look at the EU web site,[7] however, reveals that Papua New Guinea is the only Pacific island country with list-one status. Apparently, Fiji was on track to attain list-one status in 2003, with a new *Health Act* intended to prepare the Department of Health to be a Competent Authority to verify the safety of food produced by Fijian companies (Turaganivalu, pers. comm.). The department, however, failed to meet all of the recommendations of the 2003 inspection rounds, so Fiji remains on list two (Batty, pers. comm.). This means Fijian companies can export only to EU countries with which there are bilateral agreements to accept imports.

Government services

According to Solander managers, the licensing system operating in Fiji has been complex, with licences taking too long to come through, discouraging investment. There was low security of tenure with the annual licence process, which Solander managers felt made banks less willing to lend to fisheries businesses (Hufflett, pers. comm.). Solander managers also cited taxation rules on depreciation as discouraging investment in the tuna sector. Taxation relief for fisheries industries was complicated and had changed over time.

Fuel prices

Fuel prices were a major problem for longline companies around the globe, especially in 2004–05. In 2004, Fiji Fish could buy fuel for US$330 a metric tonne; in September 2005, the price was US$710 a metric tonne. In order to try to save on fuel costs, Fiji Fish was planning to add transport vessels to its fleet, to minimise the time spent by fishing vessels steaming to and from port.

Governing tuna industries

In 2002, the Ministry of Fisheries and Forestry established the Management Services Division within the Fisheries Department to manage Fiji's tuna fisheries. The division was run using the management fees of F$6,000 included in tuna-fishing licences (Government of Fiji 2002). With 60 licences, this budget amounted to $360,000 in 2005. The division has cost just slightly more than that to run (Turaganivalu, pers. comm.), with the shortfall being covered by the ministry's general budget. The division performed duties such as data collection and analysis, international fisheries negotiations, licensing, monitoring, control and surveillance, and administration of fisheries development policies and projects.

In the Tuna Management and Development Plan, it was intended that a National Fisheries Authority (NFA) along the lines of Australia's Fisheries Management Authority and Papua New Guinea's NFA be created. The Fijian NFA would be governed by a board of directors representing 'the major interests in the fishery' (Government of Fiji 2002). Its role would be to control the issuing, renewal and replacement of licences, to collect licence fees and to enforce regulations (with the navy and police). As of 2005, the plan for an NFA was still being considered by Cabinet.

Data on catches had been unreliable up to the time of the SPC tuna development strategy report, so the Tuna Management and Development Plan committed to improve accuracy of the database for the purpose of management decision making (Government of Fiji 2002). By 2005, the Ministry of Fisheries and Forests, in conjunction with the SPC, had greatly improved data collection and analysis for Fiji's tuna fisheries.

Interviewees identified a couple of areas where fisheries management could be improved through human resources development in the Fisheries Department. The department did not have a legal officer in 2005; it had been using legal expertise from the Fijian Attorney-General's office and from the FFA (Turaganivalu, pers. comm.). Some industry interviewees felt fisheries bureaucrats could benefit from training in principles of business management (Hufflett, pers. comm;Stone, pers. comm.).

Consultation between government and industry

Fiji's fishery managers were aware of the importance of consultation with industry and had developed the Tuna Management and Development Plan (with FFA and SPC input) with a schedule of consultations with tuna company managers. All industry players were consulted widely during the formation of the plan in 2001 (Turaganivalu, pers. comm.). Effective consultation, however, in which all stakeholders feel they have an active voice in decision-making processes, is difficult to achieve. Some tuna industry interviewees said that although they had been consulted on the plan, and in principle approved of it, they felt it was delivered to them as a government policy rather than as something they had had a real role in shaping, and therefore 'owned' (Lucas, pers. comm.).

There has been active industry–government consultation in the past few years. Fiji Fish's Grahame Southwick estimated that he spent about 80 per cent of his time doing 'fish politics' instead of running his business. Since 2002, industry players have been consulted through meetings more than once a year in order to set up management measures from available options under the legislative framework for the next licensing period. A meeting for offshore fisheries was held on 28 September 2005 to discuss the latest data on stock assessments nationally and regionally, licensing measures for 2006 and harmonisation of national management measures with any regional measures that might come out of the 2005 WCPFC meeting. The outcome of the meeting was that industry would form three working groups to come up with suggestions for three different issues affecting the Fijian longline fishery: criteria for licences for 2006, subsidies for fuel and a more flexible model of access fees based on profit rather than a flat fee—to make it easier for vessels to cover their costs during years of no profit (Turaganivalu, pers. comm.).

At the time of fieldwork in 2005, veteran local companies, Fiji Fish and Solander, were lobbying government to institute regulations to require companies operating with demise charters on foreign-owned vessels to present financial records showing the local company, *inter alia*, i) paid market rates for chartering the vessel/s, ii) was properly registered and approved by the relevant domestic authorities, iii) put all operational costs through a local bank, iv) complied with Reserve Bank of Fiji regulations, and v) was not managed by the vessel owner in any way (Southwick, pers. comm.).

One of the questions industry raised during the offshore fisheries meeting in September 2005 was what was being done with the management fees paid as part of tuna-fishing licences. Apparently, industry people had not visited the Management Services Division to be shown what was done there, and had not been shown the division's comprehensive annual report.

The biggest concern industry has had about government regards unregulated, increased investment in longline fisheries in the early 2000s. The major problem identified was that the licensing system approved by Cabinet in 1994 needed urgent redress. One of the issues was that senior officials were selling 'approval-in-principle' licences (options for companies to reserve licences before finding a vessel). Many more spaces were sold in 2001 than there were licences to issue (Turaganivalu, pers. comm.). The Tuna Management and Development Plan addressed shortfalls in the licensing regime and investigations into licensing problems were launched by Cabinet in 2003, first through the Public Service Commission, to assess the practices of Fisheries Department staff in terms of the Public Service code of ethics. One senior official was suspended and demoted. The police began criminal investigations in 2005.

Fees and licensing were regularised under the Tuna Management and Development Plan, and accountability was enforced by the Public Service Commission and criminal prosecution process, but some industry interviewees still felt that too many licences were being issued (Hufflett, pers. comm.; Southwick, pers. comm.). These interviewees also worried that recent generosity by the Chinese government in large public construction projects in Fiji might be linked to increased fisheries access by the growing Chinese fleet. The licence numbers had declined by 2005 for economic reasons without government intervention, but these industry interviewees wanted government limits imposed on the fishery as well.

Despite progress in enforcing accountability in fisheries management, industry interviewees still saw room for improvement in the governing of Fiji's tuna fisheries. According to Jean-Claude Guenegan of Bumble Bee, who worked at the Pafco plant in Levuka, 'politics gets in the way' of Fiji's tuna industry. He was referring to the 2000 coup, and also said that business was disrupted each time there were elections: 'Fiji has the resources to have really good tuna fisheries development but sometimes the government messes up the opportunities' (Guenegan, pers. comm.). One example he cited was the government rejecting offers from FCF Fishery and Japanese aid to fund slipway and fishing jetty infrastructure at Lautoka and Lami. He also referred to what he saw as overzealous enforcement of Institutional Strengthening Programs (ISPs) by Fijian officials. In September 2005, managers from Pafco's international partner, Bumble Bee, visited Fiji and said that government red tape, especially regarding ISPs, was threatening the economic viability of the Pafco plant and therefore all the jobs at Levuka. Bumble Bee representatives said Fiji was being stricter about compliance with security standards than even the United States, and since Pafco competed directly with Pago Pago these requirements were decreasing Pafco's competitiveness (Guenegan, pers. comm.).

Creating an enabling business environment

Some aspects of the Fijian government's approaches to tuna industries showed an interventionist tendency, such as the ideas for small-scale fisheries development in the Tuna Management and Development Plan, and the affirmative action indigenisation policies. On the whole, however, in most government approaches to Fiji's tuna industries, the aim was to provide infrastructure and an environment conducive to private-sector development.

Table 4.1   **Fiji: indicators of domestic development, 2001**

	Locally based vessels active	Cannery/loining facilities	Sashimi packing facilities	Fijian nationals jobs on vessels	Fijian nationals jobs on shore	Frozen tuna exports (mt)	Fresh tuna exports (mt)
Fiji Fish	23 LL	0	1	300	200	272	529
Solander	11 LL	0	0	109	33	416	1,037
Other companies	62 LL	1	4	459	407	820	1,970
Tosa Bussan	1 PL	0	1	25	56	74	94
Pafco	0	1	0	0	800	0	0
Total	96 LL 1 PL	2	6	893	1,496	1,582	3,630

Notes: mt: metric tonnes. LL: longline. PL: pole-and-line.
Source: Gillett, R., 2003. *Domestic tuna industry development in the Pacific islands. The current situation and considerations for future development assistance*, FFA Report 03/01, Pacific Islands Forum Fisheries Agency, Honiara, Solomon Islands.

Conclusion

The development of Fiji's domestic longlining industry has been a success story that emerged independently from the private sector (Tables 4.1 and 4.2). For a period, Fiji's longline fishery and related fresh-fish processing businesses were clearly financially viable, but they have been hit hard in recent years with falling CPUE and rising fuel prices. Service and supply industries for trans-shipping longline fleets and small-scale gourmet processing businesses were also clearly economically sustainable. While Pafco has required large inputs of government funding, it has at least provided jobs and human resource training opportunities for people outside Suva. The way in which the tuna industry has been used as a tool to address self-determination issues through affirmative action policies has been problematic, and has contributed to the downturn in the fishery. The most pressing issue for Fiji's tuna fisheries is to implement sound fisheries management, domestically and regionally through the WCPFC, to return economic viability to the longline industry. The next steps will be to improve training and infrastructure to support fisheries, service and supply, and processing industries. Bringing more indigenous Fijians into leadership and ownership roles is a long-term vision requiring a great deal of training and building experience in business management.

Development aspirations and tuna

The aspirations for tuna resources contained in interviews with Fijians and the various documents about tuna management and development examined for this report covered roughly three main areas: wealth generation, social and political issues, and ecological sustainability. This combination is evident in various expressions of the aims and objectives of the Tuna Management and Development Plan (Government of Fiji 2002), which are to

Table 4.2   Fiji: indicators of tuna development, 2004–2005

Company	Domestic vessels: no. and type	Processing facilities: no. and type	Jobs for nationals: no. and type	Annual exports: volume and type	Annual domestic sales: volume and type	Distant water: vessels no. and type
Solander Pacific	10 longline	1 ULT freezing machine (processing and packing contracted out)	~ 100 fleet ~ 30 shore base	1,263mt frozen whole tuna 424 mt chilled fresh fish	0	0
Pafco	0	1 cannery/loining plant	800 factory	cooked frozen loins using 30,000mt round fish inputs 38,000 cases of 48 cans	200,000 cases of 48 cans	0
Fiji Fish	40 longline 1 carrier	1 sashimi packing plant	370 fleet 150 shore base	most of 377mt bigeye and 18mt yellowfin exported chilled(some frozen); (some chilled) most of 2,236mt albacore exported frozen	10 per cent of frozen by-catch (2,747mt in 2003)sold locally	0
Tosa Bussan	1 pole-and-line	1 sashimi and tataki processing plant, including ULT facilities	25 vessel 70 shore base	1,200mt ULT skinless loins and tataki	0	0
Other companies	~ 10 longline 13 pole-and-line	3 sashimi packing plants	-	-	-	0
Stonefish	0	1 small-scale gourmet processing plant	-	cold smoked tuna, and billfish tuna jerky, tuna ham	Tuna jerky	0
Total:	~ 60 longline 14 pole-and-line 1 carrier	5 sashimi, 2 ULT 1 gourmet 1 cannery/loining	>1,500	Cans, loins, round whole chilled fish, round whole frozen fish, smoked and other processed fish	0	0

Notes: Apart from Tosa Bussan's local vessel, the other pole-and-line vessels active in Fiji were Japanese vessels using 'trip-based' licences in 2004. It was not clear whether these vessels also operated again in 2005. Fiji Fish's export figures are from 2003.

Sources: Interviews conducted September 2005. Amoe, J., 2005. *Fiji Tuna and Billfish Fisheries*, First Meeting of the Scientific Committee of the Western and Central Pacific Fisheries Commission, Noumea, New Caledonia. Government of Fiji, 2005. *MS–Offshore 2004 Annual Report*, Offshore Management Services Division, Fisheries Department, Suva, Fiji.

- develop for maximum utilisation of the resource 'without compromising the long-term economic, political and resource sustainability'
- establish what the sustainable limit of fishing effort is, set a sustainable catch limit, conserve and manage tuna resources
- distribute licences according to criteria that uphold government objectives, limit the number of licences issued and limit the TAC to optimise the returns to holders
- maximise economic returns by providing policy directions for government for development to increase economic gains from tuna fishing, recommending institutional changes that will increase revenue raised through licence fees, export and processing permits
- set licence fees to support management of the fishery and also provide benefits for all Fijians, have a 'fair' distribution of wealth from tuna industries
- establish a development program to address shortcomings in port facilities, legislation, training, social and gender issues and coordination across government agencies
- recommend institutional changes that will improve transparency and accountability, strengthen fisheries institutions, improve public confidence in tuna management and development
- have a well-trained industry.

Some of the kinds of development envisaged as helping to achieve these aims and objectives included

- continuation of the domestic longline fleet
- assistance to indigenous Fijians to become vessel owners
- further development of Suva as a longline trans-shipment port through improving service industries for fishing vessels
- promotion of tuna developments in the outer islands
- training for captains, engineers and other crew, training for processing employees and business training for indigenous resource owners
- staff development for the Fisheries Department (Government of Fiji 2002).

Wealth generation for the domestic economy

Most of the aspirations expressed regarding tuna resources in Fiji centred on the aim of capturing more wealth.

Licence fees. Fiji's domestication policy banned distant water fleets, so distant water access fees were not a factor in the equation in Fiji, apart from small amounts paid retrospectively by the Japanese fleet when it strayed over the EEZ boundary. Domestic licence fees, however, were divided into a management fee, paid by all licensees, and an access fee, paid by all non-indigenous Fijian licence-holders. The management fees largely supported the Management Services Unit while the access fees went into consolidated revenue. Licence fees were thus a handy source of revenue, but were not nearly as significant an economic contribution in Fiji as in countries such as Kiribati. On the whole, capturing more wealth in the Fijian economy was about the domestic private sector generating economic activity.

Trans-shipping, ports and service industries. At the time of interview in September 2005, the government's strategy for making the most of the region's tuna resources was to develop Fiji as a hub for the regional longline industry. The Tuna Management and Development Plan targeted service industries as an area for further development through provision of processing licences to foreign companies that offload their catch in Suva, and through building a larger slipway to attract more vessels to be repaired in Suva (Government of Fiji 2002). It was also proposed that the government could tie trans-shipping access to the supply of reliable records of catch, and to employ Fijians as crew members, to allow vessels to set up a base of operations in Fiji without being licensed to fish in the Fijian EEZ (Government of Fiji 2002).

This strategy had been in place since 2000, but had not progressed due to local opposition to fisheries wharf developments in the planned areas (Lami and Lautoka). In addition, industry interviewees said there was not the full range of the necessary trades and skills for service industries available in Suva (Hufflett, pers. comm.). So, although the Fisheries Department had continued to address the needs of the service industries in meetings with other relevant government agencies for five years, there was still some way to go before the government fully realised aspirations to develop Fiji as a hub for the region's longline fleets (Turaganivalu, pers. comm.).

Processing. Aspirations regarding processing included maintaining the Pafco plant and trying to encourage indigenous Fijians to invest in processing businesses, including a long-term plan that 50 per cent of processing licences would go to indigenous Fijians. Development aspirations were generally focused more on indigenously owned fisheries development and ports infrastructure than on processing. When asked whether the Fisheries Department saw small-scale value adding as a direction to pursue, the reply was that this market was a small niche market, not as reliable or large as the sashimi market.

Human resources and training. The government intended to improve training facilities and programs to increase the numbers of Fijian skippers and engineers (Government of Fiji 2002).

Solander managers felt that local welding skills were very good, but in other areas there were not enough proficient local tradespeople. They felt that the Fijian government would have to either improve training or loosen immigration requirements, so that tradespeople could be brought in until the local pool of skills increased. At the time of interview, the government had no plan to employ foreigners to fill gaps in skills, or to target training of locals (Turaganivalu, pers. comm.).

Solander managers also felt that Fiji should have more post-harvest expertise (Hufflett, pers. comm.). They pointed out that Fiji was a major producer in the region—yet there was not one seafood industry food technologist. Solander sent its employees to the USP HACCP course and found it useful, but said they would like more coordination between that course and the various post-harvest courses offered under aid schemes, and also that a wider range of courses and more places would be helpful (Hufflett, pers. comm.; Lucas, pers. comm.).

Public-sector human resources were identified by the government as in need of improvement through 'institutional strengthening'. This was specifically with regard to environmental and fisheries science, training for observers and port samplers, and implementing a comprehensive logsheet and landings data collection scheme (Government of Fiji 2002).

The Tuna Management and Development Plan recognised the need for business training as well as fisheries training for success in owning and managing businesses, as did private sector managers.

Social and political issues

The 2000 coup damaged tuna industries for a period. Fall-off in tourist flights meant lack of freight capacity for sashimi exports. The Pafco cannery was occupied by militants, which nearly caused Bumble Bee to pull out of Fiji (Navuetaki c.2002). Fiji had largely recovered economically and in terms of government administration by 2005. A legacy of the coup is visible in government policies for affirmative action to encourage greater participation by indigenous Fijians in ownership of tuna businesses.

While ethnic issues dominated aspirations regarding social and political aspects of the future of tuna industries, there were also aspirations expressed about minimising social impacts more generally. The Tuna Management and Development Plan included a social impacts fund to be created from a portion of the access fees charged to the industry. The government also hoped to improve social and political problems in relation to tuna fisheries through greater consultation in decision making. A Social Consultative Committee was to examine regularly social impacts from the industry (specifically alcohol abuse and STIs) and distribute the social impacts fund accordingly. In addition, a training module was to be implemented for seafarers and their families to try to reduce the negative impacts on communities from tuna industries. Government recognised the need for more public awareness of fisheries and intended to address this through school curricula (Government of Fiji 2002).

Outer-islands tuna development

Fiji's aspirations for tuna development included distribution of opportunities and benefits from tuna industries in rural and remote areas. The Tuna Management and Development Plan included a FAD program for rural communities including technical assistance from the SPC, data collection systems and the building of three fisheries centres. Local fishers were to be subsidised to buy skiffs, outboard motors and fishing equipment. Fisheries training modules were to include money management, small business principles and community and family responsibilities in fisheries. A local business training institute was to devise these courses in conjunction with the SPC (Government of Fiji 2002). Pafco employed a Public Relations Officer to assist local communities to develop spin-off businesses to take advantage of the opportunities created by Pafco's operations on Ovalau (Navuetaki, pers. comm.).

Indigenisation

There were strong aspirations for indigenous Fijians to become leaders as well as employees in tuna industries. These aspirations focused largely on vessel ownership. Aspirations for greater participation by indigenous Fijians as reflected in the plan and in interviewees' comments equated vessel ownership with 'real' participation in the industry. Behind this idea is the desire to have the power and status of leadership in the sector. The main affirmative action mechanism to encourage indigenous Fijians to become owners of businesses in the tuna plan was the SCARF program's interest-free loans as seed funding to help indigenous Fijians and Rotumans become owners of vessels.

One problem with government policies aiming to have indigenous Fijians own medium-scale longlining businesses was that these businesses were costly, and therefore risky, and the marketing and trading involved was financially complex.

Going from a position of very little training, experience or knowledge in business management straight into ownership is fraught with risk. Robert Stone felt that the affirmative action policies were problematic in giving people money to own boats before they learned how to run a business.

Gender

Gender issues were raised as one of the social factors to be considered in aspirations for Fiji's tuna industries in the Tuna Management and Development Plan. Women bear the brunt of domestic violence from men's employment in fishing fleets, and the worst effects of social dislocation from prostitution occurring around fleets.[8] Women's groups were some of the stakeholders consulted in generating the plan (Government of Fiji 2002). A Social Consultative Committee comprising women's and community groups was to be set up to distribute money from the social impact fund. The plan stipulated that information concerning opportunities in the fisheries sector was to be made available to 'young people and women in rural areas' (Government of Fiji 2002), and the ministry was to be 'proactive in recruiting and promoting women employed with the [Fisheries] Division, and ensuring that women are not only confined to office and secretarial duties' (Government of Fiji 2002).

Women made up a large proportion of the workforce in the Management Services Unit, not only in secretarial positions. Women were administering the data collection system TUFMANA and a woman was the acting CEO of the Department of Fisheries at the time of fieldwork in September 2005. Women made up a large proportion of office staff in the private sector too, as well as the bulk of the workforce at the Levuka Pafco plant and tuna-processing facilities in Suva. Agape Fisheries Limited had a woman CEO Betty Wong. However men tend to hold most senior management positions in the public and private sector.

Ecological sustainability

The Fijian government has given thought to ways in which the Tuna Management and Development Plan would ensure ecological sustainability. For example, environmental groups' concerns about by-catch of other species were to be addressed through the observer program (Government of Fiji 2002). The Implementation Schedule of Activity linked sustainability to activities and responsibilities such as the setting of quotas, creation of reliable catch and by-catch databases, setting TAC limits according to stock assessment, and recommendations for mitigating environmental problems caused by fishing (Government of Fiji 2002). A commitment to resource management was manifest in improved data collection from logsheets, observer coverage and port sampling. Nevertheless, some industry interviewees still felt in 2005 that Fiji's fisheries management was not protecting the resources properly and that fishing effort (licences) needed to be reduced even further (Southwick, pers. comm.; Hufflett, pers. comm.). Some of the aspirations for improved management of Fiji's tuna resources included greater transparency and accountability, improved public confidence in Fiji's fisheries management, as well as improved effectiveness of government policies.

Recommendations

Despite having less rich tuna resources than some of the other Pacific island countries in this study, Fiji has greater opportunities and fewer constraints on developing industries to generate wealth from tuna because it has more infrastructure, and because its economy and society are more capitalistic.

Although licensing was subject to corruption in 2001–03, the fact that accountability was then imposed by the public service and justice systems at the insistence of the private sector showed that governance in Fiji was healthier than in many other Pacific island countries. In respect of governance, it is important for Fiji to

- maintain high levels of transparency and accountability for fisheries management and development decisions
- keep working on consultation with industry, and streamlining bureaucratic processes
- show industry what is being achieved with its management fees, for example, by the Management Services Division offering *ad hoc* tours for industry members and adapting the internal annual fisheries report for external use, thereby disseminating information about the fishery and its management to interested members of the public as well as industry.

Fiji's ethnic affirmative action policies have thus far not worked well in terms of facilitating indigenous Fijians' leadership in the sector through ownership of businesses. Indigenous vessel owners are struggling financially, and foreign investors have used the SCARF program to enter the Fijian fishery. To address this, it is suggested that

- potential investors be made aware that it is difficult for people with little business experience to be successful in their first attempt
- inappropriate and ill-advised indigenous investment be discouraged to reduce the impact of business failures

- as an alternative to subsidising vessel ownership through large up-front loans, promote a step-wise scheme to enable interested indigenous Fijians to gain training and experience in business management and/or in owning smaller fishing businesses before moving onto tuna enterprises requiring large loans
- consideration be given to tying licences to apprenticeship and training schemes for indigenous Fijians in financial and management aspects of business, and sponsoring indigenous Fijians to undertake tertiary business education combined with internship-style training in tuna businesses.

All the indicators suggest that the fishing end of the business has been increasingly competitive and decreasingly profitable in recent years, especially in the longline industry. Linking aspirations for indigenous participation and wealth generation only to vessel ownership, therefore, could be misguided. It might be better to

- give a range of tuna-related businesses equal weight with vessel ownership, such as service industries, marketing/trading and processing
- recognise that since most seafood trading and marketing occurs in centres such as Bangkok, Tokyo and Manila, consider sending trainees overseas for work experience, as well as tertiary education in business studies and training in Asian languages
- consider the employment of women as well as men in marketing, trading and processing.

To encourage trans-shipping and the accompanying service industries, wharf facilities in Suva need to be improved. The following measures would encourage the use of Suva as a major trans-shipping and service port and minimise adverse impacts

- survey vessel owners about what would affect their choice to use Suva for maintenance work and whether there are sufficient tradespeople available
- if adequate skilled labour is not available, consider an immigration scheme to import tradespeople in the short term and a training scheme to increase the supply of Fijian tradespeople in the medium term
- deal with the social impacts that come with a trans-shipment port by developing the particular kinds of health and welfare services needed to deal with STIs, gender-based violence, social dislocation of women involved in prostitution, substance abuse and physical and mental health care of fishing crews.

Fiji's large tourist industry has been helpful in creating conditions that facilitate tuna development. To nurture these synergies, consider the following

- having representatives from the tourism and fisheries sectors participate in decision making, for example, future upgrades in planes for tourists should take into consideration any potential impacts on cargo space when selecting planes
- collaborate on expanding training for food safety and hygiene, since the tourism industry also needs employees to be able to handle food safely.

Notes

[1] For further information on the Fijian economy, see 'Fiji' (ADB 2005a; ADB 2005b).

[2] SPC scientist Adam Langley said the drop in CPUE for albacore in 2003 was likely to have been caused by oceanographic effects, as the CPUE increased again in 2004 without a reduction in fishing mortality (Langley 2005).

[3] As of 2005, China still did not have a 'Head Agreement' between governments in the Pacific; fishing access was negotiated between locally based agents and relevant Pacific island government authorities (McCoy and Gillett 2005).

[4] For information on cost structures for the Chinese fleet, see McCoy and Gillett 2005.

[5] According to Robert Gillett (pers. comm.), however, many of the Chinese vessels based in Suva have not reflagged as Fijian vessels.

[6] In 2003, the number of licences reserved for indigenous Fijians was increased to 25 (plus 70 in the 'Open' category and 15 for processing companies). In 2004, the Cabinet revised the categories of licences to just two: 'Open' and 'Indigenous', to be apportioned in the ratio 54:46 (Turaganivalu, pers. comm.).

[7] Available from http://forum.europa.eu.int/irc/sanco/vets/info/data/listes/ffp.html, accessed May 2006.

[8] For further perspectives on the effects on women of economic development in Fiji, including from tuna industries, see Emberson-Bain 1994.

5

Kiribati

Population: 93,100
Land area: 811 km²
Sea area: 3,550,000 km²

Kiribati is made up of 33 main islands in three groups: the Gilbert Group, the Phoenix Group and the Line Islands. Along with what is now Tuvalu, these islands were part of the British colonial territory Gilbert and Ellice Islands. The Gilbert, Phoenix and Line Islands groups are spread across 5,000km of the Pacific Ocean from just east of Nauru to south of Hawai'i, separated by stretches of international waters and the Exclusive Economic Zones (EEZs) of other countries. The ratio of land to water surface area in Kiribati is 1:4,377. Most of the islands are low lying, about one metre above sea level, with limited possibilities for agriculture and no topographically generated precipitation. Fresh water comes from groundwater lenses and captured rainwater. Kiribati's geography means a limited range of land-based economic activity is possible. Money from phosphate mining in the colonial period was put into a trust fund, which now produces dividends to contribute to Kiribati's revenue. Apart from that, overseas aid and distant water fisheries access make up the bulk of government revenue, with small amounts being contributed by other schemes such as the sale of passports.

Potential of tuna fisheries

Kiribati's tuna resources are excellent, with a huge EEZ containing some of the richest skipjack fishing areas in the region. Longline fishing is good around the Line Islands in the east. The small size of Kiribati's economy, however, its distance from major trade routes and shortages of land and fresh water probably mean that shore-based processing developments will be so high cost as to be uncompetitive.

History of development

In the 1960s and early 1970s, Japanese, Taiwanese and Korean distant water longline and pole-and-line fleets operated in what is now Kiribati's EEZ. They fished year round and caught between 1,000 and 25,000 metric tonnes annually (Chapman 2003). When Kiribati

Map 5.1   Kiribati

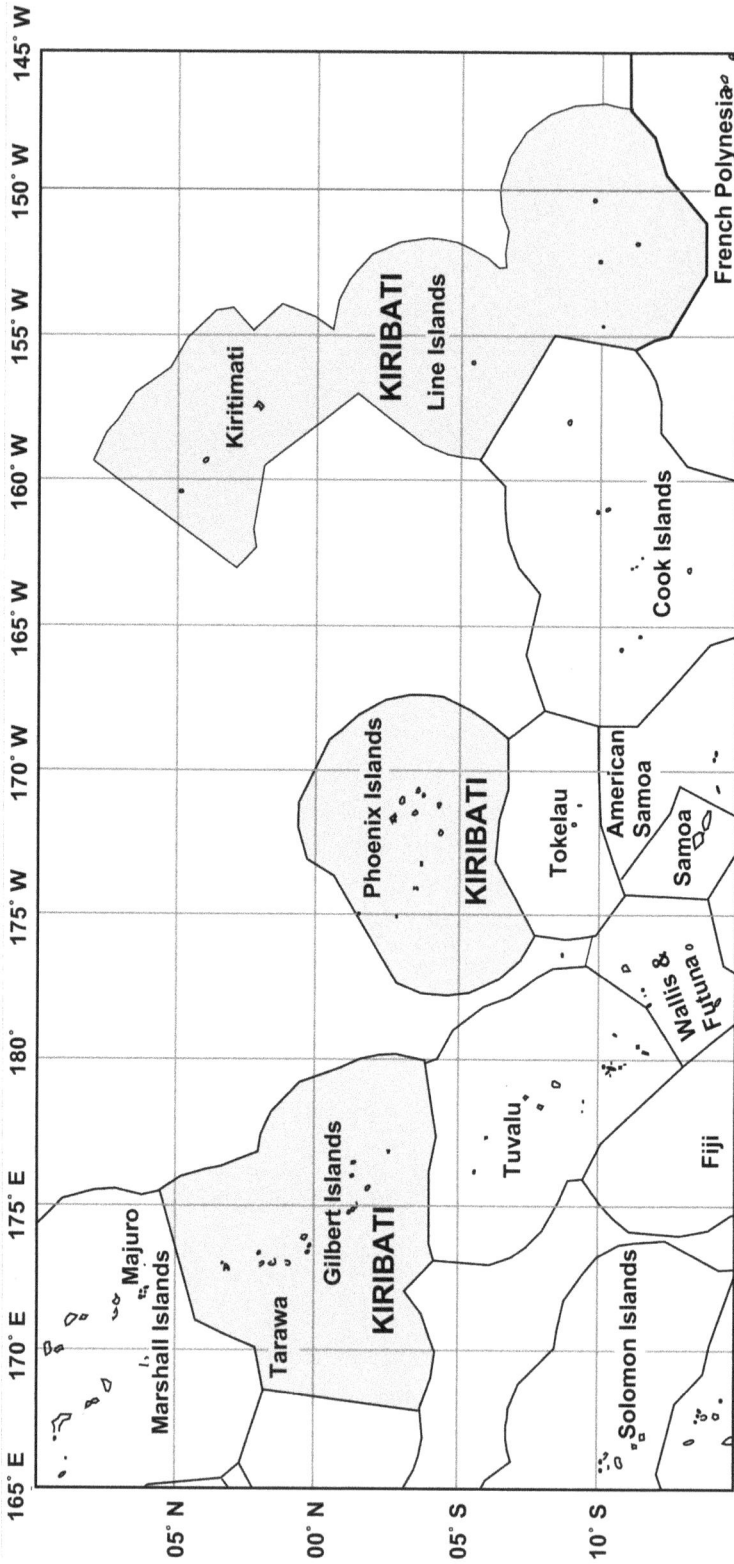

Source: Youngmi Choi, Secretariat of the Pacific Community, Noumea, New Caledonia.

declared its EEZ in 1978, it was therefore known that the huge area of ocean had great potential for development of tuna industries. Distant water fleets remained active in Kiribati waters after independence and the total amount of access fees they paid increased to make up one-third or more of the government's annual revenue. Tuna fees replaced the money from phosphate mining, which had been the country's economic mainstay (Tables 5.1 and 5.2).

In order to establish a locally based fishery, several fishing and bait-fishing surveys were conducted during the 1970s by a range of organisations, including the Teikaraoi Fishing Company, the Secretariat of the Pacific Community (SPC), Japanese fishing companies and the Japan International Cooperation Agency (JICA). All of these surveys reported problems securing an adequate supply of bait (Rawlinson et al. 1992; Chapman 2003). Bait fish have been supplied by a long-running milkfish aquaculture pond system near the airport on Tarawa (Chapman 2003), but have not been used consistently for industrial tuna fishing.

Te Mautari, a government-owned company that began in pole-and-line fishing in 1979, had the first cold stores, blast freezer and ice machines in Kiribati. These were built in 1981 when the aim was to produce frozen tuna for export to canneries. Japanese aid funded an extension to the facility in 1984 and a further upgrade in 1989 at the same time as the building of a jetty complex. In 1988, the US government provided a new office complex for Te Mautari. The cold stores were refurbished with Japanese aid in 1992–93, then fell into disuse. Another round of Japanese aid refurbished the facilities again (1999–2003), this time reorienting them for fresh fish for the local market and export in conjunction with the Outer Islands Fisheries Program (Chapman 2003).

Table 5.1   **Kiribati: indicators of domestic development, 2001**

	Locally based vessels active	Cannery/ loining facilities	Sashimi packing and other value-adding facilities	Kiribati nationals jobs on vessels	Kiribati nationals jobs on shore	Frozen tuna exports (mt)	Fresh tuna exports (mt)	Processed exports (mt)
Central Pacific producers Fisheries	1 LL	0	1	15	40	0	-	0
Division	1 LL	0	0	4	-	0	-	0
Kao	1 PS	0	0	0	-	0	-	0
Teikabuti	-	0	1	0	8	0	-	0.6 (jerky)
Total	2 LL 1 PS	0	2	19	48	0	-	0.6 (jerky)

Notes: LL: longline; PS: purse-seine
Source: Gillett, R., 2003. *Domestic tuna industry development in the Pacific islands. The current situation and considerations for future development assistance*, FFA Report 03/01, Pacific Islands Forum Fisheries Agency, Honiara, Solomon Islands:176-77.

Table 5.2   **Kiribati: distant water fleets (2005) and catches (2004)**

Flag country	Purse-seine vessels	Longline vessels	Purse-seine catch (mt)	Longline catch (mt)
China	6	0	0	0
Spain	4	5	625	-
Federated States of Micronesia	1	0	689	-
Japan	34	7	4,169	685
Korea	26	121	750	5,029
New Zealand	1	0	4,869	-
Philippines	1	0	0	-
Taiwan	18	27	17,394	559
United States of America	2	0	19,299	-
Vanuatu	6	2	-	-
Totals	99	162	47,795	6,273

Source: Riinga, T., 2005. Kiribati fisheries report, First Meeting of the Scientific Committee of the Western and Central Pacific Fisheries Commission, Noumea, New Caledonia.

In 2001, a Cabinet decision consolidated the three government-owned fisheries companies—Te Mautari, Kiritimati Marine Exports Limited (KMEL) and the Outer Islands Fisheries Project (OIFP)—into Central Pacific Producers Limited (CPP). Te Mautari's office, jetty facilities and cold store became CPP's main base. When CPP started, the company took on all the staff from the previous companies, totalling 104, including fishers from Te Mautari, which by then had no functioning fishing vessels (CPP c.2003). In the next few years these fishers were relocated when CPP's agency business found them jobs on distant water fleets (Onorio, pers. comm.). Te Mautari's carrier vessel, the *Moamoa*, had been chartered to foreign fleets to use as a mothership to take their fish to canneries at Pago Pago and Levuka. CPP decided this was not a good use of the vessel so brought it back to Tarawa, where it was used mainly for carrying reefer and dry cargo and fuel between Tarawa, Majuro and Kiritimati. There was a shortage of cargo freight between the islands so this was quite a lucrative business for CPP.

Pole-and-line

The government-owned Te Mautari Limited started off with two pole-and-line vessels, one donated in 1979 by the United Kingdom (the *Nei Manganibuka*) and one by Japan in 1980 (the *Nei Arintetongo*). In 1983, Te Mautari acquired two new pole-and-line vessels, the *Nei Kaneati* and the *Nei Tiaroa*. In 1987, it was given two more vessels built in Fiji, funded by the European Economic Commission. By 1988, one of the first two vessels was decommissioned due to increasing maintenance costs as the vessel aged. The second of the first two vessels followed suit in 1990, bringing the fleet back to four vessels. Te Mautari's catch rates fluctuated from a low of 434mt with four vessels in 1987, to a high of 2,273mt with five vessels in 1989. Te Mautari exported frozen fish by container to Hawai'i via

Marshall Islands. In 1990, the company attempted to fish from Solomon Islands, but it lost money, leading to a suspension of operations. Fishing restarted with three vessels and continued until 1992–93. Difficulties with transporting the catch to market and storage capacity limited the company's production rates, as did persistent maintenance problems (Chapman 2003). On top of this, prices for the main catch, skipjack, were declining, from $1,000 per metric tonne when the company started to a low of $600/mt in the 1990s. Te Mautari's fleet dwindled to nothing by the early 2000s, when the remaining two vessels sank at the wharf.

Longline

One of the options investigated for Kiribati's tuna industry development potential was the development of a small to medium-scale domestic longline fishery. A vessel that was suitable for local conditions and which could be constructed and repaired locally was developed by UN Food and Agriculture Organisation (FAO) designer Oyvind Gulbrandsen and built by FAO boat-builder Mike Savins at Betiraoi Boatbuilding in Betio, with technical assistance from the SPC, under a Japanese aid program in the late 1990s (Beverly 2004). Based roughly on an outrigger canoe style, with a platform joining the two hulls, this multipurpose vessel was trialled for longlining. It was about 13 metres long and supported a crew of up to eight. The *Tekokona* vessels cost about $150,000 to build, so they were considered feasible in terms of price and catching capacity for small-scale fishing. Joe Stanley, an FAO consultant who had been working on the review of CPP, was investigating Samoa's super-*alia* model as another possibility (Onorio, pers. comm.).

The Fisheries Division periodically used *Tekokona II* for trial fishing and training in longlining methods around Tarawa. Staff said that apart from continuing problems with the hydraulics for the reel, the vessel was good for fishing (Temwaang, pers. comm.). There were no established market routes to export longline product to sashimi markets, so the trials were not seriously aiming at developing an export fishery around Tarawa. The catch was distributed to staff or sold to CPP (Tioti, pers. comm.). In 2005, there was no solution to the problem of market access for Kiribati sashimi exports (Tioti, pers. comm.).

One purpose the *Tekokona II* trials were fulfilling was to give locals who thought they would like to work on distant water vessels some training. This training, in conjunction with the International Maritime Organisation (IMO) accredited Standards for the Training and Certification of Watchkeepers (STCW) safety course offered through the Maritime Training Centre, meant they could be employed by distant water vessels. The Fisheries Training Centre trained crew specifically for the Japanese fleet and had quite high educational requirements (high school graduate), so the Fisheries Division training was aimed at village fishermen who had not finished school and who might work on the Korean or Taiwanese fleets (Tioti, pers. comm.).

Though the *Tekokona II* had various structural limitations, many of these problems were fixed in the *Tekokona III* (Chapman 2003). In 2005, the *Tekokona III* was being used by CPP in Kiritimati for fishing trials and training. It was intended that the *Tekokona III* would be in commercial use for export markets by then (Beverly 2004), but the lack of reliable airfreight—among other problems, such as a lack of trained and experienced skippers and engineers (Chapman 2003)—meant that an export-oriented commercial longline fishery had not yet taken off in Kiritimati.

Kiritimati seemed the logical place to have a tuna industry because it was relatively close to the market in Hawai'i. Unfortunately, the small population (about 3,000) and its distance from any other population centre meant it was a difficult location from which to run a longline fishery.

Ministry of Fisheries and Marine Resource Development (hereafter referred to as the Ministry of Fisheries) official David Yeeting spent six years in the 1990s based in Kiritimati working for CPP's predecessor, KMEL. During that time he saw many privately owned Hawaiian medium-scale fishing vessels come through Kiritimati and it made him wonder how Kiribati could develop the same kind of industry. He also thought Kiribati could learn from the Maldives experience in small-scale longline fishing.[1] Yeeting also wanted to learn from innovations in small-scale tuna longlining he had heard about in the Philippines. He was confident that the *Tekokona* type of vessel could work in future when the fishery was ready to expand (Yeeting, pers. comm.).

Since Kiritimati is close to Hawai'i, and is known in Hawai'i as a good place for fish, it always seemed that Kiritimati would be the natural location for fisheries exports, but the lack of freight capacity is a major inhibitor. Aloha Air was chartered by the Kiribati government for flights between Kiritimati and Honolulu during the late 1980s and 1990s. The main customer for these flights was a Japanese satellite program. The flights used a Boeing 727, a DC8 and a Boeing 727 Combi that was split between passengers and cargo. These planes were useful for exporting fish and, for several years, the government-owned KMEL was making good money sending a substantial tonnage of chilled reef fish, crayfish and occasionally tuna to Honolulu. The priorities and budget of the Japanese space program changed in the mid 1990s and the flights became less reliable. There were no flights for a while, then the route used a Lear jet, with no significant space for cargo. Eventually, the terms of the contract with Aloha were renegotiated and a 737 was used again, but under the new terms various businesspeople on Kiritimati were competing for cargo space and things went badly for KMEL. In 2002, there were plans for an Air Pacific flight from Nadi to Honolulu stopping at Kiritimati (Chapman 2003), but that route did not become established until October 2005. With the new flight, there was hope that fisheries export businesses in Kiritimati would revive.

Infrequent sea freight runs meant it was difficult and expensive to buy any supplies in Kiritimati. All sea freight had been going via Tarawa. Goods were expensive to begin with in Tarawa because of its remoteness and the lack of an economy of scale. Once goods spent another couple of weeks being shipped from Tarawa to Kiritimati, they became prohibitively expensive (Onorio, pers. comm.). CPP began using the *Moamoa* for cargo runs between Kiritimati and Tarawa to supply the Kiritimati CPP fishing base and earn income with paid cargo. Kiritimati is much closer to Hawai'i than to Tarawa, so it would make sense to have sea freight runs between Kiritimati and Honolulu. For a longline industry Kiritimati really needed a dedicated freight run, so CPP was working with the

Ministry of Communications and Transport to have a regular sea freight connection to Honolulu established (Onorio, pers. comm.).

Another reason why the Kiritimati longline operation had not started by 2005 was that the fishing system was still not fully developed. *Tekokona III* was an improvement on *Tekokona II* but the model still needed work (Onorio, pers. comm.; Beverly 2004). It was not yet clear whether the tuna resources around Kiritimati Islands were suitable. From SPC records, it seems that foreign longline vessels operate north and south of the Kiritimati area because Kiritimati itself is in a fishing 'shadow'. If this is so, CPP vessels would need to steam further south or north to fish on more productive grounds. The *Tekokona* vessels might not be large enough to make trips of that length (Onorio, pers. comm.; Beverly 2004).

Purse-seine

Kiribati has never had a locally based purse-seine fishery. Purse-seine activity by the distant water fleet expanded greatly in 1990 and has stayed high since then, reaching more than 250,000mt in 2001 (Government of Kiribati 2003). In 1994, the Kiribati government signed a joint venture with the Japanese Kao Fishing company to own a purse-seine vessel, which was flagged in Kiribati but fished in Kiribati's EEZ only occasionally (Chapman 2003). For the first four to five years, the Kao vessel went well and was profitable. Then the profitability declined. Since 2002, the Kiribati Government has had difficultly maintaining contact with its Japanese counterpart.

Distant water fleets

Before independence, fleets from several different countries had fished the waters around the groups of islands that became Kiribati. After 1978, they had to negotiate access to the EEZ as distant water fishing states. Japan was the first country to do this, with a two-year agreement in 1978–80 to pay US$600,000 for several pole-and-line and longline vessels. In 1979, Korea signed a contract for US$185,000 for several longline vessels to catch up to a certain daily limit for one year. Japan did not renew the access agreement in 1980 because it wanted to reduce the fee and Kiribati refused. Fisheries aid from Japan also stopped for a year, then in late 1981 a new fisheries agreement and bilateral aid program was negotiated. In 1984–85, fleets from Japan, Korea, the United States and the Soviet Union worked the Kiribati EEZ, paying combined access fees of US$4 million. The core of the distant water fleet operating in Kiribati's EEZ in the late 1980s and early 1990s was Japan, Korea, and the United States. Total access fees rose to A$12.3 million in 1991 and $12.9 million in 1992, largely because of increased US purse-seine activity in Kiribati waters under the US multilateral treaty. In 2001, access fees reached A$47 million (Government of Kiribati c.2003). Taiwanese purse-seiners made up an increasingly large proportion of the distant water fleet from the mid 1990s, with the Korean proportion also expanding, and the Japanese proportion shrinking. The main problem with distant water access fees as a contribution to government revenue was the volatility due to oceanographic climate cycles reducing catches significantly every few years.

In 2000 and 2001, eight and 11 purse-seine vessels, respectively, from a Spanish company joined the distant water fleet licensed to operate in Kiribati (Chapman 2003). The vessels mostly did not fish in the Kiribati EEZ. Some of the vessels were flagged in Latin American countries. Other Pacific island countries were annoyed that Kiribati licensed these vessels because the Pacific island countries had agreed as a group not to license any vessels from the European Union until further negotiations for a partnership agreement were completed.[2] After the partnership agreement was signed, Spanish vessels could fish in Kiribati as part of the EU fleet, but the vessels owned by the Spanish company flagged outside the European Union could not. In 2005, there were four purse-seine vessels and five longline vessels from the European Union licensed to fish by Kiribati (Tumoa, pers. comm.).

Kiribati received generous amounts of aid from Japan as a distant water fishing state, and in recent years also from Taiwan. Additionally, distant water companies agreed to employ a certain number of Kiribati nationals on their vessels.

I-Kiribati crews

Kiribati was unusual among Pacific island countries in that it trained and recruited I-Kiribati to work on foreign fleets. This started as an offshoot from the Maritime Training Centre (MTC), which had trained and recruited I-Kiribati for the German merchant marine since the 1960s (Hughes, pers. comm.). The industry organisation Japan Tuna noted the positive effects of the MTC on employment for I-Kiribati, and was also looking for a source of cheaper crews, so decided to set up something similar for training fishers. This became the Fisheries Training Centre (FTC), established in 1989.

In 2005, there were about 325 I-Kiribati crew contracted to the Japanese fleet, and 100–200 more contracted to the Korean and Taiwanese fleets (Bauro, pers. comm.; Tekaata, pers. comm.). Remittances from seamen including fishermen were listed along with dividends from the government's reserve fund (the trust fund from phosphate mining in previous decades), EEZ fishery access fees and sales of passports to foreigners as 'crucially underpin[ning] current levels of public and private disposable income, which in turn yield domestic tax revenues' (Government of Kiribati c.2003).

At the FTC, Japan Tuna funded the salaries of two Japanese instructors, two local instructors and the costs of running the longline training vessel, *Tiakawa*, including the crew (Bauro, pers. comm.). Japan Tuna channelled resources for the FTC and recruited graduates from its fleet via a business called the Kiribati Fisherman's Service, with an office in Bairiki also staffed and funded by Japan Tuna (Bauro, pers. comm.). The FTC was under government obligation to train at least 72 young men between the ages of 18 and 30 each year, and usually trained only this many because Japan Tuna paid for the training and did not want to train more crew than it needed. As a result, all of the trainees had a job to go to on graduation and the course was popular among young Kiribati men because of chronic unemployment problems in Tarawa (Kabure, pers. comm.).

The FTC conducted two courses a year, each with 36 trainees, which lasted between eight and nine months. Usually about one-third of each cohort left before graduation. The college then ran a second round of recruitment for a special fast-track, intensive course for replacement trainees, so that the right number would graduate on time ready to work on the Japanese fleet. The economic contribution made by this opportunity for I-Kiribati to work on the Japanese fleet was significant. About 325 I-Kiribati were employed on the Japanese fleet in 2004 and earned a total of A$1,695,230 for the year (an average of $5,281 per person). A similar number were employed in 2005 (Kabure, pers. comm.).

The business of providing crew for foreign fishing fleets was becoming more and more competitive. Kiribati fishermen competed against Indonesian and Vietnamese fishermen on Japan's distant water tuna fleets, and there was talk that China would also like to start supplying crews for the Japanese fleet (Bauro, pers. comm.). In the distant water fleet as a whole there was also competition from Filipinos and Taiwanese (Kabure, pers. comm.). In light of this, it was important that Kiribati crew proved themselves as productive as crews from any other country.

Working on distant water vessels bought economic benefits, however, the scheme also entailed some social costs. Crews were away from home most of the year, returning for perhaps only one or two weeks (a normal holiday length for Japan). This was hard for single men, but for married men it was particularly difficult. There were sometimes problems with wives of crew working on foreign vessels leaving their husbands because of their long periods of absence (Bauro, pers. comm.). Some crew also developed long-term alcohol abuse problems, or picked up a sexually transmitted infection (STI) from sexual liaisons overseas, both of which caused marital problems at home.

The Japanese tuna fleet was in severe economic trouble by the mid 2000s and needed to maximise productivity while keeping costs down. In the past decade, the Kiribati Fisherman's Service had to redeploy crew from at least three Japanese vessels that went bankrupt (Bauro, pers. comm.). Another new direction was that Japan Tuna was organising with the FTC and the Kiribati Fisherman's Service to train and recruit officers. Until 2005, they had only ever recruited ordinary crew from Kiribati. This move was probably a response to declining interest in going to sea among young Japanese, as well as the prohibitive cost of employing Japanese crew, and meant a significant increase in the type of opportunity the FTC could offer young Kiritbati men (Bauro, pers. comm.; Kabure, pers. comm.).

In 2005, CPP was recruiting Kiribati fishermen to work on foreign fleets other than the Japanese fleet (served exclusively by the Kiribati Fisherman's Service). In the past, CPP had supplied crew to fleets from Korea and New Zealand, and British fleets operating from Africa. In 2005, for the first time, they supplied 60 fishermen to the Taiwanese tuna-boat owners' association. Negotiations were almost complete in October 2005, with some of the Kiribati fishermen having signed their contracts while another group was holding out for better pay.

The FTC was thinking about expanding its operations, for example, into training crew for the Taiwanese distant water fleet. It was hoped that they could be trained along with the Japanese crew, but this plan had yet to be confirmed with Japan Tuna, which funded the FTC. Japan Tuna was apparently happy for the FTC to be used to train recruits for other distant water fleets, as long as Japan Tuna resources were used only to train students that worked on its fleet (Bauro, pers. comm.).

Bait fishery

Consistent findings from fishing trials that bait-fish stocks were insufficient to support a pole-and-line commercial tuna fishery in Kiribati led to the establishment of a bait-fish project funded by the United Kingdom and implemented by the FAO and the UN Development Program in 1971. This pilot project led to the establishment of the Temaiku fish farm on Tarawa in 1975, also funded by the United Kingdom. The ponds used milkfish, some of which were purchased as fry, and some of which were recruited naturally. Since pole-and-line fishing under Te Mautari did not develop to a point where it needed large amounts of bait fish on a continuing basis, the ponds also produced fish as food for the local market, and small amounts of bait. During an extension to the Temaiku ponds in the 1980s, a sluice gate was opened to let in milkfish fry from Tarawa Lagoon. Tilapia that were already present in brackish ponds contaminated the newly built ponds and led to predation on the incoming milkfish fry and fingerlings. Milkfish production was inhibited by the tilapia in waves in the 1980s, with some years being better than others. Since 1998, Japan Tuna has been involved in providing technical advice for the fish farm, introducing integrated farming methods with pigs and chickens to increase algae levels in the ponds and thus help the milkfish to grow faster. They were trying to eliminate tilapia from the ponds. One option considered was to have Japan Tuna run the ponds commercially. Under government management, the ponds had not reached full productivity potential (Chapman 2003).

Fisheries Division officers who conducted training on the *Tekokona II* for longline fishing said that the milkfish from the aquaculture ponds on Tarawa were sometimes not the right size to target large tuna, so they wanted a source of wild bait fish as well. The last time a bait-fish project had been conducted was on the Australian Council for International Agricultural Research project in the 1990s (Rawlinson et al. 1992), and Fisheries Division coastal fisheries staff thought it was time for another bait-fish project, so were planning to apply for funding (Tioti, pers. comm.).

There is the potential for the bait fishery to be developed further for export for longline or pole-and-line fisheries. If Tarawa was to attract longline or pole-and-line vessels for trans-shipment and servicing of these vessels, there would be a market for bait fish. If domestic pole-and-line or longline fisheries were to be further developed they could use local bait, either live or frozen. There were ponds on Kiritimati that could be adapted for commercial bait-fish production but this potential had not been explored (Chapman 2003). As well as the farmed milkfish, wild bait fish could be harvested from Tarawa and Kiritimati Lagoons (Chapman 2003). If the longline fishery were to take off on Kiritimati, a local supply of bait fish, or a supply from Tarawa, could be cheaper than the source CPP intended to use: carrier vessels selling to distant water fleets in the region.

Fish aggregating devices (FADs)

FADs were used by distant water fleets offshore. In addition, there had been several schemes for small FADs in near-shore areas to support small-scale coastal tuna fisheries. FADs were considered to be important for the outer islands, where people fished in very small vessels such as canoes paddled by hand, so they needed to be able to fish close to the shore. FADs had worked well for coastal fisheries in Nuie and Nauru, and so would probably work well in Kiribati too (Tioti, pers. comm.). Fisheries Division trials with various methods of small-scale tuna fishing in the mid 1990s found that FADs would greatly enhance the productivity of small-scale tuna fisheries (Chapman 2003). There had been several donor-funded projects to install FADs for small-scale fisheries since the 1980s, but because Fisheries Division projects tended to be donor funded rather than funded by the government, there had never been a continuing government-funded program to maintain FADs (Tioti, pers. comm.).

Twelve FADs for the small-scale fishery were deployed in 1988 around Tarawa and neighbouring islands. They were all lost soon after deployment. Eight FADs were deployed in the Line Islands from 1989 to 1993, and all but one of these also disappeared soon after being deployed. The one that survived was productive and used by local fishers for four years before it disintegrated. Economic development fund money administered by the FFA from the US multilateral treaty was used to deploy 20 FADs around the outer islands in 1994. Fourteen of these were lost in the first week, with the remaining six lost soon after, so the project was put on hold (Chapman 2003).

The last FAD program was a New Zealand government-funded project during the 1990s. All of the FADs deployed during that project were lost. Fisheries Division staff were planning to make an application for funding for a new coastal FAD project in 2006, based on lessons learned from failed FAD projects in the past (Tioti, pers. comm.).

Game fishing

As of 2002, there were between five and 10 game-fishing vessels engaging in monthly tournaments around Tarawa (Chapman 2003). There was an active international sports-fishing tourist industry in Kiritimati. Anglers for fly-fishing came from the United States via Hawai'i, mostly to fish for bonefish and trevally in the lagoons of the Line Islands (Chapman 2003). There could be potential to attract international game fishers to Kiritimati for tuna and billfish via the same route.

Small-scale fisheries

There have been various projects to support small-scale fisheries around Kiribati.

In 1979, a Marine Exports Division was established on Kiritimati for the Kiribati government using Japanese aid money. This comprised a six-metre aluminium boat, ice plant, blast freezer and cold storage for buying lobster and reef fish from local fishers, and tuna when available. The Marine Exports Division exported milkfish and a small amount of tuna to Hawai'i, the US west coast and Nauru. During the 1980s, exports fluctuated with freight, supply and marketing problems, then collapsed in 1991 when the flights from Kiritimati stopped. The company was renamed Kiritimati Marine Exports Limited (KMEL) and exports started again in 1992 with a new air service. Business continued, with supply problems caused by lack of fishermen and limits on exports of crayfish. In 1997, 2001 and 2002, Japanese aid money upgraded the ice-making and cold-storage facilities on Kiritimati.

In 2002, the company was amalgamated with the other government-owned fishing companies in CPP (Chapman 2003). In 2005, the Kiritimati cold store was being upgraded with Japanese aid once more, as part of an upgrade of the whole Kiritimati CPP base. It was still unclear whether small-scale fisheries from Kiribati could be economically viable.

In 1988, the Outer Islands Fisheries Project (OIFP), funded by the United Kingdom, was established on Abemama and Butaritari in the outer islands of the Gilbert Group. The aim of the project was to extend the government fishing company, Te Mautari's, fish-buying services to small-scale fishermen in the outer islands. Tuna was intended to be one of the target species but fishers tended to focus on reef fish instead. The financial break-even point for the centres was 180mt a year but the highest achieved was 120mt in 1989. The centres operated at a loss and were closed down in 1992. Even while these centres were closing, other fishery centres were started on Abaiang, Maiana, Kuria and Aranuka. There were difficulties with maintaining equipment and getting product to market in Tarawa from the outset. Furthermore, there were problems with poor processing facilities in Tarawa and administration of payments to fishers. Until 1999, the project continued operating at a loss despite attempts to solve transport difficulties by filleting fish on the islands before sending it to Tarawa and with islands managing their own transport. Then the United Kingdom's funding ceased.

Japanese funding for the project began in 2000 as part of an integrated project that included upgrades to the Te Mautari processing and cold-storage facilities in Betio. Under the Japanese project, production increased and transportation improved. During the Japanese project, OIFP became part of CPP (Chapman 2003). As well as establishing the processing plant and cold-storage facility in Betio, the Japanese project refurbished four outer-islands fisheries centres with ice-making machines and cold storage, and provided fishing vessels in those locations. The Japanese team developed a system for collecting fish from the outer islands, processing and reselling it in the Tarawa market (Onorio, pers. comm.). Fifteen or so canoes were supplied by the Japanese aid project to fishermen in the areas where each of the four outer-islands fisheries centres were established.

Under CPP, fish from the three closer fisheries centres was brought to Tarawa several times a week by boat. The outer-islands project produced some tuna for CPP, but the main focus was crayfish and reef fish. Outer-islands fishers were paid about $1 a kilogram, and CPP sold it on for $2/kg. [3] For this mark up, CPP covered all the operating costs of the fisheries centres and transportation. The fourth fishery centre, which was further away, was filleting the fish and sending it by airfreight to Tarawa.

Sometimes outer-islands fishers chose not to fish full time. Recently, when copra prices boomed, many villages put their energy into copra for a while, and fishing dropped off. It picked up again when copra prices went back down. There was a plan for more fisheries centres further south in the Gilbert Group of islands. There was potential for this plan because people in those southern islands tended to be more focused on fishing than people closer to Tarawa, who had a wider range of economic options. There would, however, be problems working out a viable collection system because of the distance (Onorio, pers. comm.).

One of the options that had been considered was that outer-islands people could process the fish in the outer islands. They could then store a large amount of preserved fish for large freight runs, making the runs more cost effective. It would also reduce the space and weight of the freight and add value. Outer-islands production of tuna jerky had been trialled but had not progressed since 2004.

The ministry saw the support of small-scale fisheries in the outer islands as a priority. There were plans to construct more fish centres in outer islands that did not yet have them to provide income for those communities. The viability of these projects, however, would rest on finding a way to get products to market in Tarawa or overseas in a cost-efficient manner.

In 2005, Tarawa's small-scale tuna troll and pearl-shell pole fishery was still working well. The SPC *Development Options Report* cited this as the only successful private-sector tuna initiative in Kiribati (Chapman 2003). Since 1983, the FAO had been involved in developing various craft for small-scale fisheries around Tarawa, most based on adaptations of the outrigger canoe. The project employed several boat builders with assistants and labourers at Betio and produced more than 550 vessels to 1992 (Chapman 2003).

There were about 1,000 small-vessel owners operating from Tarawa in 2005. Fisheries Division coastal fisheries staff said that some of the small-scale fishers had made quite good money so more people entered the fishery, to the point that by 2005 the fishery was 'quite crowded'.

The Tarawa Fishermen's Cooperative imported fishing gear for small-scale fishers and sold it on to them. It also sold fuel and ice. The cooperative was established by the government in 1994 using Japanese aid money to provide the building, some cold-storage facilities, an ice machine, some marine outboard motors, a standby generator and a displacing pump for fuel. The Tarawa Cooperative had not received continuing funding or any grant aid since its inception. It continued by covering its costs through sales of gear, ice and fuel (Baiteke, pers. comm.; Baree, pers. comm.).

The majority of the small-scale catch from around Tarawa was sold by women at roadside stalls. Small-scale fishers knew more in 2005 than they did in the past about fish quality and the importance of gutting and icing fish. Because ice was expensive, however, they still tended to hold off on using ice unless they thought they would not be able to sell the fish before it started to deteriorate visibly (Tioti, pers. comm.).

The SPC report into development options and constraints recommended that the government support the existing small-scale trolling and poling fisheries by setting up a FAD program and providing training for small-scale tuna fishing techniques. It was suggested that this could be funded through taking a small percentage of distant water access fees as a 'development fee' (Chapman 2003). This had not occurred by 2005.

Tarawa's small-scale tuna markets had been damaged by discards from trans-shipping vessels. Discards were collected on the wharf then sold on the roadside in direct competition with the freshly caught fish, for a cheaper price. Consumers could see that the freshly caught fish were much better quality but still bought the discards because they were cheaper, causing the price of fresh fish to drop (Tioti, pers. comm.).

Anecdotally, expatriate recreational fishermen said that over the years their game-fishing efforts had produced less and less catch. They blamed illegal 'pirate' fishing by foreign industrial vessels close to shore for this. Nauan Bauro said that small-scale fishermen had been complaining in recent years that they had to go further out and fish for longer to find big fish, and he had also noticed that the fish for sale in 2005 were smaller than they had been previously (Bauro, pers. comm.). On the other hand, interviewees from the Tarawa Fishermen's Cooperative Society felt that the coastal resources were healthy (Baiteke, pers. comm.; Baree, pers. comm.). The Fisheries Division had no plans to try to manage the fishery because it seemed to them to be self-managing, in that once the numbers of a species decreased or the price in the market decreased, fishers moved on to another species. Fisheries Division staff felt that Kiribati's coastal fisheries, including tuna, were still quite productive, so no management was necessary (Temwaang, pers. comm.; Tioti, pers. comm.).

Smoked processed and other tuna

One processing plant for smoked tuna, Teikabuti, exists in Kiribati. Plant operations were put on hold temporarily when owner, Mike Savins, an expatriate living in Kiribati, left the country in 2005, but there were plans to resume operations in 2006. CPP also produced tuna and clam jerky for the local market.

Trans-shipping, service and supply

Tarawa's lagoon and proximity to the fishing grounds mean it has the potential to be a major trans-shipment hub, especially for purse-seine fleets; however, it suffers from a lack of fresh food and water, and the country's isolated geography and poor transport connections are inhibitors. Tarawa has no access to suitable airfreight to export sashimi or longline fleet catches. Purse-seine vessels could offload to reefer carrier vessels but ships could not buy enough fresh vegetables in Tarawa to ensure a good diet for their crews. Tarawa has only an inadequate supply of locally grown cabbages and bananas. All other fruit and vegetables are imported, and are thus expensive and not always available in large quantities. Fresh water is also a problem. Nevertheless, because of its proximity to the fishing grounds, Tarawa does significant purse-seine trans-shipping business most years.

While trans-shipping represents an economic opportunity for Kiribati, it also brings social costs in the form of influxes of ship crews ready to 'party'. Alcohol abuse and prostitution are common occurrences around trans-shipping fleets. In 2005, Kiribati society was struggling to cope with increasing numbers of women, some extremely young, visiting the vessels moored in port at Betio (ABC 2005b).

The principal of the FTC said that prostitution in the port area was 'really, *really* against our custom' and 'a big national issue', but he felt that conservative Christian mores, especially among older community leaders, were preventing frank and open discussion of the issues (Kabure, pers. comm.). He saw prostitution as a problem that came with modernity for which I-Kiribati would have to work out their own solution.

One cause of prostitution was that young women had virtually no employment possibilities, especially girls who did not finish school. Boys could get work via the MTC or FTC, but options were more limited for girls.

Agencies to represent and act on behalf of distant water fleets are one of the business opportunity spin-offs from trans-shipping. One of the recommendations in the SPC report on options for tuna development was that the government-owned CPP not be involved in the agency business because it had advantages over private-sector businesses and thus discouraged private-sector development (Chapman 2003). There were two private-sector agencies in Betio (Shipping Agency Kiribati and Kiribati Shipping Services) and one in Korobu (Kiribati Maritime Agency), all three handling a much smaller volume of business than CPP (Tumoa, pers. comm.).

Nevertheless, in 2005, CPP was the largest agent in Tarawa for distant water purse-seine fleets, and was possibly favoured because it was under the same ministry that issued fishing licences. Ministry officials said they promoted CPP to vessels contacting them about registration and licence issues because the ministry wanted CPP to learn about the industry. As agents, CPP arranged for pilots for vessels coming into Tarawa Lagoon, port entry formalities, provision of food, fuel and water, trans-shipment licences, repatriation of crews and treatment of sick and injured crew (Tekaata, pers. comm.). Being the legal representatives of vessels in Kiribati, agents were responsible if vessels or crews were involved in crimes or accidents (Tumoa, pers. comm.).

The migratory and seasonal nature of the resource had major effects on the agency business; in the years when the fishing around Tarawa was poor, fleets did not trans-ship in Tarawa. In 2001, CPP acted as agent for about 90 vessels; in 2002, for 120. In 2003, only two vessels and, in 2004, only three vessels trans-shipped in Tarawa (Riinga 2005). The business picked up again in 2005 with about 100 vessels trans-shipping by October. For CPP, this fluctuation was manageable because the company had other businesses, but it would be difficult for a private-sector company to work only as an agent under these conditions (Tekaata, pers. comm.).

Processing

The processing facility at the CPP base on the wharf area at Betio was upgraded with Japanese aid between 1999 and 2003 to enable CPP to loin or fillet fresh fish and freeze it for export. Since government power supplies were unreliable, the plant had its own generators, which were still on hand for back up, although power supplies had improved by 2005. Because of fresh water quality and supply issues, the plant also had a desalination plant. This was expensive to run in terms of fuel, especially since fuel price increases in 2004–05. The plant also had a blast freezer and large cold storage. The cold storage was so large CPP had never used more than a fraction of the space, so it rented storage places to local food processors (Tekaata, pers. comm.). The facility was used to sell CPP products to the public as well as discards from trans-shipping vessels.

Japan responded to the Kiribati government's aspiration to do more processing by donating equipment (a steaming oven and a vacuum-sealing, plastic-packing machine) for a small loining operation in the CPP plant. It was planned that CPP would start processing one to two metric tonnes of whole fish into loins a day for export markets, moving up to 10 tonnes per day by 2007 (CPP c.2003). In 2005, CPP was processing one metric tonne of raw material (skipjack and yellowfin) per day into vacuum-packed frozen cooked loins for sale in the local market (Onorio, pers. comm.). CPP paid A$0.75 an hour for unskilled labour in its processing plant. This was lower than government wage levels, but because of the training nature of the project and high unemployment in Tarawa, people were willing to work for this amount (Onorio, pers. comm.).

In 2005, there was a plan for multinational fishing company Trimarine to conduct a feasibility study for a large-scale loining plant like the one in Marshall Islands (which by 2005 had closed down). The rationale for the idea seemed to be that if Marshall Islands could have one, Kiribati should be able to have one too, since the two places are geographically very similar. A key difference, however, was that Marshall Islands' close relationship with the United States and the presence of a large US military installation on Kwajalein meant that Marshall Islands had frequent and reasonably priced sea freight that could take processed loins on to destination canneries. Kiribati did not have such freight connections and thus logistics were likely to become an onerous operational cost for a loining plant in Kiribati, just as they were for Pafco in Fiji. Water supply is also likely to be a key issue.

President Anote Tong was very much in favour of a loining plant and convinced the Asian Development Bank (ADB) that its fisheries aid to Kiribati should go to this project. In 2004, staff from the Ministry of Fisheries and Marine Resource Development visited the United States and spoke with representatives of Bumble Bee, who told them about the huge market for loins in the United States, and a supply shortage problem (Tumoa, pers. comm.). There would be a demand for the product, it seemed, provided it could be produced at a competitive cost in Kiribati.

A Korean purse-seine company had suggested during licensing negotiations that it bring a processing vessel to work from Tarawa Lagoon (although this possibility had not been followed up by the government) (Yeeting, pers. comm.). In 2005, Taiwanese businessmen were also in contact with the Office of the President about a potential processing investment.

Small-scale loining for the local market at CPP had exposed to the government some of the constraints that needed to be overcome before a large-scale loining plant could be viable in Tarawa. As well as problems with supplies of fresh water and fuel, it was difficult to maintain a regular and reliable supply of raw materials.

In 2003, the SPC report into development options and constraints mentioned one small plant producing tuna jerky: Teikabuti. The plant employed 10 women and had a Hazard Analysis Critical Control Point (HACCP) plan in place, meaning it could export without fear of food safety scandals (Chapman 2003). Apparently, Teikabuti had been exporting jerky to a buyer in Fiji, who repacked it and exported it on. The SPC report recommended exploring this type of small-scale value adding, as well as salting and drying, which was a possibility for the outer islands, especially if focused towards the local market (due to the difficulties in establishing adequate systems for export-standard food safety and hygiene in outer-island areas) (Chapman 2003).

Future prospects

Since independence, the government has been looking at Kiribati's large EEZ and wondering how to make more from its tuna resources (Onorio, pers. comm.). In 2002–03, there was a thorough examination of policies and plans regarding tuna industries as part of working up the Tuna Development and Management Plan (Government of Kiribati 2003), which was contributed to by the FFA, the SPC and Canadian Government aid.

By 2005, the plan had not been taken forward by Kiribati. One reason for this was that the plan needed further work and review, especially in light of the new fisheries legislation that was needed. Kiribati was using its old *Fisheries Act*, which had been amended from time to time, and which the FFA was helping to revise in 2005. The tuna plan called for the establishment of an authority along the lines of Papua New Guinea's National Fisheries Authority or Australia's Fisheries Management Authority, which would be funded by vessel registration fees.[4] The legislation needed to be revised so that a statutory authority could be established (Tumoa, pers. comm.). The Tong government's main hope for development from tuna resources was some form of processing factory. It intended to have a feasibility study undertaken and eventually have a processing facility built either in Tarawa or in Kiritimati (Tira, pers. comm.).

In 2005, the FAO was conducting a review of CPP as the main domestic company involved in tuna businesses, which included discussions with all the stakeholders, including the ministries, the high commissions and the fishermen's associations (Onorio, pers. comm.). It was possible this review would form a new direction for fisheries development to replace the Tuna Management and Development Plan. Since the early 2000s, the government had emphasised processing rather than fishing, although as a result of the 2005 review it seemed to CPP that the government had gone back to thinking some form of domestic industrial tuna fishery would also be good (Onorio, pers. comm.) (Table 5.3).

Determinants of success

The generally low level of economic development in Kiribati has inhibited fisheries development. The institutions, geography and infrastructure for industrial business development simply do not exist.

Freight

Freight is a major problem for any kind of economic development in Kiribati. Distance from major trading ports and the very small volume of freight coming in and out of Kiribati ports pushes up freight prices. In addition, port facilities at Betio in Tarawa are not large enough or deep enough for large vessels. Large freight vessels moor in the lagoon and freight is unloaded from the vessel to a barge, then brought to the wharf and unloaded again. The wharf built in Kiritimati was for the Japanese–United States satellite program for very big vessels bringing rocket parts, so it was too high for fishing vessels to use (Onorio, pers. comm.). The wharf on Kiritimati also has insufficient shelter from bad weather.

Table 5.3   **Kiribati: indicators of tuna development, 2004–2005**

Company	Domestic vessels: no. and type	Processing facilities: no. and type	Jobs for nationals: no. and type	Annual exports: volume and type	Annual domestic sales: volume and type
Central Pacific Producers (CPP)	1 carrier 1 small longline	1 medium-sized multipurpose	21 on carrier vessel 8 on longline vessel 29 in the office 20 at fish markets/fisheries centres 2 miscellaneous		~300mt frozen vacuum-packed loins 250mt fresh fish small amounts jerky
Fisheries Division	1 small longline	-	-	-	-
Ministry of Fisheries	1 purse-seine (joint venture)	0	0	0	-
Teikabuti	-	1 small tuna jerky	10 I-Kiribati, 1 expatriate	-	-
Totals	1 carrier 1 purse-seine 2 small longline	2 facilities	~90	No regular exports in 2005	>550mt from CPP, unrecorded amounts in roadside stalls

Note: Teikabuti was not operating in 2005.
Sources: Interviews conducted in October 2005.

The 2003 SPC study into opportunities and constraints for tuna industries development in Kiribati recommended two purpose-built fisheries wharves, one for Tarawa and one for Kiritimati, with a 500-metric tonne capacity slip for Tarawa, and a smaller tonnage capacity with side-slipping capabilities in Kiritimati (Chapman 2003:18–19).There were no port redevelopment projects in Tarawa in 2005, although the Ministry of Fisheries prioritised port upgrades as vital infrastructure and was looking for donors willing to fund such a project (Yeeting, pers. comm.). Port upgrades and an increase in the volume of freight would bring the price of freight down (Tira, pers. comm.).

In 2002, there was one small, old slipway in Tarawa and no functioning slipway in Kiritimati (Chapman 2003). In late 2005, a fishing wharf and associated facilities were under construction in Kiritimati. This was an A$8 million Japanese aid project along similar lines to the fishing wharf, cold store and processing facilities built for CPP in Betio, Tarawa. The jetty and shore base was smaller than the government had wanted, as the focus of the JICA project was for local fishermen using current boats, but it was a start (Yeeting, pers. comm.).

Airfreight was also expensive and the routes did not suit exports of fresh fish. Air Kiribati had collapsed, leaving Air Nauru as the only international carrier servicing Tarawa, and its freight prices were too expensive for fish exports (Tioti, pers. comm.). Air Nauru's route to Nadi in one direction and Majuro in the other would line up with flights to Japan, however, so it might be feasible to export sashimi this way if the price were right. Fiji Fish had apparently conducted a trial with the Fisheries Department to explore this option but department staff were unaware of the outcome of the trial (Tioti, pers. comm.). Central Pacific Producers in 2005 had discussions with Air Nauru for favourable freight rates for marine products out of Tarawa through Brisbane, Nadi or Majuro. The Air Pacific route between Nadi, Kiritimati and Honolulu was a potential commercial link for chilled fish exports from Kiritimati to the United States (Onorio, pers. comm.).

Some interviewees expressed a sense of defeatism about Kiribati's geographic location. For example, one ministry interviewee said that Kiribati probably could not compete in the loining industry because it was too far from the markets for loins in Europe and the United States. However, Kiribati is no further from these markets than the other main suppliers, Fiji, American Samoa and Thailand. And, although Kiribati might be far from the markets, it is very close to the fishing grounds (Tumoa, pers. comm.).

Land, water and power

As well as difficulties with freight, development on Tarawa is constrained by an extreme shortage of land. Tarawa is overcrowded and customary tenure systems make it difficult and expensive to negotiate use rights for land. Land is more plentiful and is not held under customary tenure on Kiritimati (all land is government-owned there as it was previously uninhabited) (Chapman 2003). Because Tarawa probably could not support more urbanisation due to land and fresh water shortages (Government of Kiribati c.2003), the government was considering that some or most future fisheries developments should be based in Kiritimati (Tumoa, pers. comm.). The fisheries wharf complex being built with Japanese aid in Kiritimati was to be CPP's base for a fleet of small longline vessels with shallow drafts similar to the *Tekokona* design. The ministry also hoped to develop trans-shipping and service facilities for longliners and to attract foreign vessels to base themselves at Kiritimati, as in Suva. These vessels would be encouraged to employ I-Kiribati crew as part of the licensing process (Yeeting, pers. comm.).

As the centre of population, government and other commercial activities, Tarawa would be an easier location from which to operate than Kiritimati. Reclaiming land would be one solution, as would the use of factory ships moored in the lagoon.

Other problems for establishing tuna businesses in Tarawa, especially processing businesses, include a shortage of fresh water and insufficient and expensive fuel supplies. In Tarawa in 2005, diesel cost A\$0.89 per litre while in Majuro it cost A\$0.51, so CPP did not buy from the government-owned Kiribati Oil (KOIL) but from the tankers that supplied the distant water fishing fleets in the area. CPP used the *Moamoa* to bring fuel from Majuro to operate the generators and desalination plant for their processing facility at Betio (Onorio, pers. comm.). The fuel problem was partly a function of the wharf facilities and partly due to a year-long stand-off between the supplier, Mobil, and the government-owned distributor, KOIL (Chapman 2003). Because the KOIL fuel tanks were quite small, and because the wharf was not deep enough for a large tanker, Mobil had to use a special small tanker to bring oil to Kiribati and charged correspondingly high rates (Onorio, pers. comm.). The local electricity supply was also unreliable, with blackouts of several hours every couple of weeks.

Fresh water was in short supply because atolls rely on rainwater collected from roofs or groundwater that collects in lenses accessed by well or pump. Overcrowded Tarawa's groundwater supply was not very clean and there was not enough of it for a large industrial factory, so some kind of desalination plant would be needed. The problem with desalination plants is that they consume a lot of fuel.

Human resources: training, business skills and government capacity

In order for tuna industries to be based in Kiribati, or for service industries to be able to support distant water fleets using Tarawa, training for various trades and skills is necessary. According to the SPC *Development Options Report*, there were enough tradespeople in Tarawa for carpentry, welding, fibreglassing and diesel engineering, but not enough with skills in refrigeration or hydraulics. There were also not enough tradespeople in Kiritimati (Chapman 2003).

Training and education were also needed for institutional strengthening in the Fisheries Division, so as to enable staff to be able to implement data collection and analysis (including observer programs) and the monitoring, control and surveillance required for a tuna management plan (Chapman 2003). Fisheries Division employees were regularly sent overseas for a range of fisheries management and extension training to SPC courses in New Zealand and OFCF and JICA courses in Japan.

Part of the problem for establishing trading links and for I-Kiribati starting up and running businesses in tuna industries was the generally low level of interest in business in Kiribati society.

The Ministry of Fisheries had long wanted small-scale fishers to move up in scale to buy larger vessels and run them commercially. The Development Bank was supportive of this idea and willing to lend to local fishers, but the ministry was unable to encourage any local fishers to put forward a proposal. The Permanent Secretary for Fisheries, David Yeeting, felt this was probably because the local fishers did not feel comfortable about taking the risk involved in a loan. 'Kiribati people are excellent fishermen, but they lack exposure to the business world.' Lack of exposure to the business world is a major constraint for domestic fisheries development in Kiribati. Tarawa's successful small-scale fishers did not operate their fishing vessels as businesses, but as part of the production of the household economy. When the household had money for fuel, gear and ice they went out fishing and sold the surplus, with the money going back into the household or being spent on consumables. They did not keep track of costs relative to profits for fishing activities. Doing small-scale fishing thus developed fishing skills, but did not develop business skills. Operating a vessel as a business would be a completely new way of doing things. Likewise, observing carefully while working on a distant water fishing vessel would mean learning about the operations of a large-scale vessel, but the business was conducted mostly in shore-based offices, so crew did not have the opportunity to learn much about business while working on the distant water fleets. Small-scale fishermen and crew from the distant water fleets thus did not have the experience to be able to step straight into business ownership.

Kiribati society offers few opportunities for I-Kiribati to develop business skills. Partnerships with foreign businesspeople in the short to medium term, or teaming up with someone who already has a track record in business, would probably be necessary before these fishers could run fishing businesses.

The SPC report on options for development recommended that the Ministry of Fisheries collaborate with the Tarawa Technical Institute vocational training school to develop fisheries-specific business courses (Chapman 2003). This had not happened by 2005, although AusAID had funded a training scheme with an instructor from Australia's Technical and Further Education (TAFE) colleges, who conducted three courses on fish handling, safety and quality and principles of small business. Such courses go some way towards addressing the lack of exposure to the business world among I-Kiribati, but courses alone are probably not enough preparation for taking out a large loan to buy a small industrial fishing vessel or equipment for a processing plant. Gaining experience running a smaller, less risky business for several years would probably be prudent before taking out a large loan.

Government capacity and aid dependency

The government did not have enough revenue to manage fisheries independently so it relied on aid. When government staff wanted to initiate a project, the normal procedure was to write a proposal to the ministry, which would then look for suitable donor funding (Tioti, pers. comm.). Projects in fisheries tended to be tailored to what donors would fund. After nearly 30 years of fisheries aid from a range of donors, the Kiribati government had become somewhat disillusioned. 'With all this aid for so many years one tends to wonder why we aren't moving' (Yeeting, pers. comm.). Government officials felt they were usually not given exactly what they had asked for from donors. By 2005, the Kiribati government was trying to be careful about the aid it accepted to make sure it really helped development, rather than becoming an additional cost to government.

Governing tuna industries

Tuna fisheries management in Kiribati comes under the Ministry of Fisheries, with offices in downtown Bairiki. Coastal small-scale fisheries and aquaculture extension work is carried out by the Fisheries Division, with offices and aquaculture facilities at Tanaea. Functions to do with the distant water fleet and most of the administrative work are carried out by the ministry office.

The FFA has been working with the Kiribati government to detail the necessary changes to legislation to accommodate the Western and Central Pacific Fisheries Commission (WCPFC), with the international and regional obligations membership of the commission entails. As of 2005, it was not clear whether Kiribati needed new legislation or could get by with amendments to the old act. Another issue being worked through was whether Kiribati should move towards having a fisheries authority.

As with other tuna management plans in the region, the Kiribati Tuna Development and Management Plan called for a tuna management committee to be established for consultative decision making on tuna issues. This had not been established by 2005 and, along with most other recommendations in the plan, was indefinitely on hold. *Ad hoc* cross-ministry consultation was conducted on particular issues—for example, alcohol abuse and prostitution in the fishing industry (Yeeting, pers. comm.)—but there was no continuing mechanism for cross-sectoral consultation on tuna-related issues (Tumoa, pers. comm.).

State-owned enterprise

Kiribati was unusual among the countries visited for this report in that the government still believed that public-sector companies were a viable option for development. No government-managed tuna business in the Pacific has ever been financially successful, and most have ended up costing governments far more than they generated in development benefits, so most other Pacific island countries have moved away from government involvement in tuna businesses.[5] One reason some interviewees gave for continued government involvement in tuna businesses in Kiribati was that no local people had the capital to go into a fisheries business (Yeeting, pers. comm.), especially something on a large scale. Only small private companies were possible. It was easier for the government to extend control over such public-sector businesses, and ensure government access to data about the company's operations (Yeeting, pers. comm.). Ministry of Fisheries officials knew that public-sector companies were unlikely to achieve development alone.

The government aim was to have development driven mostly by the private sector with government-owned CPP trailblazing to encourage private-sector development by showing people that a certain business could work and how to do it. The SPC report on tuna development options said that far from encouraging the private sector, CPP inhibited private-sector development in its areas of business (trade in fresh and frozen fish, fish processing, agency and recruitment for distant water fleets, and cargo) (Chapman 2003). Despite CPP's presence in the market in Tarawa, however, local sales from Tarawa's fleet of small vessels were thriving in 2005. A small privately owned tuna-jerky facility producing for export had emerged and there were a couple of private-sector agents for distant water vessels.

Nevertheless, CPP's close connection to the Ministry of Fisheries could have undercut the private businesses, and CPP had all its facilities, offices and training provided under aid projects. In any case, by 2005, CPP had not managed to develop any significant export businesses itself, nor had it succeeded in encouraging the private sector to do so. The SPC report recommended the roll back of state involvement in various areas to enable private-sector development to emerge, including privatisation of CPP (Chapman 2003), but this was not part of the government's plans in 2005.

Another way to get around the 'lack of capital' problem in developing tuna businesses in Kiribati would be to have joint ventures with foreign companies (Baiteke, pers. comm.; Baree, pers. comm.; Tumoa, pers. comm.). While the public sector was seen as having a role to play in ownership and management of tuna industries, 'public–private partnerships with reputable foreign investors' for fishing and/or processing were also seen as desirable (Baiteke, pers. comm.; Baree, pers. comm.; Tumoa, pers. comm.; Government of Kiribati c.2003).

Foreign private investors were seen as a source of expertise, as well as of capital for infrastructure. Some interviewees also felt that allowing wholly foreign-owned ventures might be a good thing, as long as the company employed I-Kiribati, since foreign investors might be unwilling to invest if they had to hand over some of the shareholdings to the government (Tumoa, pers. comm.). As of 2005, however, the only substantial joint venture with overseas companies was the government share in the Japanese purse-seiner, *Kao*, possibly because the difficult business environment of Kiribati discouraged foreign investors.

Governing to encourage private-sector development

As of 2005, Kiribati's government had made limited headway in 'enabling' the private sector. One of the problems noted in a 2002 study was the high rates of taxes/duties on inputs for fishing-related businesses. As of 2005, import duties had been removed from most fisheries-related equipment, such as bait for longlining, fish boxes and most fishing gear (Onorio, pers. comm.), but the government still needed to do more to be seen to be providing a business-friendly environment.

The usual first step in the process to gain business approvals for fisheries was for prospective investors to go to the Fisheries Department for an informal discussion. After this, if it looked like the business was something the government would agree to, the investor was required to apply officially to the Foreign Investment Commission, which had representation from a number of different ministries, including Fisheries. In theory, if the business representatives had all their paperwork in order, this process could take two weeks. Once a business has this approval, they have to seek approvals from the other ministries concerned, including Immigration, Labour and Fisheries. According to ministry official David Yeeting, businesspeople applying for the approval usually told him that the process was very bureaucratic and time-consuming.

One of the features likely to discourage investors in Kiribati is that policies tend to change quite markedly from government to government. One of the reasons given for the failure to take up the Tuna Development and Management Plan was that the plan reflected the policies of the previous government. It was expected that the new government (which, in 2005, was more than halfway through its term) would want to make its own policies for tuna industries (Onorio, pers. comm.; Tumoa, pers. comm.). Policy stability is another area the Kiribati government needs to work on to enable private-sector development.

Fish management

The main conservation measure instituted for tuna fisheries in Kiribati thus far has been that industrial-scale vessels are prohibited from coming within 60 nautical miles of the coast, so as to conserve coastal resources for 'our own people' (Tumoa, pers. comm.). No total allowable catches (TACs) for the national fishery (by gear or species) or limits on licences for industrial tuna fishing had been set by 2005 (Tumoa, pers. comm.; Yeeting, pers. comm.). The ministry was not sure whether the TACs recommended by the SPC in the Tuna Development and Management Plan were the right level, and thought they could be higher (Tumoa, pers. comm.).

Observer coverage had a high priority in the Ministry of Fisheries because it was linked to access fees, as well as the value of accurate logsheets for data collection for stock assessments (Yeeting, pers. comm.). Kiribati was trying to increase observer coverage and reduce inaccuracies in logsheet reporting from distant water fleets. Observer coverage was limited because of the numbers of observers available, and because distant water fleets were reluctant to accept observers (Tumoa, pers. comm.). Observers were also employed by contract to do port sampling when vessels trans-shipped in Tarawa. Port sampling coverage depended on how many vessels were trans-shipping at the same time and how many observers were in town (as opposed to being out on vessels) (Tumoa, pers. comm.).

The observer program started in 2002 and the ministry had 20 observers, who did up to 10 trips a year. More than 300 vessels were licensed to fish by Kiribati each year. The aim was to have 20 per cent coverage but this was difficult because many of the vessels never came to Tarawa. Sometimes the ministry sent observers to board vessels in Majuro, but this was very expensive. If the vessel was in the Federated States of Micronesia (FSM) or other countries, it was even more expensive (Tumoa, pers. comm.).

Surveillance was costly and logistically difficult for an EEZ the size of Kiribati's so the government received assistance from Australia. Because of the difficulties of doing surveillance for any one Pacific island country alone, the PNA group was exploring a joint surveillance program. It had been agreed to in principle by late 2005 (Yeeting, pers. comm.).

The Tuna Development and Management Plan recommended that Kiribati's catch-data collection systems be improved because there were problems with under-reporting by distant water vessels, trying to reduce their access fees (Government of Kiribati 2003). It was not clear whether catch data from the foreign fleet were more accurate by 2005. The Foreign Licensing Unit enforced logsheet submission by fining vessels that failed to submit logsheets (Tumoa, pers. comm.).

In 2005, tuna fishing licences, which were mostly distant water access, were still administered under the old institutional arrangement from an office in the ministry rather than through the Fisheries Licensing and Law Enforcing Authority (FLLEA) recommended in the Tuna Development and Management Plan (Tumoa, pers. comm.). Kiribati has achieved the same rates (about 5 per cent of the sold value of the catch) for distant water access fees as other Pacific island countries receive (Reid, pers. comm.). In addition to fees, Kiribati has negotiated benefits from DWFNs including a great deal of aid from Japan and Taiwan, and has negotiated to have I-Kiribati crew employed on distant water fleets. One possible improvement to distant water negotiations suggested by ministry official Raikaon Tumoa was to have the negotiations conducted in Kiribati, so that more stakeholders could contribute (Tumoa pers. comm.). It was also hoped that overall fees could be increased by a change to fisheries licences being considered in 2005

Conclusion

There are a range of necessary inputs for development in the marine sector: fish, fishing vessels and gear, crews, wharves, fuel, fresh water, ice, slipways, maintenance facilities, spare parts for maintenance, tradespeople, land and freight (air and sea). In 2005, Kiribati had only some of these: fish, crews and some vessels (*Tekokona II* and *III* and the fleet of privately owned small-scale boats). The resources are very rich and Kiribati is centrally located to them, local fishermen are plentiful and willing to work, although there is a shortage of crew with higher-level qualifications and experience, as well as a shortage in some of the other trades needed for fisheries and processing service industries. Freight was one of the most pressing disadvantages for any kind of industry because the lack of scale made air and sea freight expensive, air routes were not suitable for fresh fish exports, and there were inadequate sea and air port facilities. Fuel was expensive and in short supply, as were land and fresh water. Local companies lacked marketing expertise and trade networks, and the very high food safety standards of the most valuable markets in the European Union and the United States were another barrier to exports. Finally, the government had not created a macroeconomic environment that encouraged private-sector development. It could be that Kiribati's fragile land environment and small economy mean shore-based tuna development is never going to be competitive. Focusing on access fees, supplying crew for distant water fleets, development trans-shipping businesses (especially in trading) and sound management of near-shore fisheries could be the best policy mix for Kiribati.

Development aspirations and tuna

Aspirations for tuna development were contained in the objectives and strategies specified in the 2003 SPC study of options for development and the Tuna Development and Management Plan (Government of Kiribati 2003; Chapman 2003). These included

- providing an enabling environment for private-sector development in commercial fishing, sports fishing, processing and support sectors
- providing environmentally responsible domestic development and harvesting for food and for export-oriented income
- maximising benefits to I-Kiribati, local communities and the Kiribati economy
- generating employment and income for I-Kiribati, including in the outer islands
- ensuring accurate data collection, including by-catch and interactions with protected species
- making domestic fisheries development and regulation compatible with regional and international obligations
- reducing and replacing foreign fishing access with Kiribati-owned and operated vessels.

The following strategies were listed in relation to these objectives

- develop infrastructure
- maximise external funding
- develop tuna longlining as the most feasible domestic fishery development
- develop post-harvest activities to add value
- develop data collection and analysis systems
- review government taxes and duties to remove disincentives to invest
- train small-scale fishers in fishing techniques and business management
- have a continuing FAD program for small-scale fishers
- explore options for owning (such as cooperatives) and marketing for viable outer-islands fisheries businesses
- build capacity in the Fisheries Ministry for better fisheries management.

As has already been discussed, however, the Tuna Development and Management Plan was not taken forward by the government and, according to interviewees, the government in 2005 had a slightly different set of policies and aspirations in mind for tuna development. The aspiration that came through most strongly in interviews was that I-Kiribati felt that collecting access fees was not enough. There had long been a desire to do something more with the fishery, something owned and operated by I-Kiribati.

Kiribati's general development aspiration as detailed in the National Development Strategies was 'enhancing growth and ensuring the equitable distribution of development benefits to the people of Kiribati according to principles of good governance' (Government of Kiribati c.2003). This aim was to be achieved through

- partnership of public and private investment in infrastructure and production
- equitable distribution of services and economic opportunity

- improved efficiency in the public sector
- equipping people to manage social and economic change as individuals, communities and as a nation
- using our natural resources and physical assets sustainably
- preserving our financial reserves while making use of them to finance development.

Employment

One of the main development challenges facing Kiribati is unemployment. About 2,000 young people leave school each year but only 500 jobs become available. Forty-one per cent of the population is less than 20 years of age. Two out of three jobs are in the public sector (four out of every five dollars of pay come from the public sector), with two out of three of these jobs concentrated in the south Tarawa area (Government of Kiribati c.2003). As well as continued employment opportunities with distant water fleets, it was hoped that developing a domestic fishing fleet and onshore fish processing would generate many jobs (Tumoa, pers. comm.).

Not only were there too few cash-paying jobs, those that did exist were too concentrated in south Tarawa. There were already problems with overcrowding, expensive and lengthy processes to secure land for businesses, and lack of clean fresh water in Tarawa, so it seemed best that employment-generating development should occur outside Tarawa. The outer-islands fisheries project selling fish to Tarawa under CPP was one way that fisheries, including tuna, contributed to the development aim of distributing benefits equitably and slowing the consolidation of the population in Tarawa. Developments on Kiritimati would also further this aspiration.

Spreading development outside Tarawa

Kiritimati in the Line Islands is the largest atoll in Kiribati, has more easily available land than elsewhere and is the fastest growing population centre in the country (Government of Kiribati c.2003). Because of its location close to Hawai'i, Kiritimati seemed a good location for export-oriented tuna development. The Office of the President was considering Kiritimati as the site for a loining plant, although port and infrastructure development would be necessary before such development. Kiritimati had recently been targeted by cruise liners, so it could be developed as a tourist centre, which would create a local market for tuna, among other seafoods. The 2005 establishment of the Air Pacific route from Fiji to Hawai'i stopping off at Kiritimati was a good first step in the direction of tuna industries in Kiritimati. The government has been encouraging air force planes travelling across the Pacific to stop for refuelling at Kiritimati (Tira, pers. comm.) and hoped it would become a hub for planes.

Another way interviewees hoped to ensure continued employment opportunities outside Tarawa was through I-Kiribati working as crew on distant water fleets. With economic problems threatening the future of the Japanese fleet, and increased competition from other nationalities, it was not clear whether this opportunity would last into the future. The step to train officers, and the establishment of recruiting services for fleets other than Japan's, are positive moves (Bauro, pers. comm.).

Environmental and social issues

One of the factors complicating the aspiration to have more people employed as crew on distant water fleets—alcohol abuse by crew—was related to another general aspiration about 'equipping our people to manage social and economic change' (Government of Kiribati c.2003). Two paragraphs in the Tuna Development and Management Plan assigned the government responsibility for working with community groups to address a range of negative social impacts associated with tuna fisheries (Government of Kiribati 2003). No significant initiatives in this direction had been made by 2005.

According to Ministry of Fisheries official David Yeeting, changing gender relations and roles were part of the mix of issues understood as having negative social impacts. The MTC had started training young women to work in the German merchant marine, which was a controversial move opposed by some of the older, more conservative members of society. In recent years, some men have begun to take their wives out fishing (Yeeting, pers. comm.), and ways of raising girls in Kiribati are slowly changing.

There was an aspiration to mitigate negative environmental effects, through sustainable management of tuna resources. Ministry staff felt that in order to realise this aspiration domestic management should dovetail with regional management through bodies such as the FFA, the SPC and the WCPFC (Tumoa, pers. comm.; Yeeting, pers. comm.). They also felt it was important to achieve a balance between domestic and regional management for the purposes of sustainability, and to balance present gain against future gain from the fishery. Building the human resources capacity in the Ministry of Fisheries was seen as another necessary component for realising aspirations towards effective resource management, as well as management for economic development. Other areas where ministry and Fisheries Division staff could benefit were from studies in fisheries and business management (Tumoa, pers. comm.).

Processing

The primary aspiration of President Anote Tong's government to generate more jobs and wealth in the domestic economy from the EEZ's tuna resources was through a loining plant (Onorio, pers. comm.; Tumoa, pers. comm.; Yeeting, pers. comm.). In order to develop loining, Kiribati would have to develop various services and infrastructure to make the port area suitable, and to enable the country to meet the strict standards of importing countries. It was seen as important that Kiribati not export before it could meet these standards as it could damage the reputation of the fishery if Kiribati fish made people sick.

Increasing returns from distant water fleets

While I-Kiribati would prefer to run tuna businesses themselves, the revenue generated from access fees has been so significant to the economy that most interviewees saw a continued role for access agreements. Increasing the numbers and rank of I-Kiribati employed on distant water fleets was another aspiration, to generate more income from distant water fleets. They aspired to increase distant water fleets' payments to Kiribati for access to the EEZ. 'Cost effective use of economic diplomacy to sustain [economic] flows from abroad has been an important arm of Kiribati's development strategies' (Government of Kiribati c.2003:13). Skilful negotiations for fisheries access in exchange for aid has been part of that strategy.

Trans-shipping service and supply

In addition to processing tuna and increasing access fees, the Kiribati government had aspirations to capture some of the wealth of regional distant water tuna fisheries by making Tarawa and Kiritimati trans-shipping hubs, for purse-seining and longlining, respectively. Overcoming obstacles to trans-shipping was one of the medium-term strategies listed in the Tuna Development and Management Plan (Government of Kiribati 2003). In 2005, port developments to encourage trans-shipping were still a government priority, although no concrete plans were under way. The Ministry of Fisheries was looking for donors interested in funding expensive wharf developments in Tarawa. Since the Line Islands have long been popular with longline fleets, especially from Korea, Kiritimati has the potential to be a longline trans-shipment hub, like Suva, but lack of port facilities, service industries and logistical problems with air and sea transport have meant Kiritimati has not hosted any trans-shipping businesses.

So as to develop trans-shipping capacity, in 2005 the government regarded a purpose-built fisheries port area with processing facilities as a desirable development. If facilities were improved, the government could require distant water fishers to offload part of their catch to Kiribati's processing facility. In addition, a better port would generate many beneficial spin-offs for the wider economy via cheaper cargo. An economy of scale in freight would be achieved with more vessels coming and going with provisions for the fishing fleet, meaning cheaper imports of food and fuel.

With better facilities in the port area, more trans-shipping service industries could develop for repair and maintenance of vessels and hospitality industries for visiting crews. Distant water vessel owners had indicated to the Kiribati government in licence negotiations that it was expensive for them to steam away from Kiribati to offload if they fished around Kiribati, so it was likely that spin-off businesses from trans-shipment could flourish if Tarawa offered more in terms of service and supply.

Trading and marketing

While interviewees were aware of fishing, processing and service industries as potential development strategies, on the whole they were less aware of marketing and trading as equally important facets of tuna industries. Trading and marketing expertise is an important deficit in the local economy constraining Kiribati from realising its aspirations for development from tuna resources.

Fishing

Notwithstanding the current government's aim was to undertake tuna processing, the majority of interviewees aspired for I-Kiribati to do the fishing. Ministry of Fisheries official Raikon Tumoa said he would like I-Kiribati to be involved in fishing and to have their own fleets, to replace some of the distant water fleets (Tumoa, pers. comm.). Nauan Bauro also felt that Kiribati should have the means to reap its own huge tuna resources. He thought it would be good for the government to continue giving some licences to foreign fleets, while also developing a local fleet (Bauro, pers. comm.).

Fisheries Division interviewees said they would like to see the foreign fleets replaced by Kiribati fishing companies in the future (Temwaang, pers. comm.; Tioti, pers. comm.).

Nauan Bauro, as head of the Japan Tuna-funded Kiribati Fisherman's Service, knew that the Japanese fleet faced financial difficulties, but he felt the surest way to safeguard I-Kiribati employment opportunities on tuna vessels was for Kiribati to have its own fleet, or to attract more foreign-owned vessels to be based in Kiribati. Through developing a large fleet and controlling fishing conducted in Kiribati's EEZ, FTC principal Teorae Kabure hoped Kiribati would be able to control the market for tuna and keep the prices at beneficial levels

This research, as well as other reports into similar topics cited here, show that these kinds of aspirations to fish tuna might not be economically viable. CPP General Manager, Barerei Onorio, noted that in the 2005 FAO review of CPP, when stakeholders were asked what they wanted for the future of tuna industries in Kiribati, many did not know enough about the background of fishing in Kiribati or about tuna businesses to be able to give realistic answers (Onorio, pers. comm.). This lack of knowledge of the history of failure of most Pacific island government-owned tuna-fishing ventures is one explanation for the apparently naïve expectations that if I-Kiribati were given the capital to start they could make a financial success of tuna fishing.

Recommendations

While many challenges face the domestication of tuna fisheries in Kiribati, the following are some areas that could yield benefits

- increase the understanding of tuna fishery-related developments, especially what is likely to generate real long-term benefits to the Kiribati economy, then align activities to focus on realising the most promising developments
- improve freight and transport infrastructure and management
- seek to build on the undoubted capabilities of I-Kiribati seamen, possibly by undertaking a feasibility study for a private-sector joint venture based on a medium-scale, domestically based tuna fleet using and expanding on the existing CPP facility
- reconsider the advice provided by the FFA and the SPC in terms of strategies for tuna management and development
- encourage development of business training and experience
- support industry training and develop new training for trades and business development.

To maximise the benefits from distant water fleets, it will be important to

- gain an improved understanding of the economics and dynamics of the Western and Central Pacific Ocean distant water tuna fleets to engender a better understanding of what benefits can be realistically extracted from DWFNs

- build on the current use of Tarawa (and possibly Kiritimati) as a trans-shipment port by providing competitive service industries and business-friendly approaches as per the Marshall Islands' model

- consider ways of maximising access revenue with the FFA and other Pacific island countries, for example, by examining the nature of existing agreements, including the contracting party (individual licences versus association-based agreements)

- vigorously pursue subregional (PNA) and FFA-wide cooperative arrangements to maximise the long-term benefits arising from the vessel days scheme and to secure equitable allocations and acceptable management measures at the WCPFC, in a reasonable timeframe

- continue to train and find employment for fishing crews, recognising that competition from Chinese and Southeast Asian crews is likely to increase

- avoid expenditure of government revenue on high-risk tuna-fishing developments.

Notes

[1] The previous Permanent Secretary made a study tour of the Maldives but was transferred soon after returning to Kiribati, so his study was not utilised by the Ministry.

[2] Kiribati steadfastly reserved the right to license EU vessels throughout the negotiation of the WCPF Convention and signalled this intent during discussion and agreement of a resolution at the third MHLC negotiating session in Hawai'i in 1999, calling on states to 'exercise reasonable restraint in respect of any regional expansion of fishing effort and capacity'.

[3] Observations of roadside stalls in October 2005 showed the basic price for fish in Tarawa was between A$1 and $2.50 a kilogram.

[4] In Papua New Guinea, the entire fishing access fee went to the National Fisheries Authority, but in Kiribati access fees were too large a part of the country's revenue, so only the vessel registration part was considered for funding an authority.

[5] The only other people interviewed for this project who believed government-owned companies could be successful were the managers of government-owned Soltai Fishing and Processing in Solomon Islands, and some interviewees, not NFA officials, in Papua New Guinea.

6

Marshall Islands

Population: 61,200
Land area: 726 km²
Sea area: 2,131,000 km²

The Republic of the Marshall Islands is made up of 29 coral atolls and five single islands from just north of the equator to 15°N latitude (Figure 6.1) (Chapman 2004a). The atoll geomorphology (narrow ribbons of land around lagoons) means there has been a limited range of agriculture possible and there have often been shortages of fresh water for agriculture and domestic use. Most areas rely on lenses of fresh water in the ground of the atolls and any rainwater that can be caught. The marginality of Marshall Islands' land for human habitation means the Marshallese have historically relied considerably on cooperation between islands in the two main groups (Ralik and Ratak) for resources when storms or drought made conditions difficult on particular islands (Spenneman 2005). With most land only a metre or so above sea level, Marshall Islands is one of the Pacific island countries most at threat from global warming.

After sporadic contact with Spanish, British, Russian and American ships from the 1500s, the Marshall Islands were claimed as a German protectorate in 1885. Along with all other German colonial territories north of the equator, Marshall Islands was given to Japan as part of the Treaty of Versailles settlement after World War I. Marshall Islands remained a Japanese territory, with extensive migration from Japan for fisheries, general business and military purposes, until the end of World War II. In 1947, the United Nations gave Marshall Islands to the United States as a Strategic Trust. Until 1954, the United States conducted 67 nuclear tests in, above and around the Bikini and Enewetak Atolls. Most notable was the 'Bravo' bomb. Exploded on the reef of Bikini Atoll in 1954, this bomb caused massive damage to the atoll and irradiated thousands of Marshallese on neighbouring atolls. Unexpected fallout from the detonation—intended to be a secret test—poisoned the crew of *Daigo Fukuru Maru*, a Japanese fishing boat, and created international concern about atmospheric thermonuclear testing.

An increasing desire for independence from the United States culminated in Marshall Islands joining the United Nations. Since 1986, Marshall Islands has been self-governing in free association with the United States (MIVA 2003). Under the Compact of Free Association, the United States provides military defence, guaranteed financial assistance and grant funding, and special immigration provisions to Marshallese citizens in exchange for exclusive military access to Marshall Islands. Of particular strategic importance to the United States is Kwajalein Atoll, operated by the US Army since 1944, now home to the Reagan Anti-Ballistic Missile Testing Facility. Controversies continue to surround the use of the base. Today, in spite of continuing protests from landowners, a number of islands on Kwajalein Atoll are still leased to the United States for about US$15 million a year.

Map 6.1   **Marshall Islands**

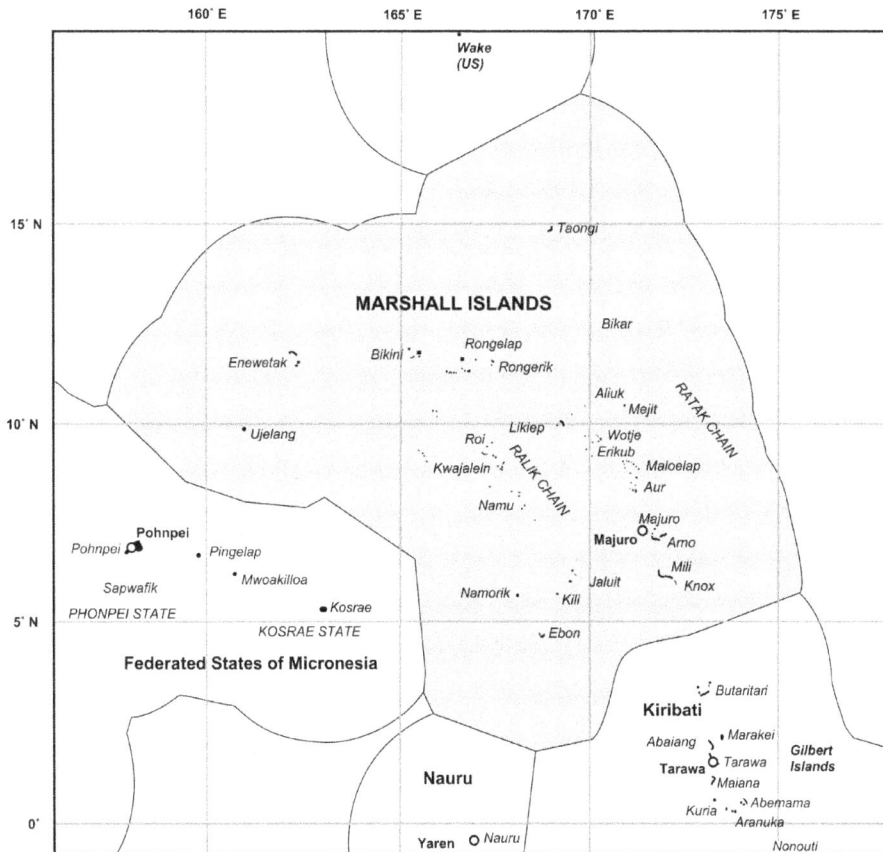

Source: Youngmi Choi, Secretariat of the Pacific Community, Noumea, New Caledonia.

Potential of tuna fisheries

Marshall Islands is in the equatorial belt of the Western and Central Pacific Ocean, which is rich in tuna resources, particularly skipjack. Oceanographic effects on water temperatures mean that in some years the pole-and-line and purse-seine surface fisheries of skipjack (including juvenile yellowfin and bigeye) are less rich. Marshall Islands also hosts many longline companies, although due to the warm water temperatures yellowfin and bigeye from Marshall Islands do not fetch the highest prices in the Japanese sashimi market.

The fresh water, power and freight situation in Marshall Islands is more viable for tuna industries than many other geographically similar Pacific island countries. Despite being an atoll, Majuro has a reliable supply of potable water through a catchment and reservoir utilising rainwater from the airport runway. Land is scarce in Majuro, but it could be possible to develop floating facilities within the lagoon. As well as large-scale loining or canning, it could be possible for Marshall Islands to develop small-scale processing—salting, drying or smoking—as has been tried in Fiji, Cook Islands and Kiribati. Another kind of processing that could be established on Majuro is a fish-meal plant utilising fish rejected from other facilities (Gillett 2003). Freight volume is relatively high and competitively priced because of the US military presence. The availability of chilled and other cargo space on vessels returning to the US west coast also presents an opportunity for cost-effective transport of tuna-related products. Regional air connections mean Marshall Islands is convenient for trans-shipping vessels wishing to fly in crews from countries such as Indonesia and China for whom it is difficult to get transit visas for US ports (Ishizaki, pers. comm.).

Since Marshallese have residency and working rights in the United States, and remuneration for public servants is among the highest in the region, wage levels are quite high (Joseph, pers. comm.), meaning Marshallese labour is expensive for tuna industries compared with China and Southeast Asia, which are the main competitors.

History of development

Fishing has always been a central part of the Marshall Islands' nutritional and social life. Tuna and other pelagic species were originally trolled for from outrigger sailing canoes. From the 1980s, these canoes were replaced with outboard engine-powered fibreglass or aluminium vessels (Chapman 2004a). Industrial commercial fishing has been conducted mainly by distant water fleets. Commercial fishing in the Marshall Islands started with Japanese pole-and-line fishers in the 1920s (Chapman 2004a), which continued until the end of World War II. Japanese longline and pole-and-line fishers returned in the 1960s and dominated the fishery until 1990 when the presence of other distant water fishing nations (DWFNs) increased (Table 6.1).

Longline

The Japanese fleet dominated the longline fishery in Marshall Islands' Exclusive Economic Zone (EEZ) until 1990. With regular flights to and from Guam and Hawai'i, Majuro has

Table 6.1　Fishing vessels with access to the Marshall Islands' EEZ, 2003

Country/company	Access type	Gear	Number of vessels	Flag
USA	Multilateral, regional, administered by FFA	Purse-seine	26	USA
Japan	Bilateral, government to government, administered by MIMRA	Purse-seine	34	Japan
		Longline	23	Japan
		Pole-and-line	74	Japan
Taiwan	Bilateral, industry to government, administered by MIMRA	Purse-seine	42	Taiwan
Korea	Bilateral, industry to government, administered by MIMRA	Purse-seine	27	Korea
FSM Arrangement	Multilateral, subregional, administered by FFA	Purse-seine	23	Variousa
Fong Seong	Bilateral, industry to government, administered by MIMRA	Purse-seine	2	Vanuatu
Shandong Fishery	Bilateral, industry to government, administered by MIMRA	Purse-seine	2	China
Shanghai Fishery	Bilateral, industry to government, administered by MIMRA	Purse-seine	2	China
MIFV	Bilateral, industry to government, administered by MIMRA	Longline	30	China, Taiwan
New Zealand	Bilateral, industry to government, administered by MIMRA	Purse-seine	4	New Zealand
Edgewater Fishery	Bilateral, industry to government, administered by MIMRA	Longline	5	FSM
Totals:	Purse-seine: 162			
	Longline: 58			
	Pole-and-line: 74			

Notes: FSM Arrangement vessels included vessels flagged to Federated States of Micronesia, Republic of Marshall Islands (5), Kiribati, Solomon Islands and Papua New Guinea. The single vessel from Papua New Guinea was operated by Fair Well Fishery. This vessel was Vanuatu flagged but probably Taiwanese owned. The five Vanuatu vessels were operated by a company called Fong Seong.
Source: Marshall Islands Marine Resources Authority (MIMRA), 2005. Fisheries report—Marshall Islands, Paper read at First Meeting of the Scientific Committee WCPFC-SC1, Noumea, New Caledonia.

far better air connections to Japan and the United States than many other Pacific island countries, making it logistically a good location from which to engage in longlining for sashimi tuna. According to a former Japanese longline fishing master, however, the quality of tuna that can be caught around Marshall Islands is not as good as other parts of the Pacific in terms of value for Japanese sashimi markets. Japanese distant water longline fisheries are allocated fishing grounds around the world by a lottery system. Vessels that draw equatorial waters such as those around Marshall Islands consider themselves unlucky compared with vessels that draw cold-water areas, where the higher-value bluefin species as well as yellowfin and bigeye have higher body-fat content and more desirable flesh quality (Ishizaki, pers. comm.).

After the 1990s, the numbers of Japanese vessels reduced to about 30 a year, while numbers of Korean, Taiwanese and Chinese vessels increased (Table 6.2). Locally based

Table 6.2   **Longline vessels operating in Marshall Islands' EEZ by flag country, 1978–2003**

	China	Federated States of Micronesia	Japan	Korea	Marshall Islands	Taiwan	Total
1978	0	0	3	0	0	0	3
1979	0	0	40	0	0	0	40
1980	0	0	188	1	0	0	189
1981	0	0	177	0	0	0	177
1982	0	0	178	0	0	0	178
1983	0	0	144	0	0	0	144
1984	0	0	145	0	0	0	145
1985	0	0	103	0	0	0	103
1986	0	0	99	0	0	0	99
1987	0	0	88	2	0	0	90
1988	0	0	70	1	0	0	71
1989	0	0	88	13	0	2	103
1990	0	0	83	7	0	5	95
1991	0	0	80	1	0	7	88
1992	0	0	104	7	6	4	121
1993	11	0	83	2	5	1	102
1994	109	1	82	2	0	13	207
1995	138	0	60	2	1	12	213
1996	74	2	40	2	0	37	155
1997	45	1	15	0	0	37	98
1998	28	3	35	1	0	13	80
1999	0	4	46	0	0	3	53
2000	0	7	34	0	0	3	44
2001	3	7	40	0	0	3	53
2002	36	7	21	0	0	10	74
2003	35	4	0	0	0	4	43

Notes: Data from 2003 incomplete.
Source: Langley, A., 2004. *Marshall Islands National Tuna Fishery Status Report No.5*, Oceanic Fisheries Program, Secretariat of the Pacific Community, Noumea, New Caledonia.

Table 6.3   Japanese pole-and-line vessels operating in Marshall Islands' EEZ, 1979–2002

	Number of vessels	Catch (skipjack) in metric tonnes	Percentage of catch in Western and Central Pacific Ocean
1979	18	145	0.5
1980	171	6,584	12.5
1981	146	10,088	24.6
1982	102	8,881	54.7
1983	97	28,284	68.4
1984	77	6,352	22.4
1985	63	5,141	26.2
1986	47	4,687	9.2
1987	63	10,495	36.0
1988	49	33,977	50.1
1989	51	4,377	15.0
1990	39	2,787	15.7
1991	21	763	4.1
1992	37	7,259	37.3
1993	29	3,095	25.6
1994	31	3,990	24.6
1995	33	3,250	12.5
1996	28	3,177	34.1
1997	36	2,980	45.0
1998	40	17,843	87.1
1999	32	3,916	45.4
2000	38	8,015	64.1
2001	37	16,207	90.8
2002	35	7,312	95.0

Source: Langley, A., 2004. *Marshall Islands National Tuna Fishery Status Report No.5*, Oceanic Fisheries Program, Secretariat of the Pacific Community, Noumea, New Caledonia.

Chinese and Taiwanese vessels have operated from Majuro, supplying the Fishbase sashimi-tuna processing and packaging facility. The numbers of vessels operating from the Fishbase peaked at close to 150 vessels in the mid 1990s, when it was operated by Ting Hong (Gillett 2003). The Chinese longline vessels that have been based in Majuro are fairly small and stay relatively close to Majuro, but they are still denoted as distant water fleets, rather than 'locally based foreign' as other Pacific island countries have chosen to denote locally based foreign-owned vessels. The connections between Chinese businesses and the vessels they represent, either through charter or ownership, have not been entirely clear (McCoy and Gillett 2005).

In the early 1990s, the Marshall Islands Development Authority (MIDA) brought in five tuna longline vessels to be operated by local private-sector investors with government loans (Chapman 2004a). The vessels achieved low catch rates, never managed to cover their operating costs (Gillett 2003) and ceased operating by 2004 (Chapman 2004a). According

Table 6.4   Purse-seine vessels operating in the Marshall Islands EEZ by flag country, 1980–2003

	Australia and New Zealand	China	Japan	Korea	Philippines	Soviet Union	Taiwan	USA	Vanuatu	FSM	Total
1980	0	0	0	0	0	0	0	0	0	0	0
1981	0	0	1	0	0	0	0	0	0	0	1
1982	0	0	0	0	1	0	0	0	0	0	1
1983	0	0	0	0	0	0	0	0	0	0	0
1984	0	0	0	0	0	0	0	0	0	0	0
1985	0	0	0	0	0	1	0	2	0	0	3
1986	0	0	1	0	0	1	0	1	0	0	3
1987	0	0	0	2	0	0	0	0	0	0	2
1988	0	0	0	0	0	0	1	16	0	0	17
1989	0	0	0	0	0	0	0	10	0	0	10
1990	1	0	0	0	0	0	0	17	0	0	18
1991	0	0	0	0	0	0	1	10	0	0	11
1992	0	0	0	0	0	0	2	43	0	1	46
1993	0	0	2	0	0	0	0	32	0	2	36
1994	0	0	20	0	0	0	5	14	0	1	40
1995	0	0	0	0	0	0	0	33	0	1	34
1996	0	0	0	0	0	0	0	24	0	0	24
1997	0	0	5	4	0	0	7	5	1	0	22
1998	0	0	33	24	0	0	30	7	4	5	103
1999	0	0	35	25	0	0	37	5	7	2	111
2000	0	0	37	24	0	0	35	3	7	8	114
2001	0	0	34	26	0	0	43	12	0	14	129
2002	0	3	34	27	0	0	41	4	0	17	126
2003[b]	4	0	15	10	0	0	21	10	0	9	69

Notes: b Data from 2003 incomplete. FSM Arrangement vessels included vessels flagged to Federated States of Micronesia, Republic of Marshall Islands, Kiribati, Solomon Islands and Papua New Guinea.
Source: Langley, A., 2004. *Marshall Islands National Tuna Fishery Status Report No.5*, Oceanic Fisheries Program, Secretariat of the Pacific Community, Noumea, New Caledonia.

to some commentators, there has been considerable interest expressed in establishing another domestic longline fleet, and training in longline techniques has been continuing at the Fisheries and Nautical Training Centre (Sokimi and Chapman 2003; Ishizaki, pers. comm.). Longlining techniques based on the US style were also taught at the centre. In the early 2000s, MIMRA was investigating vessel types for small-scale coastal longline fisheries (Chapman 2004a). This was apparently to be based on the *alia* fishery in Samoa. According to Marshall Islands Marine Resources Authority (MIMRA) director Glen Joseph, local fishers and MIMRA were wary of trying to enter the commercial longline fishery again after the failures of the MIDA project.

In the mid 1990s, Ting Hong, a Taiwanese company, was the dominant presence in the Marshall Islands fishing industry. In 1994, the peak of Chinese longline presence in the Pacific, 457 vessels in Micronesia supplied fish to bases operated by Ting Hong for air trans-shipment to Japan, but business did not go well and Ting Hong departed the Western and Central Pacific Ocean in 1996 (McCoy and Gillett 2005). The influx of the Chinese vessels seems to have been poorly planned. There were insufficient port facilities and other infrastructure to support these vessels in Micronesia. The catches were also poor so the number of Chinese vessels based in Micronesia fell to only 66 in 1999 (McCoy and Gillett 2005).

Ting Hong was replaced in Majuro by the Marshall Islands Fishing Venture (MIFV), owned by Luen Thai Fishing Venture (LTFV), a subsidiary of the Hong Kong-based Luen Thai International Group, which has operations in several other northern Pacific island countries (McCoy and Gillett 2005). MIFV began operations in Majuro in 2001. It took over and refurbished the defunct cold storage, wharf and offloading area known as Fishbase (which had been used by Ting Hong) from the government for a nominal sum on a long-term lease. Base managers who spoke good English were recruited. MIFV expanded the facilities with a small loining plant for fresh sashimi loins.

In 2002, MIFV was managing 49 longline vessels. In 2004, it operated 28 longliners from the Fishbase (Chapman 2004a). MIFV owned eight of these, while the rest came from China, Taiwan, a Federated States of Micronesia (FSM) company and one from Japan (Gillett 2003). MIFV exported to Japan, Taiwan and the United States: A-grade sashimi to Japan, with B and C-grade tuna loined and sold for tuna steaks to the United States, and frozen tuna and bycatch exported to Taiwan (Chapman 2004a). In 2002, MIFV employed no Marshallese on the fleet, but about 38 were employed onshore (Gillett 2003). MIFV also acted as an agent for trans-shipping purse-seiners (McCoy and Gillett 2005).

Rather than being a fishing company *per se*, MIFV's parent, LTFV, is more a marketing and trading company. LTFV has sales offices in Japan and marketing arrangements with other companies elsewhere (McCoy and Gillett 2005), and it contracts vessels rather than owning them. It sells supplies to the vessels and markets the catch. Sometimes the agent relationship was such that vessels arrived at the fishing grounds owing large amounts to their agent and were tied to them for supplies and marketing. Due to lack of familiarity with the local society, they relied on their agent for 'almost every need', so had little scope for profitability (McCoy and Gillett 2005). Lack of profit for the vessel was not necessarily bad for LTFV's profits.

LFTV learned from some of the mistakes made by Ting Hong. It kept its vessel numbers much lower. LTFV also suffered less resentment as a foreign company than Ting Hong had because in the intervening years failures in the domestic industry showed how difficult it was to run longline businesses successfully. Whereas Ting Hong was seen as taking a business opportunity that locals could have used, LTFV was seen as a business providing locals with an opportunity to try their hand. MIFV was also seen as contributing to Majuro society; it was a major sponsor for the 2004 annual sports-fishing tournament (McCoy and Gillett 2005).

It is important to note that MIFV has not relied on passenger flights for its airfreight. Another subsidiary of the Luen Thai International Group owned Asia Pacific Air, an airfreight company with two Boeing 727s used to run mail contracts and support other Luen Thai businesses. Asia Pacific Air transported MIFV's sashimi out of Marshall Islands to markets in Japan and the United States (Gillett 2003; Chapman 2004a).

A smaller longline company, Edgewater, operated five longliners from a small base next to MIFV but targeted mostly shark.

Pole-and-line

A Japanese distant water pole-and-line fleet, targeting skipjack for the Japanese market for fresh skipjack and for smoke-dried *katsuobushi* production, has operated continuously in the Marshall Islands EEZ since the 1960s. Although the size of the fleet was much larger in the early 1980s, it has been relatively stable for many years (Table 6.3). Indeed, as indicated by the increasing percentage of the regional catch coming from Marshall Islands' waters, it could be that the fleet is gravitating towards Marshall Islands as a preferred port, perhaps due to its business-friendly environment.

Further research would be needed to confirm the reason for Marshall Islands' increased percentage of the total catch in recent years, and to ascertain whether this fleet is likely to stay active in Marshall Islands in future, considering the overall decline in Japanese distant water tuna fleets. In addition and contrary to overall trends, oceanographic effects that moved the skipjack stocks further west meant the numbers of pole-and-line vessels operating in Marshall Islands waters plummeted from 35 in 2002 to two in 2003 (MIMRA 2004).

Purse-seine

Until 1998, when purse-seine fishing in Marshall Islands' EEZ was restricted to a small number of US vessels, most purse-seine fishing was of unassociated (free-school) sets, with log sets in some years (Langley 2004). In 1998, fleets from Korea, Japan and Taiwan joined the US fleet (Table 6.4) and catches increased correspondingly (Table 6.5). Numbers of vessels flagged to countries in the FSM Arrangement have also increased. In 1998, when Japanese purse-seiners started to operate in Marshall Islands' waters, they brought with them their preferred method of drifting fish aggregating devices (FADs). Neither the Korean nor Taiwanese purse-seine fleets that also started fishing in Marshall Islands waters in 1998 used drifting FADs; they used mostly unassociated (free-school and bait-fish) sets and log sets (Langley 2004).

Table 6.5   Marshall Islands: purse-seine catches by year and species, 1980–2003

	Skipjack (metric tonnes)	Yellowfin (metric tonnes)
1980	0	0
1981	5	1
1982	766	475
1983	0	0
1984	0	0
1985	14	3
1986	49	65
1987	0	0
1988	1,381	334
1989	0	0
1990	938	1,882
1991	50	13
1992	8,841	2,203
1993	1,436	412
1994	4,279	432
1995	7,267	1,229
1996	1,181	401
1997	141	196
1998	47,984	22,458
1999	20,288	4,340
2000	21,161	1,522
2001	35,612	4,358
2002	29,733	1,858
2003	2,654	465

Notes: Data from 2003 incomplete.
Source: Langley, A., 2004. *Marshall Islands National Tuna Fishery Status Report No.5*, Oceanic Fisheries Program, Secretariat of the Pacific Community, Noumea, New Caledonia.

Although more than 100 purse-seine vessels were licensed to fish in Marshall Islands in 2004, on average, each vessel fished in the Marshallese EEZ for only 10–12 days a year. FSM Arrangement vessels had a higher average of 30 days a year, while the US vessels had an average of only two to five days a year (Langley 2004).

Marshall Islands has six registered (Marshall Islands-flagged) purse-seine vessels operating under the Palau Arrangement (MIMRA 2004; Chapman 2004a). In 2002, Koo Fishing operated five purse-seine vessels flagged to Marshall Islands. These vessels had previously been flagged in Vanuatu. The company maintains an office in Majuro and, according to MIMRA, most or all of the catch is trans-shipped in Majuro and counted as Marshall Islands exports (Gillett 2003). The Marshall Islands-flagged purse-seine fleet operates exclusively in the Western and Central Pacific Ocean under the FSM Arrangement (MIMRA 2004).

Distant water fleets

Historically, access fees have provided a relatively high percentage of gross domestic product (5.12 per cent) for Marshall Islands compared with other countries in the region (Gillett and Lightfoot 2002).[1] Licence fees from distant water fleets constitute a significant source of revenue for Marshall Islands. For the financial year 2002–03, the total fisheries revenue received by Marshall Islands was US$2,613,217.[2] Because fleets followed the fish away from Marshall Islands in 2003, this was much lower than the previous year's figure of about US$4 million (MIMRA 2004).

Reforms to fisheries management since the late 1990s have improved the business environment, leading to an increase in fleets wishing to access Marshall Islands' waters when the fishing is good in that zone, so as to be able to trans-ship in Majuro.

Marshall Islands has in the past not been able to make the most of distant water access agreements due to a lack of capacity in independently checking the market prices secured for fish caught in the EEZ. That is, fishing companies seem to have declared a lower than market value for their catch and thus paid less fees, and, due to lack of information, MIMRA was unable to challenge the reported market figures. In addition, the fee system was described as 'administratively onerous' for MIMRA's small staff to handle (FFA 2001).

Distant water fleet access to Marshall Islands is negotiated in a number of ways (Table 6.3). Some countries had a government-to-government 'Head Agreement', but there were also government-to-company negotiations at the time of writing. China did not yet have a Head Agreement in the Pacific so it negotiated fishing access through locally based agents with the relevant Pacific island government authorities (McCoy and Gillett 2005).

The increase in numbers of international vessels using Majuro has led to an increase in certain social problems. Prostitution seems to be one of the thriving service industries for trans-shipping vessels. Unfortunately, there is a lack of awareness of and services for such social and health problems, meaning a high level of sexually transmitted infections (STIs) (*Marshall Islands Journal* 2001).

Small-scale[3]

It was estimated in 2002 that the small-scale fleet took about 3 metric tonnes of tuna weekly in Majuro, and about 444 metric tonnes of fish annually in Marshall Islands, of which 5–10 per cent was tuna (Gillett 2003). As of 2004, 10 full-time and 25–30 part-time vessels were trolling for tuna and other pelagic species around Majuro, using FADs and bird patches, while an unknown number were trolling around reefs and bird patches in the outer islands (Chapman 2004a). MIMRA was sponsoring a multi-agency working group to develop community-based fisheries management programs (MIMRA 2004).

Small-scale fisheries have been supported by Japanese government aid. The first rural fishing centre, with boats and gear, was established on Arno in 1989. Freezers, an ice plant and other infrastructure were added in the early 1990s. About this time, Japanese aid was also used to build a MIMRA dock and processing facility for coastal fisheries. MIMRA's Coastal Fisheries Division had an outer-islands fishing project that collected and helped market fish through two markets and seven fish bases. Fish from the outer islands are sold retail and wholesale in Majuro from a market centre (MIMRA 2004). MIMRA has overseen several programs to develop small-scale fisheries catching tuna, among other species, including longline tuna-fishing workshops and trials.

Coastal fishing catches were purchased and transported to Majuro for resale. During the 1990s, six other outer-island fishing centres were established, with associated gear (Chapman 2004a). Japanese fisheries aid was continuing in 2005 through Japan International Cooperation Agency (JICA) and Overseas Fisheries Cooperation Foundation (OFCF) projects (MIMRA 2004).

A sociological report commissioned as part of the Asian Development Bank (ADB) fisheries management review in the late 1990s recommended establishing a trust fund for coastal fisheries community development projects, as these projects were usually of too small a budget to be eligible for international aid. In 2003, MIMRA set aside US$300,000 for such projects, with applications to be assessed and administered by a team of officials from MIMRA and the Marshall Islands Development Authority (MIMRA 2004). Although all of the Pacific island countries covered by this report included in fisheries planning documents the idea to channel some portion of commercial tuna fishing licence fees to coastal rural communities in this way, Marshall Islands was the only one that had implemented the idea.

Efforts to deploy several FADs in the late 1980s and early 1990s around Arno for small-scale fishing were unsuccessful. Four FADs were deployed around Majuro in the early 2000s, mainly for the benefit of game fishers (Chapman 2004a).

Game fishing

Game fishing has been very popular in Marshall Islands among locals and tourists. Since 1983, the biggest club has been the Billfish Club (www.billfishclub.com). In 2004, there were about 25 charter vessels operating on Majuro, and 10 between Kwajalein and Arno. There were two big annual tournaments around Majuro, as well as monthly Billfish Club tournaments, and a couple of other events around the other islands (Chapman 2004a).

Bait fishery

Bait fishing was first conducted in the Marshall Islands by Japanese pole-and-line fishers in the 1920s. There was a survey of several atolls in 1977–78 by Japanese interests, some Secretariat of the Pacific Community (SPC) bait-fishing trials in 1978, followed by some further trials in 1983 (Chapman 2004a). As of 2005, there were no bait-fishing trials or businesses operating, although in 2004 MIMRA had been considering a proposal to farm milkfish for the longline sector (Chapman 2004a). If a bait fishery could be developed, this could add to supply business for trans-shipping fleets and domesticate more of the turnover of distant water pole-and-line and longline fleets.

Trans-shipping service and supply

Acting on technical advice received during a restructuring and reorientation of fisheries management and development in the late 1990s under an ADB loan, the Marshall Islands government developed Majuro as a service and supply centre for trans-shipping. Distant water fleets operating in the region were enticed to trans-ship in Majuro by duty-free fuel, relatively straightforward bureaucratic procedures and the air and sea freight connections available there. This policy has been successful economically, netting millions of dollars worth of revenue each year, as well as reaping the economic benefits of having the trans-shipping vessels staying in port for several days each trip and buying supplies.

Several companies have provided agency services for distant water fleets, including the multinational Ting Hong in the 1990s and local company Robert Reimers Enterprises Inc. Business and revenue generated by visiting fleets became a major source of economic benefits; the expenditure was estimated by MIMRA to be US$15–20,000 per vessel, or US$5–6 million for 300 visits a year (Ching Fu Shipbuilding Company c.2003). Numbers of trans-shipments increased steadily once the policy was implemented, from 118 in 1999 to 286 in 2001 (Gillett 2003), then fell in 2002–03 due to changes in oceanographic conditions, before rising again (MIMRA 2005).

Distant water fleets did not use Majuro for their supplies and service needs. Chinese vessels dry-docked and undertook all major refits and repairs in China (McCoy and Gillett 2005). The Japanese Zengyoren longline fleet bought steak and rice in Marshall Islands, and flew in their international crew (mostly Indonesian) to board in Majuro, but sourced virtually nothing else in Majuro and did not trans-ship there (Ishizaki, pers. comm.).[4] Because Japanese vessels use Indonesian crew, many of whom are Muslim, they have had trouble securing transit visas for their crew to pass through US airports since 11 September 2001. For this reason, Japanese vessels that had based themselves at Guam or Hawai'i in the past had looked for alternative bases, and thus started using Majuro more often. They had to use the Air Nauru route for their crews as this was the only flight in to Majuro that did not go through a US airport.

Processing

In 1985, the first tuna-processing facilities were established on Majuro under a JICA project, called Fishbase. This was for processing and packing tuna from longline vessels bound for sashimi markets. The facility included wharves, freezers, cold stores, an ice-making machine, office space and two processing rooms. MIDA managed the plant for several years, until it was leased to a Hawaiian-based longline company in the early 1990s. This company upgraded the facilities somewhat and used it until the mid 1990s, when Ting Hong took over the facility. Ting Hong had a 20-year lease arrangement with MIMRA, but in 1998 MIMRA cancelled the contract because the facility was not being maintained properly. Around 2001, Fishbase was leased to MIFV.

As well as Fishbase, there were three other fresh-fish processing facilities on Majuro in 2004 (Chapman 2004a). One was a small sashimi-packing house owned by Edgewater.

There was also the MIMRA dock facility, which was used for coastal fisheries, collecting fish from outer-islands fisheries centres.

The third was the PM&O loining plant, built in 1999, which produced cooked tuna loins (for canning). This plant froze the loins and exported them to Starkist in Pago Pago, American Samoa. The plant operated under a Hazard Analysis Critical Control Point (HACCP) plan to conform to US Food and Drug Administration (FDA) standards (although in 2004 an SPC report highlighted that the plan had not been revised for several years). It employed about 500 local people in 2004, about 80 per cent of whom were women. PM&O was supplied with purse-seine-caught product by Starkist and had its own 2,000mt-capacity freezer storage area (Gillett 2003; Chapman 2004a).

In 2005, the facility had closed down, apparently due to persistent quality and financial problems after a change in management (Echigo, pers. comm.). The PM&O loining plant was successful for several years and appears to have failed for a fairly straightforward reason, so it could possibly be revived if suitable management could be found. In 2006, a Chinese purse-seine fishing company Shanghai Deep Sea Fisheries was considering reopening loining operations at the plant (Rodwell, pers. comm.).

Determinants of success

Fluctuations in tuna stocks

Catch statistics for Marshall Islands' EEZ, especially for skipjack surface fisheries, fluctuate due to oceanographic effects related to the El Niño/Southern Oscillation Index, sea temperatures and the depth of the thermocline (Langley 2004). This has consequences for the economic benefits possible from tuna resources. The purse-seine catch dropped significantly from 31,631mt in 2002 to just 3,500mt in 2003 (MIMRA 2004). This meant that distant water vessels moved away from the EEZ and did not use Majuro's port facilities. The number of purse-seiners trans-shipping through Majuro dropped by half, and the number of Japanese pole-and-line vessels dropped from 35 in 2002 to only two in 2003 (MIMRA 2004). Marshall Islands' policy of domesticating wealth from tuna fisheries through service and supply industries instead of domesticating fisheries *per se* meant that the country had a relatively low proportion of the catch in the EEZ caught by vessels flagged to Marshall Islands. The 2003 domestic industry development report raised this as a concern for Marshall Islands' future tuna aspirations, in that this could mean Marshall Islands recorded a low catch history. Depending on how allocation is worked out in the Western and Central Pacific Fisheries Commission (WCPFC), this could have negative consequences for Marshall Islands' allocation of the total allowable catch (TAC) (Gillett 2003).

Because there has not been substantial purse-seine fishing in Marshall Islands' waters for very long, there is insufficient data for scientists in the SPC to meaningfully correlate catch rates with oceanographic effects. Nevertheless, changing sea-surface temperatures and thermocline depths do seem to be significant (Langley 2004).

Scientific assessments of oceanographic affects on stocks available in the Marshall Islands' EEZ, including the effects of climate change, need to be taken into account when developing policy, especially regarding the purse-seine fleet.

Freight

The substantial US military presence on Kwajalein has meant that Marshall Islands has had a relatively high volume of sea freight. Ships regularly bring in supplies and leave relatively empty, meaning there is reliable, frequent and reasonably priced freight for frozen or canned fish exports. The PM&O loining business apparently made use of this freight advantage.

Human resources

During the 1990s, employment for Marshallese in tuna-related industries was insignificant: about 120 jobs, or 0.09 per cent of all formal jobs in Marshall Islands (Gillett 2003). This increased when several hundred people were employed in the loining factory, but in 2005, after the closure of the factory, the local employment level shrank back to levels similar to those in the 1990s. Productivity rates were not competitive because minimum-wage rates were pushed high by US work rights. Because Marshallese have the right to live and work in the United States under the Compact of Free Association, unemployment was not as pressing an issue in Marshall Islands as in some of the other Pacific island countries covered by this study. Thus, the willingness of Marshallese to work in commercial fishery industries has become a major issue (Chapman 2004a).

This lack of interest, along with relatively high expectations of remuneration, meant that Marshall Islands did not have a large, eager labour pool for domestic tuna developments. Unreliability, absenteeism and high turnover were cited as labour problems by industry interviewees in 2002 (Gillett 2003). Lack of skilled tradespeople for service industries and locally based fleets were also cited as a constraint in 2003 (Chapman 2004a). As of 2005, there was a shortage of workers skilled in ship repairs, especially in hydraulics and refrigeration. An SPC report from 2004 detailed ways in which Marshall Islands might increase the number of local tradespeople (Chapman 2004a). The foreign investment proposal for a floating dry dock included a training scheme (Ching Fu Shipbuilding Company c.2003).

The Fisheries and Nautical Training Centre (FNTC) conducted education and training in basic seamanship, marine engine and vessel maintenance and fishing techniques (including longlining), although no courses were run in 2002 or 2003 due to a shortage of funds and resources (Chapman 2004a). The College of the Marshall Islands has in the past offered vocational courses in trades relating to marine industries, as well as two-year diploma programs, which included marine-related topics. The college, however, had difficulty in encouraging students to take courses in marine studies areas, due to lack of interest in fisheries-related careers (Chapman 2004a).

Future prospects

Future prospects for the tuna industry in Marshall Islands in 2005 looked similar to those outlined by Robert Gillett in 2003. Constraints on development of tuna industries noted by Gillett in 2002 included land availability, quality and price of labour, docking facilities and services, visa problems, lack of preparation for HACCP requirements, and difficulties for local companies to compete against financially stronger Asian companies (Gillett 2003). Suggestions for improvements from Gillett include

- improved information on the likely future of the fishing fleets that Marshall Islands relies on for trans-shipping
- make sure future small-scale fisheries developments are technically and economically viable before starting
- develop a Tuna Management and Development Plan
- develop a HACCP strategy for exports
- make sure Marshall Islands is in a good position to achieve a reasonable allocation within the WCPFC
- develop the commercial code and streamline the procedures for establishing businesses, in terms of licensing and access to land.

Gillett (2003) found that one of the major advantages Marshall Islands had for developing tuna industries was that the government had made some reforms to its business environment. He found it rated highly compared with other Micronesian countries in terms of immigration and customs requirements, rates of prosecution for fishing-related violations, and the costs of ice, cold storage, stevedoring, packing materials and fuel. Marshall Islands was also seen as more attractive for tuna industries than some of its neighbours because of MIMRA's focus on industry, government incentives such as tax holidays and the quality of fisheries infrastructure. Marshall Islands attracted companies that found the business environment too difficult, for various reasons, in Guam, Palau and the Federated States of Micronesia.

Governing tuna industries

Fisheries in Marshall Islands are governed by MIMRA, which was established in 1988 under the *MIMRA Act* (1986, revised 1997). There was an extensive review of Marshall Islands' fisheries policy and institutions under an ADB loan in the mid to late 1990s (ANZDEC Limited 1997). As part of this, a national fisheries policy was drafted and adopted by the cabinet in 1997, and was followed diligently by MIMRA. The development of Majuro as a service centre for trans-shipping fleets was one of the more significant outcomes of this reform effort.

Since then, the Forum Fisheries Agency (FFA), with funding provided by the Canadian government under the CSPOD II fund, has worked with MIMRA to develop a Tuna Management Plan. The process of developing the plan has included working on the following issues: i) assessing the feasibility of options for domestic tuna development, including a longline fishery; ii) identifying constraints to further development of Marshall Islands' tuna resources; iii) identifying potential infrastructure developments that would promote tuna-related development; and iv) reviewing Marshall Islands' labour-force issues for fisheries-related industries with a view to training needs (MIMRA 2004).

The Tuna Management Plan as an overall framework was formally adopted in mid 2005 by the government, with specific provisions to be worked out during 2006 (MIMRA

2005). Possible improvements to fisheries management and development, including introducing more consultative decision making, were detailed in a *National Preparation Report* for the Global Environment Facility Strategic Action Program (Lewis 2004b). Details of MIMRA's observer scheme are available from the 2005 WCPFC Scientific Committee Marshall Islands national report (MIMRA 2005).

As in other Pacific island countries, the Marshall Islands government has in the past been involved in tuna enterprises. This included MIDA's joint-venture partnership with a US purse-seining company, which started operations in 1989, and another which started in 1991 (Chapman 2004a). These operated at a net loss (Gillett 2003). An OFCF study from 1998 found that MIDA had invested about US$12 million for tuna-industry development, largely unsuccessfully (Gillett 2003).

After these failures, the Marshall Islands government moved to a policy of providing an enabling environment for business, and having any tuna developments run by the private sector (Joseph, pers. comm.). The PM&O loining plant was an example of an entirely private-sector venture. Its failure thus cost the government nothing but the revenue and economic benefits that disappeared with the company's demise. In the case of the Fishbase, the government had worked around its ownership of the means of production by leasing it to the private sector rather than attempting to run it itself.

The Marshall Islands government has shown itself willing to follow some of the advice of technical specialists working on the ADB, SPC, FFA and CPSOD II-funded contributions to fisheries development policy. This willingness to try new ideas is probably why the Marshall Islands has been relatively successful with its tuna developments since the mid 1990s. It has not developed a large domestic industry, but the investments that have occurred during this time were profitable while they lasted and cost the government very little even when they failed. Developing Majuro as a service sector for trans-shipping has been an economic success story, albeit currently constrained by the seasonal nature of surface fisheries in the Marshall Islands EEZ, and qualified by social problems.

Consultative processes in government

Due to the government policy of focusing on gaining wealth from distant water fishing via trans-shipment supply, servicing and processing, no industrial-scale domestic fishing industry has existed in Marshall Islands since the 1990s. In 2002, there was no commercial fisheries industry association in Marshall Islands. Larger companies such as PM&O and the MIFV were members of the Chamber of Commerce, and there was an association for tourism-related charter boats (Gillett 2003).

Conclusion

Marshall Islands has experienced a number of setbacks and generally overcome them, moving from government involvement in fishing operations to successfully encouraging and supporting private-sector investment. The resource potential, freight and transport connections, and pragmatic, relatively business-friendly approach of the government to development means Marshall Islands is in a good position to maintain and increase the wealth it generates from tuna industries (Tables 6.6 and 6.7). The shortage of local managers, a suitable labour pool and relatively high wages are constraints to tuna-industry development; these factors are at least caused partly by the ability of Marshallese to go to work in the United States. With the development of management skills and the implementation of its tuna management plan, the outlook could be improved further. The social impacts of hosting a busy international port in the lagoon detract from the economic benefits gained from tuna industries, so this is another area in need of policy attention. Finally, the fluctuations in the fortunes of the tuna sector are somewhat tied to El Niño cycle-driven resource availability, so strategies to smooth (or adapt to) this variation need to be factored into development strategies.

Development aspirations and tuna

The Marshall Islands government's general development aspirations were laid out in the *Strategic Development Plan Framework 2003–2018: Vision 2018*. Specific objectives regarding marine resources mentioned in this document included (Chapman 2004a)

- maximising rents from resources within sustainable limits
- developing income-generating activities in sustainable coastal fisheries
- ensuring all new developments are sustainable by having them approved through management plans based on scientific stock assessments
- strengthening fisheries education and training and employment opportunities for graduates
- enhancing capacities of the sector to sustainably increase fisheries production, onshore processing, trade and exports.

Table 6.6   Marshall Islands: indicators of domestic development, 2001

	Locally based vessels active	Cannery/ loining facilities	Sashimi packing facilities	RMI nationals jobs on vessels	RMI nationals jobs on shore	Frozen tuna exports (mt)	Fresh tuna exports (mt)	Cooked loin exports (mt)
PM&O Processing	0	1	0	0	395	0	0	3,852 (9,632mt raw tuna inputs)
MIFV	49 LL	0	1	0	38	0	76	0
Koo Fishing	5 PS	0	0	5	4	36,598	0	0
Edgewater	5 LL	0	1	0	20	0	0	0
Total	54 LL, 5 PS	1	2	5	457	36,598	76	3,852

Notes: LL: longline PS: purse-seine MIFV: Marshall Islands Fishing Venture.
This figure is not representative of MIFV's annual production because it started production late in 2001. In 2002, MIFV exported 1,121mt of fresh whole fish and loins and 1,120mt of frozen tuna and by-catch. Edgewater started up in late 2001 and did not start exporting until 2002.
Source: Gillett, R., 2003. *Domestic tuna industry development in the Pacific islands. The current situation and considerations for future development assistance*, FFA Report 03/01, Pacific Islands Forum Fisheries Agency, Honiara.

Table 6.7   Marshall Islands: indicators of tuna development, 2004–2005

Company/fleet	Domestic vessels: no. and type	Processing facilities: no. and type	Jobs for nationals: no. and type	Annual exports: volume and type	Annual domestic sales: volume and type
	10 full-time and 25–30 part-time small-scale vessels operating around Majuro Several other small-scale vessels operating in outer-islands areas	7 fisheries centres around the country, including one in Majuro	-	0	Fresh chilled and frozen tuna for domestic consumption
MIFV (vessels included in Chinese DWFN)	38 longline	Fishbase, sashimi packing plant	0-	A-grade tuna to Japan as sashimi B and C-grade to US as loins/steaks	—
Totals	38 longline several dozen small-scale	9 fresh-fish processing facilities	-	-	-

Notes: Edgewater fished and processed shark; it was unclear whether it also fished and processed tuna. Of the Japanese longline fleet, 11 vessels were not directly from Japan but were cited as being from the company Pacific Food and Services Inc. and 14 were from the Guam subsidiary of the company, Sanko Bussan. Of the 38 MIFV longline vessels listed here as Chinese, an unspecified number were Taiwanese owned.
Sources: Interviews conducted in June 2005. Marshall Islands Marine Resources Authority (MIMRA), 2005. Fisheries report—Marshall Islands, Paper read at First Meeting of the Scientific Committee WCPFC-SC1, Noumea, New Caledonia. Chapman, L., 2004b. *Nearshore domestic fisheries development in Pacific islands countries and territories*, Information Paper for Fourth Heads of Fisheries Meeting, Secretariat of the Pacific Community, Noumea, New Caledonia.

The picture of development from marine resources, including tuna, emerging from this list closely resembles the picture of development that emerges from MIMRA's policy and vision statement (MIMRA 2003).

Policy. Improve economic benefits from the fisheries sector within sustainable limits, promote responsible, private-sector led fishery developments, and strengthen institutional capacity to facilitate the responsible development and management of the nation's fisheries resources.

Vision. To develop the Marshall Islands into a major fishing port and centre for maritime activity within the Western and Central Pacific region.

Marshall Islands' aspirations for development from tuna resources are also listed in the tuna management plan as follows (MIMRA 2004)

- provide an enabling environment that will promote and encourage private-sector development in the commercial fishing, charter/sport fishing, processing and support sectors in Marshall Islands
- promote sustainable and responsible domestic development and harvesting of the tuna resource in the Marshall Islands EEZ in an environmentally friendly way, to provide food for local consumption and export-oriented income
- maximise the benefits and economic returns to Marshallese—local communities and Marshall Islands as a whole
- create employment and income-generating opportunities for Marshallese, including those in outer islands
- collect accurate data from all tuna fishery activities in Marshall Islands, ensuring that all by-catch and any interactions with protected species are recorded
- ensure that all development within the Marshall Islands tuna fishery is consistent and compatible with any obligations or requirements as set out in local legislation and/or international agreements that affect the Marshall Islands
- eventually reduce and replace foreign fishing access with Marshallese-owned and operated vessels.

Domestic fishery development

MIMRA's pragmatic approach to development from tuna industries meant that, in light of the disastrous longline project in the 1990s, development of domestic fisheries was much less of a priority in Marshall Islands than in other Pacific island countries. Developing a domestic longline fishery was mentioned in early drafts of the Tuna Management Plan and SPC assistance had been sought to investigate possibilities, but in 2005 the director of MIMRA saw little likelihood that an economically viable domestic longline fishery could be established in the near future (Joseph, pers. comm.). Instead, the government's plan was to continue to domesticate wealth from fishing done by foreign-owned companies through processing the catch onshore and through service and supply industries. Other possibilities for domestic fisheries development mentioned in the 2003 Gillett report into domestic development for Pacific island countries included developing an albacore fishery in the north of the country, and developing a longline base at Enewetak close to concentrations of yellowfin and bigeye tuna, but these were not being pursued in 2005.

Domestic processing

In the early 1990s, there had been talk of building a cannery in Majuro, pending access to land and a fresh water supply (Gillett 2003). In 2005, however, canning was not part of the Marshall Islands government's plans for increasing onshore production. One of the areas noted in 2002 as needing work to facilitate development of processing and tuna exporting was implementing a HACCP plan (Gillett 2003). By 2004, MIMRA had completed a HACCP plan with assistance from an FAO-funded consultant. Marshall Islands still needed to enact the regulations, set up an inspection laboratory and be approved as a Competent Authority by the European Union in order to be able to export processed foods to the European Union and had applied for 'pre-approved' status. MIFV was upgrading its facility in anticipation of changes being required in order to be able to export tuna loins and steaks to the European Union as well as to the United States (MIMRA 2004).

Developing port infrastructure

Marshall Islands could boost its economic benefits from servicing international fleets further if it developed the capacity for ship repairs, such as a dry dock and a net-repair facility. Ships coming to Majuro for repairs might then stay in port for seven to 10 days, whereas for trans-shipping they stay an average of only five (Ching Fu Shipbuilding Company c.2003). Marshall Islands' existing dry-dock facilities were not large enough, but MIMRA had received proposals to develop port infrastructure, including a floating dry-dock facility (Ching Fu Shipbuilding Company c.2003).

Aspirations will have to overcome these difficulties for this kind of venture to work. Repair facilities would have to be reliable and their costs low enough to make it cheaper than for vessels to steam to and from cheap shipping repair centres in China. Another constraint for this type of industry is the seasonal nature of the Marshall Islands surface fishery.

Marshall Islands also has logistical difficulties with obtaining spare parts and other materials necessary for repairs. Since Marshall Islands seems to have more favourable freight conditions than other Pacific island countries covered by this report, the main issue appears to be that local businesses have not yet picked up on this demand. Possibly MIMRA could encourage local trading companies to import parts to enable service industries to be more competitive.

Human resources development

Other benefits, such as meeting employment aspirations, could come from human resources development, if operations effectively trained and employed Marshallese labourers, technicians and managers. These kinds of jobs might be more desirable to Marshallese than working on fishing vessels. Because of the training required and because Marshall Islands' wage rates are high by regional standards, commercial proposals to develop ship-repair facilities have included requests for government assistance with training costs, and for reductions in the minimum-wage standard (Ching Fu Shipbuilding Company c.2003). Considering the wage levels in Marshall Islands compared with China, where the Chinese and Japanese fleets based in Marshall Islands went for repairs (McCoy and Gillett 2005; Ishizaki, pers. comm.), it seems unlikely that ship-repair services in Marshall Islands could be competitively priced.

Environmental issues

The word 'sustainable' was used in just about every aspiration listed in the Marshall Islands government documents relating to fisheries quoted in this report. The Minister for Resources and Development and chair of the MIMRA board, John Silk, wrote in his preface to the 2002–03 MIMRA *Annual Report*: 'I cannot emphasize enough the fragility of our fishery environment and the need to ensure its sustainable use' (MIMRA 2004). Other Pacific island countries covered by this report also used the word copiously in government documents about fisheries, but Marshall Islands was one of only two (the other being Papua New Guinea) that had committed itself through aid projects to a survey of coastal resources. Deep-sea offshore tuna fisheries are much more robust than near-shore fisheries, so it would be worthwhile for the Marshall Islands to consider management of near-shore fisheries, deflecting effort when necessary and possible to offshore tuna fisheries.

Recommendations

- Maintain and progress advances made in the following areas
  - an enabling environment for private-sector development, especially in trans-shipping, viable onshore processing and service and supply areas
  - environmental monitoring of near-shore fisheries and the effects of pollution
  - a trust fund for small coastal development projects, emphasising the need for pre-assessment of projects to determine economic and biological sustainability.
- Improve capacity in MIMRA and the private sector, especially in the area of negotiating and administering distant water fleet access, and to ensure an adequately skilled workforce to support domestic industry development.
- Fully implement the Tuna Management Plan, including the development of management measures for tuna stocks.
- Develop and pursue clear negotiating objectives and strategies that maximise the long-term national benefits of regional and multilateral cooperation in tuna management.

Notes

[1] Kiribati was the highest in this study, with an estimated 42.81 per cent of GDP coming from access fees in 1999. For Cook Islands, the figure was 0.21 per cent; for Papua New Guinea, 0.17 per cent; for Solomon Islands, 0.10 per cent; and for Fiji, 0.01 per cent (Gillett and Lightfoot 2002).

[2] This amount included licence fees as well as other fees collected by MIMRA from vessels under multilateral and bilateral access agreements.

[3] For a history of all the small-scale coastal fisheries development projects in Marshall Islands, see Chapman 2004a.

[4] The Japanese distant water longline fleet must trans-ship in Japan, so has not trans-shipped in Marshall Islands. They have ultra-low temperature (ULT) freezing capacity so stay out at sea for months or more than a year before needing to offload.

7

Papua New Guinea

Population: 5,836,000
Land area: 426,840 km²
Sea area: 2,400,000 km²

Of the countries included in this study, Papua New Guinea is the largest in terms of land size and population. It is made up of one very large mountainous island shared with the Indonesian-controlled West Papua to the west, with numerous smaller islands to the north and east. The most striking characteristic of PNG society is its diversity. There are hundreds of distinct language and cultural groups, with differences in facial features and skin colour between peoples of the Highlands, south coast, the islands and Bougainville. Before World War I, the northern part of what is now Papua New Guinea was colonised by Germany. After the war, the whole of what is now Papua New Guinea was under Australian colonial rule, until independence in 1975.

Papua New Guinea has a formal capitalist economy—which is dominated by the government and a few large corporations in the mining and forestry sectors—and an informal economy. Some of the informal sector is also capitalist (such as stalls selling fresh fish by the side of the road or smoked fish in markets), but the bulk of it operates mostly without cash according to indigenous norms (such as village fish catches being distributed as per social obligations).[1] The formal economy has grown through resource-extraction industries—such as mining, forestry and fisheries—but it is widely felt that these industries have failed to bring benefits at the village level, except perhaps to a small proportion of landowners.

In the 30 years since independence, government services and infrastructure have deteriorated markedly (Manning 2005). The national government has undertaken a range of financial and economic reforms in recent years, but there continue to be serious concerns about governance, corruption and capacity. The investment environment remains erratic and high risk (Government of Australia 2005). Compared with other Pacific island countries, Papua New Guinea has far more agricultural, mineral and marine resources, as well as land, labour and potable water, but thus far it has been unable to convert this resource potential into sustained development gains for the majority of its population.

Map 7.1   Papua New Guinea

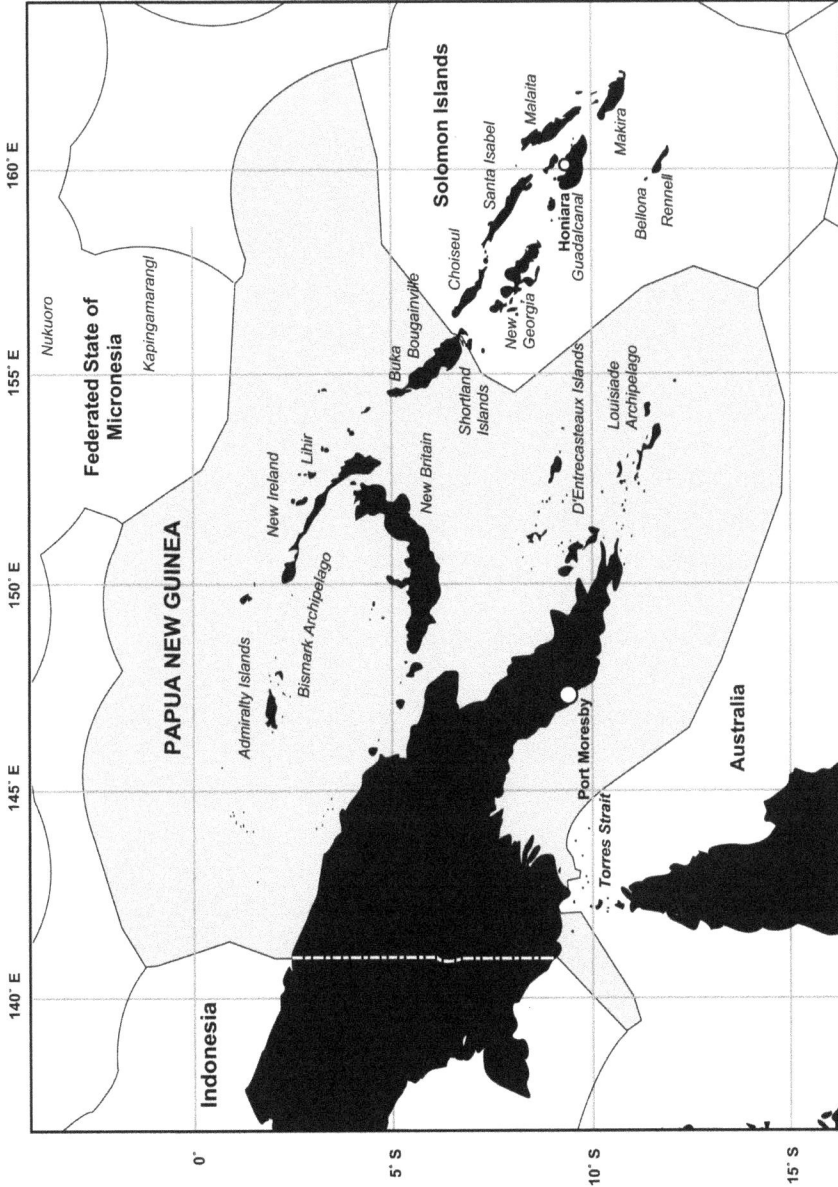

Source: Youngmi Choi, Secretariat of the Pacific Community, Noumea, New Caledonia.

Potential of tuna fisheries

The potential of Papua New Guinea's tuna resources is probably the best of any of the countries included in this report. Papua New Guinea's Exclusive Economic Zone (EEZ) includes some of the richest purse-seine fishing grounds, with the highest annual catch. While the longline-caught bigeye and yellowfin tuna in PNG waters do not have the value of the colder-water fish of the same species, the longline fishery is potentially very productive, especially to the north of the country. Furthermore, Papua New Guinea has relatively well-developed infrastructure, plentiful land, labour and potable water, and is close to important markets in Southeast Asia.

History of development

Early domestic industry development

In the 1970s, Papua New Guinea had a Japanese pole-and-line industry, as did many countries in the region. This fishery targeted skipjack, some of which was processed at an *arabushi* skipjack smoking facility in Kavieng.[2] The pole-and-line fishery peaked in 1974 with a catch of 74,649 metric tonnes. The fishery was based around Rabaul and Kavieng. The Japanese pole-and-line vessels caught fresh live bait each evening for the next day's fishing. There were difficulties with the bait fishery in Papua New Guinea, because it was under provincial government jurisdiction and the regulations were not uniform across provinces.

A Japanese distant water longline fleet had operated around Papua New Guinea until the mid 1980s, with a peak catch of 20,000mt in 1978. There were also US purse-seine vessels operating in PNG waters from the 1970s. The Japanese pole-and-line vessels and the US purse-seine vessels exported to Starkist canneries. Starkist promised to establish a cannery in Papua New Guinea. In order to encourage fishing companies to establish employment-generating onshore processing facilities and 'value add' in Papua New Guinea, the government introduced duties on exports of unprocessed tuna. At first the duties were 2.5 per cent but later they peaked at 15 per cent. The policy did not work as intended. Starkist never built a cannery. The Japanese pole-and-line fleets withdrew in 1986. Japanese longliners allowed the bilateral fishing access agreement to lapse in 1987 and ceased operating in PNG waters.

Throughout the 1980s and early 1990s, the main benefit Papua New Guinea derived from commercial tuna fisheries was the access fees paid by distant water purse-seine fleets, mainly from Taiwan but also from the Philippines and the United States. The fact that Papua New Guinea managed to capture only a small contribution to GDP in terms of revenue from its tuna resources via access fees from these fleets, and no employment or spin-off activities in the local economy, means that these were wasted years in terms of capturing wealth from tuna.

Reform and development since 1995

During the late 1990s and early 2000s, there was substantial restructuring of PNG fisheries administration under an Asian Development Bank (ADB) loan. The old Department of Fisheries and Marine Resources was downsised and reoriented from fisheries research and extension work, particularly in the provinces, to providing services for large-scale commercial fisheries. It became a self-funding (through access and licence fees), non-commercial statutory authority, the National Fisheries Authority (NFA).

Industry representatives interviewed as part of this study said the NFA administrative reforms had a positive influence on tuna business development in that policies became more transparent and therefore reliable. For example, several industry managers interviewed cited the introduction of transparent licensing procedures as encouraging their investment because they knew in advance what needed to be done to secure a licence and could anticipate what it would cost. Gillett (2003) also found that improved fisheries governance in Papua New Guinea in this period was one of the factors causing the growth in domestic tuna industries.

In the mid 1990s, changes in fisheries policy breathed new life into Papua New Guinea-based tuna fisheries. The duty on tuna exports was lifted and the new tuna longline industry, under a national management plan, became reserved for PNG citizens and local companies with only a minority (49 per cent maximum) foreign shareholding permitted. Local investors (mostly non-indigenous PNG citizen businessmen) moved into medium-scale longline fishing. At various stages, domestic longline vessels operated from Port Moresby, Lae, Kimbe, Kavieng, Wewak and Manus (Table 7.1). Vessels were all either locally or foreign owned under a 'bare boat' (or 'demise') charter to a local company. A cold-store facility was built at Port Moresby airport to store chilled fish before it was freighted out. Based on large catches adjacent to Papua New Guinea's EEZ in the north, the northern part of the EEZ appears to be the optimal longline fishing area. Longline wharves were provided under ADB loans in Kavieng and Lobrum (Manus) (Kumoru 2005). This area has only ever been lightly fished, however, due to difficulties freighting fish to sashimi markets from outside Port Moresby.

Papua New Guinea's catch in 2004 was 3,918mt, made up mostly of yellowfin (47 per cent), bigeye, albacore and others. Albacore was more common in the Coral Sea area. According to longline company interviewees, the best way to deal with their catch is to fly the A-grade tuna to the Japanese sashimi market. The next best product is sold in the Australian and Southeast Asian sashimi markets. B and C-grade product that cannot be profitably sold as fresh chilled sashimi was then further processed and packed as chilled or frozen loins or tuna steaks. These are exported to Australia, the United States and Asia. There is demand for these products in Europe, but the logistics of sending fresh chilled or frozen product to Europe from Papua New Guinea are difficult, largely because of a lack of scale (Paru, pers. comm.). Airfreight is expensive and the routes and schedules of passenger flights have not been appropriate for fresh-fish markets. Frozen product could be shipped, but Papua New Guinea's sea freight has been controlled by one international

Table 7.1   Papua New Guinea: indicators of domestic development, 2001–2002

	Locally based vessels active	Cannery/ loining facilities	Sashimi packing facilities	PNG nationals jobs on vessels	PNG nationals jobs on shore	Frozen tuna exports (mt)	Fresh tuna exports (mt)	Cases canned tuna
Latitude 8	9 longline	0	1	102	34	42	1,050	0
Neptune	9 longline	0	1	95	35	256	360	0
Coco	6 longline	0	0	22	20	166	0	0
Other companies	16 longline	0	5	130	70	32	600	0
RD	10 purse-seine	1	0	25	2,500	15,888	0	1,464,158
Frabelle	5 purse-seine	0	0	60	23	9,092	0	0
South Seas Tuna	5 purse-seine	0	0	7	20	26,975	0	0
Fair Well	3 purse-seine	0	0	15	2	0	0	0
Pacific Blue Sea	1 purse-seine	0	0	4	3	5,080	0	0
Total	40 longline 24 purse-seine	1	7	460	2,707	2,010	59,532	1,464,158

Notes: Other companies included: Equatorial Marine Resources (EMR, a joint venture with Sanko Bussan), Blue Haven, Kidu Kidu, Longline Tuna, Manus Provincial Government, MAPS Tuna, Molina, Nako, Niugini Islands Sea Products, Yuwan Fisheries and PNG Fresh Tuna. There was a discrepancy between the NFA reported exports of fresh tuna for 2001 (1,745mt) and the FFA report of imports of PNG fresh tuna in the Japanese market for that year (2,015mt).
Source: Gillett, R., 2003. *Domestic tuna industry development in the Pacific islands. The current situation and considerations for future development assistance*, FFA Report 03/01, Pacific Islands Forum Fisheries Agency, Honiara, Solomon Islands:70.

Table 7.2   Papua New Guinea: export values of marine products, 1996–2002
('000 kina)

	1996	1997	1998	1999	2000	2001	2002
Tuna	3,584.02	14,066.67	85,703.49	76,553.65	100,339.30	156,629.43	220,875.38
All marine products	25,880.22	37,150.44	138,172.60	124,583.80	157,544.70	218,749.18	282,855.64

Notes: Data for 2002 are provisional. All marine products: tuna, various crab products, crayfish products, various fish products (non-tuna), various shark products, frozen shrimp and 'sedentary' resources including *bêche-de-mer* and shell products such as buttons, pearl etc.
Source: Gomez, B. (ed.), 2005. 'PNG's robust tuna industry', in *Papua New Guinea Yearbook*, Yong Shan Fook, Port Moresby.

consortium. In addition to the price inflation caused by this monopoly, inefficiencies in ports and the low volume of shipping make sea freight expensive.

Raw packaged tuna loins and steaks can be further processed with 'gas' or 'tasteless smoke'. In this process, carbon monoxide is injected to preserve the red colour of the flesh, which makes the product look fresh (red tuna meat turns brown after exposure to air or freezing). Companies in Lae and Kavieng using this process in 2004 were trading with a Dutch company Anova. The process is controversial because it can be used to mask substandard product, so is banned in many markets. For that reason only some PNG operators were anticipating using gas processing in future.

Several of the longline companies had sashimi packing and fresh-tuna loining facilities. In addition, there were some facilities not owned by longline companies. These included

- an NFA-owned facility in Kavieng, built with AusAID funding, which was being used for tuna in 2004 until the local longline fleet ceased operating in early 2005, and is currently used primarily for deep-water snapper and reef fish
- the Frabelle facility in Lae, completed in early 2005
- a facility planned for Lae to be built with Chinese aid money (to be owned by the NFA)
- a facility planned for Madang, intending to process handline catch (private investment by a company called Japan Foods).

In addition to the domestic longline tuna industry, since the mid 1990s distant water purse-seine companies have been enticed to base some of their fleets locally and to establish processing facilities in exchange for being licensed as 'domestically based foreign-owned' vessels. Being licensed as domestically based instead of distant water brought two main benefits to purse-seine fishers: i) they avoided access fees, and ii) distant water fishers who were not included in the 205-vessel cap on distant water purse-seine vessels in the region set by the Parties to the Nauru Agreement (PNA) would, as locally based vessels, be preferentially included in the cap under the FSM Arrangement.

By 2002, Papua New Guinea was looking like a model for development of commercial tuna fisheries. Since the domestication policy was introduced in the mid 1990s, annual export revenue from locally based tuna companies grew from K3.6 million to K221 million. Fisheries exports exceeded the value of forestry exports for the first time (Lewis 2005). The RD tuna cannery, established in 1997, was profitable and employed about 2,500 people in Madang (see Table 7.2). Several other processing facilities were planned for Lae, Manus, Kavieng and Wewak.

Export destinations for PNG tuna were as follows: chilled tuna to Japan and Australia; frozen tuna to the Philippines, Japan and Taiwan; canned tuna to Germany, the United Kingdom and small amounts to Melanesian Spearhead Group trading bloc countries; loins to Europe and the United States; and fish meal to Australia and Japan (Kumoru 2005).

Papua New Guinea was a site for tuna trans-shipment, especially Port Moresby. There were net-mending facilities at Lae and Madang, with a facility being built in Manus. Vessels trans-shipped at Kavieng, with provincial fisheries staff monitoring their activities.

Decline of domestic longline industry since 2002

The value of tuna exports for Papua New Guinea peaked in 2002 at about US$64 million, then declined in the next few years by 10 per cent. The domestic tuna longline fleet, which had grown since starting in 1995 and suffered a downturn after 2002. There were several years of poor catches with small fish not suited to the most valuable Japanese market (Brownjohn, pers. comm.). It is possible that PNG longline fisheries were thus suffering the catch per unit of effort (CPUE) decline noted for the region as a whole for bigeye and yellowfin—the species targeted by sashimi-oriented longline fisheries. In addition, fuel cost increases and increased airfreight costs in the aftermath of the 11 September 2001 terrorist attacks hit the domestic longline fishers hard. During 2004, it became uneconomical to do tuna longlining from anywhere in Papua New Guinea other than Port Moresby, because of the extra leg of transport required to get the tuna to Port Moresby before it was sent overseas. By early 2005, all tuna longliners outside Port Moresby targeting the sashimi market had ceased operating (some longliners remained, targeting shark).

While airfreight and fuel costs had stifled the industry outside Port Moresby by 2005, longlining based in Port Moresby was still viable, although most companies had wound back operations due to decreased margins. One company, Equatorial Marine Resources (EMR), was expanding. It was a joint venture between a local businessman with a background in logistics, Blaise Paru, and Sanko Bussan, a Japanese longline sashimi-tuna company with 30 years' experience. All of EMR's product was pre-sold through Sanko Bussan's connections, meaning it avoided the risks of auction. EMR had a new processing facility on its wharf in Port Moresby, and had invested in a freezer vessel to collect catch from the fishing vessels to enable them to stay fishing (Paru, pers. comm.).

Air Niugini bears some responsibility for the collapse of the longline fishery outside Port Moresby. When Australian airline Ansett collapsed in 2001, Air Niugini also nearly folded and since then it had focused on profitability, charging as much as it could for its services and trying to maintain its monopoly status. As well as being expensive, schedules and the size of the planes operating in regional centres meant Air Niugini was not able to provide a suitably speedy and reliable service for sashimi-tuna exporters. Even from Port Moresby, Air Niugini's service was not ideal for sashimi exports to Japan because it could not get tuna to market quickly enough. When tuna exporters tried to bring in chartered freight flights, Air Niugini lobbied relevant government departments to refuse approval, arguing that Air Niugini had the capacity to do tuna airfreighting.

Eventually EMR in Port Moresby achieved approval for regular charter flights and was using this service successfully in 2005, but by this time the operators outside Port Moresby had already withdrawn from the fishery. Air Niugini prevented EMR using any of the cold storage or loading equipment at the airport (*The National* 2005b; Paru, pers. comm.).

The domestication policy of the 1990s was being rethought in 2005, in light of the stagnation of the domestic longline industry in 2004 and 2005. Even in its heyday, the domestic fleet had not taken the nominal annual total allowable catch (TAC) of 10,000mt, so the banning of distant water longline fleets could be seen as a missed opportunity in terms of revenue (Gillett, Preston and Associates 2000). With the decline in the domestically owned industry, the NFA board agreed in 2005 to allow limited access by foreign longline vessels (Kumoru, pers. comm.). A new access agreement for the Japanese fleet was signed in 2006. It was hoped that having distant water longliners in Kavieng would build the fisheries sector in the area, thus enabling domestic fisheries enterprise (Barnabas, pers. comm.).

Another planned change is that ultra-low temperature (ULT) freezing vessels will be allowed to work in PNG waters.[3] The high technology and high cost of these vessels means they are not easily localised so they had been banned under the old domestication policy. Industry interviewees outside Port Moresby, however, for whom airfreight was such a problem, said the ban on ULT freezers was a constraint on the domestic longline industry.

Purse-seine fishery

In terms of volume and value, the purse-seine fishery has been the biggest in Papua New Guinea, making up about 99 per cent of the commercial catch. Eighty per cent of the PNG purse-seine catch was recorded as skipjack, with the rest being yellowfin (Table 7.3).

Papua New Guinea's purse-seine fishery is made up of a distant water access fleet and a locally based foreign-owned fleet. In 2005, the distant water fleet licensed to operate in Papua New Guinea's EEZ included 98 active purse-seine vessels (several of the US vessels were licensed for but did not operate in Papua New Guinea) (Kumoru 2005). In 2005, 19 purse-seiners were regarded as domestic; 12 of these were non-Papua New Guinea-flagged vessels operating from Siar near Madang, supplying the RD cannery. There were 18 locally based foreign vessels, mostly Vanuatu flagged, which fished around the region under the FSM Arrangement (taking about 30 per cent of their catch in Papua New Guinea's EEZ). The domestic and locally based foreign proportion of the PNG catch has

Table 7.3   **Papua New Guinea: tuna exports by volume, value and product, 2000–2004**

	Total catch	Chilled tuna		Frozen tuna		Canned tuna		Tuna loins		Fish meal	
	mt	mt	US$	mt	US$	mt	US$	mt	US$	mt	US$
2000	282,005	1,196	5.1m	33,004	13.5m	10,298	18.1m	0	0	1,690	0.4m
2001	162,999	1,857	8.2m	34,656	22.2m	9,858	17.6m	0	0	1,438	0.5m
2002	170,175	2,106	8.4m	33,908	30.4m	12,214	23.4m	0	0	1,670	0.6m
2003	374,542	2,092	9.3m	31,275	16.5m	13,753	28.0m	0	0	1,791	0.7m
2004	313,027	2,111	9.6m	10,968	7m	15,252	35.3m	1,724	0.9m	2,973	1.2m

Notes: The total catch included distant water as well as local fleets, while the exported amounts were from the local and locally based fleets only. Canned tuna is not usually measured in metric tonnes but in cases of 48 cans. It is possible the figure for volume of exports of canned tuna referred to the amount of whole fish put into exported cans.
Source: Kumoru, L., 2005. Tuna Fisheries Report—Papua New Guinea, First Meeting of the Scientific Committee, Western and Central Pacific Fisheries Commission, Noumea, New Caledonia.

been more than 30 per cent in recent years (Kumoru 2005). Since 2000, the PNG purse-seine catch averaged about 260,000mt annually, making up about 20 per cent of the total Western and Central Pacific Ocean purse-seine catch.

The 1990s' domestication policy operated differently in the purse-seine fishery than it did in the longline fishery. Purse-seine vessels are larger, more high tech and much more expensive than longline vessels, so local businesses did not move into purse-seining. Rather, the domestication approach was to encourage foreign fleets to base some of their vessels in Papua New Guinea and establish a PNG-registered branch of their company. Since purse-seiners stay out at sea for months on end, import most of their inputs and are not slipped and repaired in Papua New Guinea, simply having purse-seine vessels based there is not economically better than having them based overseas and paying access fees as a distant water fleet. Locally based foreign vessels employed up to five PNG nationals on each vessel and there were some benefits from having company finances go through Papua New Guinea's economy, but these would not offset the loss in access fees.

The PNG government aimed to gain from having purse-seiners based in Papua New Guinea by tying their licences as 'locally based foreign' to commitments to develop onshore processing facilities, and to supply fish to those facilities (Kumoru 2005). Under the PNG Tuna Management Plan, licences for locally based foreign purse-seiners required the fishing company to own part of a large capacity (greater than 60 metric tonnes a day) processing facility and/or to supply an 'approved portion' of its catch to a local processing facility (Government of Papua New Guinea 2004). By 2005, this policy had resulted in the RD cannery in Madang (established in 1997), the South Seas Tuna loining plant in Wewak (established in 2004) and the Frabelle cannery and loining plant (which opened in Lae in 2006). Other processing facilities were being planned, including a 200mt-a-day cannery to join RD in Madang (Kumoru 2005) (Table 7.4).

Papua New Guinea's domestically based fleet tended to be made up of smaller purse-seine vessels that fished around fish aggregating devices (FADs) (Kumoru 2005). The domestically based purse-seine fleet could therefore feel directly the effects of any management measures aimed at restricting purse-seine catches from FADs to protect juvenile bigeye and yellowfin stocks that might arise in the Western and Central Pacific Fisheries Commission (WCPFC). The PNG government thus has an interest in regional management measures that could affect this domestic development initiative, such as changes to the FSM Arrangement from the 205-vessel cap to the Vessel Days Scheme (VDS).

Canneries and loining plants supplying tuna ready for canning were the central pillar of government aspirations for development from tuna resources in Papua New Guinea. Domestically based purse-seine vessels started off exporting about half of their catch in the mid 2000s but gradually landed more and more of the catch to local processing plants such that, according to government figures, the volume exported dropped to about 10,000mt in 2004 (Kumoru 2005). This figure seems very low. Solomon Islands' NFD manager, Adrian Wickham, estimated that the FCF purse-seine vessels (Taiwanese owned, Vanuatu flagged) supplying the South Seas Tuna loining plant each caught about 6,000mt a year—a total of 72,000mt for the fleet of 12. The loining plant had a throughput of 100mt

Table 7.4   Papua New Guinea: indicators of tuna development, 2004–2005

Company	Domestic vessels: no. and type	Processing facilities: no. and type	Jobs for nationals: no. and type	Annual exports: volume and type	Annual domestic sales: volume and type
Latitude 8	10 longline (7 active)	1 sashimi packing	-		Sold non-export-grade fish in Port Moresby shops
Neptune	3 longline	0	-		
Equatorial Marine Resources (EMR)	19 longline	1 sashimi, fresh loin/steak, packing	105 fleet 105 shore	Whole chilled and frozen fish, fresh loins/steaks	
Other companies	- longline	-	-		
RD	12 purse-seine	1 cannery	35 fleet 3,000 shore		
Frabelle	7 purse-seine	1 cannery 1 fresh loin	35 fleet 80 shore		
South Seas Tuna ,m	12 purse-seine	1 cooked loin	- fleet 1,400 shore	2,800mt frozen loins	
Pacific Blue Sea	- purse-seine	-	-		
NFA	0	1 small smoking, fresh fillet/loin, packing	-		
Total	42 longline (39 active) 23 purse-seine (D) 19 purse-seine (LBF)	>2 fresh loin >3 sashimi packing 3 cannery/cooked loin	>4,760	Fresh chilled and frozen, whole or cut up, cooked loins, cans	Fresh chilled/ frozen fish

Notes: D: domestic; LBF: locally based foreign. Other domestic longline companies included: Coco, Molina, Fair Well, Gensbel, Longline Tuna, PNG Fresh Tuna and Kidu Kidu. Of EMR's vessels, nine were owned by Sanko Bussan, a Japanese company in joint venture with EMR, and 10 were owned by other companies. Neptune's vessels were targeting shark and frozen tuna for export to Taiwan, not sashimi tuna.
Sources: Interviews and personal communications 2005. Kumoru, L., 2005. Tuna Fisheries Report—Papua New Guinea, First Meeting of the Scientific Committee, Western and Central Pacific Fisheries Commission, Noumea, New Caledonia.

Table 7.5   **Purse-seine catches in Papua New Guinea's EEZ, 2000–2004**
            (metric tonnes)

	2000	2001	2002	2003	2004
D and LBF	52,184	53,178	72,275	107,001	101,300
DWFN	217,137	104,378	92,223	254,043	205,743
Total	269,291	157,556	164,498	361,044	307,043

Notes: D: domestic; LBF: locally based foreign; DWFN: distant water fleet
Source: Kumoru, L., 2005. Tuna Fisheries Report—Papua New Guinea, First Meeting of the Scientific Committee, Western and Central Pacific Fisheries Commission, Noumea, New Caledonia.

a day; if it operated six days a week, 52 weeks a year, this would consume 31,200mt. So Wickham felt that the locally based foreign fleet supplying South Seas Tuna alone was probably exporting more than 35,000mt annually; and the locally based foreign fleet as a whole would still have been exporting more than half of its catch (Wickham, pers. comm.). According to manager, Pete Celso (pers. comm.), RD processed almost 100 per cent of its catch and had tried to buy more locally caught purse-seine catch from other companies but most companies were tied into contracts to supply Thai processors.

In order to preserve Papua New Guinea's tuna resources for the long term, as well as to alleviate damage being done to bigeye and yellowfin stocks now, Papua New Guinea's purse-seine fishery will have to be carefully managed. Commentators who believed there were governance problems with the NFA's licensing procedures were concerned that Papua New Guinea could give out too many licences under pressure from foreign purse-seine companies, undermining the long-term sustainability of the fishery (Brownjohn, pers. comm.; Lewis 2005).

RD

In 1995, the NFA signed an agreement with the Philippines company RD, whereby it could establish a locally based foreign purse-seine fleet after 75 per cent completion of a large cannery on the outskirts of Madang. The fleet and the cannery started operating in 1997. The cannery at Siar became profitable within a few years and, in 2004 and 2005, expanded production capacity from 100 to 150 metric tonnes a day (Celso, pers. comm.). Average throughput was 130mt a day (Kumoru 2005). The RD cannery was the first fully private-sector, profitable, large-scale, onshore processing facility in the Pacific. Government revenue was forgone in the incentive package negotiated with RD, but no government or aid donor money was used to build RD's facilities, and the government was not involved in management or direction of the company. In 2005, RD employed about 3,000 PNG nationals in the cannery, and contracted various spin-off businesses owned and run by PNG nationals for catering, security, stevedoring, transport and so on.

According to management, RD Tuna Canners' profitability was completely dependent on preferential trade access to the European Union under the Cotonou Agreement.[4] Preferential access for PNG products was negotiated on a five-year basis. RD's viability was vulnerable if the European Union dropped or reduced the 24 per cent tariff on canned tuna as a result of continuing pressure to liberalise trade, or if the quotas of tariff-free product from non-ACP Southeast Asian countries were increased. In either of these cases, PNG product would have to compete on a level playing field against product from Thailand, the Philippines and Indonesia, and since production costs were higher in Papua New Guinea, this would mean the end of Papua New Guinea's tuna processing industry.

Production costs are high in Papua New Guinea in a range of areas, particularly freight. In 2005, it cost US$2,500 to send a container from Papua New Guinea to Hamburg—RD's main export destination—whereas sending a container from Bangkok to Hamburg cost US$1,000 (Celso, pers. comm.). The lack of competition in container shipping in Papua New Guinea was part of the problem with freight costs, but it was also a matter of scale. In order to address these issues, RD had been promoting a marine industrial park scheme to attract other marine-product export enterprises to set up near the cannery, using the wharf facilities developed by RD. Despite promoting the scheme internationally for a couple of years, RD was still operating alone in 2005.

Other areas where production costs are higher in Papua New Guinea than elsewhere relate to labour. Wages rates were competitive and no manager suggested that the hourly wage rate was a cost they wanted to reduce, but the productivity rate was low. RD wages were above the legal minimum wage at about K0.70 an hour, they included an attendance bonus of K20 for working 10 days in a fortnight, and there were subsidised meals offered at the RD canteen (*The Nation* 2003a). The yield rate (the amount of export-grade flesh retrieved from each fish), however, was lower than in Southeast Asia, and there were such high levels of absenteeism it restricted production on some days, and meant the company had to employ more cannery workers than it needed (Celso, pers. comm.). In addition, whereas in competitor countries employees organise and pay for their own commuting costs, the custom in Papua New Guinea is for employers to provide transport to and from the place of work. To get about 3,000 employees to and from the base across two shifts six days a week cost RD almost K50,000 each week (Celso, pers. comm.).

Production was also constrained by an unreliable power supply and insufficient water supply.

Since starting up, RD has been dogged by social opposition. In 2005, the company had court proceedings against people it felt had slandered the company. There was a web site apparently authored by some local people calling for a boycott of RD's products (Friends of Kananam c.2003). The company had a scandal in 2004 when fishers who went on strike were charged with the serious offence of 'mutiny' when they returned to Philippines (Stinus-Remonde 2004). It is commonly believed that RD has not allowed a union, although according to management Papua New Guinea's labour laws guarantee that all workplaces must have a union, so RD has an in-house union (Celso, pers. comm.).

Landowners felt they had not been adequately recompensed for what they saw as the illegitimate use of their land (Sullivan et al. 2003).[5] On the other hand, some interviewees with an independent perspective and knowledge of fisheries in Papua New Guinea said that, on the whole, RD was a socially responsible company that was contributing to Papua New Guinea's economy (Kinch, pers. comm.; Walton, pers. comm.).

RD has undertaken improvements to waste management at the cannery over the years (*The Nation* 2003a, 2003c). Some environmental problems around Sek Harbour are also the responsibility of national and provincial government environmental monitoring and regulating agencies, which, like most PNG government departments, have serious capacity problems. A 2003 World Wide Fund for Nature report into water quality in Madang Lagoon, including Sek Harbour, found that while the lagoon as a whole was relatively pristine, samples from coastal and river areas showed higher than permitted bathing levels for faecal coliforms—indicating sewerage management problems in villages—as well as abnormal readings around Siar village—indicating some pollution being caused by RD's factory (Benet Monico 2003).[6]

Other tuna processing

Apart from a short-lived *katsuobushi* factory in Kavieng in the 1970s, no tuna smoking had been tried on a commercial basis in Papua New Guinea as of 2005. The NFA factory in Kavieng was suitable for gourmet, small-scale processing to produce cold smoked fish, tuna jerky and tuna ham, but no private operator was using the factory for this purpose. The factory had been provided under the AusAID National Fisheries College refurbishment project. In 2004, the facility was used for loining and gassing tuna, but with the collapse of the Kavieng longline fishery the facility was processing reef fish only. A similar kind of facility was planned using Chinese aid money in Lae.

Small-scale coastal

Tuna, along with other pelagic fish, have long been fished and consumed by coastal communities in Papua New Guinea. For many villagers, tuna is important in the informal sector as a food fish and as a product to sell at markets. Coastal fisheries target tuna, among other species, and are an important source of nutrition and income for Papua New Guinea's rural coastal areas. Many aid projects have targeted small-scale fisheries, and the government focus in the past has been on extension services to train coastal small-scale fishers in a range of fishing techniques. There had been persistent problems, however, in small-scale rural coastal fishers moving into more commercial kinds of arrangements. The constraints in Papua New Guinea seemed to be similar to those listed for other Pacific island countries: the high cost of producing fish and getting it to urban markets from rural areas compared with the prices it is sold at; logistical difficulties getting fresh fish to market in time; infrastructure not being maintained; village fishers' lack of experience with (or interest in) commercial business principles; and villagers' prioritising of other social obligations higher than business commitments.

In 2005, there were two large continuing aid projects working on small-scale coastal fisheries in Papua New Guinea: the EU-funded Rural Coastal Fisheries Development Program and an ADB loan-funded Coastal Fisheries Management and Development Project, which collected and analysed socioeconomic survey data for village fisheries in several rural coastal areas. The EU program, based in Madang but also operating in Lae, Port Moresby and Kavieng, represented a new approach to rural small-scale fisheries development, based on commercial principles rather than the charity model. Participants had to devise a business plan and take out a loan at commercial rates for the vessel provided by the program. Established private-sector partners—RD in Madang, MAPS Tuna in Lae—then administered the loan. The private-sector partners bought fish from the participants, setting a portion of the sales money off against the loan, and subtracting costs for ice and fuel purchased through the private-sector partner. The program was running into problems in Madang (Kinch et al. 2005), but had worked quite well in Lae in 2004 (until MAPS Tuna scaled back operations when it stopped its own tuna fishing), and was working quite well in Kavieng (Marriot, pers. comm.; Paka, pers. comm.).

Near-shore FADs are a way to boost the production of tuna and other pelagic species for small-scale coastal fisheries. Papua New Guinea's reef fisheries appear to be under pressure in heavily populated areas, so redirecting effort to pelagic species could be advisable. By concentrating stocks, FADs can make targeting pelagic species more viable for small-scale fisheries. This was one of the strategies being considered by the EU program (Kinch et al. 2005).

Bait fishing to supply industrial tuna fleets is another potential opportunity for rural coastal fisheries. A bait fishery existed in Papua New Guinea for the Japanese pole-and-line fleet in the 1970s and early 1980s. There is the potential for a commercial bait fishery to supply domestic longline fleets, and also distant water longline and pole-and-line fleets if they start to operate in Papua New Guinea in the future, although there would likely be difficulties in governing coastal waters under customary tenure and provincial jurisdiction. [7]

Game fishing was not mentioned as having great economic development potential by interviewees or in reports on Papua New Guinea's potential for development from tuna resources. Papua New Guinea's small tourist industry has some game fishing, mostly trolling using lures. As with the other Pacific island countries covered by this report, Papua New Guinea had small active game-fishing clubs in each of the major coastal towns, holding regular tournaments (Chapman 2004b).

Handline/pump-boats

This category was included in the 2004 revision of the Tuna Management Plan, to encourage the development of small-scale commercial tuna fisheries in coastal regions (Government of Papua New Guinea 2004).

The idea behind the pump-boat plan was to emulate small-scale tuna fisheries in the Maldives, Samoa and the Philippines, which had enabled small-scale village-level fishers to enter the commercial tuna fishery. Thus far, small-scale village-based fisheries in Papua

New Guinea have been unable to participate significantly in commercial tuna enterprises due to: i) fuel inefficiencies for small-scale operators; ii) the difficult logistics of getting perishable tuna from remote villages to commercial centres in good condition; and iii) the cultural economies of villages not being suited to fishers making continuing full-time commitments to a single cash-earning activity.

Pump-boats are small wooden outrigger vessels with inboard diesel engines that carry crews of less than 10 using handlines around FADs. In 1996–97, a feasibility study was conducted around Milne Bay. The trial was not very successful, apparently due to an unexpected El Niño effect meaning tuna fishing in that region was below usual productivity, but interest remained high. A second trial was conducted in 2003 by the PNG company Popiyacop Ltd (Go, pers. comm.).

Initially, the pump-boats are to be operated by experienced Filipino fishers in partnership with local fishers (the vessels must be owned by PNG citizen companies), but it is intended that the relatively low cost and low technology, 'learn-by-doing' nature of the fishery means it will be quickly taken up by PNG fishers.

The handline method can catch larger tuna suitable for fresh (chilled or frozen) loin markets. Frabelle in Lae and another planned loining facility called Japan Foods in Madang (Celso, pers. comm.) hoped to utilise this kind of catch from the pump-boats.

Challenges facing the nascent handline tuna fishery include

- developing appropriate legislation for licensing
- establishing a management plan that will prevent overfishing and other negative environmental impacts from the fishery
- maintaining export quality in vessels with no refrigeration capacity, by fishers with no experience or training in commercial food handling
- safety issues for small vessels operating on the open sea
- achieving localisation when most previous attempts to establish small-scale commercial fisheries owned and operated by PNG nationals have failed for logistical and cultural reasons.

The pump-boat initiative in Lae as at early 2006 was progressing with a total of seven vessels taking good catches of yellowfin and bigeye, which were being landed and processed at Frabelle. A number of the challenges outlined above are being overcome, although it will be some time before the model can be declared a success.

Governing tuna industries

The meteoric rise of tuna fishing and processing industries in Papua New Guinea in the past decade was largely the result of improvements in governance. Better administration led to better policies, and the great potential of Papua New Guinea's tuna resources began to be realised. The NFA's administration has been as good as that in any sector in Papua New Guinea. As a statutory authority, the NFA has been in a position to pay its employees better than normal public servants and to expect a higher standard of work from them. The NFA offices are equipped to a standard similar to government departments in wealthy countries. Each year, the NFA collects tens of millions of kina in distant water fleet access fees and domestic fleet licence fees. After deducting its operating costs, the NFA gives the remaining tens of millions of kina to central revenue in publicised ceremonies.[8]

Improved governance under the NFA resulted in increased revenues. According to the former managing director of the NFA, improved negotiations for distant water fleet access meant that, in 2002, it secured about K40 million (US$9.1 million) (Lewis 2005). This was a great improvement from 1999, when the estimated total access fees were only US$5.8 million (Gillett and Lightfoot 2002).

One of the lessons to be drawn from the NFA experience in Papua New Guinea, however, is that administrative improvements in one sector can be limited if governance as a whole remains problematic. The problems of corruption in Papua New Guinea, within the context of a generally high level of crime in society, are well known. Improved profitability in the sector and the NFA's revenue-raising capacity unfortunately meant that political interference became visible in tuna fisheries soon after the change of government in 2002. A former managing director of the NFA estimated that on the basis of the large purse-seine catch in 2003, access fees of K60 million should have been generated, but by late 2004 only about K25 million had been deposited into consolidated revenue, and it was unclear what had happened to the balance. According to Antony Lewis (2005), the NFA's governance problems included

- licences came to be approved 'in principle' without going through the recently established transparent NFA licensing procedure
- politicians pressured the NFA to issue licences for foreign purse-seine vessels in contravention of the NFA's rationale for licensing taking into consideration regional efforts to limit purse-seine effort
- the NFA board, which was supposed to be a safeguard for governance reforms, was 'dysfunctional' by the end of 2003
- the stakeholder meetings that had helped keep the NFA in tune with various stakeholder perceptions as well as to disseminate information became infrequent and irregular
- concerns about fisheries governance at the most senior level of the NFA and Cabinet led the major donor in the sector, the ADB, to withhold funds in 2003 and 2004.

Interviewees in 2005 (names withheld) suggested a range of areas in which they thought corruption might be extant

- issuing of fishing licences
- launching of policies (one draft of a policy being negotiated among stakeholders then a different draft being signed off by the NFA or relevant politician)
- monitoring activities (observers on vessels and officials checking compliance with environmental or safety regulations around onshore and waterfront facilities).

It should be pointed out that the existence of corruption *per se* need not prevent capitalist development (China is a case in point), although it has been argued that is has costs in terms of economic development (Rose-Ackerman 1999). Managers from tuna industries interviewed for this project, however, all cited corruption as one of the constraints on development of their industry. The reasons they gave were that corruption added to uncertainty about costs and reliability of government services, and uncertainty about resource sustainability (for example, corrupt officials might not make the necessary decisions about managing purse-seine fisheries to conserve stocks).

Industry interviewees said some of the concrete effects on their businesses after the post-2002 decline in governance included problems with over-zealous enforcement, such as longliners being taken to task for not complying with rules intended to govern the purse-seine fleet. In some cases, annual licences applied for long before the expiration date did not arrive until months after the expiration of the old licence, leaving operators open to prosecution for operating without a licence. Such situations clearly contain the potential for unofficial 'fees' to be requested or proffered. Governance issues also seem to have contributed to the slow-down in private-sector onshore investments during 2003 and 2004; investors were wary of the security of their investments in the less transparent environment (Lewis 2005).

In the past few years, several initiatives have been undertaken to address problems connected to corruption in Papua New Guinea, such as the passing of the *Organic Law on Political Parties and Candidates* to try to stem tendencies to cross the floor and topple governments by stabilising party membership (Baker 2005), the creation of the Independent Commission Against Corruption and the Australian government-sponsored Enhanced Cooperation Package. In addition, the first-past-the-post electoral system, which had been identified as a contributing factor in poor behaviour by politicians (Pitts 2002), was changed to a preferential system in 2005 (Reilly 2005). The Papua New Guinea chapter of the non-governmental organisation (NGO) Transparency International has an active leader in Michael Manning. Manning has been talking to tuna-industry people about how to address problems in their sector (Paru, pers. comm.). Continuing government efforts, as well as personal efforts by Papua New Guineans and foreign investors to contribute to good governance through their voting patterns and relations with government officials, are needed to remove the constraints of corruption on economic development.

According to Maurice Brownjohn, a longline fishing company owner and chairman of the Fisheries Industry Association, the decline in governance since 2002 distorted the domestication policy that saw such dramatic improvements in the GDP generated from Papua New Guinea's tuna resources from the mid 1990s to 2002. Carefully prepared and negotiated agreements in the early years of the policy saw a totally domestic longline fishery emerge, and substantial domestic economic engagement from foreign companies such as RD through facilitating domestic licences tied to processing. Brownjohn feels that recent agreements, however, have not been scrutinised to ensure that foreign companies will significantly contribute to the PNG economy in return for being licensed as 'locally based'.

Notwithstanding some backsliding since 2002, fisheries administration at the national level in Papua New Guinea was still much better resourced and organised than in some other Pacific island countries covered by this study.

When asked about problems in the NFA, manager, Norman Barnabas, said he felt there had been a lack of consistency in leadership in a period of major change. Since the late 1990s, the NFA has had no less than seven different managing directors, each with a distinct management style that altered the way the organisation functioned. He said there was a need to develop and maintain a consistently strong senior management team within the NFA to ensure stability and well-developed policies (Barnabas, pers. comm.).

It is possible that another reason why some of the NFA reforms have not 'stuck' is that some of these managing directors were non-nationals. According to interviewees, the non-nationals were highly competent managers (as were the national managing directors) who were effective in achieving positive reform and organisational change, while they were in position. One of the main problems noted with development projects in the Pacific in the past three decades is sustainability after the project funding ceases and the technical advisors leave. While non-nationals have less attachment to the status quo and have no cultural ties that can complicate governance issues, when the leaders have been non-nationals Pacific islanders tend not to take ownership of projects, meaning any changes might not survive in the long term. While better governance in fisheries helped Papua New Guinea's tuna industries take off, broader and deeper fisheries administration and policy improvements would help them develop even further.

Industry representation was secured on the board of the NFA. Since 1991, Papua New Guinea has had an active Fisheries Industry Association (FIA), which has participated as a stakeholder in policy forums. Papua New Guinea has correspondingly had fewer of the problems that other Pacific island countries have in terms of misunderstanding private-sector needs and priorities by the government (Gillett 2003). Nevertheless, the relationship between industry and government is not as healthy as it could be.

Government administration is particularly important for sustainable fisheries. Logsheet data on the longline catch was poor until 2002. The first Scientific Committee meeting for the WCPFC in August 2005 highlighted that bigeye and yellowfin were being overfished (WCPFC 2005). Good management of purse-seine fishing in Papua New Guinea's EEZ will be crucial in the coming years. Papua New Guinea's EEZ has accounted for about 20 per cent of the regional purse-seine catch since 2000 (Kumoru 2005). Its domestically based purse-seine fishery, which by 2005 made up more than 30 per cent of the purse-seine catch in Papua New Guinea's EEZ, was mostly taken around anchored FADs. This kind of fishing was identified as one of the main causes of damage to bigeye and yellowfin stocks. Observer data from Papua New Guinea indicated that as much as 60 per cent of the FAD-associated purse-seine sets might be bigeye and yellowfin (Kumoru 2005).[9]

In 2004, Papua New Guinea's observer program employed 87 observers on 168 trips, funded by access agreement levies and direct cost recovery. Observers were stationed at major landing posts to cover purse-seine and longline vessels, trans-shipments and FAD deployments (Kumoru 2005).

Port sampling, observer, monitoring and enforcement activities were undertaken from provincial fisheries departments as well as the NFA. Provincial governments have on the whole been less well run than the national government and the provincial fisheries offices visited for this project in Madang and Kavieng had not been allocated their operating grants for some years. There were staff, whose salaries were paid, and they had offices, but there was no money for office supplies, computing or fax equipment, or fuel for cars or boats to do extension work. So provincial fisheries officers had been unable to do much work for several years. In order for provincial fisheries officers to be able to undertake monitoring and enforcement work, the NFA had utilised a legislative initiative to improve connections between provincial governments and the national government to devolve these duties to the provincial level, and also to set up a user-pays system whereby the NFA paid fisheries departments directly for tuna-related activities. This was revitalising provincial fisheries departments.

Fish aggregating devices (FADs)

The National Tuna Management Plan included a FAD management plan, one of the first by any Pacific island country. Interviewees with experience in longline fisheries were concerned about the overall number of FADs, the positions of FADs being accurately recorded on charts, and deploying companies being held responsible for FADs when they eventually disintegrated and floated freely under the surface of the water (Brownjohn, pers. comm.; Kanawi, pers. comm.). It can be quite dangerous, and expensive, when longline gear becomes fouled in invisible floating FADs. In 2005, the government reiterated its commitment to manage FADs in Papua New Guinea's EEZ, by restricting the number deployed, and by restricting the purse-seine effort around FADs, as this seems to be having negative impacts on bigeye and yellowfin stocks (Kumoru 2005).

Conclusion

In terms of the full range of raw materials and infrastructure required for successful domestic industry development, Papua New Guinea is in the best position of any of the Pacific island countries included in this study. In addition, Papua New Guinea's tuna resources are so rich it can make a great deal of money from distant water fleets. While some impressive progress had been made, one main factor constraining Papua New Guinea from achieving its development aspirations was the incapacity of the government to improve the business environment.

Proving the domestication model is possible despite a challenging competitive environment, RD has been more commercially viable than previous attempts by Pacific island countries to trade access fees for onshore development. The company has not relied on aid money and its taxation holiday finished in 2002. RD, however, still relies on preferential trade deals to offset competitive disadvantage. Continuing improvements to the business environment will consolidate RD's position and facilitate further investment along these lines.

Of particular concern to legitimate industry and investors has been the uncertainty surrounding governance, in particular the management and politicisation of decision-making at the NFA. The other main factor affecting Papua New Guinea's ability to capture wealth from tuna is implementing sound management of the fishery for its long-term sustainability.

Development aspirations and tuna

Overall development aspirations

The PNG government's general development aspirations are contained in the *Medium Term Development Strategy 2005–10* (*MTDS*) (Government of Papua New Guinea 2005). The cover of the *MTDS* document includes photographs of a child washing under a tap, a child studying at school, some policewomen, a woman selling produce at a market and a road-construction scene. From these images, one could deduce that the government sees sanitation, education, law and order, grassroots income generation and transport infrastructure as development priorities, and that women and children are at the forefront of these goals. This image is reinforced in the subtitle of the document, 'Our plan for economic and social advancement'. The first couple of pages of the *MTDS* list 10 guiding principles. This list conveys a somewhat different vision of development from that communicated by the cover images

- private sector-led economic growth
- resource mobilisation and alignment
- improvements in the quality of life
- natural endowments
- competitive advantage and the global market
- integrating the three tiers of government
- partnership through strategic alliances
- least-developed areas intervention
- empowering Papua New Guineans and improving skills
- 'sweat equity' and Papua New Guinean character.

This list prioritises economic growth driven by the private sector, through engagement with global markets, in areas in which Papua New Guinea is competitive, and through coordinated mobilisation of Papua New Guinea's resources. National cohesion is raised in three of these principles—in terms of integration between levels of government, partnerships between institutions within society and evening out development benefits across the country by targeting least-developed areas. Health and education services and the informal sector are only implied in these principles.

The picture shifts slightly again on page iii of the *MTDS*. Here, its role is identified as providing a guiding framework for expenditure in line with the government's Program for Recovery and Development, characterised as comprising good governance, export-driven economic growth, rural development, poverty reduction and empowerment through human resource development (in that order). Further down the page, the government development strategy is described as incorporating these features, plus the promotion of sustainable agriculture, forestry, fisheries and tourism. The expenditure priorities listed on this page return to the vision of development in the pictures on the cover of the document

- rehabilitation and maintenance of transport infrastructure
- promotion of income-earning opportunities

- basic education
- development-oriented informal adult education
- primary health care
- HIV/AIDS prevention
- law and justice.

The general development aspirations that emerge from the *MTDS* are about improvements in material standards of living for Papua New Guineans. The document prioritises a range of public services, it notes the importance of promoting national cohesion and good governance, and it accords a central role to private-sector capitalist activity as an engine for economic growth. Special mention is made of internationally competitive export industries making sustainable use of Papua New Guinea's natural resources.

Development based on tuna resources fits within the *MTDS* vision as generating economic growth through exports and providing opportunities for Papua New Guineans to generate income and learn new skills. The role and nature of government in tuna development includes the notion that different levels of government should be coordinated, and should include stakeholders from various sectors of society in policymaking. The *MTDS* does not indicate that government should drive enterprise, rather it should facilitate the private sector to generate and run businesses. This marks a change from previous decades when Papua New Guinea and other Pacific governments felt it was appropriate to own or manage tuna businesses (Gillett 2003; ADB 1997).

Specific aspirations for development using tuna resources from the PNG government perspective are spelled out in the National Tuna Management Plan, section 2.4 'Objectives' (Government of Papua New Guinea 1999)

- encourage development of the tuna fishery, with optimal development of onshore processing and downstream value-adding processing, so as to maximise economic and social benefits to Papua New Guinea from sustainable use of its tuna resource
- foster the development of an economically viable domestic tuna-fishing industry while ensuring that the utilisation of Papua New Guinea's tuna resources is sustainable and that commercial tuna fishing has minimal impact on the marine and coastal environment and on customary and subsistence fishers
- meet Papua New Guinea's regional and international obligations to the management and conservation of tuna resources, while holding Papua New Guinea's interests paramount
- maximise Papua New Guinean participation through the wise use and development of fisheries resources as a renewable asset.

The picture of development aspirations that emerges from this list prioritises the generation of wealth from tuna resources in the PNG economy through fishing and processing industries, while minimising negative social and environmental impacts, and maximising the involvement of Papua New Guineans in these industries.

Government capacity

Although 'governance' is often used simply as a euphemism for corruption, it is a very broad term. Good governance encompasses a range of issues raised in the *MTDS*, the Tuna Management Plan and by interviewees from all levels of society. It includes the obvious factors of transparency and accountability in government, but also of creating an enabling environment for development, consultative processes that enable civil society to participate in government and setting in place measures to mitigate social and environmental problems that could emerge from economic development. In Papua New Guinea, aspirations for development from tuna also touch on improving coordination between national and provincial levels of government, and informal community governance systems.

In order to achieve this kind of governance, government departments must be adequately resourced, bureaucrats adequately skilled and systems of government must encourage best practice from officials. The NFA is a good example of this relationship.

In Papua New Guinea, where responsibility for tuna fisheries lies with the national government, but the concomitant effects in related areas fall to provincial authorities, coordination between levels of government is extremely important. While some responsibilities related to tuna fisheries have been devolved to provinces, capacity has been a problem. Provincial fisheries departments have been starved of resources for some years, and have not been reoriented from extension services to deal with industry in the same way as the NFA staff.

Human resources in government departments are a large part of 'capacity'. Several interviewees noted that PNG bureaucrats could benefit from further education in fisheries science, fisheries and business management and environmental monitoring. Interviewees involved in fisheries education and training were concerned that Papua New Guinea's tertiary education facilities were not producing enough graduates with the range of skills necessary to work as fisheries bureaucrats, covering all the areas mentioned above (Munkaje, pers. comm.; Adani pers. comm.).

Economic viability

Since most expressions of aspiration for development from tuna involved private-sector businesses, the role of government in creating an enabling environment for private-sector development is important. Improvements in macroeconomic policy as well as other aspects of governance are needed to improve the economic viability of tuna businesses.

One example of how poor government involvement could damage development in tuna businesses is problematic development projects. Aid donors as well as governments have been at fault in these situations.

Policy stability

Political stability was cited by Mike Manning as one of the highest priorities for businesspeople in Papua New Guinea (Manning 2005). Interviewees for this project, however, had a slightly

191

different take: they were not really concerned with who was in government or whether the government changed frequently, but they were very concerned about stability of policies.

For example, in 2005 companies planning to use pump boats had been given information on how many licences were likely to be issued that was inconsistent with national legislation and provincial government plans. It is obviously costly for businesses to invest based on one policy direction, only to have it changed afterwards.

Government services

Related to policy stability as a concern for business were the reliability, effectiveness, transparency, accountability and cost-efficiency of government services. Many industry interviewees expressed frustration with the quality of government services—for example, the length of time it took to receive licences.

Current moves to balance the budget are likely to restrict government resources even further, although apparently World Bank and ADB projects in public service reform, along with the *Organic Law* in this area, have been working towards 'right-sizing' rather than just 'down-sizing' to try to develop government services that are effective as well as affordable (Manning, pers. comm.).

Taxation and incentives

The PNG government has used a combination of licence conditions with incentive packages involving tax holidays to attract international fishing companies to establish shore-based processing facilities. As of 2005, the policy seemed to be successful in that two plants were running profitably, employing nearly 5,000 people between them, another was almost complete and more were planned. A cost–benefit analysis would reveal whether these benefits outweighed revenue lost through incentive packages. A study of the economics of tuna fisheries in Papua New Guinea from 2000 suggested that during the period in which the incentives applied, the costs of concessions outweighed the benefits gained in terms of local employment, probably in the order of K12–14 million each year (Gillett, Preston and Associates 2000).[10]

One potential pitfall is that the incentives and licence conditions have skewed the economic behaviour of the foreign investors to invest in an economically unsustainable business. As it is, RD claims that if preferential trade access to the European Union were to disappear, it would cease to be financially viable (Celso, pers. comm.). Most commentators agree that preferential trade access to the European Union from ACP countries will be wound back at some stage, so it would seem prudent to treat incentives as an interim plan and work harder on improving the general business environment.

Another problem with the incentives packages in Papua New Guinea is that they seem to have been negotiated individually for each fishery/processing business on an *ad hoc* basis, rather than as a standard set of incentives for all businesses in the sector (Celso, pers. comm.; Defensor, pers. comm.; Nidung, pers. comm.). The potential for corruption in individually negotiated incentives packages is obvious; at the very least, they contain the potential for differential treatment by government of industry players. They lead to a situation in which companies are seen to be asking for special favours, which sets up an unhealthy relationship between companies and government.

Human resources development

To a certain extent, the private sector will furnish its own educational and training needs, but government also needs to provide general and specialist education and training. A report into the economics of the PNG tuna industry in 2000 found that lack of qualified and trained crew was one of the major constraints on development of tuna-fishing businesses, and recommended a 50 per cent increase in the numbers proposed to be trained by the National Fisheries College (Gillett, Preston and Associates 2000). Industry and small business-oriented fisheries education services have improved greatly in recent years with the refurbishment and reorientation of the National Fisheries College in Kavieng under an AusAID project.

One of the areas in which education could help is in developing business skills among Papua New Guineans. The lack of indigenous participation in management and ownership of businesses was in part culturally based, whereby social priorities had not facilitated Papua New Guineans' success in business, and partly historical, whereby the colonial system prevented Papua New Guineans from assuming leadership positions in trade and other businesses. Greater emphasis on financial literacy and education in business studies could help encourage more ethnic Papua New Guineans to own or manage businesses.

Minimising negative social impacts

Social problems associated with tuna industries are often treated as an add-on; consultants are hired to write reports about the problems, calls for measures to mitigate negative social impacts are made in policy documents, then little or nothing is done. Social discontent left untreated had disastrous consequences at Panguna in Bougainville in the 1980s. Nothing on that scale has happened in the tuna sector in Papua New Guinea, however, the public relations problems RD has faced in the Madang area show that even relatively minor social discontent can be a constraint to business. It is possible that RD's public relations problems have dissuaded other prospective investors from onshore processing in Papua New Guinea.

Where tuna industries are causing social problems, it is important for government to take the lead in resolving the problems and to make the public aware of these efforts. Where social problems are perceived to exist or exist but are being unrealistically blamed on particular businesses, government and companies need to work together to build awareness about the facts of the situation, rather than letting negative rumours flourish.

Consultative decision making and dissemination of information about issues of public concern are two strategies that would have a positive effect on improving the social problems arising around tuna industries.

Distribution of benefits

An important aspiration for development from tuna resources in Papua New Guinea was that benefits from development should be distributed across society. The geographic distribution of benefits from tuna industries is implied in the *MTDS* principle of 'least-developed areas intervention'. One of the aspirations relating to the distribution of benefits was that tuna industries should generate benefits in villages, in part because coastal villagers are seen as oceanic resource owners (even though legally their customary tenure rights stop in coastal waters). Interviewees who have worked with coastal village communities said that the pervasive attitude about tuna industries in villages was that they had not benefited villagers (Aini, pers. comm.; Tamba, pers. comm.; Sibanganei, pers. comm.; Kinch, pers. comm.). In theory, increased revenue from tuna businesses, even distant water fleets, should lead to improved government services in rural areas, but in Papua New Guinea, government services in rural areas have declined. Not trusting the government to distribute development benefits on their behalf, people saw that villagers' direct involvement in tuna industries, either through employment or through owning businesses, was the way to secure development benefits at the village level.

The EU Rural Coastal Fisheries Development Program was one of a range of rural coastal fisheries development projects that had been conducted in Papua New Guinea and other Pacific island countries in recent decades, to try to facilitate rural coastal fishers' involvement in small-scale commercial tuna fisheries.

Notwithstanding the apparent short-term problems with the EU program at this stage, it is probable that some of the principles for economic viability contained in it could in the long term facilitate village fishers' transition to more commercial ways of operating.

Another way for villagers to benefit from tuna industries in Papua New Guinea seems to have been developed in the mining industry, whereby local landowning villagers are given preferential access to jobs and spin-off businesses. Part of the conditions under which RD was set up was that the company undertook to contract with local landowning groups to provide stevedoring and other services to RD.

While most national government employee interviewees said governments were not good at doing business and should therefore not own or run tuna enterprises, some interviewees at the provincial level said there was a role for government in assisting small-scale operators at the village level (Sibanganei, pers. comm.; Tamba, pers. comm.). They felt the commercial difficulties faced by small-scale village-based operators should be addressed by subsidies, in the form of government agencies buying their product at attractive prices and government vessels being used to travel to village fishing centres to pick up catches to transport them to urban markets.

One more way villagers could gain benefits from tuna industries would be if the NFA directed a small proportion of licence fees to a rural coastal development fund, and administered a cross-sectoral committee to allocate the fund to projects each year. This could improve public approval of industrial tuna fisheries, especially if it was combined with bringing village stakeholders into consultative decision-making processes and more active awareness programs to disseminate accurate information about tuna industries.

As well as somehow spreading development benefits from tuna industries to rural areas, many interviewees' aspirations contained the idea that industrial tuna developments should be geographically spread. Several interviewees expressed aspirations along the lines of having tuna canneries or loining plants in every province. Recent developments have indeed resulted in large-scale tuna processing in Madang, Lae and Wewak, with longline centres in Port Moresby, Lae, Kavieng and Lobrum (Manus). The problem with this aspiration, however, is that it detracts from the economic viability of those developments.

Distribution of benefits versus economic viability: industrial hubs

RD interviewees stated clearly that high operating costs in Papua New Guinea detracted from the company's profitability in relation to Southeast Asian competitors, and was counteracted only by preferential trade access to the European Union. Many of the problems for tuna industries in Papua New Guinea's business environment were related to the cost and infrequency of freight, and the costs and reliability of infrastructure and government services. RD managers could see that a consolidation of similar types of business in the Vidar area north of Madang would bring these costs down, and thus had been trying to attract other marine production industries to Vidar, and lobbying the government to reserve the area as a marine industrial park (Celso, pers. comm.). The project manager of the EU program in Madang agreed that such an industrial zone could be beneficial for fisheries, including small-scale fisheries, especially if it were to be developed along environmental 'best practice' lines, with, for example, Marine Stewardship Council accreditation (Marriot, pers. comm.).

Industrial clusters or 'hubs' such as this proposal have been used to generate economic development in several countries, including China's 'special economic zones' and 'export processing zones' on the east coast around which spectacular economic growth has been generated. Concentrations of firms with related specialisations are able to generate operational synergies, with pooled infrastructure and human resources development (Bowman 2005). Greater volumes of freight alone would solve many of RD's cost problems. Changing commuting attitudes and structures, as well as working around the utility challenges, would be easier if a group of companies could work on it together.

In order to sustain the promising levels of growth in foreign direct investment in large-scale fishing and processing enterprises in Papua New Guinea, therefore, decision makers might want to rethink the policy of geographically spreading tuna developments, in favour of consolidating them.

Minimising negative environmental impacts

The National Tuna Management Plan (Government of Papua New Guinea 1999) identified ecological responsibility as a high priority among aspirations for development from tuna. The experiences of RD show how ecological responsibility in shore-based developments is intimately related to social issues, and can also have an impact on economic issues. Some of the loudest social opposition to RD has been denouncing its environmental practices, claiming that polluted waterways, bad smells and swarms of flies have detracted from the quality of life and fishing opportunities of villagers living near the wharf and factory (Sullivan et al. 2003). While perceptions of RD's wrongdoing in this area seem to exceed RD's environmental perfidy, the fact remains that RD is seen widely as environmentally unfriendly and this perception has various social, political and economic repercussions.

One of the ways government, NGOs and aid donors could contribute to improving awareness of environmental issues around tuna industries would be to conduct baseline studies of the effects of tuna fisheries and onshore processing on coastal environments and food-fish stocks. These activities could be incorporated into continuing monitoring by the Department of Conservation. The results of monitoring could then be disseminated to local communities in a digestible manner, such as short pamphlets or speaking tours.

The other side to this coin is that being perceived as environmentally friendly can have economic benefits in RD's target markets. Ecological responsibility is an important marketing advantage in high-end seafood markets in the European Union and the United States (Marriot, pers. comm.; WWF 2005).

Some interviewees expressed concern about the management of commercial tuna fisheries, specifically whether licences were being managed for the long-term economic and ecological sustainability of the fishery, or whether they were being allocated on principles of short-term financial gain. Some commentators have expressed doubt about transparency, accountability and the following of 'proper processes' in licence approvals (Brownjohn, pers. comm.; Lewis 2005).

Domestication

The biggest aspiration for tuna development in Papua New Guinea, as for the other Pacific island countries covered in this project, was the notion of domestication: capturing more of the benefits from tuna fisheries by pulling tuna enterprises into the orbit of the domestic economy. The Medium Term Development Strategy indicates that the government intends to build on fisheries-sector growth by 'increasing the level of local participation' (Government of Papua New Guinea 2005:11). The National Tuna Management Plan aimed to encourage onshore processing—domesticating the value-added portions of the tuna commodity chain—and to foster the domestic tuna-fishing industry (Government of Papua New Guinea 1999). The aspirations of interviewees from all levels of society included ideas about domestication, often couched in terms of PNG nationals coming to be employed in, manage and own tuna businesses, and always containing the assumption that PNG nationals would contribute more to the economy than would foreign investors, managers and employees.

The main argument used to justify domestication policies is that having economic activity based in Papua New Guinea's economy generates growth at home, rather than overseas.

Some economists have argued against trying to bring tuna industries into the domestic economy, saying that Pacific island countries seem not to have competitive advantage in tuna fishing or processing, so they should instead maximise their access fees and use that revenue to facilitate economic development in other areas (Petersen 2002a).

Another take on this issue is that government involvement and inappropriate policy environments have been blocking comparative advantage by making the business environment unattractive and scaring off the private sector. According to this argument, if fisheries management and development policies are improved so that investors can trust a return on their investment, the private sector will invest in tuna fisheries. This concept fits events in Papua New Guinea since 1995, when government administration improved a great deal, until about 2002–03, and during this period the private sector boomed. Licensing conditions favouring companies making onshore investment were also a key factor. For the first time in the Pacific, Papua New Guinea has established large-scale onshore investments funded entirely by the private sector with no government ownership or donor support (albeit with tax incentives and coercion through licensing arrangements).

One of the problems with domestication policies is that often it is possible for foreign investors to fulfil the criteria for domestication but still not generate much activity in the domestic economy. Fisheries Industry Association chairman, Maurice Brownjohn, outlined a spectrum of potential locally based foreign fishing companies that could range from companies fully engaged and committed in the local economy to companies that were little more than agents for distant water fleets (Brownjohn, pers. comm.).

Even when companies do generate activity in the local economy, the quality of the activity is important. Fishing and processing industries tend to consume a high volume of imports, such as fuel, which pass through the local economy but generate few benefits, especially if there is a balance-of-trade problem.

One of the striking features of aspirations to domesticate tuna industries is the persistence of the belief that it is important for PNG nationals to work in, manage and own fishing companies. Tuna fishing is capital intensive and high risk. Wealthier companies in wealthier countries have moved out of fishing into processing and trading, and the companies that continue to fish also trade, which is presumably where they make their profit. In the words of RD's managing director, 'People think this business is all about fishing, but it's not' (Celso, pers. comm.). Papua New Guinea's aspirations for domestication include processing as well as fishing, but perhaps it would be pertinent to include marketing and trading as well.

Aspirations for domestication also include more than simply economic concerns. National self-esteem is at stake, no doubt stemming from the colonial experience. Sometimes the nationalist angle can lead to a preoccupation with complete domestication at all costs, when that might not be economically the most sensible strategy.

In the short to medium term, some business owners have expressed the opinion that preoccupations with domestication in PNG immigration regulations act as a constraint on businesses (Kingston, pers. comm.; Middleton, pers. comm.). Work visas for expatriate employees are expensive and time-consuming to apply for. The policy of encouraging employers to hire and train locals rather than bring foreigners in was no doubt intended to further domestication aspirations, but, according to interviewees, the cumbersome nature of immigration requirements to acquire human resources that were not available in the local labour pool have instead had the effect of discouraging businesses from expanding or starting up at all.

That is not to say that national self-esteem factors should be overlooked as aspirations. To do that would risk adding to existing levels of social discontent with tuna industries. In other words, optimal domestication policies require complex juggling of recognition of the importance of national self-esteem in having indigenous role models in leadership positions, with recognition of the fact that even in the long term total indigenisation might not be the best economic outcome.

Value adding through processing

With the stagnation of the domestic longline industry in 2005, the main focus of PNG government aspirations for development for tuna resources was fishing tied to onshore processing. Papua New Guinea's aspirations for this sector were very high; it saw that with cooperation and co-investment from other Pacific island countries, Papua New Guinea could challenge Thailand as the world centre of tuna processing (Barnabas, pers. comm.; Celso, pers. comm.; Natividad, pers. comm.). The Forum Fishing Agency's (FFA) deputy director described Papua New Guinea's aspirations for development from processing as visionary; he saw Papua New Guinea as 'the most obsessed with domestic development' of all the Pacific island countries (Dunn, pers. comm.).

Since Papua New Guinea has land, labour, fresh water and abundant tuna resources, it is the most suitable of the Pacific island countries for large-scale onshore processing. Industry interviewees said they hoped other Pacific island countries might collaborate with Papua New Guinea in aspiring to become the world centre for processing tuna, by funnelling catches from their EEZs to PNG processing centres instead of to Southeast Asia (Natividad, pers. comm.). One reason why other countries might support this aspiration is that for many Pacific island countries, Papua New Guinea is closer than Thailand, so it could make their fishing grounds more economical in terms of steaming time to point of sale. But many questions remain. Will other Pacific island countries see their interests as lying with Papua New Guinea in developing its processing sector, or will they see its success as a threat to their own aspirations? Will other countries invest in PNG industries? Will Papua New Guinea allow nationals of other Pacific island countries to train and work in its industries, or will it want only PNG nationals to have access to these benefits?

Potential future additional developments in onshore processing mentioned by industry interviewees included fresh chilled or frozen loins for the EU and US markets, and fully prepared and packaged fresh fish for supermarket shelves in Japan. ULT freezer vessels were in 2005 to be allowed to operate in Papua New Guinea from the enactment of the next National Tuna Management Plan (Kumoru, pers. comm.). Another possibility would be for Papua New Guinea's substantial agricultural potential to be directed to domestic production of materials needed for tuna industries. This could include ingredients for canneries, such as spices, vegetable oil and table salt. Industrial salt is also used in large quantities for brine freezers in fishing.

Recommendations

For Papua New Guinea to realise its aspirations as a leader in economic development from tuna in the Pacific, it will be important to work on governance issues within fisheries and cross-sectorally to ensure the transparent and consistent application of fisheries policies, plans and legislation. It will be important to continue with domestic processing initiatives while addressing the factors that make Papua New Guinea an uncompetitive (high-cost) business environment. For example, Papua New Guinea could develop industrial hubs rather than spreading developments around the country. Papua New Guineans themselves could improve their capacity to benefit from tuna industries by developing more self-sufficiency in attitudes towards large companies, for example, by establishing spin-off businesses independently rather than waiting for companies to make businesses for them. The government can help by continuing work on maintaining 'list-one' status for importing to the European Union.

Other factors that will sustain recent gains include addressing social and environmental issues through more consultative decision making, and carefully assessing the costs and benefits of taxation incentives. With reform to the taxation system individual tax holidays may not be necessary to help companies establish themselves. The administration of incentives for new companies could be made uniform across the sector and easier to apply for. The government could also work on ensuring locally based foreign activities, attracted by preferential access to tuna resources, fulfil investment requirements and are monitored to ensure that real benefits to the PNG economy are received. Finally, for long term sustainability it will be crucial to develop sound management for tuna fisheries in consultation with industry, including ensuring licensing guidelines are strictly adhered to, to improve business confidence in the capacity of government and the future of the industry.

Notes

[1]   Some might call this part of the economy 'traditional' or 'subsistence'. Contemporary village fishing practices have changed a great deal since first contact with Europeans and use of the word 'traditional' can imply unchanged practices. By the same token, 'subsistence' can imply fishing only to have enough to eat, but village fishing has always been about social exchange and cultural practices in addition to getting enough to eat.

[2]   According to a Japanese interviewee who worked at Nago Island, the *arabushi* venture in Kavieng was never very successful due to a lack of suitable timber to use as fuel for the smoke-drying process (Nakamura, pers. comm.).

[3]   ULT vessels freeze tuna to –60°C, which means the flesh does not oxidise and turn brown, which means it can still be sold as sashimi.

[4]   To protect canneries in Spain, Italy and France, the European Union has a 24 per cent tariff on imports of canned tuna. RD cannery's product fits within the Rules of Origin as an ACP (Africa Caribbean Pacific) product, which means it could avoid the tariff under an agreement originally set up during decolonisation to ensure Europe's continued access to the commodities of former colonies (the Lomé Convention).

[5]   RD management feels aggrieved by this belief and sees responsibility for the dispute lying with the Department of Lands. 'RD as an innocent party in good faith merely bought the land in question from the previous owner through an auction ordered by a court of competent authority' (Celso, pers. comm.).

[6]   RD management sees this report as unfair to the company because it was not given the opportunity to participate or comment on the testing procedures or results (Celso, pers. comm.).

[7]   For recent examples of disputes in coastal fisheries arising from customary tenure, see Kinch et al. 2005.

[8]   In Papua New Guinea, most government departments run at a deficit (Warner and Yauieb 2005) so the NFA's public demonstration that it not only balanced its books but contributed a substantial amount to consolidated revenue was a public relations coup.

[9]   RD management disputes this finding, saying that skipjack always makes up more than half of its catch, and also asserts that other methods could be catching large numbers of juvenile bigeye and yellowfin but that this mortality from other methods is not being picked up in logsheet reports (Celso, pers. comm.).

[10]   RD management disputes this conclusion, saying that employment benefits are not the only benefits that should have been considered in this equation. Others that could have been included are foreign exchange earnings, the kinds of taxes the company contributed in that period, such as the value-added tax and income taxes for employees, import substitution benefits and technology transfer (Celso, pers. comm.).

8

Solomon Islands

Population: 521,000
Land area: 28,896 km²
Sea area: 1,300,000 km²

Solomon Islands is made up of a double chain of six main islands surrounded by many smaller ones, and several groups of outlying islands, stretched over 1,300 kilometres. The large islands are volcanic with fertile soil and plentiful fresh water sources, while some of the smaller islands are atolls with less rich soil and limited supplies of fresh water.

When the British Solomon Islands Protectorate was granted independence in 1978, most of the economy was still non-cash and based in village production. In 1999, about 85 per cent of the population lived in rural areas, while 12 per cent lived in the capital, Honiara; the remainder lived in small provincial towns, representing a trend of rural–urban migration since 1986. The population density is low at 13 people per square kilometre. With its good natural resource base, including the potential for a wider range of agriculture, forestry and some mining, the country could support a much larger population at a higher standard of living (Government of Solomon Islands 2003). The country has struggled to develop a successful capitalist economy and thus has been heavily dependent on aid.

Solomon Islands was on the whole a peaceful society for the first two decades after independence. Then, in late 1998, long-running dissatisfactions about the lack of economic development in some areas on Guadalcanal flared along ethnic lines, with Guale militants targeting Malaitan settlers and economic installations such as Goldridge Mine and Solomon Islands Plantations Limited's oil-palm plantation. Malaitan militants responded. Sporadic incidents increased in frequency during 1999 and 2000, culminating in the overthrow of the government in June 2000. During 2000, all major industries closed or scaled down, 8,000 jobs were lost (about one-quarter of these in tuna industries) and 30,000 people were displaced. GDP declined in real terms by 14 per cent, the balance of payments nosedived to the point where there were foreign currency reserves for only two months' worth of imports, and government expenditure far outstripped revenue (CBSI 2001).

This period is commonly referred to as the 'Tensions'.[1] Law, order, justice and security broke down and, despite Australian attempts to broker a peace agreement in October 2000,

Map 8.1   Solomon Islands

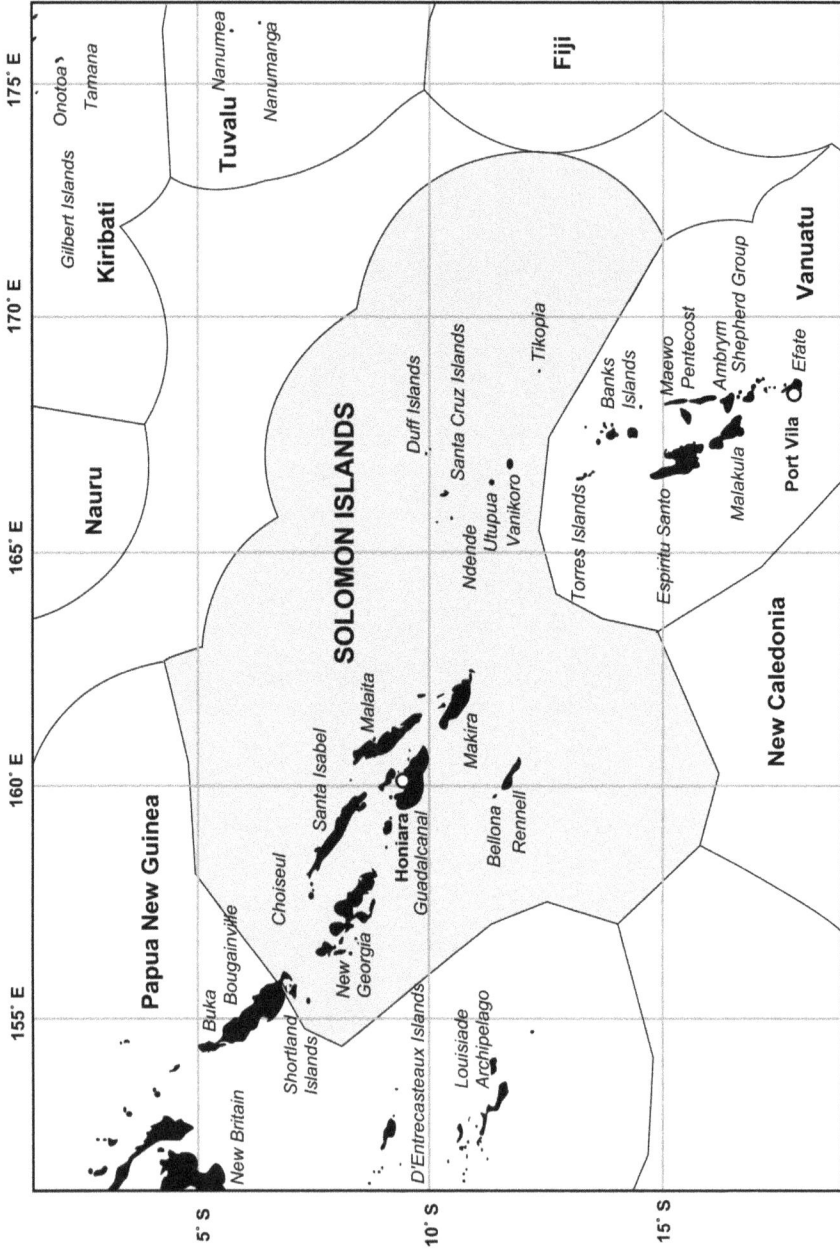

Source: Youngmi Choi, Secretariat of the Pacific Community, Noumea, New Caledonia.

the security situation remained dysfunctional until 2003, when the Regional Assistance Mission to Solomon Islands (RAMSI), led by Australian police and military personnel, re-established order.

The Tensions further set back an already challenging economic environment. All major formal-sector businesses closed or scaled down operations for a time. Infrastructure fell into even worse disrepair. Crime rates increased. Public services were not funded or protected from gangs. The informal economy also suffered from militant and gang activities, with smallholders unable to take produce to market. Since the low point in the early 2000s, there has been significant recovery in overall GDP and economic growth indicators (CBSI 2005). Nonetheless, at 2005 rates of recovery, it would take Solomon Islands 19 years just to recover to 1999 levels (Chand 2005a). In addition, social indicators of development had not yet improved, there were widening wealth disparities and increasing levels of poverty (Beseto, pers. comm.; Government of Solomon Islands 2003; Roughan, pers. comm.).

History of tuna fisheries development

Tuna, especially skipjack, has always been a culturally significant, highly valued and nutritionally important fish in Solomon Islands. In the old days, it was often caught with *kastom* hooks made from oyster shell, turtle shell and hand-spun string, trolled from dugout canoes. In recent times, it has become more common to use synthetic handlines and steel hooks from a fibreglass canoe powered by an outboard motor.

Solomon Taiyo Limited

Commercial tuna fisheries started in Solomon Islands in 1971. The British Solomon Islands Protectorate government was thinking about independence for the Solomons and saw tuna as having the potential to be one of the industries on which to base an independent Solomon Islands economy. Expressions of interest were entertained by several international tuna companies, but the responsible officer at the Western Pacific High Commission in Suva preferred the scheme put forward by Taiy GyoGyo of Tokyo because it included the development of a shore base that would add value in-country and employ locals. Japanese fishing companies were looking for Pacific island joint-venture partners at this time as a way to deal with the declarations of the 200 nautical mile Exclusive Economic Zones (EEZs) that were closing off previously open fishing grounds.

In 1971, Taiyo GyoGyo started commercial pole-and-line fishing as part of an 18-month survey of fishing conditions under the Memorandum of Understanding signed by the Governing Council (Hughes 1987). The fishing turned out to be excellent and a joint-venture agreement between Taiyo GyoGyo and the Governing Council was ratified by Parliament in 1973, giving rise to Solomon Taiyo Limited.

Solomon Taiyo had a fleet of about 20 small to medium pole-and-line vessels, and one group seiner. Originally based in Tulagi near Honiara, Solomon Taiyo moved its base to Noro in the Western Province about 1990. The shore base included a cannery, a smoking plant, brine-freezing and ice-making facilities, cold storage and wharf facilities, a waste-water treatment plant, a fish-meal plant, a boat-repair yard and a clinic.

Soon after starting operations in the 1970s, the company began employing large numbers of Solomon Islanders, the numbers increasing until, by 1999, Solomon Taiyo employed about 2,500 Solomon Islanders, and only about 60 expatriates in senior management, executive positions in crews and some technical supervision roles. Only about 10 per cent of the working-age population has ever been engaged in formal employment (CBSI 2005), and unemployment, especially among youth, has historically been considered a major social problem.

The fleet was never particularly profitable but continued for several reasons. The Japanese company Taiyo Gyogyo (which changed its name to Maruha in 1993) established trading relationships with UK supermarket chains, including Sainsbury's, which were willing to pay a premium price for pole-and-line-caught canned tuna because of its quality, the method's environmental friendliness and the large numbers of Solomon Islanders employed by Solomon Taiyo (which meant the product was considered socially responsible). Solomon Taiyo's inclusion as an Africa Caribbean Pacific (ACP) country product under the Lomé Convention (precursor to the Cotonou Agreement) also meant the product avoided the 24 per cent tariff incurred by competing products from Southeast Asia. In addition, there seems to have been a moral commitment by the Japanese partner company to the pole-and-line method—for the sake of Solomon Islands, the manufacturer of the vessels in Japan and the Okinawan fishers who worked on the fleet.[2]

Solomon Taiyo produced 'fancy' white-meat tuna exported mostly to the United Kingdom as an ACP product under the Lomé Convention. The dark meat used in the 'Solomon Blue' product was marketed locally. The company also produced smoke-dried skipjack for the Japanese *katsuobushi* market under an agreement with a small subsidiary company of the large *katsuobushi* company Yamaki. Solomon Taiyo also exported a portion of its catch frozen to be processed elsewhere, often in Thailand. In 1999, 65 per cent of Solomon Taiyo's catch was canned, 20 per cent exported frozen and 13 per cent smoked, and 2 per cent made into fish meal (Government of Solomon Islands 1999).

In the late 1990s, about 20,000mt a year of the total catch of 50–75,000mt (higher in 1998) was being processed in Solomon Islands; 15,000mt was being canned and 5,000mt was being smoked, both by Solomon Taiyo. The government wanted to increase the amount of processing done in-country, and was thinking of using access agreements to require distant water fleets to build shore-based facilities and/or employ locals (Government of Solomon Islands 1999). In 1999, Solomon Taiyo had 21 pole-and-line vessels 'operating on narrow margins' because of the age of vessels (most were more than 20 years old) (Government of Solomon Islands 1999).

National Fisheries Development

In 1978, another domestic pole-and-line company, National Fisheries Development (NFD), was started as a joint venture between Solomon Taiyo (25 per cent shareholding) and the Solomon Islands government (75 per cent shareholding) to conduct training-oriented activities (Hughes 1987). The company had several pole-and-line boats and sold its catch through Solomon Taiyo. NFD hosted an Asian Development Bank-funded project in ferro-cement boat building and ended up making and using some of these vessels for pole-and-line operations (not very profitably). In the early 1990s, NFD also operated two longliners under a Japanese aid project (Hughes 1987). In 1984, the shipbuilding and repair side of the business split from NFD and was renamed Sasape Marina. In 1988, NFD started operating two purse-seiners in addition to its small pole-and-line fleet, and started selling some of its catch outside Solomon Taiyo (Grynberg et al. 1995). During the 1980s, Solomon Taiyo relinquished its shareholding in NFD, leaving it a wholly government-owned operation; then, in 1990, the company was privatised. The first private owner was British Columbia Packers, then it was taken over by the Singapore-based company Trimarine. In 1999, NFD finally decided pole-and-line fishing was uneconomical so it divested its pole-and-line fleet to concentrate only on purse-seining. Since being taken over by Trimarine, NFD has been financially viable and a much stronger company than it was when it was government owned.

Longline fishery

The Solomon Islands longline fishery was limited to a total allowable catch (TAC) of 15,000mt, which was split among sectors—there was an amount for domestically based companies, an amount for by-catch from longliners targeting shark and an amount for distant water fleets. There was a licence limit of 120 for longlining, including 34 licences for large freezer vessels, which could be exchanged 'two for one' with non-freezer vessels. Licence allocation for longliners was to prioritise the distant water access agreement vessels, then the remaining licences were to be allocated according to a points system that favoured local ownership and management of vessels (Government of Solomon Islands 1999).

During the 1990s, there was only one tuna longline company operating out of Honiara, largely because airfreight was expensive, infrequent and the times did not always line up conveniently for getting fish to market in optimal condition. In addition, wharf facilities in Honiara limited fleet expansion potential and Solomon Islands sashimi was relatively low value. Prices might improve with better handling and increasing quality levels, but tropical tuna has always been valued lower than colder-water tuna in the Japanese sashimi market.

Since the 1990s, a Japanese-owned company Solgreen operated a few longline boats from Honiara, and flew chilled sashimi fish out by chartered freight plane to Australia to catch passenger flights to Japan. Solgreen also supplied Honiara restaurants with fish for sashimi. Solgreen had always been entirely private, and was also considered less 'domestic' than either NFD or Solomon Taiyo because it employed a much lower proportion of Solomon Islanders, preferring to source crews from China, Indonesia and the Philippines (Hamagawa, pers. comm.). Solgreen vessels were registered in Taiwan and Honduras (Gillett 2003).

Purse-seine fishery

The Tuna Management and Development Plan set a limit of 78 vessels for the offshore area. Numbers of purse-seiners in the offshore area were to be limited to less than 50 per cent of the limit set under the Palau Arrangement to prevent stock depletion, to fit within management capacities of the Fisheries Division and prevent overcrowding of vessels (Government of Solomon Islands 1999). In addition, 'a limited purse-seine fishery will be permitted, by licence endorsement, in selected parts of the Inner MGA [main group archipelago area]'. The Director of Fisheries, acting on the advice of the Tuna Management Committee, was to decide how many endorsements to issue (Government of Solomon Islands 1999). Managers from the pole-and-line company (Solomon Taiyo, now Soltai) complained about purse-seining in the MGA because they felt it scared the fish away from the surface, making it more difficult to catch with the pole-and-line method; they thought the government should show its commitment to the pole-and-line method by banning purse-seining in the MGA.

Bait fishery

Solomon Islands' pole-and-line fishery relied on an associated bait fishery. The bait fishery has been a significant source of income for rural communities whose reefs were frequently used by pole-and-line vessels, such as the Maroon Lagoon. Reef-owning communities were paid a royalty per night per vessel (Table 8.1).[3]

The data collection and bait-fish royalty payment systems were changed during the first 10 years of the fishery to improve accuracy by using the most appropriate measure of catch per unit of effort (CPUE), and also to remove the incentive for under-reporting (Blaber et al. 1993; Blaber and Copland 1990). The sudden jump in CPUE from 1981 was probably due to the introduction of a system of bait-fishing maps, logs and observers that made the records more accurate than before, rather than an increase in capacity. Statistics on bait fish held by the Fisheries Division included a caveat that figures from 1973 to 1980 were raised by a factor of 1.87 to compensate for the under-reporting of catches during those years.

The bait fishery had always been managed by the Fisheries Department in Honiara, even though jurisdiction for these coastal areas legally lay with the provincial governments. The Tuna Management and Development Plan envisioned responsibility being devolved back to the provinces (Government of Solomon Islands 1999).

Trans-shipping, service and supply

A policy to encourage and improve services for trans-shipping vessels started in 1993 after a Forum Fisheries Agency (FFA) ban on trans-shipping on the high seas. In 1994, Solomon Islands hosted 94 trans-shipments that generated S$700,000 in revenue (Government of Solomon Islands 1995). In the late 1990s, Honiara became a prime choice for trans-shipping in the central western part of the Pacific. Under the Tuna Management and Development Plan, the service and supply sector for trans-shipping was slated as a priority for development. Mothership operations were to be banned, as was bunkering at sea (Government of Solomon Islands 1999).

November to March was the peak season for trans-shipping activity in Solomon Islands. During this season, Honiara was busy with crew spending money in hotels, restaurants, pubs and clubs. The vessels also bought a lot of fresh produce from the central Honiara market. According to Fisheries Department staff, the trans-shipping vessels' crews complained that Honiara did not have enough for them to do. (Government of Solomon Islands, pers. comm.).

Skipjack stocks in particular follow a three to four-year cycle of being available for surface fisheries in Solomon Islands' EEZ (Government of Solomon Islands 1999). These fluctuations are probably due to the oceanographic effects of El Niño and the Southern Oscillation Index and mean that in some years purse-seine vessels do not fish near Solomon Islands and do not trans-ship in Honiara. Longline fleets (not a surface fishery) were generally more stable.

Table 8.1   Solomon Islands: bait-fishery catch, 1973–98

	Nights fished	Buckets hauled	Buckets per night per boat	Hauls per night	Buckets per haul	Catch (mt)
1973	1,722	118,808	69.0	0	0	488.8
1974	1,503	91,371	60.8	0	0	375.9
1975	1,563	130,587	83.5	0	0	537.2
1976	1,967	167,685	85.2	0	0	689.9
1977	2,913	225,076	77.3	0	0	926.0
1978	3,597	238,965	66.4	0	0	983.1
1979	4,858	303,741	62.5	0	0	1,249.6
1980	4,903	325,645	66.4	0	0	1,339.7
1981	4,892	645,811	132.0	10,580	61.0	1,420.8
1982	5,335	672,203	126.0	14,525	46.3	1,478.8
1983	6,844	895,631	130.9	17,543	51.1	1,970.4
1984	6,548	813,570	124.2	18,167	44.8	1,789.9
1985	7,593	1,015,539	133.8	20,024	50.7	2,234.2
1986	8,150	1,075,263	131.9	21,878	49.1	2,365.6
1987	7,372	956,323	130.0	21,671	44.1	2,103.9
1988	8,008	1,135,289	142.0	21,251	53.4	2,497.6
1989	7,347	968,301	132.0	19,281	50.2	2,130.3
1990	6,638	863,163	130.0	18,923	45.6	1,899.0
1991	7,866	1,043,811	133.0	23,261	44.9	2,296.4
1992	6,757	901,224	133.0	23,261	38.7	1,982.7
1993	6,008	881,537	147.0	18,389	47.9	1,939.4
1994	7,202	942,509	138.0	20,794	45.3	2,182.3
1995	-	1,005,973	-	20,792	48.4	2,213.4
1996	-	948,017	-	17,848	53.1	1,896.0
1997	-	405,596	-	8,468	47.9	892.3
1998	-	766,403	-	13,288	57.7	1,686.0

Notes: One bucket of bait was approximately 2.2kg wet weight of bait fish. These figures include Solomon Taiyo-owned vessels, Okinawan-owned vessels and NFD vessels from 1979. The bait-fishing season was usually nine or 10 months a year. Shorter or longer seasons account for some yearly fluctuations in catch size. For example, the 1988 bait-fish catch total was up 394mt on the 1987 total of 2,104mt because the fishing season in 1988 was 8,008 nights, while in 1987 it was only 7,372 nights (Government of Solomon Islands, 1989. Fisheries Division Annual Report 1988, Fisheries Division, Honiara, Solomon Islands.)
Sources: Solomon Islands Government Fisheries Division.

Fishing crews, especially those that have been at sea for months, are well known for enjoying a few drinks and the company of women when they are in port. In Honiara, there is a growing poverty problem and strong patriarchy means some women have extremely limited life opportunities, so some women and girls engage in prostitution or 'befriending' of fishermen. The Fisheries Department licensing officer, Selina Lipa, who visited trans-shipping vessels saw many young women on board (Government of Solomon Islands pers. comm.).

Needless to say, this causes a range of social problems, including unwanted pregnancies and unprotected sex with multiple partners in the context of an extremely limited health system, and with no domestic screening and treatment program for HIV/AIDS. Some of the women involved are extremely young; many have limited literacy and are ostracised (sometimes violently) by their families (Chiota, pers. comm.). There have been health awareness campaigns conducted by the Health Department targeting the port due to concerns about HIV/AIDS, but government health and welfare services need to be improved in a range of areas to cope with the social issues generated by international ports.

The Tensions: damage to tuna-industry development

In 1999, Solomon Islands had the largest domestic-based tuna industry of all the Pacific island countries in terms of volume and value. There were large long-running locally based companies engaged in pole-and-line, purse-seine and longline fishing, with a large long-established canning factory and a smoking plant exporting *katsuobushi* to Japan. More than 8 per cent of total formal employment was in direct tuna fishing and processing industries (Government of Solomon Islands 1999).

In 1999, Solomon Taiyo employed about 3,000 people, including about 800 women in the cannery (SPPF 1999), which was the only significant source of cash employment for rural women. This employment was connected to human resources development and training for Solomon Islanders in fishing, business administration and technical trades. The Solomon Taiyo base in Noro, with its large number of employees, generated spin-off businesses in consumer retail, wholesale, banking, fuel sales, transport, hardware sales and hospitality services, as well as a thriving fresh produce market (Noro Town Council 2004).

Thirty per cent of Noro tuna production was consumed nationally (Government of Solomon Islands 1999), replacing imports of canned mackerel and consequently assisting with the balance of payments in domestic sales as well as boosting exports. For the three decades up to 2000, the export value of tuna was 20–46 per cent of total exports in an economy whose only other major export was unsustainably high numbers of hardwood logs (Government of Solomon Islands 1999). Tuna industries generated revenue for a cash-strapped government; Solomon Taiyo alone generated about S$10 million in revenue in 1999 (SPPF 1999). A comprehensive Tuna Management Plan addressing the major issues was in place and was supported by the national government. The future of domestic tuna industries in Solomon Islands looked bright.

Then, the entire formal economy (except logging) was derailed by the Tensions. At the same time, average world prices for frozen skipjack fell from US$980 a metric tonne in

1998 and US$550 in 1999 to US$326 in 2000 (CBSI 2001). Domestic companies Solgreen and Solomon Taiyo closed operations, at least in part due to the Tensions, and NFD scaled down operations.[4] The formal fisheries sector contracted by 42.4 per cent (CBSI 2001). Fish production plunged by 55.9 per cent to 21,163mt, the lowest catch since commercial fisheries started in Solomon Islands (CBSI 2001). The temporary closure of Solomon Taiyo and Solgreen coupled with dwindling prices meant the value of fisheries exports plummeted by 77 per cent in 2000 (CBSI 2001). Access agreements also suffered. One reason for this was that the general breakdown of law and order, combined with inadequate government procedures, meant that not all of the fees were getting through to consolidated revenue (*Solomon Star* 2005; SIBC 2005a, 2005b; *Islands Business* 2005).

Unlike Goldridge Mine and Solomon Islands Plantations Limited, tuna businesses were not major targets for militants, but tuna companies were part of the capitalist system in Solomon Islands, which was perceived by some as generating an inequitable distribution of benefits, and as such were part of the cluster of factors contributing to the Tensions (UNDP 2004a). These problems were recognised to an extent before the Tensions, with the Tuna Management and Development Plan recommending awareness and public relations strategies (Government of Solomon Islands 1999). Unfortunately, with governance and revenue problems still not sorted out in the aftermath of the Tensions, most of the plan's recommendations were not pushed forward. As of 2005, the government had not initiated any strategies to improve the social acceptability of the capitalist sector, including tuna businesses.

Tuna developments since 2001

After tuna prices recovered in 2001, the domestic industry started rebuilding (Table 8.2). Solomon Taiyo had to adjust to the departure of its Japanese partner company. In 2000, Maruha pulled out and the company then reopened in 2001 with S$8 million in grant aid from Taiwan as the wholly government-owned Soltai Fishing and Processing (see above).[5] Of the 21 vessels, only 12 were useable in 2001. The national government retained its 51 per cent shareholding through the Investment Corporation of Solomon Islands (ICSI), while Maruha's 49 per cent shareholding was promised to the Western Province government. The fully nationalised company struggled to find its financial feet. Less than 10 of the company's vessels have been operational at any one time. In 2004, a senior management team from the Fisheries Division went to Noro to talk with a visiting Japanese group about aid for Soltai. They reached an agreement for two new vessels to be built at a cost of S$70 million (Diake, pers. comm.).

Soltai had record high catch rates from 2001 to 2003, but in 2003 rates fell, due in part to the seasonal fluctuations that reduce the amount of surface-swimming skipjack in the Solomon Islands EEZ in certain years.[6] In 2004, mechanical difficulties compounded the unfavourable fishing conditions, causing a 35.7 per cent drop in catches from 2003 (CBSI 2005). As of 2005, only seven of the vessels were licensed to operate (Government of Solomon Islands pers. comm.), with a couple undergoing repairs and two more retired. reopened commercial operations as Soltai Fishing and Processing. Only nine or 10

Table 8.2   Solomon Islands: indicators of domestic development, 2001

	Locally based vessels active	Cannery/ loining facilities	Sashimi packing facilities	Nationals jobs on vessels	Nationals jobs on shore	Frozen tuna exports (mt)	Fresh tuna exports (mt)	Canned tuna (cases)
Soltai	12 PL	1	0	380	368	0	0	8,800
NFD	2 PS	0	0	39	6	11,700	0	0
Solco	8 LL	0	1	45	40	0	1,200	0
Other	0	0	0	0	8	0	0	0
Total	12 PL, 2 PS, 8 LL	1	1	464	422	11,700	1,200	8,800

Notes: LL: longline. PS: purse-seine. According to the Central Bank (Central Bank of Solomon Islands [CBSI], 2001. Annual Report 2000, Central Bank of Solomon Islands, Honiara) in 2000, Solgreen (Solco) had 14 longline vessels and employed 120 people (including 50 expatriates).
Source: Gillett, R., 2003. Domestic tuna industry development in the Pacific islands. The current situation and considerations for future development assistance, FFA Report 03/01, Pacific Islands Forum Fisheries Agency, Honiara, Solomon Islands. Islands:176-77.

The main reason Solomon Taiyo had managed to stay viable in competition with cheaper purse seine caught product was that supermarket chains in the UK such as Sainsbury's had a policy of buying high quality and environmentally 'friendly' product (the pole-and-line method is environmentally friendly) and selling it for a premium price. Around 2000 this policy changed, with UK buyers wanting the same quality and environmental friendliness but for more competitive prices. In any case marketing to the UK had always been handled by Maruha, and Soltai did not have access to those trading networks. So Soltai had difficulty finding markets that would pay a higher price to enable its fishing fleet to compete with purse seiners.

Soltai's financial problems were solved partly by developing a new product: vacuum-packed frozen loins, sold by arrangement with NFD's owner company, Trimarine. Trimarine had set up a marketing arrangement with a buyer in Italy to buy the loins free on board (FOB), which meant Soltai did not have to manage the freighting process. Soltai loins were sold in Italy as ACP product and thus escaped the 24 per cent tariff under the Cotonou Agreement. Soltai managers were happy with the loining arrangement with Trimarine, apart from losing the margin on the fish it bought from NFD.[7]

Even with the loining arrangement with Trimarine, in 2005 Soltai was facing a possible sale of assets for defaulted loan repayments to the National Provident Fund. Soltai employees could see it was going to be tough for the cannery and vessels to achieve EU certification enabling the company to continue exporting loins to Italy, with an inspection team due in late 2005 or 2006.

Soltai's is the last surviving fleet of pole-and-line vessels based in a Pacific island country.[8] Solomon Islands' pole-and-line catch peaked in 1986 with 38,000mt (Reid 2005), when the fleet numbered more than 30 vessels. In 2006, the fleet was less than 10 vessels. Adrian Wickham, after running NFD's pole-and-line fleet for several years, said he did not think the kind of pole-and-line fishing Soltai conducted could be profitable, because of the extra costs of labour and running a large shore base required by that kind of fleet—at least when compared with purse-seining (Wickham, pers. comm.). Soltai managers also expressed doubts that the Soltai fleet in its current form could be profitable, suggesting instead that it be subsidised by government and aid donors because of the social benefits the fleet brought to Solomon Islands (Kukui, pers. comm.; Sibisopere, pers. comm.).

In 2004, the Earth Island Institute (EIS) created a problem for the export of loins to Italy. The Solomon Islands Fisheries Department had given a licence to a company to catch 100 dolphins for live shows. There is an indigenous dolphin fishery that kills hundreds of dolphins a year in Solomon Islands, so the Fisheries Department did not think a live export fishery would be a problem. However, when the EIS discovered that Solomon Islands was exporting live dolphins it started a campaign in Italy against the Italian company buying Soltai loins. Because of the bad publicity, the buyer stalled one shipment of loins from Soltai. The dolphin company had caught only 26 or so dolphins, but the government decided to cease the export of live dolphins at that time (Ramohia, pers. comm.; Diake, pers. comm.).

Soltai generated less spin-offs than Solomon Taiyo did, having reduced production by about two-thirds, and also because it no longer contracted local small businesses to provide services, such as transport and security. Since Soltai reduced its operations, NFD has been the largest domestic company in terms of catch since 2001, although Soltai was still the largest employer in the tuna sector, with about 800 workers. NFD employed a sixty-Solomon islander crew (three vessels were operating in 2005, with a fourth on order) and one non-national engineering manager on shore.

During 1999 and 2000, flights from Honiara international airport were disrupted periodically by militants, so the longline company Solgreen suffered financially from the Tensions and apparently changed its name to Solco about this time. Solgreen/Solco recovered in terms of production after the Tensions. In 2004, the company landed 986mt (CBSI 2005). By mid 2005, however, the company had closed and its vessels were tied up.

Since 2001, several new 'locally based foreign' companies have started up in Solomon Islands: Global, Tuna Pacific, Mako and Warken. Fisheries Department interviewees said that compared with Soltai and NFD, which they described as being 'really domestic', the others were 'more foreign than local' (Government of Solomon Islands pers. comm.). Of these, Tuna Pacific had its status changed from locally based foreign to distant water by the Fisheries Department in 2004, and Mako and Warken actually agents for distant water fishing fleets (Korean and Taiwanese respectively) rather than fishing companies in their own right. Global Investment Ltd had purse seining operations based in Tulagi (Table 8.3).

Distant water fleets

The longline and pole-and-line distant water fleets operating in Solomon Islands remained fairly stable during the 1990s, but the numbers of purse-seine vessels climbed steeply from only 31 in 1992 to more than 70 by 1998 (Government of Solomon Islands 1999) (Table 8.3).

Table 8.3 Solomon Islands: indicators of tuna development, 2004–2005

Company	Domestic vessels: no. and type	Processing facilities: no. and type	Jobs for nationals: no. and type	Annual exports: volume and type	Annual domestic sales: volume and type
Soltai	7 pole-and-line 1 carrier	1 cannery/loining plant 1 katsuobushi smoking plant 56 engineering 80 smoking 94 office	330 fleet and cold store 93 cannery/loining packs (7.5kg) frozen cooked loin	215 cartons canned tuna 270,614 plastic fishing vessels	261,928 cartons canned tuna discards from
NFD	3 purse-seine 1 carrier	0	60 fleet 15 shore base	whole frozen skipjack	–
Global	2 pole-and-line 31 longline 4 purse-seine 1 carrier	0	–	–	–
Mako	5 purse-seine 2 longline 3 carrier 4 bunkering vessels	0	0	–	–
Warken	2 purse-seine	0	0	–	–
Total	9 pole-and-line 33 longline 9 purse-seine 6 carrier, 4 bunkering	1 cannery 1 katsuobushi smoking plant	>928	Cans, cooked loins, whole frozen fish	Cans, whole frozen fish

Notes: In 2005, only seven of Soltai's vessels were licensed. Two new vessels funded by Japanese aid were delivered in 2006. NFD had purchased a fourth purse-seine vessel, which at the time of writing was awaiting a licence and therefore was not operational. Mako and Warken were officially 'domestically based foreign' but, according to Fisheries Department staff and managers of the companies themselves, they were more like agents for the distant water fleets of Korea and Taiwan respectively. Of Global Investment's longliners, three targeted shark rather than tuna.

Sources: Government of Solomon Islands (pers. comm.). Sevilleja, Alfredo, 2005. Finance Advisor, Soltai Fishing and Processing. Interview, 19 July. Noro, Solomon Islands. Kukui, Asery, 2005. Manager of Human Resources and Administration, Soltai Fishing and Processing. Interviews, Soltai office, 19–22 July. Noro, Solomon Islands. Wickham, Adrian, 2005. CEO, National Fisheries Development. Interview, NFD Office, 15 July. Honiara, Solomon Islands.

In January 2004, a bilateral agreement with the European Union for longline and purse-seine vessels was signed (Government of Solomon Islands 2005a), but no EU-flagged vessels were recorded by the Fisheries Department as being licensed to fish in Solomon Islands' waters in 2004 or 2005.

Trans-shipping, service and supply

From 2001 to 2003, no trans-shipping was documented for the Solomon Islands. Apparently fleets preferred not to use Honiara during the Tensions, and even in 2005 fisheries officers said they felt some vessels were still choosing not to come to Honiara because of law and order concerns (Ramohia, pers. comm.). Trans-shipping had been re-established in November 2003 after the RAMSI intervention. Between then and April 2004, 144 trans-shipments took place in the designated ports of Honiara, Tulagi and Noro.

Distant water fleet access fees are an important source of revenue, added to by attracting distant water fleets to trans-ship in country. As of 2005, a trans-shipment levy of US$2 per metric tonne of fish was charged. This usually amounted to S$10–15,000 per purse-seiner. From January to April 2005, there were 34 trans-shipments from Mako purse-seine vessels in Honiara. This generated trans-shipment levy revenue of US$47,682 (Government of Solomon Islands 2005a). There were also port entry fees of S$100 per vessel. Other costs included payment for the private security company that operated around the wharf, plus costs for water, fuel and other supplies bought in port.

Fish aggregating devices (FADs)

The Tuna Management and Development Plan included a comprehensive management plan for FADs, which were seen as crucial for the domestic pole-and-line and purse-seine fleets being able to operate year round in the Main Group Archipelago (MGA) waters. Foreign vessels were to be prohibited from setting anchored FADs, and FADs set for the domestic purse-seine fleet in the inner MGA were to be restricted. Anchored FADs were to be maintained on a register kept by the Director of Fisheries. FAD catches were to be monitored, and they were to be marked with the name of the company that owned it and equipped with radar reflectors. Floating FADs were to have radio beacons (Government of Solomon Islands 1999). The limited number of resources in the Fisheries Department since the Tensions has stalled the implementation of this plan.

Table 8.4   **Solomon Islands: bait-fishery catch, 2000–2004**

	Total hauls	Total buckets	Total catch (mt)	Days fished	CPUE
2000	325	126,679	278.69	781	0.4
2001	133	102,220	224.88	807	0.3
2002	306	376,406	828.09	3,289	0.3
2003	238	328,043	721.69	2,543	0.3
2004	126	198,193	436.02	1,543	0.3

Source: Government of Solomon Islands pers. comm.

Table 8.5   Solomon Islands: distant water access fleet and fees, 1994–2005

	Fee ($ million)	Number of vessels	Composition of fleet
1994	S$7.3 US$1.5	131	16 purse-seine (USA) 16 longline (Taiwan) 66 longline (Japan) 33 pole-and-line (Japan)
1998	S$8.8 124 US$1.9	3	5 purse-seine (USA) ~ 40 purse-seine (?) 18 longline (?) 31 pole-and-line (Japan)
2004	S$29.1 ~190 US$3.9	-	
2005	SB$30–40 US$4–5.4 (target for 2005 negotiations)	194	27 purse-seine (Japan) 11 pole-and-line (Japan) 19 longline (Japan) 27 purse-seine (Korea) 37 purse-seine (Taiwan) 29 longline (Taiwan) 40 purse-seine (USA) 4 purse-seine (New Zealand)

Notes: The figure for 1998 included licence fees from domestic as well as foreign fleets (Government of Solomon Islands, 1999. Tuna 2000: towards a sustainable fishery for the next millennium, National Tuna Managment and Development Plan, Honiara, Solomon Islands). Although 40 vessels were licensed under the multilateral treaty with the United States, less than half this number fished in the region in recent years, and not all of these necessarily fished in Solomon Islands' waters.

Sources: Diake, S., 2005. National tuna status report for Solomon Islands for 2004, First Meeting of the Scientific Committee of the Western and Central Pacific Fisheries Commission, Noumea, New Caledonia. Government of Solomon Islands, 1999. Tuna 2000: towards a sustainable fishery for the next millennium, National Tuna Managment and Development Plan, Honiara, Solomon Islands. Government of Solomon Islands, 2005a. Department of Fisheries and Marine Resources Annual Report 2004, Honiara, Solomon Islands. Central Bank of Solomon Islands (CBSI), 2005. Annual Report 2004, Central Bank of Solomon Islands, Honiara:20.

Table 8.6   Distant water fleet licensed in Solomon Islands, 2005

Japan	27 purse-seine 11 pole-and-line 19 longline	Japan Far Seas Purse-Seine Association, Japan Tuna Fishing Association, Japan Kinkatsukyo Fishing Association
Korea	27 purse-seine	Korea Deep Sea Fishing Association
Taiwan	37 purse-seine 29 longline	Taiwan Tuna Boat Owners and Exporters
USA	40 purse-seine	American Tuna Boat Owners Association
New Zealand	4 purse-seine	New Zealand Fishing Association
Fiji (Tuna Pacific)	17 longline	
Total	135 purse-seine 11 pole-and-line 65 longline	

Source: Licensing Section, Department of Fisheries and Marine Resources.

Canned/loined tuna

The cannery at Noro came online in about 1990. In 1999, it was upgraded to improve hygiene and employee amenities as part of the requirements for continuing exports to the United Kingdom. By 2005, most of the equipment was old and in need of renovation or replacement. The waste-water processing facility had not functioned properly since 2000, and untreated waste flowed directly into the harbour. The fish-meal processing equipment was no longer operational. Cold storage was insufficient and, in combination with infrequent freight, this was greatly inhibiting production.

There was a good market for loins and Soltai could have sold a lot more to the Italian buyer, except that lack of capital for factory repairs and new equipment were holding Soltai's production back.

Soltai's productivity was not competitive with the benchmark, Thailand, but it was similar to the level Solomon Taiyo had achieved in the 1990s, and that had improved a great deal.[9]

Smoked tuna

Arabushi, literally 'rough loin', is hot smoked loins of skipjack that are treated with a special mould to become *katsuobushi*, a widely used condiment in Japanese cuisine. Solomon Taiyo had an *arabushi* plant from the start of operations in Tulagi in the early 1970s. The Noro plant was the largest factory producing *arabushi* outside Japan. Since the 1980s, Solomon Taiyo's *katsuobushi* production had been managed under contract to a subsidiary of the *katsuobushi*-manufacturing giant Yamaki which, through a small contractor company, managed the smoking process and bought total production. Japanese managers employed by Maruha withdrew in 2000, but Yamaki's contractor company decided to continue the contract with Soltai.

Katsuobushi production capacity remained largely unaffected by Soltai's financial travails, because its requirements were simple and easily maintained. Two of the crucial inputs for *katsuobushi* are skipjack with a low body-fat content (skipjack swimming through the warm waters around the Solomons have low body fat), and timber that burns hot for the smoke-drying process. The Noro factory utilised mostly two types of local coastal timber—*qema* (*Pometia pinnata*) and *buni* (*Calophyllum spp.*) (Kukui, pers. comm.).[10] After being smoked for five to seven days, the loins—then referred to as *arabushi*—had to be kept in reefer containers at temperatures of less than –18° Celsius, then shipped to Japan where the final curing of the loins resulted in finished *katsuobushi*.

Before the Tensions, Solomon Taiyo produced 17 to 18 containers a month of *arabushi*. In 2005, with the low fish supply, production was eight to 10 containers a month. *Arabushi* production peaked in 2002 when the catches were good and there were limitations on cannery production, so more of the catch was going to smoking; up to 35 metric tonnes of frozen fish a day. Production average in 2005 was 10–20 tonnes a day.

Small-scale coastal

At the National Fisheries Workshop in Honiara in July 2005, Johann Bell (Worldfish Centre, Noumea) and Mike King (a coastal marine resource management specialist) said that although there were not enough data to say conclusively that coastal marine resources in Solomon Islands were overfished, the available evidence indicated that most coastal areas could produce no more fish than they currently were; indeed, harvesting might need to be decreased. Fisheries are important to Solomon Islands as a source of protein. On average, in 2005, each person consumed about 35kg of fish a year (Government of Solomon Islands 2005b), and, with a rapidly growing population, more fish would surely be needed. Coastal fisheries were also economically important because of income derived from selling fish. A precautionary approach to coastal fisheries would see food fisheries reorient from reef fish towards relatively healthy tuna stocks. Current tuna catches were neither abundant nor cheap enough to supply mass consumption needs.

Local fishers all say it is harder to catch tuna now than it was in the past; they have to go further from shore and fish for longer to get the same catch. They often blame commercial tuna fisheries for depleting tuna stocks, although provincial fisheries officers note that increasing population pressure, overfishing and unsustainable fishing practices are involved in coastal resource depletion (Government of Solomon Islands 2005).

In Solomon Islands, the small-scale village-based fisheries, including tuna, were similar to small-scale village-based fisheries in other Pacific island countries covered in this report. There were difficulties getting fish to the market cost effectively, and there were safety issues in fishing for tuna from small vessels. As with other Pacific island countries, production was not reliable, because fishers did not fish full-time but engaged in a range of economic activities.

Fisheries centres

Solomon Islands, like the other Pacific island countries studied for this report, had a long history of fisheries centres in rural areas falling victim to a familiar cycle. Established under aid projects, these centres were unable to sustain themselves and fell into disrepair after the end of the project. They were then periodically refurbished by new aid projects. The Japanese Overseas Fisheries Cooperation Foundation (OFCF) was particularly engaged with fisheries centres in Solomon Islands. The centres were supposed to be the responsibility of provincial fisheries departments, but these departments had neither the resources nor the capacity to maintain them. The centres had thus failed to generate much activity for small-scale fisheries even in terms of nutrition—their main aim—so there was a groundswell of opinion in favour of commercialising or privatising the fisheries centres (Atu, pers. comm.).

Problems with commercialising/privatising fisheries centres mainly revolved around how to make the centres work for local communities without skills and experience in sustaining commercial fish trading.

Determinants of success

The Central Bank of Solomon Islands cited fisheries as one of the sectors with the greatest potential to contribute to economic development in Solomon Islands (CBSI 2005). Total earnings from fisheries exports (mostly tuna but also *bêche-de-mer*, reef fish, trochus and shark's fin) had climbed steadily since the trough during the Tensions and the collapse of world tuna prices in 2000. In 2004, fisheries exports totalled S$132.1 million, representing 18.2 per cent of total exports, due largely to increased tuna-loin exports and rising international tuna prices (CBSI 2005). The potential of tuna industries, however, has been constrained by the government's inability to establish an environment conducive to business development, and by economic, social and political sustainability issues highlighted by the Tensions.

In terms of resource availability, Solomon Islands did have a comparative advantage, but in terms of cost structures it has not been competitive against the other major producer countries in Asia. In 2005, less than 30 fisheries businesses were operating. General economic constraints inhibited fisheries businesses in the same way as any other sector in Solomon Islands. For these reasons, the Foreign Investment Board was not actively promoting investment in 2005; these institutional problems needed to be rectified before Solomon Islands could be attractive to investors (Aihari, pers. comm.). To become competitive, Solomon Islands needs to reduce the costs of operations, and this requires that taxation and industrial policies complement fisheries policies. One of the main problems is that inconsistent policies undermine investor confidence.

Constraints to investment in tuna industries in 1999 listed in the Tuna Management and Development Plan (Government of Solomon Islands 1999) included

- poor infrastructure
  - lack of airport facilities restrict longlining export possibilities
  - insufficient port facilities, especially in Honiara, restricting expansion
  - existing wharf and cold-store facilities at Noro and Tulagi in urgent need of upgrading and maintenance; new facilities needed
  - roads poor
  - power expensive and unreliable
  - telecommunications expensive
- government systems obstruct investment
  - lack of transparency in administrative processes
  - chronic under-resourcing of the Fisheries Department
- freight expensive and difficult to organise
- lack of skilled human resources
  - low education and training levels
  - lack of business management experience/skills
- lack of ancillary services (such as repair, maintenance and supplies)
- lack of investment capital
- lack of land available reliably and at reasonable prices
- taxation structures inhibit investment.

Credit

By 2005, a liquidity boom temporarily alleviated prevailing credit problems in the Solomon Islands economy (CBSI 2005). NFD had no problems obtaining commercial finance locally (Wickham, pers. comm.). Soltai, however, because of its poor profitability record, did not have access to commercial finance (Sibisopere, pers. comm.). It is likely that new companies with no business track record in fisheries would also have difficulties obtaining finance through banks.

Freight

Freight has always been a major constraint for Solomon Islands' tuna-processing industry. The main competitor is Thailand, which has large ports with carrier vessels coming and going daily, meaning competition brings the price of freight down and shipments can be made easily whenever necessary. Freight to and from Solomon Islands is infrequent and expensive (Hughes and Thaanum 1995). In 2005, Soltai's production was frustrated by freight problems. Specific infrastructure requirements for fisheries development include infrastructure for freight—especially wharves and roads—and access to land (Government of Solomon Islands 2003).

Government ownership of enterprise

Soltai's status as a state-owned enterprise could be characterised as a constraint on industry development. Elsewhere it has been argued that Solomon Taiyo, while not as efficient as a fully private company, as a partially government-owned venture nonetheless offered a number of development benefits to the Solomon Islands economy (Barclay 2000). As a fully government-owned venture, however, Soltai has suffered from the lack of an experienced private-sector partner with capital and international marketing and trading expertise. Through reduced production, Soltai has contributed less to the economy and, in 2005, lack of financial viability was threatening its existence (Barclay 2005). Privatisation of some kind, connecting to established commercial expertise and trading networks, seems the best strategy for Soltai.

Governing tuna industries

Fisheries management in Solomon Islands has suffered from a lack of resources, a lack of consultation in decision making and problems with transparency and accountability. No annual report was published on fisheries between 1994 and 2004 (the Fisheries Division was still compiling them until 1999, but didn't have the resources to print them). The Fisheries Division continued to collect data for the SPC and the FFA but there was no internal reporting. Before 2000, there were 10 staff in the research section of the Fisheries Department; in 2005, there were only three (Ramohia, pers. comm.).

In the early 1990s, Solomon Islands politicians had entered into a spate of joint ventures with overseas fishing interests, which suddenly hiked up the potential catch to about 700,000mt, despite an SPC-recommended TAC of about 130,000mt. Fortunately, 700,000mt was never caught in a year; the national catch peaked at 130,000mt (domestic and foreign) in 1998 (Reid 2005). The joint ventures demonstrated that the system of management was unclear and lacked enforcement. This gave rise to a review of the 1972 *Fisheries Act* and the development of a tuna management plan facilitated by the FFA utilising funding from the Canadian government's CSPOD-II. A change of government in 1997 spurred on these reforms, including a restructuring of the Fisheries Division, new customs procedures, increased licence fees and a requirement for local involvement in purse-seining. A new *Fisheries Act* materialised in 1998 (Government of Solomon Islands 1998) and the Tuna Management and Development Plan was ratified in early 2000 (Government of Solomon Islands 1999), although it was never given legislative force.

In 2003, revenue-earning government departments, including Fisheries, were audited as part of the RAMSI measures, and it was revealed that millions of (US) dollars from distant water access fees had 'disappeared into someone's pocket' (*Solomon Star* 2005a; *Islands Business* 2005). In 2005, these cases were being investigated by the police. A new permanent secretary was appointed and departmental funding became dependent on planning documents, budget estimates and reporting procedures being in place for transparency and accountability. Annual reports were restarted (Government of Solomon Islands 2005a) and a national fisheries workshop was held as part of a planning exercise in July–August 2005 (Government of Solomon Islands 2005b). In 2005, the New Zealand government was intending to fund a project to review, restructure and build capacity in the Fisheries Department. Global Environment Facility (GEF) funding through the FFA was also to be used for capacity building and infrastructure developments in fisheries (Wickham, pers. comm.).

The original Tuna Management and Development Plan had not been taken forward by the government, partly because the Tensions made any government initiatives impossible for a while, and partly because the plan was complex and expensive relative to departmental capacity. In 2004, a review of the plan was commissioned (Aldous 2005). The review raised the possibility of turning the Fisheries Division into a statutory authority like the National Fisheries Authority (NFA) in Papua New Guinea, so that licence and access fees could be used to fund fisheries management. In light of Solomon Islands' difficulties with financial governance, however, instead of an authority it was recommended that a Tuna Management Unit be created within the Fisheries Department to govern tuna industries and implement the revised Tuna Management Plan (Aldous 2005).

Fisheries legislation needed updating as part of administrative improvements. The *Fisheries Act* had been under review since 2004. Some of the issues that needed to be taken into consideration in the review of legislation included harmonisation with Western and Central Pacific Fisheries Commission (WCPFC) obligations and community management plans for coastal, reef and lagoon areas with enforceable regulations to enable community control. Legislation was also needed to regulate for changes to policy introduced in the Tuna Management and Development Plan to better manage tuna industries, for resource conservation and industry development (Diake, pers. comm.).

Government services are among the first things needing improvement in order to enable private-sector development in Solomon Islands. This includes institutional strengthening, strong communication links and coordination of roles and responsibilities between agencies, which would require interagency cooperation, best facilitated at the ministerial level (Government of Solomon Islands 1999).

Investment approval

One of the main constraints listed by the Foreign Investment Board for the economy generally, as well as by the Tuna Management Plan for fisheries specifically, was the length of time investment approval processes took. Until 2005, the legislation did not allow for the Foreign Investment Board to work with other government departments so it had not been able to coordinate the various applications necessary for approval to start a business. The new *Foreign Investment Act*, intending to address this problem among others, was passed in November 2005.

Food safety regulation

Developing food safety and hygiene standards and systems is one of the important services needed for tuna-export businesses. In 2005, Solomon Islands was classified as a 'list-two' country, which meant Solomon Islands companies could export processed seafood to European countries only on a bilateral basis. In 2005, the Solomon Islands government signed a contract for a project with the European Union for a range of environmental health issues to do with fisheries, including building capacity such that the Solomon Islands Health Department could become a Competent Authority to approve the food safety of seafood products being exported to the European Union (for 'list-one' status, enabling free export to anywhere in Europe) (Beseto, pers. comm.).

Taxation

Solomon Islands' taxation system has inhibited fisheries development. An ADB study found in 1999 that the taxation regime worked counter to government aims of encouraging domestic industry over distant water fleets (Hand 1999). Domestic industry interviewees in 2005 still felt disadvantaged by the taxation and fee systems compared with foreign vessels. Incentive packages were implemented to offset some of the taxation costs, but even with the incentives, NFD management felt the amount of tax and other government fees it paid reduced its competitiveness considerably (Wickham, pers. comm.). As of 2005, no initiative had been made to rectify this situation for fisheries, although there was a board overseeing reform of the taxation system in general, including the introduction of a consumption tax, which could result in benefits for fisheries (Diake, pers. comm.).

The Central Bank of Solomon Islands advised that to galvanise the private sector, Solomon Islands must develop internationally competitive tax packages, streamline investment procedures and improve major investment infrastructure (CBSI 2005). Some interviewees felt government subsidies (incentives) were necessary to enable companies to be competitive because of the high-cost business environment (David Mamupio, pers. comm.).

Law and order

Since the Tensions, Solomon Islands' law and order problems could be considered a constraint to industry. In 2005, Solomon Islands became a member of the World Bank Group's Multilateral Investment Guarantee Agency (MIGA), which provides political risk insurance and technical assistance to potential investors (*Pacific Magazine* 2005). According to tuna-industry interviewees, however, law and order problems have not been a major problem in Solomon Islands. NFD managers said the Tensions did not disrupt operations. During and immediately after the Tensions, the police were 'completely ineffectual', but this was not a problem for Solomon Taiyo, partly because of the way the Tensions manifested in Western Province (Kukui, pers. comm.).[11] Since RAMSI began in 2003, the police force has been more effective. Soltai's security guards use neither guns nor attack dogs (both of which are usually deemed necessary in Papua New Guinea).

Land administration

Apart from a small amount of 'registered' (alienated) land, about 90 per cent of land in Solomon Islands is held under communal customary tenure, and is difficult to utilise for commercial purposes. The government sees the current land tenure system as an obstacle to development and has made it a priority to trace genealogies and codifiy them so as to avoid infighting and 'false' claims. This system has been further complicated by factors such as variations in matrilineal or patrilineal descent over time and across cultural groups. 'Even businesses on registered land are subject to harassment from landowners' (Diake, pers. comm.).

Monitoring, control and surveillance

Government monitoring and surveillance activities had been affected by lack of resources, but continued at a basic level. The FFA Vessel Monitoring System (VMS) continued to operate and the Australian government assisted with patrol-boat surveillance. Before the Tensions, port sampling was more regular (Ramohia, pers. comm.), but from 2000 to 2004, there was no port sampling program due to lack of funds (Oreihaka 2004). In 2004, port sampling was conducted with SPC funding during the first three months of the year, when most trans-shipping occurred (Government of Solomon Islands 2005a). In 2005, port sampling was still not conducted on all vessels; sampling staff were contracted by the Fisheries Department as funds became available (from the SPC, for example) and not employed when there were no funds (Ramohia, pers. comm.).

Role of government in enterprise

Perspectives on the role of government in enterprise varied. According to the National Economic Recovery and Reform and Development Plan (NERRDP), 'The presence of several inefficient state-owned enterprises [is] crowding out potential private investors' (p.111). This plan therefore recommended that the state-owned enterprises such as Soltai and the regional fisheries centres be privatised (Government of Solomon Islands 2003). NERRDP also included an objective to create 500 new jobs in the private-sector fisheries.

The Tuna Management and Development Plan specified that the private sector was to be the main engine for development, and that the government should move away from owning or trying to manage businesses (Government of Solomon Islands 1999).

On the other hand, the Central Bank of the Solomon Islands recommended protecting non-log-export oriented industries (which would include fisheries) as a general economic measure (CBSI 2005). Many interviewees saw a role for government ownership of enterprise as part of their aspirations for domestic development.

The development principles, visions, goals and objectives in the Millenium Development Policies planning document for Noro showed a mixed approach to the role of government in business. The private sector was described as the engine for commerce, industrial and urban development (Noro Town Council 2004), but then the document called for 'protected status' for fisheries industries because of their economic and social importance to Noro and the national economy (pp.5, 22, 26).

Consultative decision making

Domestic industry representative Adrian Wickham, head of NFD, was looking forward to the creation of a Tuna Management Unit in the Fisheries Department in the hope that it would improve government services. One of the improvements he saw as important was more transparency in the licensing regime; he wanted the government to publish a list of licence holders and the fees they paid (Wickham, pers. comm.). He also wanted communication between industry and government to improve.

The definition of stakeholders in Solomon Islands tuna fisheries is broad, since tuna industries have economic, social, cultural, political and ecological consequences. The Tuna Management and Development Plan called for cross-sectoral planning and budgeting to deal with cross-sectoral issues, as opposed to ministries doing their own budgeting and planning in isolation (Government of Solomon Islands 1999). In addition, the plan called for a Tuna Management Committee and a Tuna Management Impacts Review Committee with wide stakeholder membership, including the Ministry of Health, Women's Development Division, Environment Division, Fisheries Division, Department of Planning and Development, Department of Finance, Department of Provincial Government and Rural Development, Labour Division, a representative of an industry organisation and a representative of an NGO. The role of the review committee would be to facilitate monitoring and to develop strategies that mitigate and redress adverse social and environmental impacts.

In addition, consultative decision making could address some of the negative social impacts from tuna industries. Domestic tuna industries, as well as foreign fleets transshipping in Honiara, were seen as a magnet for social problems in Solomon Islands (Barclay 2004). Non-ethnic social problems did not directly constrain industry, but they were indirectly related in that they detracted from companies' good will.

The review committee was not mentioned in the post-Tensions review of the tuna plan (Aldous 2005), so it was unclear whether the Fisheries Department would go ahead with such a committee. The review did recommend the employment of an industry liaison officer in the Fisheries Department (Aldous 2005). The original plan included a Fisheries Advisory Council to advise the minister on management and research (Government of Solomon Islands 1999). The review made no specific recommendation regarding this council, but implied that a Tuna Management Committee was the main first step in consultative decision making.

Aid dependency

Solomon Islands is heavily dependent on aid for all aspects of government, including fisheries management. From 1990 to 2000, Solomon Islands received 73 per cent of its Fisheries Department development budget as aid (van Santen and Muller 2000). In order to balance the national budget, the whole fisheries development budget for 2003–06 was to come through aid (Government of Solomon Islands 2003).

Japan has long been a major source of aid for Solomon Islands. In January 2005, the Japanese government committed US$29.2 million in aid in the next few years. This included an upgrade to the Honiara power system and renovations of the Honiara International Airport (built with Japanese aid money in the 1990s) (SIBC 2005b). In 2005, Japanese aid money was being used to upgrade public water supplies in Honiara, Auki and Noro. As well as general aid, the Japanese government has given fisheries aid, administered by the Ministry of Agriculture, Forestry and Fisheries (MAFF), which sometimes had slightly different priorities from the mainstream aid program under the Ministry of Foreign Affairs (Tarte 1998).

The OFCF was also active in Solomon Islands, funding equipment for many of the 29 or so fisheries centres in rural areas.[12] Rehabilitation work was planned for eight centres in 2004 (Government of Solomon Islands 2005a). The OFCF paid the salaries of two Japanese technical advisors working as managers for Soltai. In 2005, the Japanese government committed US$9.5 million (S$70 million) for the 'rehabilitation of domestic tuna fisheries' (SIBC 2005b), which meant the construction of two new pole-and-line vessels for Soltai.[13]

The extent of Solomon Islands' aid dependency meant fisheries policy could potentially be influenced. The contract for Soltai's new vessels was launched in a ceremony at a Japanese shipyard with the Soltai managing director and a Solomon Islands government representative in early June 2005, a week or so before the International Whaling Commission meeting in Korea. Australia and Japan apparently used their significant aid contributions to try to pressure the Solomon Islands government into voting with them in the commission (ABC 2005c). Solomon Islands' dependency on aid also influenced the commercial directions of Soltai. The two new gift vessels influenced Soltai's decisions about keeping the fleet in its current structure although that kind of fleet was arguably economically unviable (Wickham, pers. comm.; Kukui, pers. comm.).

Conclusion

Solomon Islands has some of the best resource potential of any of the Pacific island countries covered in this study, with a rich surface skipjack fishery and viable longline fishery. It also has more land and potable water than many other Pacific island countries, and a larger population. These factors contributed to Solomon Islands being more advanced than the other Pacific island countries in 1999 in domestic tuna industry development. There were three locally based tuna operations making profits, and prospects under a strong Fisheries Minister (Stephen Aumanu) were good. During the Tensions (2000–03), there was a breakdown in law and order, no effective government, rampant corruption, escalating costs and loss of confidence, which destroyed much of the industry. The period to 1999, however, showed a 'proof of concept' for viable domestic tuna industries in Solomon Islands (Table 8.7). By 2005, the government, in collaboration with RAMSI, began broad reforms, so there is hope that the business environment will improve and Solomon Islands will be able to make more of its resources in future (Table 8.8).

For three decades, Solomon Taiyo was the mainstay of the domestic tuna industry, and indeed of the whole cash economy, providing thousands of jobs and a substantial portion of Solomon Islands' exports. Since that joint venture folded in 2000, Soltai has been less beneficial to the Solomon Islands economy. Clearly, it needs some experienced private-sector input, especially in trading, marketing and financial management.

Another point worth noting is the importance of environmental and social issues. Without good environmental management, development from tuna resources is not possible, and without good management of social issues arising from commercial developments the entire economy risks collapse.

Table 8.7   **Solomon Islands: domestic tuna production, 1997–2004**

	Total catch (mt)	Frozen tuna exports (mt)	Chilled tuna exports (mt)	Canned tuna total (cartons)	Canned tuna exports (cartons)	Smoke dried tuna (arabushi) (mt)	Fishmeal (mt)	Cooked tuna loins (mt)
1997	37,209	25,910	2,760	1,072,000	7,524	945	70	0
1998	41,158	37,292	2,153	-	1,446	149	118	0
1999	16,865	6,660	1,486	-	6,440	940	1,400	0
2000	4,680	670	804	-	2,349	504	353	0
2001	15,024	13,523	816	78,063	72	563	50	0
2002	11,283	7,750	1,385	254,224	72	1,480	596	0
2003	22,894	20,592	882	173,312	90	1,145	185	0
2004	27,496	23,331	1,116	262,144	215	574	225	2,035

Notes: According to NFD interviewees, NFD sold 5,282mt of its catch to Soltai in 2004 for processing as loins. The difference between the amount of tuna exported as frozen and the total catch is less than this, so there is a discrepancy between NFD and Fisheries Department figures.
Sources: Government of Solomon Islands (pers. comm.). Sevillejo, Alfredo, 2005. Finance Advisor, Soltai Fishing and Processing. Interview, 19 July. Noro, Solomon Islands. Wickham, Adrian, 2005. CEO, National Fisheries Development. Interview, NFD Office, 15 July. Honiara, Solomon Islands.

Table 8.8   Tuna catches from domestic and foreign fleets by gear, 2000–2004
(metric tonnes)

	Domestic PL	Foreign PL	Domestic LL	Foreign LL	Domestic PS	Foreign PS	Total
2000	2,777	0	1,197	835	2,365	3,885	11,059
2001	6,534	0	434	500	7,670	10,883	26,021
2002	9,787	0	907	1,267	6,783	10,883	29,627
2003	10,793	0	1,439	1,474	15,191	31,751	60,648
2004	6,882	0	1,174	619	16,094	70,184	94,953

Notes: LL: longline. PS: purse-seine. PL: pole-and-line. Licensing records indicate that a Japanese pole-and-line fleet was operating in Solomon Islands during this period, but the Statistics Section could not provide figures on the catch of this fleet since 1997. The fact that the 2002 and 2001 figures for 'Foreign PS' are exactly the same as the year before seems to indicate an error in the data provided by the Statistics Section for one of these years. NFD figures differ from the Fisheries Department figures for 'Domestic PS' for 2004; NFD interviewees reported their 2004 catch to be about 20,000mt, as did the 2004 Annual Report of the Central Bank of Solomon Islands (p.19), whereas the total domestic purse-seine catch recorded by the Fisheries Department figures is just less than 17,000mt.
Source: Government of Solomon Islands (pers. comm.).

Development aspirations and tuna

Overall aspirations

Solomon Islanders' overall aspirations for development for the mid 2000s were articulated in the National Economic Recovery, Reform and Development Plan (Government of Solomon Islands 2003). The key aim was 'to enhance and improve the quality of life and the living standards of all the people in Solomon Islands…increasing incomes and their equitable distribution' (p.6).

Another important thing to note is the emphasis placed on the distribution of development benefits across the various groups in Solomon Islands. This reflects concerns with island group rivalries, since antipathy between Malaitans and Guales was one of the contributing factors fuelling the Tensions.

Fisheries development aspirations were encapsulated in suggestions for a mission statement for the Fisheries Department put forward at the National Fisheries Workshop in Honiara in July 2005. Workshop participants were split into five groups and all came up with suggestions along the lines of managing fisheries resources sustainably for the benefit of all Solomon Islanders. The subtitle to the workshop—'Our sea resources, our livelihood'—also revealed the strong connection between the resources and the material well-being of Solomon Islanders. This dual aspiration was also cited as the main two objectives of the Tuna Management and Development Plan (Government of Solomon Islands 1999)

- to ensure that the tuna resources of the Solomon Islands are not exploited beyond their optimal sustainable yields
- within the limit set by the conservation objective, to harvest the resource in such a way that maximises the economic and social benefits received by the people of the Solomon Islands.

The lengthy Tuna Management and Development Plan (Government of Solomon Islands 1999) contained a plethora of aspirations in lists of development options, goals, objectives and strategies.

Goals

- sustainable stocks
- minimal environmental impacts
- increased domestic participation
- increased foreign revenue
- minimal social, cultural and gender impacts
- efficient (and effective) administrative services
- accountability.

Management strategies

- conservation management
- regional management and cooperation
- data collection and research
- monitoring, control and surveillance
- regulation of related fishing activities
- environmental impacts and by-catch
- domestic participation and development
- foreign access and investment
- social, cultural and gender impacts
- administrative support and licensing systems
- recovery of management costs
- accountability for management decisions.

An expression of aspirations for fisheries development in the 2004 *Fisheries Department Annual Report* was slightly different in that only economic objectives were included, with no conservation measures. The following objectives were listed

- to achieve and maintain self-sufficiency in supply of fish to the domestic market
- to improve cash income throughout the fisheries sector by assisting Solomon Islanders in developing their resources through self-employment
- to maximise participation of Solomon Islands nationals in commercial fishing and associated activities
- to improve the foreign-exchange position of Solomon Islands by encouragement of local processing of fisheries resources into value-added products
- to encourage farming of aquatic resources.

The National Economic Recovery, Reform and Development Plan (Government of Solomon Islands 2003) also specified specific aspirations for tuna fisheries

- facilitate the rational management and conservation of coastal fisheries and aquatic living resources through their sustainable utilisation

- rehabilitate and promote the privatisation and commercialisation of rural fisheries centres
- promote tuna fisheries development through foreign and local investment
- increase revenue through licensing of more tuna-fishing vessels under access agreements and domestic licensing arrangements
- improve the monitoring of fish catches, their exports and value and share such information with Customs, the central bank and related agencies
- review current fisheries legislation and formulate new legislation and fisheries management plans
- reform and rebuild capacity in the Fisheries Department.

Aspirations for development from tuna resources as embodied in these various government documents are not entirely consistent with each other. What is clear is that the paramount aspiration is to generate more wealth from tuna resources in the domestic economy.

Governance

Lack of transparency was also seen as one of the issues that needed to be addressed in order to foster an environment conducive to private-sector development. Improving governance in Solomon Islands will be a long battle. Notwithstanding efforts in the past few years by RAMSI, there were still indications that governance systems were weak and prone to abuse.

Governance is the key to being able to generate more wealth in the domestic economy from tuna resources. After the audit of the Fisheries Department in 2003, the amount of revenue generated from access fees improved dramatically in 2004 to make up 90 per cent of non-tax revenue (CBSI 2005). The National Economic Recovery, Reform and Development Plan included the general goals of 'good governance', 'revitalising the productive sector and rebuilding supporting infrastructure' (p.x) and overhauling and streamlining foreign investment legislation and governance (Government of Solomon Islands 2003). These general aspirations were similar to those documented as objectives in the Millenium Development Policies planning document for Noro: transparency, consultation and accountability (Noro Town Council 2004).

'Transparency' and 'accountability' were two buzzwords used in many aspirations about Solomon Islands' tuna industries. The Tuna Management and Development Plan listed strategies to establish well-informed, transparent and accountable decision-making processes, including public reporting of important policy issues and ensuring compliance with laws and regulations. (Government of Solomon Islands 1999:1–2). Public reporting was to include providing an annual report from the Fisheries Department to the Minister and Cabinet. The report would be developed in conjunction with relevant management committees, which in 2005 were yet to be established. The plan specified that stakeholders and the public should also be kept informed about fisheries matters via the media (Government of Solomon Islands 1999).

Human resources development

The government hoped to promote 'higher level employment in all sectors' of the tuna industry, in part through targeted education and training programs for fisheries-related skills and management with the School of Marine and Fisheries Studies and the Solomon Islands College of Higher Education (SICHE), so as to replace expatriate employees with Solomon Islanders (Government of Solomon Islands 1999). With basic seamanship and safety skills, more Solomon Islanders could be employed on domestically based and distant water vessels. For Solomon Islanders to develop their own tuna-related small businesses, other types of training considered in the tuna plan included small-business skills, fisheries business-management skills, value adding, catch handling, quality control and small-scale commercial tuna-fishing methods (Government of Solomon Islands 1999). Some of the human resources development improvements cited as necessary in the plan included investment in targeted education and training programs, upgrading existing training facilities, developing courses and workshops, sponsoring students to undertake studies in relevant areas and upgrading the qualifications of teaching staff (Government of Solomon Islands 1999).

The human resources of government itself needed attention before any of these improvements could come to fruition. The capacity of the Fisheries Department, as with the whole of government in Solomon Islands, was simply insufficient to carry out many of the reforms needed. Increasing the numbers of staff and upgrading their educational qualifications were some of the suggestions for improving departmental capacity (Diake, pers. comm.; Ramohia, pers. comm.). Ongoing training existed in the form of short courses sponsored by aid donors and regional organisations, and working closely with counterparts in regional organisations such as SPC and FFA.

While fisheries science is important for understanding and participating meaningfully in regional stock-assessing activities, tuna fisheries management is most often defined by Pacific island countries as managing the resource in terms of conservation and managing fisheries for development purposes. Greater expertise would therefore be useful in public policy, marine resource economics and business management. Some kind of training in business negotiations might also be useful for the Fisheries Department staff who negotiate distant water access agreements.

Improving access fees

According to Fisheries Department official Sylvester Diake (pers. comm.), since the Tensions, Solomon Islands' distant water access fees as a percentage of the market value of the total catch have been among the lowest in the region. The Fisheries Department saw this as due largely to the weak economic position of Solomon Islands in the aftermath of the Tensions, and envisaged that when the economy improved they would be in a better bargaining position, and fees would rise.

Industry representative Adrian Wickham suggested that distant water access negotiations could be more effective if they were conducted in Honiara rather than overseas, so that the negotiating team could be made up of officials from all the relevant government departments (Wickham, pers. comm.). Another option would be for the negotiating team to include a specialist negotiator from outside, such as an official from the FFA, as had happened in the past.

Regional and international responsibilities

Meeting regional and international responsibilities is especially important for tuna-fisheries management because the migratory nature of the stocks means no one state can manage them alone. Solomon Islands' aspirations as outlined in government documents placed a high priority on cooperating with regional and international management initiatives. The Tuna Management and Development Plan cited the importance of domestic management being consistent with regional and international laws and agreements (Government of Solomon Islands 1999). In addition, regional cooperation was seen as a way to increase the amount of revenue collected from foreign fishing interests (Government of Solomon Islands 1999).

Environmental issues

Managing tuna resources in terms of conserving stocks was one of the most important concerns Solomon Islanders raised regarding aspirations for development from tuna, in interviews and in government documents. For World Wide Fund for Nature representative Stephen Kido Dalipada and Environmental Health Officer Tina Mamupio, ecological sustainability was the most important aspiration for development from tuna resources (Kido Dalipada, pers. comm.; Tina Mamupio, pers. comm.). The Town Clerk of Noro, David Mamupio, noted that if tuna stocks fell, industries would also fall, so he hoped the government would limit the number of fisheries licences issued to protect the stocks, and that purse-seiners would be prevented from fishing too close to islands so that stocks would be protected for village fishers (David Mamupio, pers. comm.). Fisheries Department staff felt that as one of the main sources of income for Solomon Islands, tuna stocks should be protected by careful monitoring. They feared that lack of resources in the department prevented monitoring and enforcement and they would like to be able to institute more regulations to protect stocks.

Social issues

Aspirations for development from tuna resources specified in the Tuna Management and Development Plan highlighted the need to limit adverse social impacts, for example, by respecting customary rights, Solomon Islands culture and traditional fisheries (Government of Solomon Islands 1999). The plan pointed out gender inequity in work settings and in decision making, and asserted that addressing gender inequity would solve some of the negative effects of tuna industries on social stability and health.

The sustainability of tuna industries in Solomon Islands is made up of linked social, environmental and economic components, because of the obvious risks to industries posed by episodes such as the Tensions. The Tuna Management and Development Plan recognised that change through development of large-scale industry would bring positive and negative impacts, and the overall impact in terms of employment, nutrition, welfare and revenue needed to be considered. Equity of opportunity to participate was considered a prerequisite for sustainability, and government was responsible for identifying and addressing negative impacts such as prostitution and family/community disruption due to increased cash flow to rural settings (Government of Solomon Islands 1999). Government and industry were expected to share responsibility for adverse social and environmental impacts and 'undertake to minimise such costs'.

Concerns about social issues arising from tuna developments were often couched in terms of ensuring an 'equitable distribution of benefits' (Government of Solomon Islands 1999). This was defined in the tuna plan as being a balanced distribution of benefits across 'regions, communities, social groups and genders'. The government was to track revenue raised from tuna resources against the social and environmental costs and benefits associated with tuna industries, and institutionalise recurrent spending on services to mitigate negative social impacts.

Concerns about dissatisfaction over capitalist development becoming 'ethnicised'[14] were part of discourses about 'equitable distribution of benefits' (Government of Solomon Islands 1999:22). Consolidation of tuna industries in any one place is seen as a social problem partly because the influx of young people (mostly men) from other parts of the country looking for work is considered a bad thing. Free internal migration is not seen as legitimate in Solomon Islands, except perhaps in towns, although even then the apparent preponderance of any particular migrant island group is seen as unacceptable.

The aspiration to spread development geographically for social reasons, however, is in direct conflict with economic aspirations, because consolidating industries helps with economic viability. Because of infrastructure costs, as well as economies of scale for freight, it would make more sense economically to consolidate shore bases in Noro or Tulagi. With NFD having moved to Noro, as well as the existence of other export industries nearby in logging and copra, Noro has been developing as an industrial hub. Even Noro, however, still does not have the infrastructure and government services to make it a competitive business environment.

Domestication

Solomon Islanders want locals to own commercial tuna-fishing vessels (Government of Solomon Islands pers. comm.). Building domestic tuna industries to replace foreign-owned and foreign country-based industries was the main way Solomon Islanders saw that wealth from tuna resources in the EEZ could be captured in the domestic economy. '[T]he government aims to expand the domestic industry with a long-term view of using local resources and replacing the reliance on foreign access' (Government of Solomon Islands 1999:20). Domestication was seen as beneficial in terms of factors such as employment and revenue.

The Tuna Management and Development Plan included an extensive array of strategies for developing Solomon Islands' domestic tuna industries, through

- encouraging small-scale harvesting
- facilitating expansion of domestic operations (sashimi longlining, the pole-and-line fleet, maintaining and upgrading infrastructure, working towards local ownership of vessels, incentives for business development)
- facilitating private-sector development of shore-based facilities (link fishing access to shore-based facilities development)
- encouraging the development of a supply and service sector (local bait supply service, stevedoring, net repairs, entertainment)
- encouraging value-added processing (canning/loining on a large scale, smoking and other kinds of processing on a smaller scale)
- investing in education and training programs (upgrade existing training institutions including qualifications of teaching staff, develop courses for key areas, sponsor students from industry including in business management)
- setting licence fees such that foreign fishing vessels would pay relatively more than locally based vessels
- giving preference to the domestic industry, especially those with substantial onshore assets employing large numbers of Solomon Islanders (Government of Solomon Islands 1999).

The pull-out of the Japanese partner company from Solomon Taiyo was seen by several interviewees as a positive move in terms of localising tuna industries, especially since Western Province became involved in running the company (Atu, pers. comm.; Ramohia, pers. comm.; Sibisopere, pers. comm.). The managing director of Soltai, Milton Sibisopere, felt that Soltai's status as a wholly nationally owned company was critical for national self-esteem, and, because it was eligible for donor assistance, it could better facilitate bilateral relations with Japan. He felt that any privatisation would inevitably mean becoming in some way a foreign company because 'the private sector in Solomon Islands is all foreign' (Sibisopere, pers. comm.).

Interviewees also noted, however, that under full domestic ownership, the Soltai base at Noro looked more run down than it did before, the fleet had shrunk and production had fallen (Atu, pers. comm.). Several casual observers met in the course of fieldwork expressed the opinion that they thought it would be better if 'the Japanese came back'. In the case of Soltai, it seems the aspiration for domestic development is conflicting with aspirations for development in general.

Foreign direct investment

According to the Foreign Investment Board, in the short term, foreign investment is needed in Solomon Islands—especially in tourism, fishing and aquaculture—to show locals how to develop the resources, as well as to provide employment and opportunities for technology transfer (Aihari, pers. comm.). NFD manager Adrian Wickham noted that cash-rich investors were necessary in the volatile tuna industry because the nature of the industry, with fluctuating prices and catch rates, meant there were inevitably lean years. The Solomon Islands and Western Province governments as investors had not been able to support Soltai in this way, so private-sector foreign investors were the only alternative. According to Wickham (pers. comm.), NFD's shareholder, Trimarine, was keen to help Soltai with capital for investment and access to markets in the United States and the European Union, but so far the government had chosen to retain control of Soltai.

Foreign investment in tuna industries was viewed positively in the Tuna Management and Development Plan, as complementary for domestic development through increasing revenue and fisheries development. The policy framework for generating maximum domestic benefits from foreign investment included addressing disincentives for foreign investors, encouraging foreign vessels to base themselves locally and ensuring a 'fair return' to Solomon Islands for fisheries access (p.38). It was recommended that joint ventures with foreign investors be better negotiated, to be more clear and binding and to ensure greater returns to Solomon Islands.

Pole-and-line

Several interviewees included in their aspirations the desire for Soltai to be profitable (Kukui, pers. comm.; Sibisopere, pers. comm.; Wickham, pers. comm.). According to Adrian Wickham, this meant the pole-and-line fleet would have to go, because without a special marketing advantage over purse-seine product on the basis of social and environmental responsibility, he saw no way for Soltai's pole-and-line fleet to be profitable. Other interviewees, however, wanted the pole-and-line fleet to continue, largely because it was seen as being more environmentally sustainable than purse-seining (Kukui, pers. comm.; Mamupio, pers. comm.). Various interviewees hoped that the Solomon Islands government would support the pole-and-line method by monitoring and enforcing policies to make sure The Slot and Main Group Archipelago areas were reserved for small-scale and domestic pole-and-line fleets only (Pina, pers. comm.; Sevillejo, pers. comm.).

Village-level development

One of the most commonly cited aspirations for development from tuna resources was that villagers could somehow benefit from tuna businesses. Interviewees repeatedly pointed out that tuna fisheries gave very few returns at the village level. Rural people had very negative images about tuna fisheries because they saw fishing boats offshore and believed they were taking fish that belonged to them, with no recompense.

Intervieweees said they would like to see more involvement by local people in tuna fisheries and more benefits from tuna industries visible at the village level (Atu, pers. comm.; Ramohia, pers. comm.). Most frequently this was envisaged as villagers fishing tuna themselves for local markets, for processing and/or for export markets. The Tuna Management and Development Plan included various schemes for small-scale tuna harvesting, such as the development of a small multipurpose vessel, local ownership of fishing vessels, canoe fisheries, facilitating financing and incentives for business development.

Generating commercial export or processing-oriented small-scale fisheries at the village level, however, has proven to be difficult. It is often logistically difficult and expensive to transport fish from village fishing grounds to markets. Village-based fishers with diverse social and economic obligations rarely commit to full-time fishing, and they have limited experience and training to enable them to run a small business, either in terms of accounting or in handling food to export-destination standards for food safety and hygiene. The Tuna Management and Development Plan aimed to work around the lack of business experience in villages with small-scale processing and fishing business development training.

Considering the difficulties in linking small-scale village-based tuna fisheries to commercial markets, however, even with training, it is unlikely small-scale operators will be able to supply export markets.

There have been discussions about localising bait-fish harvesting over the years, and companies have said they would prefer to buy bait than catch it themselves, but bait-ground owners naturally prefer to be paid royalties (and not have to fish) rather than be paid for fishing. Non-bait-ground owners could possibly start bait-fishing businesses, but since bait-grounds are considered to be held under customary tenure they would likely have difficulties accessing them. If these tenure issues could be overcome, it could be possible for Solomon Islanders to harvest bait fish and freeze it for sale to the increasing numbers of longline vessels operating in Solomon Islands' EEZ.

Game fishing

Potentially, ecotourism with game fishing could be a business for rural communities, with high economic returns for each fish caught. There was a small game-fishing tourism market in Solomon Islands, but it was limited by the general tourism industry constraints: perceived health risks, unreliable and expensive air travel, expensive telecommunications, difficulties in accessing land for tourism businesses, and bad publicity surrounding the Tensions. In 2004, Solomon Islands accounted for less than 1 per cent of the tourists who visited the South Pacific (CBSI 2005).

Addressing the issues that discourage tourists and constrain tourism businesses as well as a large marketing campaign will be necessary to make game-fishing tourism a viable form of development from tuna in Solomon Islands.

Processing

Value-adding processing of tuna was another field in which Solomon Islanders hoped to become more involved. The Tuna Development and Management Plan envisaged small-scale processing (such as tuna jerky and smoking) and large-scale processing (such as canneries and loining facilities). Fisheries access licences were to be tied to sales to local shore-based processors to ensure supply for the processing sector.

In addition to the development potential of processing enterprises themselves, they generate spin-off businesses, such as security, cleaning and food sales. Solomon Islands could develop a salt industry to supply industrial salt for brine-freezing units, and produce table salt as an ingredient for the cannery. Spices and other ingredients used in canned products could be grown locally.

To make the most of processing in Solomon Islands, the trade and marketing sectors will have to improve. The absence of significant international trade and marketing expertise in Soltai is possibly the most important factor deterring success in recent years (Barclay 2005).

Service and supply industries

Other aspirations for generating more wealth in the domestic economy from tuna industries included expanding service industries for trans-shipping fleets. Such service industries would also benefit domestic fleets. Solomon Islands ports could improve their attractiveness by streamlining the paperwork, ensuring port security and improving air links. In terms of entertainment, Honiara could do with more cinemas, restaurants, shopping areas and karaoke bars. It will likewise be necessary to manage the health and welfare problems of substance abuse and sex work that inevitably emerge around active international ports.

Because of the climatic fluctuations in the surface fishery around Solomon Islands, it could be worthwhile checking out the possibility for collaborative investment in mobile service industries to follow fleets as they base themselves in different parts of the Pacific from year to year.

Unrealistic aspirations

One final point to make about aspirations for development from tuna resources is that sometimes people's expectations have been unrealistic. Representative for NGO Solomon Islands Development Trust, John Roughan, noted that tuna industries, as with many other things in Solomon Islands, had not lived up to expectations. Partly this was because the original expectations were overblown, based on a lack of knowledge about capitalism in general. He believed that the naivety of many Solomon Islanders' aspirations of development directly contributed to the dissatisfactions at the root of the Tensions, and he saw it as a failure of Solomon Islands leadership to have allowed these unrealistic aspirations to continue (Roughan, pers. comm.).

Recommendations

The main recommendations for Solomon Islands to be able to capture more wealth from its tuna resources are to continue with reforms to improve the stability of government and the economy as a whole, and to deal with governance issues. In particular

- the macroeconomic environment must be improved to build confidence, encourage reinvestment in fisheries and maximise prospects for economic viability
- government must convince investors it will not make capricious decisions relating to fisheries development initiatives and licensing applications
- the foundations for good public policy must be laid, and realistic objectives and strategies agreed on and enforced through legislation to guide development and discourage *ad hoc* arrangements.

Continuing reforms in the Fisheries Department in terms of governance is also important. When that is under control, it will be necessary to

- further develop the capacity of the department and work on improving fisheries management and development policies and administration
- ensure that adequate levels of staffing, resources and skills are available to deliver fisheries management and development objectives—this will inevitably need to include external assistance in the medium term.

Soltai remaining 100 per cent government controlled is unlikely to deliver an economically viable operation in the long term. Consequently, it is recommended that a private-sector partner be sought, possibly using a long-term licensing (access) arrangement as an incentive.

It will be important to consolidate tuna industries at Tulagi and Noro rather than develop new centres, so as to make it feasible to develop infrastructure, government services and human resources to a level where tuna industries can be competitive in Solomon Islands. To avoid exacerbating social problems with this policy, it will be necessary to deal with the problems created by internal migration and land tenure dysfunctions in relation to commercial activity. Further research could be necessary to identify policies that will enable labour migration to occur without causing significant social problems.

Notes

[1] The conflict has often been called 'ethnic tensions', but in line with the UN Development Program's Peace and Conflict Development Analysis, we believe the label 'ethnic' is inappropriate because although the conflict was 'ethnicised' it was more about land ownership, land use and distribution of benefits generated by land, control of political power, poverty and access to natural resources (UNDP 2004a).

[2] For further information on Solomon Taiyo, see Barclay 2001 and Hughes and Thaanum 1995.

[3] For further information on Solomon Islands' bait fishery, see Barclay 2001.

[4] NFD was not affected greatly by the Tensions, but it was economically unsound to continue operating at such low prices (Wickham, pers. comm.).

[5] For further information on the transition from Solomon Taiyo to Soltai and a comparison of the two, see Barclay 2005.

[6] Managers from Soltai and the other large domestic skipjack fishing company, NFD, said that their catches had been low from 2003 to 2005. Interestingly, no such drop in productivity for the skipjack fishery was noted by national or regional fisheries reports (Diake 2005; Molony 2005). According to one industry interviewee, skipjack were not available for surface fisheries when the water temperature was 29.5° Celsius or higher on the surface and the water had been this warm for many months to mid 2005. In July 2005, as the surface temperature was starting to drop, catches were recovering accordingly (Wickham, pers. comm.).

[7] Apparently, Soltai bought fish from NFD at the Bangkok price (instead of Bangkok minus the cost of transporting it there). In 2004, NFD sold 5,282mt from its total catch of about 20,000mt to Soltai for processing. The rest of its catch was sold wherever gave the best price for frozen purse-seine product, usually Thailand (Wickham, pers. comm.).

[8] Japan had a fleet of larger ocean-going pole-and-line vessels supplying the Japanese fresh skipjack market, and other companies based in Pacific island countries had one or two pole-and-line vessels but not a fleet.

[9] For further information on Solomon Taiyo's productivity, see Hughes and Thaanum 1995; SPPF 1999.

[10] Some Western Province leaders apparently invited vigilante groups of militants from Bougainville to come to Noro to protect Western Province from Malaitans, and these groups decided it was their mandate to protect Solomon Taiyo from looting (Kukui, pers. comm.).

[11] For further information on the nature of OFCF and its activities, see Tarte 1998.

[12] Vessels and other equipment procured in Japan under the Japanese aid program are often much more expensive than comparable items available elsewhere, and some observers felt that the purchase of these vessels from a Shizuoka shipyard was as much about assisting the constituency of the shipyard as it was about assisting Solomon Islands (Hughes, pers. comm.).

[13] 'Ethnicisation' refers to the process by which ethnic divisions are politicised by political or conflict entrepreneurs. In these cases, it is not ethnic groups per se that are the problem but the way ethnic relations are manipulated so that, for example, competition for employment or land comes to be framed as an 'ethnic' dispute (UNDP 2004a).

References

Australian Broadcasting Corporation (ABC), 2005a. 'Cook Islands party leader asked to resign', radio broadcast, ABC Radio, 17 August 2005. Available from www.abc.net.au/ra (accessed 12 December 2005).

——, 2005b. 'Kiribati: Catholic Church highlights prostitution concerns', radio broadcast, ABC Radio Australia, 12 July 2005. Available from http://www.abc.net.au/ra/pacbeat/stories/s1412613.htm (accessed 7 November 2005).

——. 2005c. 'The whale wars', television broadcast, ABC TV, 18 July 2005. Available from http://www.abc.net.au/4corners/content/2005/s1413252.htm (accessed 14 December 2005).

Aldous, D., 2005. *Review of the Solomon Islands Tuna Management Plan: a report for the Government of the Solomon Islands*, Forum Fisheries Agency, Honiara.

Amoe, J., 2005. *Fiji Tuna and Billfish Fisheries*, First Meeting of the Scientific Committee of the Western and Central Pacific Fisheries Commission, Noumea.

Anderson, K., 2002. Tuna politics in Oceania: the effectiveness of collective diplomacy, PhD Thesis, Department of International Relations, Research School of Pacific and Asian Studies, The Australian National University, Canberra.

ANZDEC Limited, 1997. *Republic of the Marshall Islands National Fisheries Development Plan*, Asian Development Bank TA No.2349—RMI, Auckland.

Aqorau, T., 2005. *The Fiji Customary Fisheries Bill 2004: the implications of the Customary Fisheries Bill on the management and conservation of Fiji's fisheries resources*, FFA Report 05/08, Forum Fisheries Agency, Honiara.

Asian Development Bank (ADB), 1997. *The Pacific's Tuna: the challenge of investing in growth*, *Pacific Studies Series*, Asian Development Bank, Office of Pacific Operations, Manila.

——, 1998. *Report and Recommendations of the President to the Board of Directors on a Proposed Loan to Papua New Guinea for the Fisheries Development Project*, Asian Development Bank, Manila

——, 2003. *On or Beyond the Horizon: a discussion paper on options for improving economic outcomes from the Western and Central Pacific Tuna Fishery*, ADB TA 6128-REG 226, Technical Assistance for Alternative Negotiating Arrangements to Increase Fisheries Revenues in the Pacific, Asian Development Bank, Manila.

——, 2005a. *Country Reports*, Asian Development Bank. Available from http://www.adb.org/ (accessed 9 December 2005).

——, 2005b. *Key Indicators of Developing Asian and Pacific Countries*, Asian Development Bank. Available from http://www.adb.org/Documents/Books/Key_Indicators/default.asp (accessed 13 December 2005).

Baker, L., 2005. 'Political integrity in Papua New Guinea and the search for stability', *Pacific Economic Bulletin*, 20(1):98–117.

Balint, R., 2005. *Mare nullius* and the making of a white ocean policy, paper read at Fresh and Salt: Water, Borders and Commons in Australia and Asia, 8–10 May, University of Technology Sydney.

Barclay, K., 2000. 'Solomon Taiyo Ltd—tuna dreams realised?', *Pacific Economic Bulletin*, 15(1):34–47.

——, 2001. Foreign bodies in tinned tuna: modernism, identity relations and economic practice in a Japanese joint venture in the Solomon Islands, PhD Thesis, Humanities and Social Sciences, University of Technology Sydney, Sydney.

——, 2004. 'Mixing up: social contact and modernisation in a Japanese joint venture in the Solomon Islands', *Critical Asian Studies*, 36(4):507–40.

——, 2005. 'Tuna dreams revisited: economic development contributions from a tuna fishing and processing enterprise in Solomon Islands', *Pacific Economic Bulletin*, 20(3):78–93.

Barclay, K. and Sunhui Koh, 2005. *Neoliberalism in Japan's tuna fisheries? Government intervention and reform in the distant water longline industry*, Working Papers in International and Development Economics, Asia Pacific School of Economics and Government, The Australian National University, Canberra. Available from http://apseg.anu.edu.au/degrees/idec/working_papers/IDEC05-2.pdf (accessed 6 December 2005).

Barter, P., 2004. Letter to the editor, *Post-Courier*, 30 December.

Benet Monico, A., 2003. *Madang Lagoon Water Quality Monitoring*, World Wild Fund for Nature South Pacific Program, Madang.

Bestor, T., 2004. 'Tsukiji: the fish market at the center of the world', in D. Goldstein (ed.), *California Studies in Food and Culture*, University of California Press, Berkeley.

Beverly, S., 2004. *Technical assistance provided to the longline fishing vessel F/V Tekokona III, Christmas Island, Republic of Kiribati*, Field Report No.25, Secretariat of the Pacific Community, Noumea.

Blaber, S. and Copland, J. (eds), 1990. *Tuna baitfish in the Indo-Pacific region. Honiara, Solomon Islands*, Vol. Proceedings No. 30, Australian Council for International Agricultural Research, Canberra.

Blaber, S., Milton, D. and Rawlinson, N. (eds), 1993. *Tuna baitfish in Fiji and Solomon Islands*, Vol. Proceedings No. 52, Australian Council for International Agricultural Research, Canberra.

Bowman, C., 2005. *Business development in Papua New Guinea. Opportunities and impediments to private sector investment and development*, Study for the Australian Agency for International Development (AusAID), Asia Pacific School of Economics and Government, The Australian National University, Canberra.

Cartwright, I., 2004. Report on regional NGO participation in regional arrangements for the management and conservation of oceanic fish stocks, Thalassa Consulting, Launceston.

Cartwright, I. and Willock, A., 1999. Oceania's birthright: the role of rights-based management in the tuna fishery of the Western and Central Pacific, Paper read at FishRights 99, 11–19 November, Perth.

Central Bank of Solomon Islands (CBSI), 2001. *Annual Report 2000*, Central Bank of Solomon Islands, Honiara.

——, 2005. *Annual Report 2004*, Central Bank of Solomon Islands, Honiara.

Central Pacific Producers Ltd (CPP), c.2003. *Business Plan 2004–2007*, Betio, Tarawa.

Central Province Fisheries Department, 2005. Presentation to National Fisheries Workshop, 25 July–3 August, King Solomon Hotel, Honiara.

Chand, S., 2005a. 'Facing up to the challenges of development in Solomon Islands', *Pacific Economic Bulletin*, 20(2):1–17.

——, 2005b. 'Labour mobility for sustainable livelihoods in Pacific island states', *Pacific Economic Bulletin*, 20(3):63–76.

Chapman, L., 2001. *Tuna fishery development strategy for the Cook Islands*, Field Report No.13, Secretariat of the Pacific Community, Noumea.

——, 2002. *Development options and constraints including training needs and infrastructure requirements within the tuna fishing industry and support services in Fiji*, Field Report No.15, Secretariat of the Pacific Community, Noumea.

——, 2003. *Development options and constraints including training needs and infrastructure requirements within the tuna fishing industry and support services on Tarawa and Christmas Islands, Republic of Kiribati*, Field Report No.19, Secretariat of the Pacific Community, Noumea.

——, 2004a. *Development options and constraints including training needs and infrastructure requirements within the tuna fishing industry and support services in the Republic of the Marshall Islands*, Field Report No.23, Secretariat of the Pacific Community, Noumea.

——, 2004b. *Nearshore domestic fisheries development in Pacific islands countries and territories*, Information Paper for Fourth Heads of Fisheries Meeting, Secretariat of the Pacific Community, Noumea. Available at http://www.spc.int/coastfish/Reports/HOF4/PDF/IP8/ip8.htm (accessed 14 December 2007).

Ching Fu Shipbuilding Company, c.2003. Marshall Islands investment plan, presentation to Marshall Islands Marine Resources Authority.

Clark, L., 2002. *Transformation and rights-based fisheries management regimes: application to the Western and Central Pacific Ocean*, Working Paper 4, Forum Fisheries Agency Rights-Based Management Workshop, 22–24 June, Nadi.

——, 2005. *First draft for AusAID Pacific 2020*, Fisheries Issues Input Paper.

Diake, S., 2005. National tuna status report for Solomon Islands for 2004, First Meeting of the Scientific Committee of the Western and Central Pacific Fisheries Commission, Noumea.

Duncan, R., 2005. Presentation to Parliamentary Seminar on Australia–Papua New Guinea Relations, Asia Pacific School of Economics and Government, The Australian National University, Canberra.

Emberson-Bain, A. (ed.), 1994. *Sustainable Development or Malignant Growth?: perspectives of Pacific island women*, Marama Publications, Suva.

Eminent Persons' Group, 2004. *Pacific Cooperation. Voices of the region*, The Eminent Persons' Group Review of the Pacific Islands Forum.

Forum Fisheries Agency (FFA), 2001. *A Review of the Current Access Arrangements in the Marshall Islands*, Pacific Islands Forum Fisheries Agency, Honiara, Solomon Islands.

——, 2002. *Report of Rights-Based Management Workshop, 22–24 June, Nadi, Fiji*, Pacific Islands Forum Fisheries Agency, Honiara.

——, 2005. *FFA Strategic Plan 2005–2020*, Pacific Islands Forum Fisheries Agency, Honiara.

Foreign Investment Advisory Service (FIAS), 2005. Home page, World Bank Group. Available from http://www.ifc.org/ifcext/fias.nsf/content/home (accessed 7 December 2005).

Fiji Times, 2005. 'Fiji environmentalists seek cleanup of shipwrecks', *Fiji Times*, 16 September.

Friends of Kananam, c.2003. 'The Kananam community say "NO" to RD Tuna!', web site, c.2003. Available from http://lorikeet.and.com.au/RD/rdtuna.html (accessed 17 November 2005).

Fry, G., 2005. '"Pooled regional governance" in the island Pacific? Lessons from history', *Pacific Economic Bulletin*, 20(3):111–19.

Gillett, Preston and Associates, 2000. *A financial and economic review of the PNG tuna fishery*, Technical Document No.2, Fisheries Development Project ADB Loan No.1656-PNG, Papua New Guinea National Fisheries Authority, Port Moresby.

Gillett, R., 1999. *A Comparative Study of Coastal Resource Management in the Pacific Island Region*, World Bank, Washington, DC.

——, 2003. *Domestic tuna industry development in the Pacific islands. The current situation and considerations for future development assistance*, FFA Report 03/01, Pacific Islands Forum Fisheries Agency, Honiara.

——, 2005. 'Tuna for tomorrow? Some of the science behind an important fishery in the Pacific islands', in *RETA 6128: alternative negotiating arrangements to increase fisheries revenues in the Pacific*, Asian Development Bank, Manila.

Gillett, R. and Lightfoot, C., 2002. *Contribution of Fisheries to the Economies of Pacific Island Countries, Pacific Studies Series*, Asian Development Bank, Manila.

Gillett, R., McCoy, M., Rodwell, L. and Tamate, J., 2001. *Tuna. A key economic resource in the Pacific islands*, Asian Development Bank and Pacific Islands Forum Fisheries Agency, Manila.

Gomez, B. (ed.), 2005. 'PNG's robust tuna industry', in *Papua New Guinea Yearbook*, Yong Shan Fook, Port Moresby.

Government of Australia, 2005. *Papua New Guinea Country Brief, Economic Overview*, Department of Foreign Affairs and Trade. Available from http://www.dfat.gov.au/geo/png/png_brief.html (accessed 17 June 2005).

Government of Cook Islands, 2005. *Cook Islands Annual Statistical Bulletin 2004*, Avarua.

Government of Fiji, 2002. *Fiji Tuna Development and Management Plan: a national policy for the development and management of tuna fisheries*, Fiji Government, Pacific Islands Forum Fisheries Agency, Canada–South Pacific Oceans Development Program, Secretariat of the Pacific Community, Suva.

——, 2005. *MS-Offshore 2004 Annual Report*, Offshore Management Services Division, Fisheries Department, Suva.

Government of Kiribati, 2003. *Kiribati Tuna Development and Management Plan 2003–2006. Vol. I Executive Summary and the Plan*, Ministry of Natural Resources Development, Bairiki, Tarawa.

——, c.2003. *National Development Strategies 2004–2007*, Ministry of Finance and Economic Development, Tarawa.

Government of Papua New Guinea, 1999. *The National Tuna Fishery Management Plan (Fisheries Management Act 1998)*, Port Moresby.

——, 2004. *Revised Draft Tuna Fishery Management Plan* (changes up to 26 June 2004), Port Moresby,.

——, 2005. *Medium Term Development Strategy 2005–2010*, Ministry of National Planning and Monitoring, Port Moresby.

Government of Solomon Islands, 1989. *Fisheries Division Annual Report 1988*, Fisheries Division, Honiara.

——, 1995. *Department of Fisheries and Marine Resources Annual Report 1994*, Honiara.

——, 1998. *The Fisheries Act*, Honiara, Solomon Islands.

——, 1999. *Tuna 2000: towards a sustainable fishery for the next millennium*, National Tuna Management and Development Plan, Honiara, Solomon Islands.

——, 2003. *National Economic Recovery, Reform and Development Plan 2003–2006: strategic action framework*, Department of National Reform and Planning, Honiara.

——, 2005a. *Department of Fisheries and Marine Resources Annual Report 2004*, Honiara.

——, 2005b. National Fisheries Workshop, Solomon Islands National and Provincial Fisheries Departments, 25 July–3 August, King Solomon Hotel, Honiara.

Greenpeace, c.2005. *Development Without Destruction. Towards sustainable Pacific fisheries*, the Oceans Campaign, Greenpeace Australia Pacific, Suva, Fiji. Available from greenpeace@connect.com.fj.

Grynberg, R., 1998. '"Rules of origin" issues in Pacific island development', *Development Issues*, 8, National Centre for Development Studies, The Australian National University, Canberra.

Grynberg, R. (ed.), 2003. *Fisheries Issues in WTO and ACP–EU Trade Negotiations*, Commonwealth Economic Paper Series, Economic Affairs Division, Commonwealth Secretariat, London.

Grynberg, R., Forsyth, D. and Twum-Barima, R., 1995. *Tuna industry development study country profiles: Solomon Islands*, FFA Report No.95/37, Forum Fisheries Agency, Asian Development Bank, Honiara.

Grynberg, R., Hyndman, M. and Silva, S., 2005. *Towards a new Pacific regionalism. A report to the Pacific Islands Forum Secretariat*, Pacific Studies Series, Asian Development Bank and Commonwealth Secretariat, Manila.

Hampton, J., Lawson, T. and Williams, P., 1996. 'Interaction between small-scale fisheries in Kiribati and the industrial purse seine fishery in the western and central Pacific Ocean', in R. Shomura, J. Majkowski and R. Harman (eds), *Status of Interactions of Pacific Tuna Fisheries in 1995*, Food and Agriculture Organisation, Rome.

Hand, A.J., 1999. *A Review of Fisheries Taxation and Licensing in Solomon Islands*, Asian Development Bank, Manila.

Hughes, A., 1987. 'High speed on an unmade road: Solomon Islands' joint venture route to a tuna fishery', in D.J. Doulman (ed.), *Tuna Issues and Perspectives in the Pacific Islands Region*, East–West Center, Honolulu.

Hughes, A. and Thaanum, O., 1995. *Costly connections: a performance appraisal of Solomon Taiyo Limited*, Forum Fisheries Agency Report No.95/54, Investment Corporation of Solomon Islands, Honiara.

Islands Business, 2005. 'Solomon Islands: audit revelations disclose US$53m losses', *Islands Business*, 20.

Kinch, J., Baine, M., Mungkaje, A., Dako, C., Bagi, T. and Aranka, M., 2005. *Moving Towards Management: an analysis of the socio-economic conditions and catch data of the European Union's Rural Coastal Fisheries Development Programme's fisher groups, Madang Province, Papua New Guinea*, Motupure Island Research Centre, University of Papua New Guinea, Port Moresby.

Krampe, P., 2006. Rising fuel prices and its impact on the tuna industry, Tuna 2006—Ninth Infofish World Tuna Trade Conference, 27 May, Bangkok.

Kumoru, L., 2005. Tuna Fisheries Report—Papua New Guinea, First Meeting of the Scientific Committee, Western and Central Pacific Fisheries Commission, Noumea.

Lal, P. and Rita, R., 2005. 'Potential impacts of EU sugar reform on the Fiji sugar industry', *Pacific Economic Bulletin*, 20(3):18–42.

Langley, A., 2004. *Marshall Islands National Tuna Fishery Status Report No.5*, Oceanic Fisheries Program, Secretariat of the Pacific Community, Noumea.

——, 2005. Presentation on status of tuna stocks in the Western and Central Pacific, Paper read at meeting between the Fiji Ministry of Fisheries and Forests and Tuna

Associations, 28 September, Fiji Nurses Association Conference Room, McGregor Road, Suva.

Larmour, P. and Wolanin, N. (eds), 2001. *Corruption and Anti-Corruption*, Asia Pacific Press, The Australian National University, Canberra.

Lehodey, P., Chai, F. and Hampton, J., 2003. 'Modelling climate-related variability of tuna populations from a coupled ocean-biogeochemical-populations dynamics model', *Fisheries Oceanography*, 12(4/5):483–94.

Lewis, A., 2004a. *A review of current access arrangements in Pacific developing member countries (PDMCs)*, ADB Project TA 6128-REG: Alternative Negotiating Arrangements to Increase Fisheries Revenues in the Pacific, Asian Development Bank, Manila.

——, 2004b. *Outline of SAPII Project: national project preparation reports*, Republic of the Marshall Islands.

——, 2005. Fisheries—a key economic sector at the crossroads: a review of recent developments in the fisheries sector of PNG, its current status and prospects for the future, Paper read at Institute for National Affairs, Papua New Guinea.

Looking Glass Design, c.2001. 'The Fiji Coup and Unrest', Looking Glass Design. Available from http://www.lookinglassdesign.com/fijicoupmay2000/fijicoup.html (accessed 12 December 2005).

Mani, L., 1994. *An Assessment of Fish Cannery Effluent Discharge on Pollution Status of the Noro Sea Front, Western Province*, Solomon Islands College of Higher Education, Honiara.

Manning, M., 2005. 'Papua New Guinea thirty years on (policy dialogue)', *Pacific Economic Bulletin*, 20(1):145–58.

Marshall Islands Journal, 2001. 'Sexually transmitted diseases on the rise in Marshall Islands', newspaper article posted in the *Pacific Islands Report*, Pacific Islands Development Program, East–West Center, 2001. Available from http://archives.pireport.org/archive/2001/february/02%2D21%2D05.htm (accessed 12 December 2005).

McCoy, M.A. and Gillett, R.D., 2005. *Tuna Longlining by China in the Pacific Islands: a description and considerations for increasing benefits to FFA member countries*, Pacific Islands Forum Fisheries Agency, Honiara.

Marshall Islands Marine Resources Authority (MIMRA), 2003. Introduction to Marshall Islands Marine Resources Authority, Powerpoint presentation, Majuro, Marshall Islands.

——, 2004. *Marshall Islands Marine Resources Authority Annual Report 2002–2003*, Majuro, Marshall Islands.

——, 2005. Fisheries report—Marshall Islands, Paper read at First Meeting of the Scientific Committee WCPFC-SC1, Noumea.

Mitchell, J., 2001. *Cook Islands Offshore Fisheries 1994–2000*, Cook Islands Ministry of Marine Resources, Avarua.

Ministry of Marine Resources (MMR), c.2003. *Cook Islands Tuna Long Line Fishery Summary 2002*, Cook Islands Ministry of Marine Resources, Avarua.

——, 2004. *Cook Islands Long Line Catch Summary 2003*, Cook Islands Ministry of Marine Resources, Avarua.

——, 2005a. *Cook Islands Long Line Catch Summary2004*, Cook Islands Ministry of Marine Resources, Avarua.

——, 2005b. *The commercial tuna longline industry*, Information Paper for Cabinet, Cook Islands Ministry of Marine Resources, Avarua.

MIVA (Marshall Islands Visitors Authority), 2003. Visitor Leaflets: A Brief History of the Marshall Islands. Available online at www.visitmarshalislands.com

Molony, B., 2005. *Solomon Islands National Tuna Fishery Status Report No.7*, Oceanic Fisheries Program, Secretariat of the Pacific Community, Noumea.

Navuetaki, I., c.2002. *Bose Ni Yasana Ko Lomaiviti (Notes on Pacific Fishing Company Limited)*, Levuka.

Niesi, P., 2005. 'Caught out. 20 illegal fishing boats herded into Alotau', *Post-Courier*, 11–13 Febuary:1.

Noro Town Council, 2004. *Millenium Development Policies: Policy Objectives, Development Strategies, Projects, Program of Actions 2005–2009*, Noro, Western Province.

Oreihaka, E., 2004. Tuna fisheries in the Solomon Islands in 2003, Seventeenth Meeting of the Standing Committee on Tuna and Billfish, Secretariat of the Pacific Community, Noumea.

Owen, A.D., 2001. *The relationship between the world price for skipjack and yellowfin tuna raw material for canning and supply from the WCPO and FFA member countries EEZs*, FFA Report 01/32, Pacific Islands Forum Fisheries Agency, Honiara.

Pacific Fishing Company Limited (Pafco), 2000. *A Big Fish in the World's Biggest Pond*, marketing pamphlet, Pacific Fishing Company Limited, Suva.

Pacific Islands Forum, 2005. 'A Pacific Plan for Strengthening Regional Cooperation and Integration (Final Draft)', Pacific Islands Forum Secretariat. Available from http://www.sidsnet.org/pacific/forumsec (accessed 25 November 2005).

Pacific Islands Forum Secretariat, 2004a. 'Forum Leaders' Communique', Thirty-Fifth Pacific Islands Forum, 5–7 August 2004, Apia. Available from http://www.sidsnet.org/pacific/forumsec/ (accessed 24 November 2005).

——, 2004b. *Gender issues in the Pacific tuna industry*, Background Reports to National Tuna Management and Development Plans, Pacific Examples, Vol.2, Pacific Islands Forum Secretariat, Canada–South Pacific Ocean Development, Secretariat of the Pacific Community, Suva.

——, 2005. 'Forum Leaders' Communique', Thirty-Sixth Pacific Islands Forum, 25–27 October 2005, Madang. Available from http://www.sidsnet.org/pacific/forumsec (accessed 23 November 2005).

Pacific Islands Trade and Investment Commission (PITIC), 2002. Homepage, 2002. Available from http://www.pitic.org.au/index.htm (accessed 27 October 2005).

Pacific Magazine, 2005. 'Solomon Islands joins world bank group agency', Pacific Basic Communications. Available from http://www.pacificislands.cc/pina/pinadefault2.php?urlpinaid=18386 (accessed 12 December 2005).

Peebles, D., 2005. *Pacific Regional Order*, Asia Pacific Press, The Australian National University, Canberra.

Petersen, E., 2002a. 'Economic policy, institutions and fisheries development in the Pacific', *Marine Policy*, 26:315–24.

——, 2002b. 'Institutional structures of fishery management: the Fortuna in the South Pacific', in R. Garnaut (ed.), *Resource Management in Asia Pacific Developing Countries*, Asia Pacific Press, The Australian National University, Canberra.

Pitts, M., 2002. *Crime, Corruption and Capacity in Papua New Guinea*, Asia Pacific Press, The Australian National University, Canberra.

Post-Courier, 2005. 'Condom in tinned fish probed', *Post-Courier*, 31 May:2.

Ram-Bidesi, V., 2004. *Report of the Sixth Session of the Preparatory Conference for the Establishment of the Commission on the Conservation and Management of Highly Migratory Fish Stocks in the Western and Central Pacific Ocean, 19–23 April, Bali, Indonesia*, Marine Studies Program, University of the South Pacific, Suva.

Rawlinson, N., Milton, D. and Blaber, S., 1992. *Tuna Baitfish and the Pole and Line Industry in Kiribati*, Australian Centre for International Agricultural Research, Canberra.

Reid, C., 2005. Presentation to Solomon Islands National Fisheries Workshop, 25 July–3 August, King Solomon Hotel, Honiara.

Reid, C., Bertignac, M. and Hampton, J., 2006. *Further development of, and analysis using, the Western and Central Pacific Bioeconomic Tuna Model (WCPBTM)*, Technical Paper No.2, ACIAR project, Maximising the Economic Benefits to Pacific Islands Nations from Management of Migratory Tuna Stocks. Available from http://www.business.latrobe.edu.au/public/staffhp/jkennedy/ACIARTechPapers_files/aciarTP2Further%20DevelopmentsWCPOBTM.pdf (review of reviewed item).

Reilly, B., 2005. Electoral reform, Presentation at the Papua New Guinea Update, Divine Word University, The Australian National University, Institute of National Affairs, National Research Institute, 20 May, Madang.

Riinga, T., 2005. Kiribati fisheries report, First Meeting of the Scientific Committee of the Western and Central Pacific Fisheries Commission, Noumea.

Rose-Ackerman, S., 1999. *Corruption and Government: causes, consequences and reform*, Cambridge University Press, Cambridge and New York.

Sasabe, M., 1993. *A Woman's Story: Japan's economic involvement in the Pacific*, Pacific Conference of Churches, Suva.

Schurman, R., 1998. 'Tuna dreams: resource nationalism and the Pacific islands' tuna industry, *Development and Change*, 29:107–36.

Secretariat of the Pacific Community (SPC), 2004a. Demography/Population Programme, Population Statistics, available at http://www.spc.int/demog/en/index.html (accessed 14 December 2007).

—— 2004b. *Report of the Scientific Committee*, Working Paper WCPFC/Comm.2/22, Secretariat of the Pacific Community, Noumea.

——, 2005. 'Tuna, fisheries and climate variability', Secretariat of the Pacific Community Oceanic Fisheries Program. Available from http://www.spc.int/oceanfish/Html/TEB/Env&Mod/index.htm (accessed 29 November 2005).

Sokimi, W. and Chapman, L., 2003. Horizontal Tuna Longline Fishing Workshops and Fishing Trials, Including Correct Handling, Processing and Chilling Practices in Majuro, Marshall Islands. Secretariat of the Pacific Community (SPC), Field Report No. 21.

Solomon Islands Broadcasting Corporation (SIBC), 2005a. 'Audit on Department of Fisheries', Solomon Islands Broadcasting Corporation, 16 November.

——, 2005b. 'Japan commits $29 million to Solomons projects', Solomon Islands Broadcasting Corporation, 17 January.

——, 2005c. 'Millions lost in uncollected fisheries fees', Solomon Islands Broadcasting Corporation, 20 November.

Solomon Star, 2004. 'Fishermen monitored for HIV/AIDS', Solomon Star, 12 November.

——, 2005a. 'Audit shows problems in Solomons Fisheries Department', Solomon Star, 15 November.

——, 2005b. 'Fisheries small business', Solomon Star, 25 July.

——, 2005c. 'Govt denies receiving cash for whale vote', Solomon Star, 20 July.

South Pacific Forum Secretariat, 2000. Gender issues in the tuna industry, Background Reports to National Tuna Management and Development Plans, Pacific Examples, Vol.1, South Pacific Forum Secretariat, Canada–South Pacific Ocean Development, Forum Fisheries Agency, Secretariat of the Pacific Community, Suva.

South Pacific Project Facility (SPPF), 1999. Report on the Valuation of the Solomon Government Investment in Solomon Taiyo Limited, South Pacific Project Facility, International Finance Corporation, World Bank, Sydney.

Spenneman, D., 2005. Water as the defining parameter of an atoll existence in Micronesia, Paper read at Fresh and Salt: Water, Borders and Commons in Australia and Asia, 8–10 May, University of Technology Sydney.

Stinus-Remonde, M., 2004. 'Mission impossible: a tremendous impact', The Manila Times, 2004. Available from http://www.manilatimes.net/national/2004/oct/19/yehey/opinion/20041019opi2.html (accessed 18 November 2005).

Sullivan, N., Warr, T., Rainbubu, J., Kunoko, J., Akauna, F., Angasa, M. and Wenda, Y., 2003. Tinpis Maror: A Social Impact Study of Proposed RD Tuna Cannery at Vidar Wharf, Madang, Nancy Sullivan and Associates, Madang.

Tai, B., 2004. 'High freight costs hurt PNG tuna exports', The National, 2004. Available from www.thenational.com.pg (accessed 21 October 2005).

Taipei Times, 2002. 'EPA to block shipment of waste to Solomon Islands', Taipei Times, 20 February 2002. Available from http://www.taipeitimes.com/News/local/archives/2002/02/20/124611 (accessed 13 December 2005).

Tamate, J., 2002. Air freighting tuna products: challenges and opportunities for Pacific island fresh tuna exporters, FFA Report 02/26, Pacific Islands Forum Fisheries Agency, Honiara.

Tarte, S., 1998. Japan's Aid Diplomacy and the Pacific Islands, Asia Pacific Press, The Australian National University, Canberra.

——, 2002. 'A duty to cooperate: building a regional regime for the conservation and management of highly migratory fish stocks in the Western and Central Pacific', in

E.M. Borgese, A. Chircop and M.L. McConnell (eds), *Ocean Yearbook*, University of Chicago Press, Chicago.

——, 2003a. *Report of the Fifth Session of the Preparatory Conference for the Establishment of the Commission on the Conservation and management of Highly Migratory Fish Stocks in the Western and Central Pacific Ocean*, Rarotonga.

——, 2003b. *Report on the Fourth Session of the Preparatory Conference of the Establishment of the Commission on the Conservation and Management of Highly Migratory Fish Stocks in the Western and Central Pacific Ocean*, Nadi.

——, 2004. Managing tuna fisheries in the Pacific: a regional success story?, Paper read at Thirty-Ninth Foreign Policy School, 25–28 June, University of Otago, New Zealand.

The Nation, 2003a. 'Department of Labour inspection of RD', *The Nation*.

——, 2003b. 'Letters to the editor', *The Nation*, 6 October.

——, 2003c. 'MP stirs up stink over RD Tuna', *The Nation*.

The National, 2005a. 'Commentary: EU should finance fish harvesting capacities', (from Peter Donigi, lawyer and diplomat, former Papua New Guinea Permanent Representative to the United Nations), *The National*, 23 August.

——, 2005b. 'Tuna cold war', *The National*, 17 June.

United Nations, 2004. 'Small islands big stakes. Small island developing states and territories', United Nations. Available from http://www.un.org/smallislands2005/indicators.pdf (accessed 13 December 2005).

United Nations Development Program (UNDP), 2004a. *Peace and Conflict Development Analysis. Emerging priorities in preventing future conflict*, United Nations Development Program and the National Peace Council, Honiara.

——, 2004b. *United Nations Development Program Human Development Reports.* Available from http://hdr.undp.org/statistics (accessed 17 June 2005).

van Santen, G., 2005. *Economic Tuna Industry Indicators: proposals for a simple annual system to monitor key parameters of the tuna fishery and its impact on FFA members*, World Bank and Forum Fisheries Agency, Sydney and Honiara.

van Santen, G. and Muller, P., 2000. *Working Apart or Together: an analysis of selected benefits and costs of a common approach to management of the tuna resources in Exclusive Economic Zones of Pacific island countries*, World Bank, Honiara.

Wallis, I., 1999. *Noro Fish Processing Facility Waste Water Treatment and Effluent Disposal*, World Health Organisation, Geneva.

Warner, R. and Yauieb, A., 2005. 'The Papua New Guinea economy', *Pacific Economic Bulletin*, 20(1):1–13.

Western and Central Pacific Fisheries Commission (WCPFC), 2004. *Western and Central Pacific Fisheries Commission Tuna Fishery Yearbook*, Report, Western and Central Pacific Fisheries Commission. Available from http://www.spc.int/oceanfish/Docs/Statistics/WCPFC_Yearbook_2004.pdf (accessed 13 December 2005).

——, 2005. *Report of the First Regular Session of the Scientific Committee of the Commission for the Conservation and Management of Highly Migratory Fish Stocks in the Western and*

Central Pacific Ocean, 8–19 August, Western and Central Pacific Fisheries Commission, Noumea.

Williams, P. and Reid, C., 2005. *Overview of tuna fisheries in the Western and Central Pacific Ocean, including economic conditions*, Working Paper WCPFC-SC1, Western and Central Pacific Fisheries Commission, Noumea.

World Bank, 2005. *World Development Indicators 2005*, World Bank. Available from http://web.worldbank.org/WBSITE/EXTERNAL/DATASTATISTICS/0,,menuPK:232599~pagePK:64133170~piPK:64133498~theSitePK:239419,00.html (accessed 13 December 2005).

World Wide Fund for Nature (WWF), 2005. 'Europeans prefer responsibly sourced seafood', Press release, World Wild Fund for Nature. Available from http://panda.org/news_facts/newsroom/index.cfm?uNewsID=53680 (accessed 14 December 2005).

Personal communications

Adani, John, 2005. Deputy Principal, National Fisheries College. Interview, 25 May. Kavieng, Papua New Guinea.

Aihari, Derick, 2005. Interview, Foreign Investment Board, 26 July. Honiara, Solomon Islands.

Aini, John, 2005. Trainer, Ailan Awareness NGO and Data Management Specialist, PNG National Fisheries Authority Coastal Fisheries Management and Development Project (ADB Project). Interview, 26 May. Kavieng, Papua New Guinea.

Armstrong, Glenn, 2005. General Manager, The Porter Group, Cook Islands Fish Exports. Interview, 21 September. Avarua, Cook Islands.

Atu, William T., 2005. Deputy Program Manager, The Nature Conservancy. Interview, 12 July. Honiara, Solomon Islands.

Baiteke, Maerere, 2005. Manager, Tarawa Fishermen's Cooperative Society. Interview, 14 October. Bairiki, Tarawa, Kiribati.

Baree, Bateriki, 2005. Chair of Board of Directors, Tarawa Fishermen's Cooperative Society. Interview, 14 October. Bairiki, Tarawa, Kiribati.

Barnabas, Norman, 2005. Manager, Provincial and Industry Liaison Division, National Fisheries Authority. Interview, 30 May. Port Moresby, Papua New Guinea.

Batty, Mike, 2006. Fisheries Development Policy Specialist, EU DevFish Project, Forum Fisheries Agency. Emails, May.

Bauro, Nauan, 2005. General Manager, Kiribati Fisherman's Services Company Limited. Interview, 13 October. Bairiki, Tarawa, Kiribati.

Bell, Johann, 2005. Principal Scientist, Natural Resources Management, World Fish Centre. Personal communications, 26–28 July. Honiara, Solomon Islands.

Bertram, Ian, 2005. Secretary, Ministry of Marine Resources. Interviews, 19–23 September. Avarua, Cook Islands.

Beseto, Pauline, 2005. Interview, office of the Ministry of Development and Planning, 12 July. Honiara, Solomon Islands.

Boatwood, Ian, 2005. Manager, South Seas Tuna. Personal communication, 20 June.

Broadhead, Garth, 2005. Director, Maritime Cook Islands. Interview, 21 September. Avarua, Cook Islands.

Brownjohn, Maurice, 2005. Fisheries company owner and Chairman of the Papua New Guinea Fisheries Industry Association. Interview, 1 June. Port Moresby, Papua New Guinea.

Bugotu, Tione, 2005. Personal communication, 26 July. Honiara, Solomon Islands.

Celso, Pete C., 2005. Managing Director, RD Tuna Canners Limited. Interview, 17 May. Vidar, Madang, Papua New Guinea.

Chiota, Judy, 2005. Women's Officer, Church of Melanesia Diocese. Interview, 14 July. Honiara, Solomon Islands.

Chow, Adrian, 2005. Director, Neptune Fisheries Limited. Interview, 12 May. Lae, Papua New Guinea.

Cooper, Jack, 2005. Factory Manager, Blue Pacific Foods. Interview, 20 September. Avarua, Cook Islands.

Defensor, Nestor, 2005. Resident Director, Frabelle (PNG). Interview, 12 May. Lae, Papua New Guinea.

Diake, Sylvester, 2005. Undersecretary, Fisheries Department, Solomon Islands government. Interview, 15 July. Honiara, Solomon Islands.

Dunham, Russell, 2005. Group Business Director, Fiji Fish Marketing Group Limited. Interview, 27 September. Lami, Fiji.

Dunn, Steve, 2005. Deputy Director, Forum Fisheries Agency. Interview, 12 July. Honiara, Solomon Islands.

Echigo, Manabu, 2005. Near-shore fisheries management consultant. Interview, 7 June. Majuro, Marshall Islands.

Epati, Navy, 2005. Co-owner Fish Bites Incorporated fishing company. Former Secretary, Ministry of Marine Resources. Interview, 20 September. Avarua, Cook Islands.

Garnier, Frances, 2005. Owner fishing company Matira South. Interview 22 September. Avarua, Cook Islands.

Gillett, Robert, 2005. Fisheries management consultant. Email, 25 December. Suva, Fiji.

Gloerfelt-Tarp, Thomas, 2005. Senior Natural Resources Specialist, Pacific Operations Division, Asian Development Bank. Interview, 28 September. Suva, Fiji.

Go, Wilson, 2005. Lecturer in Business Studies, University of Papua New Guinea. Interview, 2 June. Port Moresby, Papua New Guinea.

Government of Solomon Islands, 2005. Statistical data collected during fieldwork and interviews with staff, 28 July, Fisheries Department, Honiara, Solomon Islands.

Graham, Peter, 2005. Legal Adviser, Ministry of Marine Resources. Interviews, 19–23 September. Avarua, Cook Islands.

Guenegan, Jean Claude, 2005. General Manager, Pacific Fishing Company Limited in partnership with Bumble Bee Seafoods Incorporated. Interview, 26 September. Levuka, Fiji.

Gupta, Joy Prakash, 2005. Financial Controller, Pacific Fishing Company Limited in partnership with Bumble Bee Seafoods Incorporated. Interview, 26 September. Levuka, Fiji.

Hamagawa, Masaharu, 1998. Manager, Solgreen Limited. Interview, 6 November. Sarahama, Irabu Island, Okinawa Prefecture, Japan.

Hufflett, Charles, 2005. Chairman, Solander Group. Interview, 16 September. Walu Bay, Suva, Fiji.

Hughes, Anthony, 2005. Former Solomon Islands public servant who had been involved with Solomon Taiyo in a senior capacity for many years. Interviews, 12 September, 11 October. Sydney, Australia, and Tarawa, Kiribati.

——, 1999. Interview, 22 July. Agnes Lodge, Munda, Solomon Islands.

Hunter, Carl, 2005. Director, Pacific Affairs, Ministry of Foreign Affairs and Immigration. Interviews, 22–23 September. Avarua, Cook Islands.

Ishizaki, Takuzo, 2005. Former longline Fishing Master. Agent, Central Pacific Maritime, Zengyoren Fishing Boats (Japan), Robert Reimers Enterprises Inc. Interview, 7 June. Majuro, Marshall Islands.

Joseph, Glen, 2005. Director, Marshall Islands Marine Resources Authority. Interview, 9 June. Majuro, Marshall Islands.

Kabure, Teorae, 2005. Principal, Fisheries Training Centre. Interview, 13 October. Bikenibeu, Tarawa, Kiribati.

Kanawi, Samol, 2005. Master Fisherman—Commercial Fishing Operations. National Fisheries College. Interview, 25 May. Kavieng, Papua New Guinea.

Kido Dalipada, Stephen, 2005. Country Manager, World Wide Fund for Nature Solomon Islands Program. Interview, 13 July. Honiara, Solomon Islands.

Kinch, Jeff, 2005. Coastal Fisheries Advisor, Motupore Island Research Centre, University of Papua New Guinea. Personal communications, 16–20 May. Madang, Papua New Guinea.

King, Mike, 2005. Coastal fisheries management consultant. Personal communication, 16 June.

Kingston, Keith, 2005. Lae businessman and recreational game fisherman. Personal communication, 15 May. Lae, Papua New Guinea.

Kukui, Asery, 2005. Manager of Human Resources and Administration, Soltai Fishing and Processing. Interviews, Soltai office, 19–22 July. Noro, Solomon Islands.

Kumoru, Ludwig, 2005. Manager, National Fisheries Authority. Personal communication, 19 June.

Lalley, Barry, 2005. Trainer, Bismark Ramu Group NGO. Former volunteer with the Solomon Islands Development Trust NGO. Interview, 17 May. Jais Aben, Madang, Papua New Guinea.

Lucas, David, 2005. Director, Solander Pacific. Interview, 16 October. Walu Bay, Suva, Fiji.

Mamupio, David, 2005. Town Clerk, Noro Town Council. Interviews, 21–22 July. Noro, Solomon Islands.

Mamupio, Tina, 2005. Environmental Health Officer, Noro Town Council. Interview, Noro Town Council, 22 July. Noro, Solomon Islands.

Manning, Michael, 2005. Personal communication, 20 May. Madang, Papua New Guinea.

Marriot, Sean, 2005. Project Manager, European Union Rural Coastal Fisheries Development Program. Interview, 19 May. Madang, Papua New Guinea.

Maru, Pam, 2005. Ministry of Marine Resources employee working in the areas of monitoring, control, surveillance and licensing. Interviews, 19–23 September. Avarua, Cook Islands.

Merin, Tet and Sete, Lyanna, 2005. Financial Controller and Exports Officer, MAPS Tuna. Interview, 13 May. Lae, Papua New Guinea.

Middleton, Ian, 2005. Managing Director, Bismark Barramundi. Interview, 18 May. Dylup, Madang, Papua New Guinea.

Moeka'a, Myra, 2005. Legal Adviser, Ministry of Foreign Affairs and Immigration. Interview, 19 September. Avarua, Cook Islands.

Mungkaje, Augustine, 2005. Fisheries biologist, University of Papua New Guinea. Interview, 2 June. Port Moresby.

Nakada, Masao, 2005. Former Operations Manager of Solomon Taiyo. Interview, Forum Fisheries Agency office, 11 July. Honiara, Solomon Islands.

Nakamura, 2005. Manager, Smoking Department, Soltai Fishing and Processing. Interview, Soltai office, 22 July. Noro, Solomon Islands.

Nakano, Toru, 2005. Director, Tosa Bussan (Fiji) Limited. Interview, 27 September. Walu Bay, Suva, Fiji.

Natividad, Augusto C., 2005. Director, Frabelle Fishing Corporation (PNG). Interview, 15 May. Lae, Papua New Guinea.

Navuetaki, Inoke, 2005. Public Relations Officer, Pacific Fishing Company Limited. Interview, 26 September. Levuka, Fiji.

Nidung, Masio, 2005. Deputy State Solicitor—Treaties, Department of Attorney-General, Government of Papua New Guinea. Personal communication, 10 June. Majuro, Marshall Islands.

Onorio, Barerei, 2005. General Manager, Central Pacific Producers Limited. Interview, 12 October. Betio, Tarawa, Kiribati.

Operations Manager, 2005. Blue Pacific processing plant Operations Manager. Interview, 20 September. Avarua, Cook Islands.

Paka, Roboam, 2005. Principal, National Fisheries College. Interview, 23 May. Kavieng, Papua New Guinea.

Paru, Blaise, 2005. Managing Director, Equatorial Marine Resources and Resident Director, Sanko Bussan (PNG). Interview, 31 May. Port Moresby, Papua New Guinea.

Pina, John, 2005. Deputy Cannery Manager, Soltai Fishing and Processing. Interview, 21 July. Noro, Solomon Islands.

Preston, Garry, 2005. Fisheries management consultant, Gillett, Preston and Associates. Personal communication, 17 December.

Ramohia, Peter, 2005. Research Officer, Fisheries Department. Interview, 15 July. Honiara, Solomon Islands.

Reid, Christopher, 2005. Economist, Forum Fisheries Agency. Interview, 28 August. Honiara, Solomon Islands.

Roughan, John, 2005. Interview, Solomon Islands Development Trust Office, 13 July. Honiara, Solomon Islands.

Rodwell, Len, 2005. Economics and Marketing Manager, Forum Fisheries Agency. Interview, 11 July. Honiara, Solomon Islands.

——, 2006. Email, 28 June.

Scales, Ian, 2005. Academic and consultant on forestry in Western Province, Solomon Islands. Email, 3 August.

Sevillejo, Alfredo, 2005. Finance Advisor, Soltai Fishing and Processing. Interview, 19 July. Noro, Solomon Islands.

Short, Mark, 2005. CEO, Development Investment Board. Interview, 21 September. Avarua, Cook Islands.

Sibanganei, Terry, 2005. Provincial Fisheries Program Advisor, Madang Provincial Government. Interview, 18 May. Madang, Papua New Guinea.

Sibisopere, Milton, 2005. Managing Director, Soltai Fishing and Processing. Interviews, Soltai Office, 18–19 July. Noro, Solomon Islands.

Southwick, Grahame, 2005. Owner, Fiji Fish Marketing Group Limited. Interview, 27 September. Lami, Fiji, and email about charter conditions in Fiji's domestic longline fishery, sent 19 September.

Stone, Robert, 2005. Owner of small gourmet fish-processing factory, former owner of a skipjack fishing company. Interview, 16 September. Pacific Harbour, Fiji.

Tamba, Emmanuel, 2005. Fisheries Extension Officer, New Ireland Provincial Government. Interview, 26 May. Kavieng, Papua New Guinea.

Tarte, Sandra, 2005. Senior Lecturer, Department of History and Politics, University of the South Pacific. Interview, 28 September. Suva, Fiji.

Tekaata, Ariera, 2005. Supervisor, Vessel and Agency Services, Central Pacific Producers Limited. Interview, 12 October. Betio, Tarawa, Kiribati.

Temwaang, 2005. Fisheries Extension Officer, Fisheries Division, Ministry of Fisheries and Marine Resources Development. Interview, 11 October. Tanaea, Tarawa, Kiribati.

Tioti, Beero, 2005. Senior Fisheries Officer, Fisheries Division, Kiribati Ministry of Fisheries and Marine Resources Development. Interview, 11 October. Tanaea, Tarawa.

Tira, Teea, 2005. Permanent Secretary, Office of the President. Interview, 18 October. Bairiki, Tarawa, Kiribati.

Tumoa, Raikon, 2005. Senior Fisheries Officer, Kiribati Ministry of Fisheries and Marine Resources Development. Interview, 14 October. Bairiki, Tarawa, Kiribati.

Tupa, Vaitoti, 2005. Director, Cook Islands National Environment Services. Interview, 20 September. Avarua, Cook Islands.

Turaganivalu, Apolosi, 2005. Director, Management Services Unit, Fiji Ministry of Fisheries and Forests. Interview, 29 September. Suva, Fiji.

Walton, Hugh, 2005. Fisheries development consultant, Gillett, Preston and Associates. Interview, 12 May. Lae, Papua New Guinea.

Watt, Peter, 2005. Consultant on community-based resource management project in Samoa in the early 2000s. Interview, 26 May. Kavieng, Papua New Guinea.

Wickham, Adrian, 2005. CEO, National Fisheries Development. Interview, NFD Office, 15 July. Honiara, Solomon Islands.

Yeeting, David, 2005. Permanent Secretary, Ministry of Fisheries and Marine Resources Development. Interview, 17 October. Bairiki, Tarawa, Kiribati.

York, Trevor, 2005. Master Fisherman and co-owner Land Holdings Ltd tuna-fishing business. Interview, 20 September. Avarua, Cook Islands.

Zamudio, Danilo D., 2005. Assistant Vice-President, Export and Processing Division. Interview, 17 May. Siar, Madang, Papua New Guinea.

Appendix

Table A1.1 **Key fisheries indicators by country**

	Cook Islands	Fiji	Kiribati	Marshall Islands	Papua New Guinea	Solomon Islands
Active domestic fishing vessels						
Longline	33 (2004)	84 (2004)	2 (2003)	4 (1995)	50 (2004)	9 (2004)
Pole-and-line	0	1 (2004)	...	0	...	10 (2004)
Purse-seine	0	0	1 (2004)	6 (2004)	37 (2004)	14 (2004)
Tuna catches, metric tonnes and per cent						
Longline	3,004 (2004)	19,617 (2004)	8 (2003)	23 (1995)	6,164 (2004)	1,174 (2004)
Albacore	1,630 (54%)	11,290 (58%)	0	0	1,640 (27%)	267 (23%)
Bigeye	343 (11%)	1,254 (6%)	1 (13%)	10 (43%)	396 (6%)	357 (30%)
Yellowfin	458 (15%)	4,164 (21%)	2 (25%)	12 (52%)	2,526 (41%)	538 (46%)
Other	573 (20%)	2,909 (15%)	5 (62%)	1 (5%)	1,602 (26%)	12 (1%)
Pole-and-line	...	475 (2001)	5 (1997)	...	9,300 (1985)	6,882 (2004)
Skipjack	...	431 (91%)	4 (80%)	...	8,370 (90%)	6,625 (96%)
Yellowfin	...	44 (9%)	1 (20%)	...	930 (10%)	257 (4%)
Purse-seine	...	...	14,600 (2004)	46,672 (2004)	202,189 (2004)	16,094 (2004)
Skipjack	...	...	3,816 (83%)	42,078 (90%)	175,201 (87%)	6,817 (42%)
Yellowfin	...	...	644 / 2.64 (14%)	3,632 (8%)	23,166 (11%)	7,208 (45%)
Bigeye	...	...	140 (3%)	962 (2%)	3,749 (2%)	2,069 (13%)
Other	...	...	0	0	73 (0.03%)	0
Fisheries contribution to GDP, US$m	8.62 (11.3%)	18.62 (1.7%)	4.97 (12%)	7.23 (7.4%)	18.68 (0.6%)	...
Value of fisheries exports, US$m	2.91 (2002)	29.2 (2002)	1.48 (2002)	0.47 (2002)	48.1 (2002)	35.5 (1997)
Fisheries exports as a per cent of all exports	81.9	6.0	16.9	6.2	1.8	20.0
Estimated value of access fees, US$m	0.17 (1999)	0.21 (1999)	20.6 (1999)	4.98 (1999)	5.84 (1999)	0.27 (1999)
Access fees as a per cent of GDP, 1999	0.21	0.01	42.81	5.12	0.17	0.1

Source: Western and Central Pacific Fisheries Commission (WCPFC), 2004. *Western and Central Pacific Fisheries Commission Tuna Fishery Yearbook*, Report, Western and Central Pacific Fisheries Commission (WCPFC). Available from http://www.spc.int/oceanfish/Docs/Statistics/WCPFC_Yearbook_2004.pdf (accessed 13 December 2005).

Table A1.2 **Key development indicators by country**

	Cook Islands	Fiji	Kiribati	Marshall Islands	Papua New Guinea	Solomon Islands
Total population, 2004	20,300	847,000	89,700	61,200	5,836,000	521,000
Urban population (per cent of total)	70.2 (2003)	51.7 (2003)	47.4 (2003)	65.0 (2005)	13.2 (2003)	16.5 (2003)
Surface area—land (sq km)	236	18,274	726	181	462,840	28,896
Surface area—EEZ (sq km)	1,830,000	1,260,000	3,550,000	2,131,000	2,400,000	1,300,000
GDP per capita (US$)	8,488 (2003)	3,385 (2003)	784 (2004)	1,957 (2003)	645 (2003)	760 (2001)
Structure of GDP (per cent)	(2003)	(2002)	(2004)	(2002)	(2002)	(1990)
Agriculture	15.7	15.9	9.7	10.4	33.1	45.5
Manufacturing	3.4	14.3	0.9	0.3	10.6	3.7
Mining	...	0.9	...	4.5	16.1	0.5
Construction	3.0	4.6	8.6	11.4	7.3	2.6
Trade	36.5	16.9	11.2	17.1	10.8	7.8
Transport, communications	14.5	15.0	4.5	5.1	4.6	4.7
Finance	8.5	12.7	0.9	15.6	3.0	13.8
Public administration	11.5	20.0	49.3	13.1	10.1	18.5
Aid, 2002 (per cent of GNI)	...	2	26	48	7	11
Adult literacy rate, 2000–04 (per cent)	93	99	95	91	65	...
Life expectancy at birth, 2003 (years)	M: 68; F: 74	M: 66; F: 71	M: 62; F: 67	M: 60; F: 63	M: 59; F: 62	M: 69; F: 73
Infant mortality rate (per 1,000 live births)	18	16	49	53	69	19
Total fertility rate (births per woman)	3.2	2.9	4	5.4	4.0	4.4

Exports, by principal commodity (US$m)

	Cook Islands	Fiji	Kiribati	Marshall Islands	Papua New Guinea	Solomon Islands
	(2004)	(2004)	(2002)	(2000)	(2004)	(2004)
	Pearls (2.28)	Garments (156.0)	Copra (0.42)	Diesel fuel (6.6)	Gold (707.7)	Logs (63.8)
	Fish (2.08)	Sugar (108.5)	Shark's fin (0.19)	Copra (1.35)	Crude oil (417.3)	Fish (18.0)
	Clothing (0.15)	Gold (53.8)	Seaweed (0.08)	Coconut oil (1.11)	Copper (396.5)	Cocoa (5.50)
	Fruit/vegies (0.09)	Fish (51.8)	Fish (0.01)	Pet fish (0.45)	Palm oil (112.7)	Copra (3.48)
	Live fish (0.09)	Textiles, etc. (7.8)		Handicrafts (0.01)	Logs (109.9)	
		Molasses (6.0)			Coffee (72.9)	
		Coconut oil (2.2)			Cocoa (56.0)	

Notes: GPD: gross domestic product, the total domestic economy. GNI: gross national income, including exports (used to be called gross national product)

Sources: Asian Development Bank (ADB), 2005b. *Key Indicators of Developing Asian and Pacific Countries*, Asian Development Bank. Available from http://www.adb.org/Documents/Books/Key_Indicators/default.asp (accessed 13 December 2005). Gillett, R. and Lightfoot, C., 2002. *Contribution of Fisheries to the Economies of Pacific Island Countries, Pacific Studies Series*, Asian Development Bank, Manila. United Nations Development Program (UNDP), 2004b. *United Nations Development Program Human Development Reports*. Available from http://hdr.undp.org/statistics/ (accessed 17 June 2005). United Nations, 2004. 'Small islands big stakes. Small island developing states and territories', United Nations. Available from http://www.un.org/smallislands2005/indicators.pdf (accessed 13 December 2005). World Bank, 2005. *World Development Indicators 2005*, World Bank. Available from http://web.worldbank.org/WBSITE/EXTERNAL/DATASTATISTICS/0,,menuPK:232599~pagePK:64133170~piPK:64133498~theSitePK:239419,00.html (accessed 13 December 2005).

Index

www.ingramcontent.com/pod-product-compliance
Lightning Source LLC
Chambersburg PA
CBHW061239270326
41926CB00067B/4670